The Destruction of the *Bismarck*

The Destruction

David J. Bercuson and Holger H. Herwig

of the *Bismarck*

THE OVERLOOK PRESS
WOODSTOCK & NEW YORK

First published in paperback in the United States in 2003 by
The Overlook Press, Peter Mayer Publishers, Inc.
Woodstock & New York

WOODSTOCK:
One Overlook Drive
Woodstock, NY 12498
www.overlookpress.com
[for individual orders, bulk and special sales, contact our Woodstock office]

NEW YORK:
141 Wooster Street
New York, NY 10012

Maps on pages xiv-xvi from *The Bismarck Chase* by Robert J. Winklareth, Chatham Publishing. Used by permission.

Library of Congress Cataloging-in-Publication Data

Bercuson, David Jay.
The destruction of the Bismarck / David J. Bercuson and Holger H. Herwig.
p. cm.
1. Bismarck (Battleship). 2. World War, 1939-1945—Naval operations, German.
3. World War, 1939-1945—Naval operations, British. I. Herwig, Holger H. II. Title
D772.B5 B37 2001 940.54'5943—dc21 2001036017
Printed in the United States of America
ISBN 1-58567-397-8
3 5 7 9 8 6 4 2

Contents

	Acknowledgments	vii
	Maps	ix
	Prologue	1
Chapter 1	Battleship Bismarck: The Pride of Hitler's Navy	13
Chapter 2	Rhine Exercise: The March to the Denmark Strait	47
Chapter 3	The King's Ships, but Tovey's Men	81
Chapter 4	Deadly Encounter	125
Chapter 5	Hot Pursuit	155
Chapter 6	Roosevelt's Dilemma	181
Chapter 7	Search and Destroy	223
Chapter 8	The Kill	263
	Epilogue	301
	Notes	315
	Glossary	337
	Table of Equivalent Naval Ranks	349
	A Notes on Sources	351
	Index	359

Acknowledgments

MANY PEOPLE HELPED US in the preparation of this book. Robert Hodgins-Vermaas worked tirelessly in the Public Record Office at Kew, at the Churchill College Library at Cambridge, and at the Maritime Museum in Greenwich ferreting out the key Royal Navy sources. Tamara Sherwin gathered information and material about warships, gunnery, naval aviation, and much other lacunae. David Quayat researched the relevant files and records at the Franklin D. Roosevelt Library in Hyde Park, New York, and at the U.S. National Archives in Washington, D.C., and College Park, Maryland. Nancy Pearson Mackie helped prepare the list of Royal Navy sources to be consulted and gathered much material by telephone, courier, and mail. John Hattendorf shared his knowledge of the U.S. Navy, the Battle of the Atlantic, and Newport, Rhode Island, in the early 1940s. James Levy generously shared some of the excellent material he has gathered on the Home Fleet in World War II, which will appear shortly in his doctoral dissertation. Art Nishimura helped us with photographic restoration. David Kahn gave us many invaluable tips and much information regarding ULTRA. Dr. Jürgen Rohwer was helpful with opinions and information bearing on the *Bismarck* and the Kriegsmarine. Timothy K. Nenninger at the National Archives (College Park) was more than generous with his time and information. Michael Simpson helped us track material on the Royal Navy at the outbreak of World War II. Dan Harris sat for an interview in Ottawa.

It is somewhat customary to thank archival staffs, but we thank the people at the following institutions with much gratitude: United States Coast Guard; Roosevelt Library; National Archives, Washington, D.C.; National Archives, College Park; Bundesarchiv at Freiburg and Koblenz; Bibliothek für Zeitgeschichte at Stuttgart; Churchill College Library; and Public Record Office.

Our agent and very good friend, Linda McKnight, encouraged us from the start and guided us throughout this project. No one who has not worked with Linda can ever really know how much she cares about her authors, and not just about their books.

Our dear wives, Lorraine Herwig and Barrie Bercuson, pored over every word of this manuscript. Our staunchest supporters but toughest critics, Lorraine and Barrie helped shape our ideas, challenged our assumptions, and were always there to encourage us when fatigue set in. They are as much responsible for this book as we are. We dedicate this book to them with our deepest love and gratitude.

David J. Bercuson
Holger H. Herwig

Maps

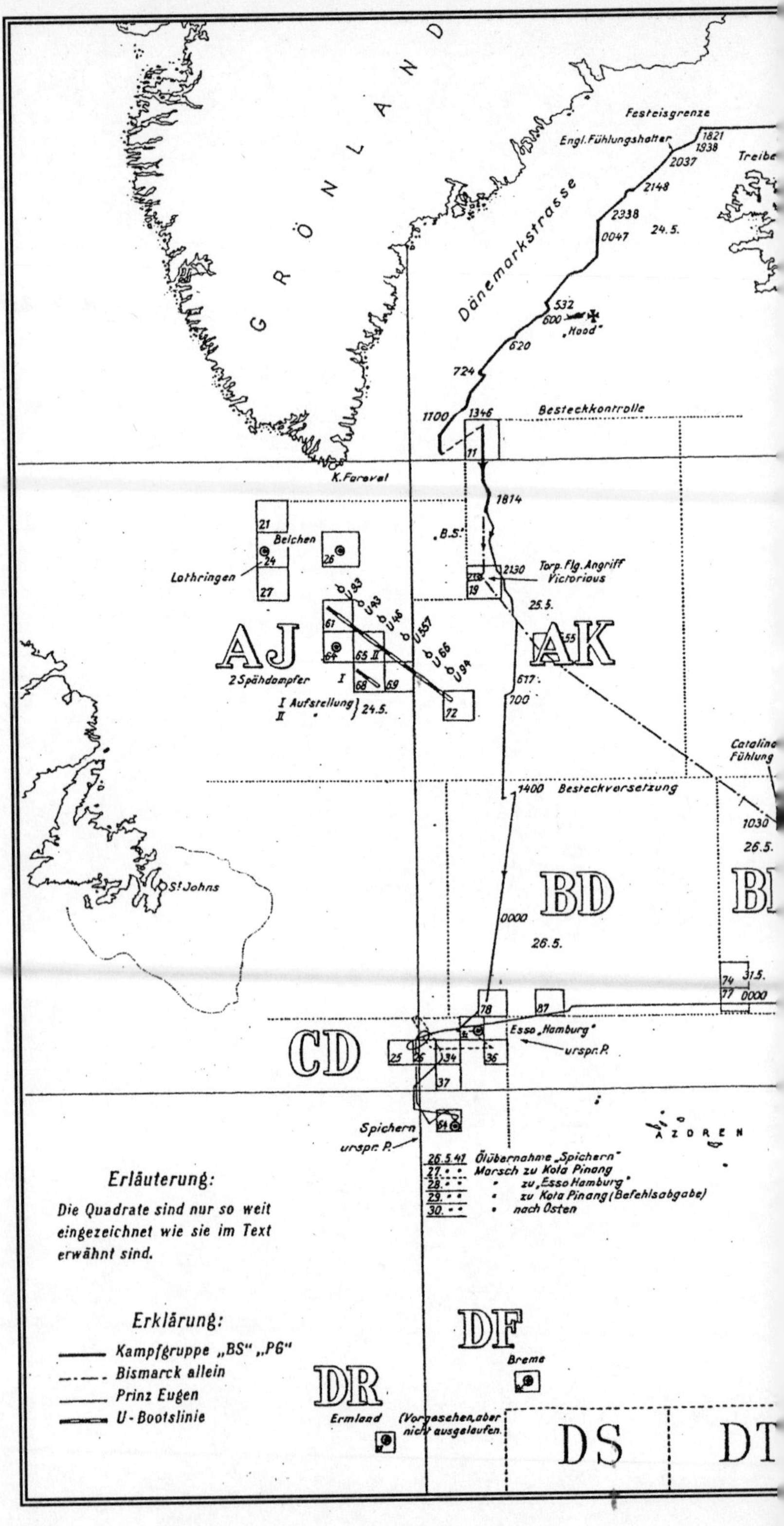

GRÖNLAND
Dänemarkstrasse
Festeisgrenze
Engl. Fühlungshalter
1821
1938
2037
2148
2338
0047
24.5.
532
600
„Hood"
620
724
1100
1346
Besteckkontrolle
11
K. Farvel
1814
21
Belchen
Lothringen
24
26
27
.B.S.
2130
Torp. Flg. Angriff
Victorious
19
25.5.
U 93
U 43
U 46
U 557
U 66
U 94
AJ
AK
55
61
64
65
II
68
69
I
72
2 Spähdampfer
I Aufstellung
II
24.5.
617
700
Catalina
Fühlung
1400 Besteckversetzung
1030
26.5.
BD
St Johns
0000
26.5.
74
77
31.5.
0000
78
87
Esso „Hamburg"
urspr. P.
CD
25
26
34
36
37
Spichern
urspr. P.
64
AZOREN
26.5.41 Ölübernahme „Spichern"
27. Marsch zu Kota Pinang
28. zu „Esso Hamburg"
29. zu Kota Pinang (Befehlsabgabe)
30. nach Osten
Erläuterung:
Die Quadrate sind nur so weit eingezeichnet wie sie im Text erwähnt sind.
Erklärung:
Kampfgruppe „BS" „PG"
Bismarck allein
Prinz Eugen
U-Bootslinie
DF
Breme
DR
Ermland
(Vorgesehen, aber nicht ausgelaufen.)
DS
DT

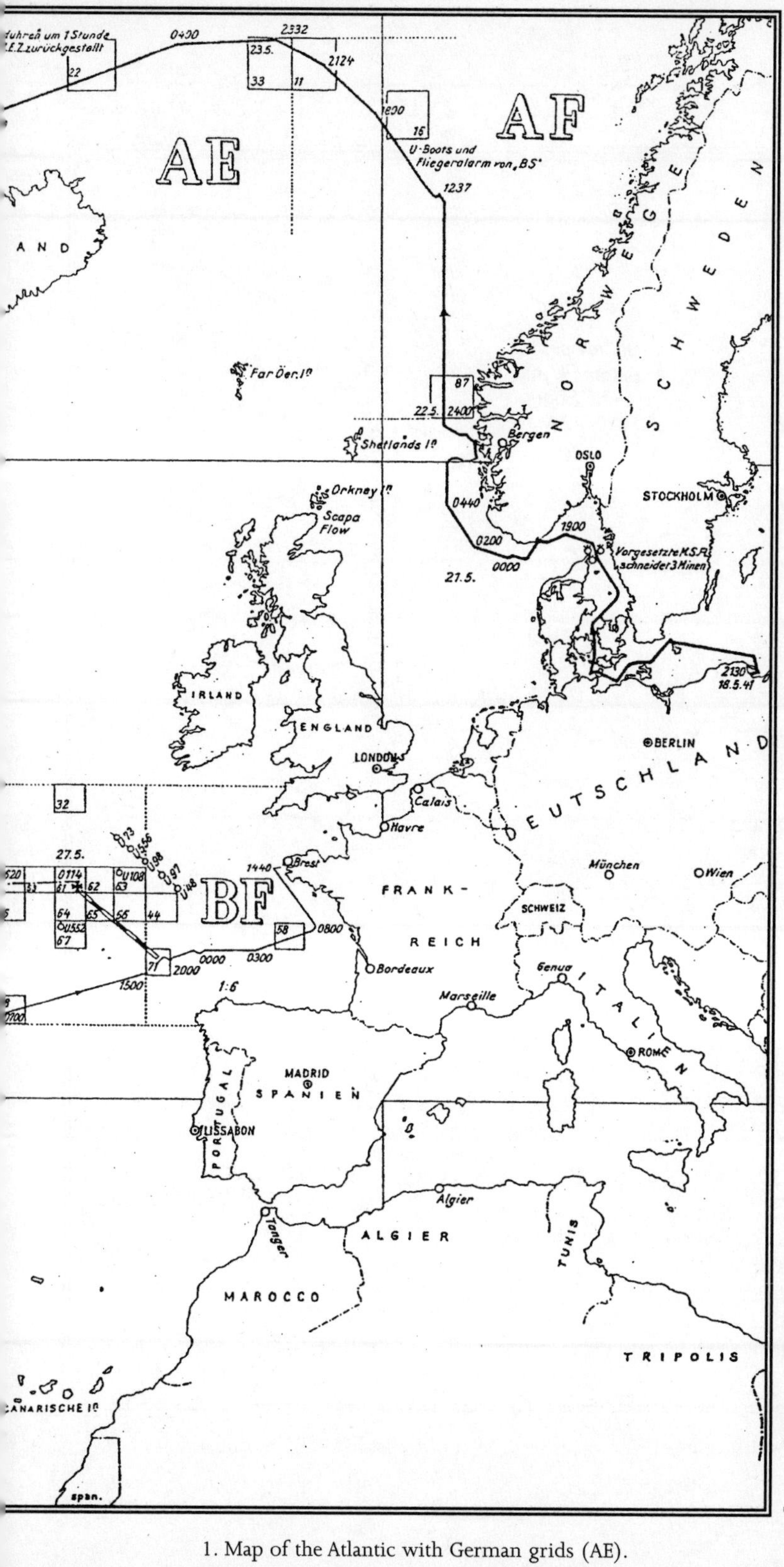

SOURCE: BUNDESARCHIV, GERMANY

1. Map of the Atlantic with German grids (AE).

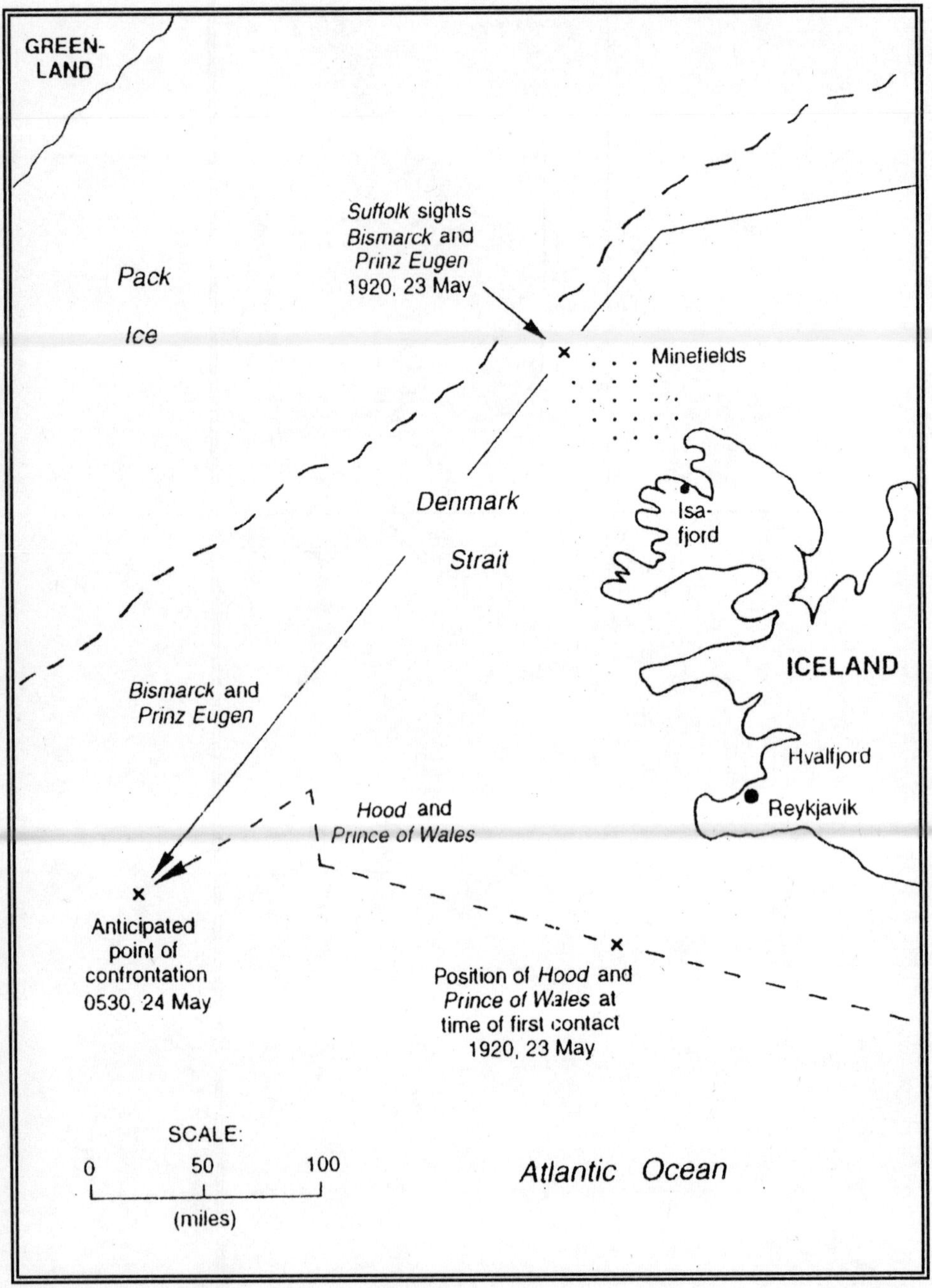

2. Movements of British and German forces prior to confrontation on the morning of 24 May.

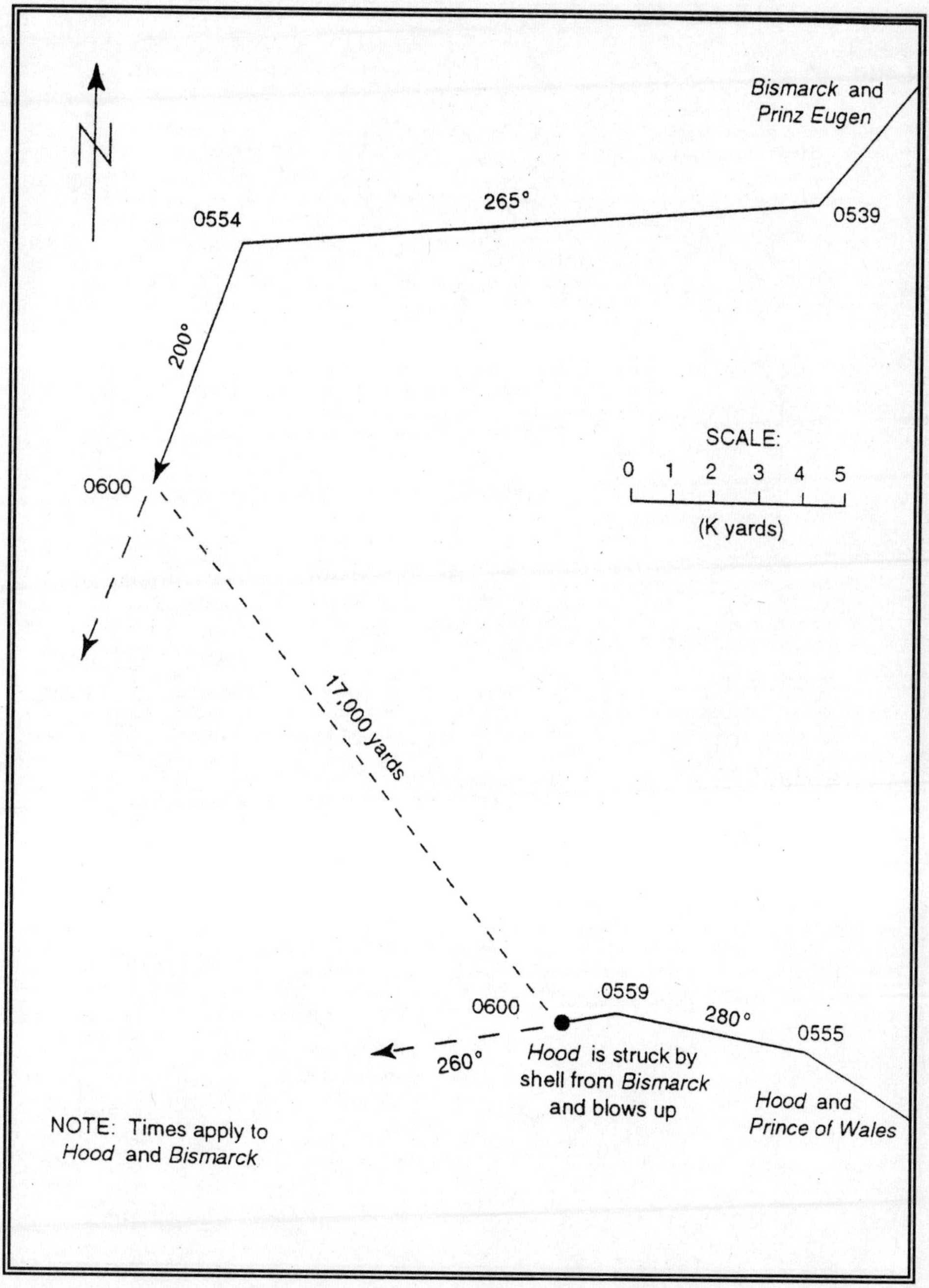

3. Position of British and German forces when HMS *Hood* was hit by shell from the *Bismarck*.

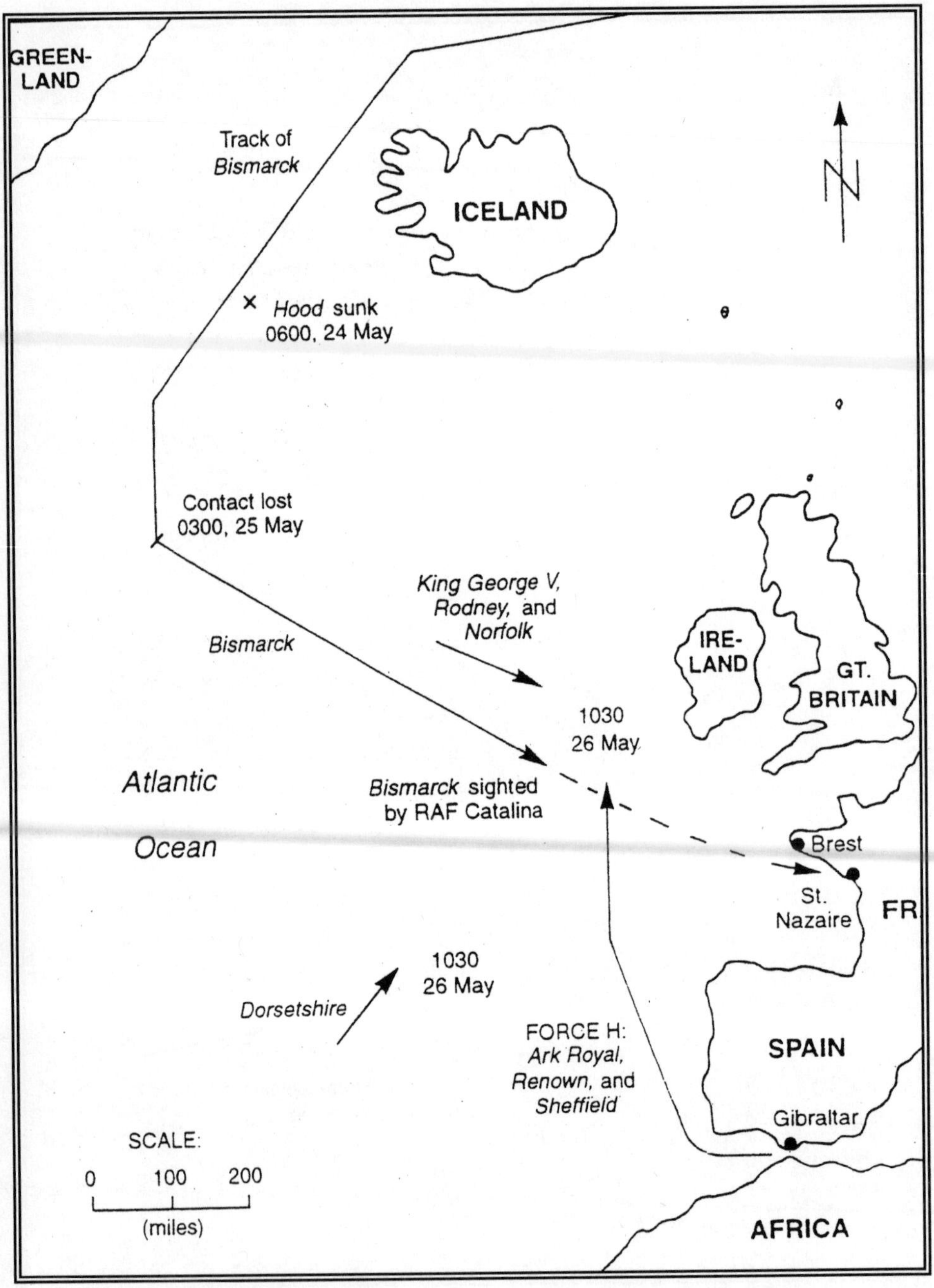

4. Deployment of British forces at time of discovery of the *Bismarck*.

PROLOGUE

Amid the torrent of violent events one anxiety reigned supreme. Battles might be won or lost, enterprises might succeed or miscarry, territories might be gained or quitted, but dominating all our power to carry on the war, or even keep ourselves alive, lay mastery of the ocean routes and the free approach and entry to our ports.

Winston S. Churchill

ADOLF HITLER'S BOMBERS LEFT the smoke-shrouded skies over London in the early morning hours of 11 May 1941, not to return en masse for three years. The London Blitz was over. The nonstop German bombing of the capital and other cities that had started in the waning days of the Battle of Britain in the late summer of 1940 was over. Behind them, the bombers left the smoking and blasted ruins of London, Coventry, Liverpool, Southampton, Birmingham, Bristol, and Plymouth. During the blitz the German air force—the Luftwaffe—had reached out as far as Northern Ireland to strike at Belfast. The Germans had attacked commercial and transportation centers, port cities, and industrial towns across England, Scotland, and Northern Ireland, but mostly they had tried to destroy London. They did not succeed, but hundreds of square miles of the city had been flattened. Thousands of homes, shops, factories, government buildings, schools, hospitals, pubs, theaters, and nightclubs had been leveled.

From early September 1940 through the cold winter, until 11 May

1941, the Germans had bombed Britain by night to protect their aircraft from the Royal Air Force's (RAF) fighters. Beginning their attacks just after twilight and continuing almost until dawn, the fleets of Luftwaffe bombers had been hidden by the long hours of darkness. At that early stage of the war, Britain's antiaircraft defenses were almost useless at night. The RAF had no airborne radar; the British antiaircraft guns shot blindly into the sky while searchlights waved about in vain. A handful of German bombers were lost, but they were a mere fraction of the attacking forces. For the most part, the Germans roamed the skies over Britain at will, their nightly arrival heralded by the long wails of air raid sirens and the crump of the antiaircraft guns. Then they bombed and bombed and bombed as the people of Britain—most often Londoners—took to their garden dugouts or their basement bomb shelters, or scurried to the deep tunnels of the London Underground, and struggled to live through yet another night.

When the Luftwaffe flew away from Britain for the last time in the early-morning hours of 11 May 1941, they left 43,000 civilians dead behind them and another 139,000 wounded. But by the time they flew away, British prime minister Winston S. Churchill knew that the danger of a German invasion had passed. Britain would survive and fight on as Churchill had declared to the world after the fall of France in June 1940. But mere survival was not Churchill's objective, nor was it enough. His real aim was to liberate Western Europe, destroy Hitler's regime, and restore civility and sanity to the international order. The truth was that on the morning of 11 May 1941 he was even farther from that goal than he had been a year earlier, when he had assumed the offices of prime minister and minister of defense.

Churchill was Britain's—and the world's—last hope. When Britain joined France to declare war on Germany on 3 September 1939, the ostensible reason for that declaration had been to come to the aid of Poland, attacked by the forces of the Third Reich forty-eight hours earlier. In fact, that was not the primary reason for Britain's entry into the war, because there was never any real hope that

Britain and France might save Poland. London and Paris went to war because their leaders—Prime Minister Neville Chamberlain of Britain and President Paul Reynaud of France—had finally realized that Germany's leader, Adolf Hitler, was a lawless and ruthless international renegade who would stop at nothing to achieve German domination of the international order. Hitler lied. Hitler plotted. Hitler broke international treaties and agreements at will. Hitler murdered his enemies to achieve his aims. By allowing Hitler almost free rein from 1933 to 1939, British and French leaders had given him leeway to build the most powerful army and air force in the world and gain great geographic advantages in Central Europe without even resorting to war. When Hitler invaded Poland, Chamberlain and Reynaud decided they had already waited too long to act; they must fight or be forever relegated to satellites of the Nazi regime, perhaps even victims.

Germany quickly swallowed Poland, sharing part of its spoils with Hitler's newfound ally, Josef Stalin's Soviet Union. Britain and France did virtually nothing to bring the Nazis to account. Over the dreary winter of 1939–40 they waited timidly for Hitler's next move, almost afraid to awaken the Nazi tiger, while Hitler secretly prepared to strike in the west. In April 1940 he invaded Norway and Denmark; in May his forces smashed their way into the Netherlands, Belgium, and finally France itself. Outfought and outmaneuvered, the French gave way as the Dutch and Belgians surrendered. The British Expeditionary Force retreated to Dunkirk, on the Channel coast, and was evacuated over ten dramatic days. At Dunkirk the British saved the core of their army but lost thousands of men and virtually all their tanks, guns, and heavy equipment. Then they stood virtually defenseless against possible German invasion.

With the German invasion of Norway and Denmark, Chamberlain's position in the British Parliament grew weaker and weaker. The people of Britain largely blamed him for the prewar policies of appeasement that had left their island nation so weak compared to Germany. Thus Hitler's move west was the death knell for his government. He resigned, to be replaced on 10 May 1940 by Churchill, who had warned the world about Hitler since 1933 and who had spent years in the political wilderness fighting his own party's government for more defense spending and more spine in its dealings with Hitler. Churchill convinced his cabinet that the struggle against Hitler must be a fight to the finish, that the war could end only when Nazism was destroyed.

On 20 June 1940 Italy declared war on France and Britain and thereby, in U.S. president Franklin D. Roosevelt's words, "plunged the dagger into the back of its neighbor." It was the final blow to France, which surrendered to Germany and Italy two days later. In the ensuing weeks Hitler tried to entice Churchill into an armistice, but the British leader was determined to fight on. Thus in the high summer of 1940 the Battle of Britain began. The Luftwaffe's task was to destroy the Royal Air Force and prepare the way for an invasion. The RAF fought back desperately and, in the end, denied the Germans the aerial victory they needed. Hitler then postponed and eventually canceled the invasion (Operation Sea Lion) as his bombers went about the task of destroying Britain's cities. The Nazi dictator was determined to conquer the Soviet Union in the summer of 1941 and decided to leave Britain to his bombers and his submarines. If he could not conquer Britain by invasion, perhaps he could blast and starve the British people into reason. By 11 May 1941 even that goal had become a forlorn hope.

On 11 May 1941 the British could take some comfort in having survived one of the worst years in their history, but the war still was going very badly for them. Along the German-Soviet border, three German army groups awaited the final order to attack Russia. Hitler had gathered one of the largest invading forces in history—about 3.6 million men—to do what Napoleaon had failed to do over a century before, namely, sweep quickly across the broad Russian plains, destroy the Soviet armed forces, capture Russia's major cities, and occupy and exploit its grain- and oil-producing regions. Churchill had no doubt what would happen after that. Fortified by the resources of all of Europe, Hitler would surely turn west again.

He would swallow up the remains of the French Republic—then under the control of Marshal Philippe Pétain's Vichy government—march across southern Spain to capture Gibraltar, and finally turn again to the enterprise of invading Britain.

Without Gibraltar, Britain's lifeline to her important naval bases at Malta and Alexandria, and her access to the oil of the Middle East and the reinforcements that could be provided by the Indian, Australian and New Zealand armies would quickly dissolve. So too would her lifeline to the Far East—to Singapore, Hong Kong, Malaya, Burma, and India itself. Churchill worried intensely that the Spanish dictator Francisco Franco might accede to German pressure and allow Hitler's forces to attack the Rock from the back door. That remained a distinct danger throughout 1941.

But even though Britain still held Gibraltar on 11 May 1941, the Axis was piling victory upon victory in North Africa, on the broad seas of the Mediterranean, and in the Balkans. After Italy's clumsy and unsuccessful attempts to drive the British out of Egypt and conquer Albania and Yugoslavia, German forces joined the fight for the Balkans and North Africa. Yugoslavia fell quickly. Greek troops were pushed back to the sea; British and Anzac forces sent to Greece to shore her up were withdrawn to Crete, with heavy losses. In North Africa the Desert Fox—General Erwin Rommel—and his Afrika Korps drove the British out of Libya and back to the borders of Egypt. The Royal Navy fought desperately to keep its sea lines of communications to Malta, Alexandria, and Suez open against the combined Italian and German air forces and the smaller but far more modern Italian fleet. It was touch-and-go through most of 1941.

In the Far East Japan had launched all-out war against China in 1937. Now, in early May 1941, Japanese ships, men, and aircraft were using bases extorted from the Vichy French in Indochina to prepare for further thrusts south, toward the Dutch East Indies and Malaya to the vast stores of oil, rubber, and tin that awaited them there. War fear grew by the day, and even though Churchill continued to express confidence in Britain's ability to defend her interests in the area, and in the strength of the vast new British naval base at Singapore, he also knew how weak the landward defenses of Singapore and Hong Kong were and how overwhelming was the local superiority, in Asian waters, of the imperial Japanese navy.

Churchill knew that Britain's only hope—to come to her aid if Japan attacked, to hold out against Hitler, eventually to defeat the Axis—lay far over the horizon to the west, in the New World, with the United States. Unlike Chamberlain, or even Chamberlain's predecessor, Prime Minister Stanley Baldwin, Churchill understood the potential power of the United States. He deeply admired American political institutions and knew the strength of American democracy. His knowledge came not only from his American-born mother, but also from his many visits to the United States beginning in the era of the Spanish-American War. His books, newspaper columns and articles, and magazine pieces were widely read in the United States. His lecture and book tours took him to most of its major cities and gave him the opportunity to meet and befriend hundreds of important and powerful Americans from coast to coast. He was an assiduous student of American history, especially the Civil War, and a staunch admirer of President Abraham Lincoln. He counted on the Americans—the other great anchor of what he called "the English-speaking peoples"—to eventually join the struggle against Hitler not simply for the self-interested motive of staving off defeat, but because of his deep conviction that the hour had struck for those English-speaking peoples (Britain, the British Commonweatlth, and the United States) to save civilization.

Churchill and the world were fortunate to have in the White House a man who instinctively understood America's mission in this dark night of global war and who also knew that Britain was the United States' last line of defense against the so-called Rome-Berlin-Tokyo axis. Roosevelt was a great liberal. He understood Nazism and feared it as much as he hated it. He and most of his defense and foreign policy advisors agreed with Churchill that the United States could not stay neutral over the long run. They knew especially that if Britain fell, the United States would be face-to-face with a Hitler who would control the resources, the war factories, and maybe even the air forces, navies, and armies of all of Europe. But until the American people were ready to enter the war on Britain's side, all the United States could do was supply Britain with the tools of war.

The United States began to do that in the fall of 1940 when it swapped fifty World War I destroyers for leases to bases on British territory in Newfoundland, Bermuda, and the Caribbean. The American public accepted Roosevelt's carefully worded explanation for the arrangement. But when the London Blitz began, most Americans were appalled by what they saw in the newsreels playing at their movie theaters or heard over their radios. American public opinion swung irresistibly toward Britain as Nazi bombers blasted Britain's cities night after night over the winter of 1940–41. More and more Americans concluded that the United States must do all it could, short of war, to help Britain while seeing to its own still weak defenses.

Roosevelt's most daring and far-reaching step to aid the British was Lend-Lease, pushed through Congress in early 1941 and finally signed into law on 11 March of that year. Under Lend-Lease, the United States ostensibly loaned, or leased, war material to any nation whose defense was vital to the interests of the United States. Britain was the first nation so designated. Others such as the Soviet Union and China would follow later in the war. In fact, the planes, tanks, guns, trucks, and ships of Lend-Lease were given away in a gesture that combined magnanimity and self-interest. But once given, those munitions still had a long way to go to reach their destinations.

Virtually every bullet, submachine gun, tank, truck and fighter plane that went to Britain under Lend-Lease had to go by sea. So did the cheese, beef, bacon, flour, oil, and gasoline that kept the British people fed and warm and healthy. The cargoes moved in huge convoys of freighters and tankers—large and small, slow and fast, old and modern—that plodded slowly across the North Atlantic from the east coast of Canada to the United Kingdom. Protected by the Royal Navy and the Royal Canadian Navy, the ships and their merchant seamen crews challenged the German navy, the German air force, and the power of the ocean itself to keep the Atlantic lifeline open. Churchill dubbed this struggle the "Battle of the Atlantic." It was the longest battle of the war and the most epic. It was also the one battle Britain could not lose lest she herself fall. But in the spring of 1941 the outlook for Britain was beginning to dim.

To stem the tide of American goods, Hitler's air force and navy deployed a growing fleet of submarines using "wolf-pack" tactics, surface warships, and long-range bombers to sink the ships carrying Britain's lifeblood. The Royal Navy and its smaller partner, the Royal Canadian Navy, were hard pressed to defend the convoys. Germany's first line of attack was its growing U-boat fleet under the command of Admiral Karl Dönitz. In the first four months of 1940 his submarines sank 135 Allied and neutral ships, a total of about 446,000 tons of shipping. His objective was simplicity itself: sink more merchant ships faster than Allied shipyards could replace them. Not only would the cargoes and the men who bravely crewed the ships be lost, but shipping capacity would diminish by the month. Eventually Britain would lose all hope of striking back at Hitler and would even be unable to feed her people. Inevitably, she would die.

The U-boat war intensified after the fall of France. The German navy immediately took control of French ports on the Bay of Biscay and shifted most of their U-boat flotillas there. The submariners then were spared the long dangerous journey from the Baltic to the North Atlantic and were able to sortie directly into the North Atlantic and patrol far to the west, close to the coast of North America. Allied shipping losses mounted dramatically.

In the second third of 1940 the German submariners accounted for 177 ships and close to a million tons of shipping, or double the toll of the first four months of the year. In all of 1940 the U-boat fleet sank 520 ships, amounting to more than 2.4 million tons of shipping.

In January 1941 powerful storms ravaged the sea lanes of the North Atlantic, and merchant shipping losses fell, not only because there were fewer ships, but because the submarines could not find them amidst the towering seas. But fairer weather brought increased losses once again the following month. By the end of May 1941 the U-boats had destroyed 215 Allied or neutral ships with a total of 1.2 million tons of shipping. Month by month these losses were added to by long-range German bombers flying from bases on the coast of France and Norway. These four-engine Condors ranged far out to sea, sinking hundreds of ships and thousands of tons of shipping while they also helped the submarine fleet track the convoys and laid mines that destroyed even more shipping. In some months the Condor kills added a quarter or even a third to the total of Allied shipping destroyed.

The German navy's small but very modern surface fleet was the third major threat to Allied shipping. In the late 1930s, German naval chief Admiral Erich Raeder envisioned the construction of a major surface fleet based on battleships and aircraft carriers. The "Z-Plan," as he called it, proposed a rapid naval construction program that would see in place by 1947 at the latest, a fleet that would be able to challenge the Royal Navy for control of the Atlantic. When the war broke out on 1 September 1939, however, the German navy was still far short of Raeder's ultimate goal. The only effective role that his big ships—heavy cruisers, battle cruisers, pocket battleships, and still-under-construction battleships—might play would be to hunt and destroy enemy commerce, like pirates of old, as individual raiders or in small fleets made up of a handful of ships.

In the fall of 1939 one of Raeder's pocket battleships, the *Graf Spee*, was hunted down by the Royal Navy in the South Atlantic. After a ferocious sea battle with three cruisers, two British and one New Zealand, the German warship took refuge in neutral Montevideo Harbor before its commander, Captain Hans Langsdorff, ordered the ship scuttled and killed himself. The German surface raiders did not sortie again until the fall of 1940 when the heavy cruiser *Hipper*, the pocket battleship *Admiral Scheer*, and the battleships *Scharnhorst* and *Gneisenau* set forth in succession between September 1940 and March 1941 to destroy close to a quarter million tons of Allied and neutral shipping. Though not as deadly as the U-boats in putting Allied and neutral ships on the bottom, the German warships tied up dozens of Royal Navy battleships, cruisers, and aircraft carriers for weeks and even months at a time. And while the German surface raiders sallied forth, or threatened to do so while waiting ominously in French, German, or Norwegian ports, the greatest threats of all—the giant 45,000-ton sister battleships *Bismarck* and *Tirpitz*—lay a-building in German shipyards.

As the 11th of May 1941 passed into history, the jet stream of high-altitude winds that blew from west to east dozens of miles above the earth, and which determined most of the weather over North America and the North Atlantic, began to form a lazy whorl over the land mass of northern Canada. The small isolated weather station at Fort Smith in the Northwest Territories first detected and reported it to Canada's Dominion Meteorological Service in Ottawa. Within days, barometric readings from remote weather stations and soundings from high-altitude weather balloons plotted the new low-pressure system on the world's meteorological charts. As the low tracked eastward across the mouth of Hudon Bay, across the Ungava Peninsula, toward southern Greenland and the Denmark Strait beyond, it intensified. The pressure gradients drew tighter around it; the counterclockwise winds around its center increased in speed. Far below, the gray seas began to heave and roil as snow shipped across the seascape. By 20 May this low, and a smaller low-pressure system some 500 miles to the southwest of it, began to break across the convoy lanes. Soon they joined into one of the most intense storm systems of the season.

As the Fort Smith storm system began its long, slow journey from northern Canada to the Norwegian Sea, another storm, this one man-made of steel and explosives, gathered its strength several thousand miles further to the east, on the coast of the Baltic Sea. This storm was the battleship *Bismarck*. It too was about to break across the North Atlantic shipping lanes. Between them, these storms would determine the fate of the Battle of the Atlantic.

CHAPTER 1

BATTLESHIP *BISMARCK*:

THE PRIDE OF HITLER'S NAVY

THE FIFTH OF MAY 1941 was a clear, blustery day in the eastern Baltic Sea. The newly commissioned fleet flagship, the *Bismarck*, rode at anchor in Gotenhafen (now Gdynia) Roads, off Danzig. The fleet chief, Admiral Günther Lütjens, and the *Bismarck*'s skipper, Captain Ernst Lindemann, anxiously peered over the railings at the approaching dispatch vessel *Hela*. Lindemann had mustered his officers and crew in their finest uniforms on the upper deck. As the *Hela* offloaded her small boarding party at 10:20 A.M., a special pennant snapped up the battleship's mainmast: the "Führer's Standard." The band struck up "Deutschland, Deutschland über alles" and the Nazi party's anthem, the "Horst Wessel Lied." Adolf Hitler was piped over the side. Accompanying him were Field Marshal Wilhelm Keitel of the Supreme Command of the Armed Forces (OKW) and two service adjutants, Major Nicolaus von Below of the air force and Commander Karl Jesko von Puttkamer of the navy.[1] The Führer, who had come to inspect both the *Bismarck* and her sister ship, the *Tirpitz*, looked pale and sullen. "On land I am a hero," he liked to boast, "at sea I am a coward."[2] Grand Admiral Erich Raeder, commander in chief of the Kriegsmarine, was conspicuously absent. It was the first time that he had not accompanied Hitler on an inspection tour.[3]

After reviewing the honor guard and assembled crew, Hitler toured the battleship. Fascinated by technology, he chatted with specialists about numerous pieces of equipment. The Führer was especially taken with the *Bismarck*'s intricate fire-control system, and in the after gunnery tower he received a detailed briefing from Lieutenant Friedrich Cardinal. A lance corporal in the Great War, Hitler keenly paid attention to the ratings. "You are the pride of the navy," he assured them. In the admiral's cabin, Lütjens briefed Hitler on the details of his recent sortie into the Atlantic Ocean (Operation Berlin) with the battleships *Gneisenau* and *Scharnhorst*, during which he had ranged as far south as Sierra Leone and as far west and north as Halifax. The raid had destroyed twenty-two Allied merchant ships totaling 115,622 tons and had disrupted the British convoy system. The *Bismarck*, with 15-inch guns, he explained to Hitler, was more powerful than the *Scharnhorst* class, with 11-inch guns, and hence ideally suited to prey upon even well-protected convoys. The admiral brushed aside the Führer's rejoinder that the Royal Navy's numerical superiority needed to be kept in mind.[4] The *Bismarck*, Lütjens patiently explained to Hitler, was superior in firing and staying power to any single British unit. Still, Lütjens conceded that hostile seaborne airpower remained a concern. Privately, Hitler did not share Lütjens' enthusiasm about Operation Berlin. "The U-boats do these things better and faster," the Führer confided privately to Puttkamer, "and without such incredible expenditures."[5] But he was not about to cross Raeder or Lütjens.

Lunch, a simple one-course vegetarian meal specially catered for the Führer, was served in the wardroom. Hitler was uncharacteristically silent. Not a word about the 50,500-ton (fully loaded) marvel of German naval engineering. Not a word about her intended sortie into the Atlantic. Not a word about the proposed date of departure. Not a word about the fact that battleships were not designed to act as high-seas commerce raiders. Not even a word about Admiral Raeder's absence.[6] When Captain Lindemann showed Hitler Franz von Lenbach's prized portrait of Otto von Bismarck and suggested that it might be put ashore during the sortie, Hitler cut him short: "If anything happens to the ship, the picture might as well be lost too."[7]

Then, as if on cue, Hitler delivered one of his celebrated monologues. It ranged from the Transylvanian Germans in Romania, whom he intended "to haul back into the Reich in short order,"[8] to the possible entry into the war of the United States, which he dismissed because of the Republic's poor combat performance in the First World War. When Captain Lindemann responded that American intervention in the present struggle should not be easily dismissed, the lunch abruptly ended. Admiral Lütjens closed the four-hour visit with a brief, general overview of the impending Atlantic raid, and vowed to crush British ships wherever they appeared. Hitler left the *Bismarck* at 2:18 P.M. Alongside the jetty he next inspected the *Tirpitz*, whose commander requested permission to accompany the *Bismarck*, and then returned to Berlin.

Throughout the meeting with Hitler, Lütjens had spoken only in generalities about another projected sortie in the Atlantic. He had avoided any discussion concerning the detailed planning for what in Raeder's innermost naval circles was officially classified as the top-secret Rhine Exercise (Operation Rheinübung). This was to be the greatest naval sortie of the war, including not only the battleships *Gneisenau* and *Scharnhorst*, but also the world's two newest and most powerful battleships, the *Bismarck* and the *Tirpitz*.

In fact, Hitler would learn about Rhine Exercise only on 22 May 1941—when the task force was already steaming into the northern end of the Denmark Strait.

Erich Raeder had good reason to remain in Berlin. For eight years he had labored hard to keep naval planning and operations as far away from Hitler's scrutiny as possible. He had argued over and over that Hitler, a native of Austria and a man who had spent much of his life in south Germany, was a stranger to the sea. A disciple of Alfred Thayer Mahan, the high priest of "blue-water" battle fleets,

Raeder had dedicated his life to resurrecting the High Sea Fleet, scuttled at Scapa Flow on 21 June 1919. Sea power could be wrested from Britain and then maintained only by a superior battle fleet; submarines, the weapon of the weak, could at best damage British maritime power but never break it. Hitler was of a different opinion. He regarded the High Sea Fleet of World War I as a "romantic plaything," a "parade piece." The scuttling at Scapa Flow in 1919 had constituted "dishonor." Above all, the kaiser's battleships had not altered the outcome of the war. Instead, they had lain idle at anchor for much of that struggle. In 1941 Hitler feared the risk of losing such a prestige object. Indeed, on his way back to Berlin, the Führer confided to General Alfred Jodl, head of the OKW's Operations Staff, that capital ships were on the endangered-species list, at the mercy of naval airpower. But Hitler shied away from a direct confrontation with Raeder, since he believed that a battle fleet would be needed once Germany had her Lebensraum on the Continent.

Hitler's inspection of the *Bismarck* and the *Tirpitz* at Gotenhafen had brought together the small coterie of players on whom the great ship's fate depended, at least in Germany—Adolf Hitler, Admiral Lütjens, and Captain Lindemann. In the shadows at naval headquarters back in Berlin lurked the final arbiter of German maritime affairs, Admiral Raeder. All three naval commanders had been trained in the Imperial German Navy; all three had served in the First World War; all three had bided their time under the Weimar Republic; and all three had embraced the Third Reich as the guarantor of rearmament and expansion.

Erich Raeder was born in Hamburg-Wandsbek on 24 April 1876 and entered the Imperial German Navy in 1894. Three years later, he graduated from the Naval School at Mürwik, first in his class. After service in the Far East and a year in Russia to learn the language, Raeder in 1912 was appointed to the post of first admiralty staff officer, Scouting Forces. During World War I he took part in the battles of the Dogger Bank (1915) and Jutland (1916), both times on the bridge of the battle cruiser *Seydlitz*. Raeder ended the Great War as commandant of the light cruiser *Köln*. In the 1920s he held a series of administrative positions, including that of head of the Baltic Naval Station. On 29 September 1928 he was promoted to the rank of admiral and appointed head of the navy.

A stiff disciplinarian and workaholic, Raeder was known throughout the service for his exceedingly formal, indeed distant behavior. Pedantic to a fault when it came to the social appearance and public bearing of his officers, Raeder advocated "discipline tempered with affection." Above all, he was sensitive to any form of criticism, preferring to discuss matters confidentially "under four eyes" and to keep "a very tight rein on things."[9] To this end, Raeder kept close and direct control of all operations, showering his front commanders with detailed instructions before operations and equally detailed criticism afterward. He tolerated little in the way of individual initiative. In his relations with Hitler, Raeder was at worst insecure, at best wary. His close ties to the Hohenzollerns in the 1920s did not sit well with Hitler, who was a radical tribune. Yet Raeder fully shared the latter's faith in Germany's resurrection as a great power, both on land and at sea.

Rhine Exercise's task force commander was a study in contrast. Born on 25 May 1889 at Wiesbaden, Günther Lütjens had entered the Imperial German Navy on 3 April 1907. He graduated twentieth in a class of 160 and spent most of the prewar years on cruisers as well as with the Torpedo Division.[10] For the first two years of the Great War, Lütjens served with the First Torpedo Division. Then in 1917–18, as flotilla leader, he took part in a series of raids against Dunkirk, rising in grade to *Kapitänleutnant* (lieutenant) and receiving the Iron Cross, First Class, in August 1916 and the Knight's Cross of the Royal House of Hohenzollern in December 1917.

In the 1920s Lütjens alternated ship and shore commands, serving first with the torpedo branch and then on the predreadnought battleship *Schlesien*. From 1925 to 1929 he was with the North Sea Naval Station at Wilhelmshaven, and thereafter assumed command of his former posting, the First Torpedo Boat Flotilla. Promoted to the rank of captain on 1 July 1933, Lütjens undertook a tour of duty in the Naval Personnel Office at Berlin, and in September 1934 was given command of the light (training) cruiser *Karlsruhe*. Lütjens was promoted to the grade of rear admiral in October 1937 and vice admiral in January 1940 (as commander of all Scouting Forces). In March 1940 Lütjens, acting as deputy for the ill fleet chief, Admiral Wilhelm Marschall, commanded the battleships *Gneisenau* and *Scharnhorst* as covering forces for Narvik and Trondheim during the German occupation of Denmark and Norway. Lütjens was awarded the Knight's Cross in recognition of his services in Norway. In July 1940 he was appointed fleet chief and on 1 September promoted to the rank of admiral.

A dour, dry, almost colorless personality, Lütjens' severe face resembled an iron mask. Tall and lean, with closely cropped hair, sharply chiseled lips, and dark, serious eyes, he was known for his personal courage, steel will, naval dash, and an "overriding temperament." Few dared to cross him. Those who served under him remembered Lütjens as silent, inflexible, taciturn, and aloof. The word *compromise* was not in his vocabulary. Lütjens was ambitious and stubborn. Above all, he had a burning sense of patriotism. And he possessed moral fortitude. In 1936–37, during his second stint as head of the Naval Personnel Office, Lütjens did nothing to enforce the "Aryan paragraphs" of the Nürnberg Racial Laws of 1935 in the navy. In November 1938 he was not afraid to show Raeder his aversion to the attack on Jews and their property that accompanied the so-called "Kristallnacht."[11] The admiral wore the imperial navy's dirk (rather than the Kriegsmarine's, adorned with a swastika), and he continued to greet even Hitler with the naval salute rather than the party salute. Lütjens' fellow officers found him to be highly competent and professional. But he was not known as a lucky commander; in fact, the superstitious among his crews regarded him as a "Jonah." For his part, Lütjens preferred to keep his inner thoughts to himself. He disliked long conferences and tedious discussions. He reached his decisions alone and rarely, if ever, changed them.

The *Bismarck*'s skipper, Ernst Lindemann, was another study in contrast, this time from Lütjens. Born on 28 March 1894 at Altenkirchen in the Westerwald region of the Rhineland, Lindemann had entered the Imperial German Navy on 1 April 1913—"on probation" because of his slender physique.[12] His classmates remembered him as being unselfish and professional, a man whose zeal and concept of duty were "exemplary." Lindemann never completed the full term at the Naval School at Mürwik due to the outbreak of the First World War. His early career centered on the big ships: he served on the elderly battleship *Lothringen* until March 1916, and ended the war on the new dreadnought *Bayern*. By 1918 Lindemann stood fifth in a class of about 210 lieutenants. He received the Iron Cross, Second Class, and then First Class, during the Great War. Unusual concentration and strength of will overcame a medium build. Sharp-chiseled features, sparkling blue eyes, large ears, and straight hair brushed back flat accentuated Lindemann's appearance. He was known as a stern taskmaster, but one with both heart and spirit. Cool and levelheaded, Lindemann's only vices seemed to be too many cigarettes and too much coffee.

In the 1920s Lindemann turned his attention to naval gunnery, alternating tours of duty as gunnery officer on the predreadnought battleships *Hannover, Elsass,* and *Schleswig-Holstein* with shore assignments on the Naval Staff in Berlin as well as at the Baltic Naval Station. In 1931–32 Lindemann served as instructor at the Naval Gunnery School at Kiel. Next came tours of duty on the battleship *Hessen* and the pocket battleship *Admiral Scheer*. In August 1938 Francisco Franco awarded Lindemann three Spanish service medals for the *Admiral Scheer*'s supportive role during the Spanish Civil War. Lindemann was promoted to the rank of commander in April 1936 and to captain in April 1938. After a brief stint at the Naval Gunnery School in 1939–40, Lindemann was given command of the *Bismarck* on 1 August 1940.

All three naval commanders were painfully aware that Hitler was not enamored of battle fleets and big ships. None could have failed to notice the attention Hitler lavished on both his army and his air force. As a veteran of the German army of 1914–18, the Führer considered himself an expert on all matters pertaining to land warfare; shortly after the start of the Second World War, Hitler would bask in the radiance of the audacious title "Greatest Military Commander of All Time." But therein Raeder especially saw an opening. Might not the Führer, after conquering the European heartland, need a fleet to protect that greater Germany against assault from across the Atlantic Ocean? For much of the 1930s, Hitler repeatedly assured Raeder that Germany planned no war with Great Britain. Hitler would not repeat the mistake of Kaiser Wilhelm II in attempting to establish German hegemony on the Continent simultaneously with challenging "perfidious Albion" for control of the seas.

But in May 1938, when Czechoslovakia partially mobilized its army as a warning to Berlin after Hitler's *Anschluss* of his homeland, Austria, the Führer shattered Admiral Raeder's comfortable world of make-believe. In short, clipped words, Hitler informed Raeder "that France and England will line up against us" in any future war.[13] Therewith, the problem of a future confrontation between Germany and Britain again rose to the forefront of German naval planning. Still, Hitler assured his admiral that Germany would not have to be prepared to meet a major enemy in the Atlantic until the Führer had "solved" Germany's "territorial problems" in Europe, at the latest by 1944–45.

In concrete terms, on 27 January 1939 Hitler assigned top priority to the navy's ambitious Z or Ziel Plan. This called for the construction, by 1948 at the latest, of a symmetrical battle fleet: 10 battleships, 15 pocket battleships,[14] 4 aircraft carriers, 5 heavy and 44 light cruisers, 68 destroyers, 90 torpedo boats, 27 ocean-going submarines, and 222 smaller U-boats. There is no question that this mammoth fleet was designed for control of the Atlantic, and in all probability as a force to be deployed against both Great Britain and the United States. And implicit in the decision was Raeder's and the Führer's rejection of a U-boat-dominated navy, as desired by Karl Dönitz, then a captain.

To drive the point home, Hitler traveled to Hamburg on 13 February 1939 to preside over the launching of "Battleship F." The Third Reich's first true battleship was officially listed at 35,000 tons—6,000 tons less than the world's largest warship, HMS *Hood*—and thus at the upper limit of the 1922 Washington Naval Treaty. The launch was a Nazi public spectacle at its best.[15] At Friedrichsruhe, just outside the Hanseatic city, Hitler laid a wreath at the grave of Germany's "Iron Chancellor," Otto von Bismarck. At 12:15 P.M. the next day, the Führer left the posh Hotel Atlantic and boarded the yacht *Hamburg*. Accompanied by a twenty-one-gun salute from the pocket battleship *Admiral Scheer*, the "First Soldier of the Reich" crossed the Elbe River to the Blohm & Voss Shipyard, where he formally christened the vessel in the name of Germany's founder and greatest statesman. Admiral Raeder thanked his Führer for naming the ship after "the blacksmith of the Second Reich" and vowed that its 103 officers and 1,962 warrant officers and ratings would honor Bismarck's name "to their last breath."

Finally, Dorothee von Loewenfeld-Bismarck, the daughter of the chancellor's second son, Wilhelm (Bill) Otto, cracked the champagne bottle against the ship's bow: "On the order of the Führer, I baptize you with the name 'Bismarck.'" A few on the launch platform appreciated the obvious irony: never a friend of battleships nor an enemy of Britain, the Iron Chancellor hardly would have wanted his name attached to this behemoth. For the superstitious, an omen: for an anxious few seconds, the hulk refused to slide away from the launching platform. Wags in the audience joked that the portly Field Marshal Hermann Göring personally had to push her before she budged from the rails.

But the *Bismarck*'s launch was just the start of a busy few months for Hitler. On 1 April, Bismarck's birthday, the Führer rushed by special train to Wilhelmshaven and presided over the launching of "Battleship G." He was in a foul mood: London the day before had "guaranteed" Poland's independence. Hitler was determined to pour the British "a devil's drink."[16] Around noon, the Führer inspected a Kriegsmarine honor guard and then motored to the Naval Shipyard—where for the first time ever he spoke from behind an armored-glass shield. Then, amid a chorus of "*Sieg Heil*" from the eighty thousand onlookers, Ilse von Hassell, the daughter of Grand Admiral Alfred von Tirpitz, architect of Kaiser Wilhelm II's High Sea Fleet, hurled the champagne bottle against the bow of the 35,000-ton hulk. "By order of the Führer and Supreme Commander of the Wehrmacht, I baptize you with the name 'Tirpitz.' "

There could have been no clearer anti-British act than to christen Germany's newest battleship with the name *Tirpitz*. Within minutes of the ceremony, Hitler promoted Raeder to the rank of *Grossadmiral* (grand admiral). The inscription on the baton read: "To the First Grand Admiral of the Third Reich. Adolf Hitler." Later that day, on board the battleship *Scharnhorst*, the Führer reportedly dictated provisional orders for "Case White," the planned attack on Poland later that year.[17]

Hitler then boarded the Nazi pleasure ship *Robert Ley* on its maiden voyage to Helgoland Island. It was Hitler's first (and last) holiday outing.[18] While cruising in the North Sea, the battleship *Scharnhorst* sliced into view at full speed and fired a twenty-one-gun salute. The crew was assembled in review formation along the railings. Raeder hailed the Führer with his new grand admiral's baton—and then the *Scharnhorst* veered away smartly from the *Robert Ley*. A scene worthy of Wilhelm II and Tirpitz.

With two heavy units safely down the slipways, Admiral Raeder turned his attention to devising a strategy for their eventual deployment. In May 1939, ably assisted by Admiral Hermann Boehm, then fleet chief, Raeder devised his so-called double-pole strategy for a war against Britain.[19] Its cardinal tenet was "*the attack upon* Great Britain's *oceanic maritime lanes and operations* [and] upon the English fleet in the North Sea." In plain language, Raeder opted to build two fleets, each centered on three battleships and one aircraft carrier, screened by several light cruisers and destroyers. While a traditional "fleet-in-being" composed of four elderly battleships tied the Royal Navy down in the North Sea, the two powerful main fleet groups were to operate in the Atlantic Ocean against British convoys and their escorts.

Hitler's attack on Poland in the early morning hours of 1 September 1939 rudely interrupted Raeder's grand strategic musings. The grand admiral was deeply disturbed. He had available only two antiquated battleships against Britain's fifteen modernized vessels; no aircraft carriers to the Royal Navy's six; and two heavy cruisers to Britain's fifteen. The Führer had bitterly disappointed him, Raeder allowed, with the early timing of the war.

On 3 September Erich Raeder nervously paced up and down in his office, then slipped behind his massive desk at the Naval High Command on Berlin's Tirpitzufer to record his impressions of the war that had just broken out. Overlooking the Landwehr Canal, into which twenty years earlier right-wing veterans of the Great War had thrown the murdered bodies of Germany's most famous Communists, Rosa Luxemburg and Karl Liebknecht, Raeder remembered his role in the Weimar Republic's turbulent beginnings all too well. In 1920 he had rushed from Hamburg to Berlin to support the right-wing Kapp Putsch, designed to overthrow the hated Social Democratic government and President Friedrich Ebert. In fact, the navy had been heavily implicated in the attempted coup, and Raeder had to be banished to the "archives"—that is, the service's historical section—for several years to write part of the official history of the war at sea between 1914 and 1918.

Thus it was partly the admiral and partly the historian who scribbled furiously in his diary on 3 September 1939. Memories of Germany's lack of preparedness at sea in 1914 flooded Raeder's mind. History seemed to be repeating itself. "On this day the war against England and France broke out, with which, in the Führer's previous declarations, we did not have to reckon until 1944, and which the Führer right up to the last moment believed he could avoid."[20] The fleet "in the fall of 1939 is in no way sufficiently armed for the great struggle with England." By 1944–45, assisted by the battle fleets of Italy and Japan, it could have effected its double-pole strategy against Britain.

Still, what to do? Raeder remembered the ignominious end of the Kaiser's imperial navy: rebellion in July 1917, revolution in

October 1918, and scuttling in June 1919. He was determined to avoid a repetition. There was only one thing to do: "to show that [the fleet] knows how to die gallantly and thereby lay the foundations for a future reconstruction." The shame and humiliation of the past were to be exorcised from the service. With these fateful words, the grand admiral closed his war diary.

At first the fleet seemed not to get the message. On 17 December 1939 Captain Hans Langsdorff scuttled the pocket battleship *Graf Spee* in the River Plate at Montevideo after a brief encounter with the heavy cruiser HMS *Exeter* and the light cruisers HMS *Ajax* and HMNZS *Achilles*. Hitler was "very upset" that the *Graf Spee* had not fought to the death. He lectured his grand admiral that whereas the British fought to the last shell, the Germans needed to understand the concept of "dying gallantly." Raeder, painfully aware of the parallel to the 1919 scuttling at Scapa Flow, immediately issued a stern general order: "The German warship fights with the full deployment of its crew until the last shell, until it is victorious or goes down with flag flying."[21]

This time the fleet got the message. On 9 April 1940 it put out to sea in full force during Operation Weserübung, the occupation of Denmark and Norway. The fleet paid a heavy price: three cruisers, ten destroyers, and four submarines lost in action. But the Wehrmacht quickly eclipsed this debacle. On 10 May it invaded Luxembourg, Belgium, the Netherlands, and France. The French capitulated on 22 June in the forest of Compiègne—in the same railroad car in which imperial Germany had been humbled on 11 November 1918. Thereafter, Hitler burned the car. The Kriegsmarine now had direct access to the Atlantic Ocean, outflanking Britain, the "mortal enemy," from Norway in the northeast and from Brest, Cherbourg, Lorient, St. Nazaire, La Pallice, and Bordeaux in the southwest. All Raeder needed to take advantage of this geographic-strategic position was a fleet.

To show the British that he had not abandoned the Atlantic, Raeder sent his remaining units out to hunt convoys. The pocket battleship *Admiral Scheer*, Captain Theodor Krancke commanding, raided the Atlantic and Indian oceans for 161 days, leaving the North Sea via the Denmark Strait in October 1940. Raeder was ecstatic. On 14 November he joyfully informed Hitler that the *Scheer* had destroyed 85,000 tons of shipping out of a "Canada-route" convoy. Overall, Krancke would dispatch twenty-one vessels totaling 155,000 tons.[22] The ship's success had created "*advantageous preconditions for a new raid by other fleet units on the north Atlantic routes.*"[23] That same month Raeder dispatched the heavy cruiser *Admiral Hipper* on another raid.

On 3 December 1940 Admiral Raeder informed Hitler and General Jodl that overseas supplies were the Achilles' heel of the British Isles. "Concentration of all available surface vessels" was the only means of bringing "perfidious Albion" to her knees; all other operations merely dispersed German strength. The "national character" of the British "as Germanic peoples is tough, their leadership hard and determined." Still, Raeder argued, there was only one enemy. "England is the principal adversary in our fight for survival."[24]

On 28 December 1940 Raeder ordered the battleships *Gneisenau* and *Scharnhorst* out on a raiding mission. The task force was under the command of Admiral Lütjens, the Kriegsmarine's new (and third) fleet chief. But sea damage encountered by the *Gneisenau* and several destroyers forced cancellation of the Atlantic raid. Operation Berlin was rescheduled for the first opportune moment.

The *Gneisenau* and the *Scharnhorst* sortied in the Atlantic from 22 January to 23 March 1941. They destroyed twenty-two vessels and in the process forced the Royal Navy to assign at least a battleship or battle cruiser to escort convoys in the northern passages. Lütjens barely managed to elude a British force composed of three battleships, eight cruisers, and eleven destroyers. Still, Raeder was delighted, deeming Operation Berlin to have been a "singularly successful operation." The surface ships had proved their ability to raid the Atlantic "for months and without bases."[25] Brest was to be completed as the navy's new sally port. All the while, Raeder pressed Hitler (to no avail) to assign air units to the navy—and urged completion of the *Bismarck* and the *Tirpitz*. At the end of March he ordered Lütjens to haul down his flag on the *Gneisenau* at Brest and to proceed to Berlin to prepare himself for what Raeder termed "a greater task."

In fact, Grand Admiral Raeder, along with his chief of operations, Rear Admiral Kurt Fricke, had been hard at work for months devising plans for a grandiose assault on Britain's Atlantic convoys. At a critical meeting with Hitler on 27 December 1940, Raeder for the first time had unveiled a new offensive strategy: the battleships would replace the smaller heavy cruisers and pocket battleships as oceanic raiders.[26] Armed with contingency studies undertaken by his staff in August, the admiral assured his Führer that there was little to choose, in terms of either quality or quantity, between the Royal Navy, on one hand, and the combined German and Italian fleets, on other. To be sure, Britain enjoyed a "decided advantage" in battleships and destroyers. But fourteen of Britain's sixteen battleships were old and slow; the ten German and Italian battleships were new and fast. Moreover, Germany and Italy were superior in U-boats (256 to 73). Above all, Britain was tied to a "strategically defensive" policy—namely, that of securing overseas supplies—and this allowed Germany, albeit the "weaker opponent," a "free hand operationally."

The acquisition of naval bases in Norway and France had shifted even the geographic balance in Germany's favor. As soon as the new 15-inch battleships *Bismarck* and *Tirpitz* could augment the 11-inch battleships *Scharnhorst* and *Gneisenau*, Raeder informed Hitler, vast new "opportunities to attack British convoys" would offer themselves. When Hitler, ever leery of losing a heavy ship, queried Raeder concerning the purpose of sending these ships into the Atlantic, Raeder replied: "First and foremost battle against supplies. Goal is always the convoys, not the escorts, which are to be evaded if they are not significantly weaker." Admiral Raeder's double-pole strategy seemed within reach.

While Admiral Raeder instructed Hitler on the newly developed "opportunities to attack British convoys" with heavy surface ships, work on the two super battleships had proceeded throughout 1940. At Hamburg, an army of welders and fitters, carpenters and electricians, shipwrights and plumbers worked around the clock to ready the great ship for her sea trials. In August Captain Lindemann surveyed his new charge: almost three football fields long and one football field wide, with seven decks below the waterline and as many again above, the *Bismarck* would shortly become the world's most powerful ship. At 50,000 tons, she was easily 15,000 tons larger than the *Scharnhorst* and 12,000 tons more than her British contemporary, HMS *Prince of Wales*. She was given the task of terrorizing Britain's vital Atlantic sea lanes to Canada and the United States.

Shortly after the fall of France in June, Lindemann was ordered to host a surprise party: a special Swedish naval delegation headed by special envoy Stig Ericson and the Danish naval attaché to Germany, Fritz Kjølsen. Lindemann resented both the intrusion on his time and the revealing of *Bismarck*'s size and armament; Ericson had been educated at the French Naval War College and was known to be pro-British.[27] Lindemann was sure that Ericson would report on his findings, both to Swedish Intelligence and to the British Legation in Stockholm. Still, orders were orders, and Lindemann was not about to cross Admiral Raeder on the matter. After two months of further work at Blohm & Voss, the *Bismarck* was formally placed into service at Hamburg on 24 August 1940. Captain Ernst Lindemann was her first skipper.

"Attention! Face to starboard," barked the *Bismarck*'s first officer, Fregattenkapitän (Commander) Hans Oels, as he lined his divisions up on the deck's planks. A sleek white motorboat sporting the battle ensign and commission pennant smartly came up alongside the battleship. A bugler sounded the signal, the honor guard presented arms, and Lindemann was piped on board. "Crew formed for commissioning ceremony," Oels reported. The *Bismarck*'s captain reviewed the crew and then addressed his new charges. "Seamen of the *Bismarck*! Commissioning day for our splendid ship has come at last." Lindemann stated that the hour of decision in the war would soon be at hand, that military force alone could resolve Germany's fate. Next the captain reminded the crew of Otto von Bismarck's famous "iron and blood" approach to international relations. In fact, Lindemann had taken the Iron Chancellor's motto, *Patriae inserviendo consumor* (I am consumed in the service of the fatherland), to heart. Lindemann's first order was that the *Bismarck* be addressed only in the masculine form. "So powerful a ship as this could only be a *he*, not a *she*."[28] Apprentice Machinist Hermann Budich gained the impression that the "Old Man" radiated an aristocratic calm. A man to sail with!

Lindemann and his band of about thirty executive and engineer officers spent weeks and months at the Blohm & Voss Shipyard at Hamburg getting acquainted with their new ship. She was not at all what her official statistics suggested. In truth, the *Bismarck*, built at a cost of 196 million Reichsmarks, displaced about 41,200 tons empty (same as HMS *Hood* after revisions in 1939) and 50,500 full.[29] The Kriegsmarine's chief naval designer, Hermann Burckhardt, had reached back to the last class of battleships produced by the imperial navy—the *Bayern* and *Baden*, completed in 1916—for guidance. Like them, the *Bismarck* was powered by steam-driven turbines, but she carried a main armament of 15-inch guns. Germany's locks, docks, and canals dictated her dimensions. Only a single pen at the North Sea base of Wilhelmshaven could accommodate *Bismarck*'s beam of 39 yards; there were only three dry docks in Germany (at Bremerhaven, Hamburg, and Kiel) that could hold her 50,000 tons; and the Kiel Canal, with a depth of 12 yards at full water level, just barely managed *Bismarck*'s draft of 11 yards. In short, the *Bismarck* reached the outer limits of Germany's docks, locks, and canals.

Whereas the kaiser's battleships had been designed to operate off the German coast, that is, within the confines of the North Sea, Admiral Raeder demanded that all his capital ships be fit for extended tours of duty out in the broad reaches of the Atlantic Ocean. This forced Burckhardt to design battleships that had *both* speed and endurance—an almost impossible task, as high speed ravaged the fuel supply. Thus *Bismarck* was given a triple-turbine, Curtis-type power plant that produced 150,170 horsepower maximum, and drove the trio of three-bladed 5-yard propellers for a best speed of 30.1 knots under ideal conditions—about 2 knots slower than the *Hood*. The *Bismarck*'s range was roughly 8,500 nautical miles at 19 knots, 6,600 at 24 knots. For extended operations on the 4.1 million square miles of the Atlantic, this was insufficient. The ship could bunker 8,294 tons of main and supplementary fuel, 306 tons of fresh water, and 160 tons of lubricating oil. Four electric plants, each with two 4,000-kilowatt diesel generators, produced 7,910 kilowatts at 220 volts. An electric steering gear operated the ship's two balance-type parallel rudders, each with an area of 24 square yards. Commander Walter Lehmann, as chief engineer, was in charge of her heavy machinery.

A gunnery expert, Captain Lindemann paid special attention to the *Bismarck*'s primary armament. It consisted, like that of the *Hood*, of eight 15-inch guns, mounted in pairs in four centerline superimposed turrets (A and B, or "Anton" and "Bruno," forward; C and D, or "Cäsar" and "Dora," aft). The big guns, each barrel weighing 244,000 pounds, had a muzzle velocity of 890 yards per second and could penetrate 12 inches of armor plate at 27,000 yards. In theory, the *Bismarck* could fire 3.3 shells per barrel per minute; in reality, as Lindemann would discover during her workup trials, it was two rounds per minute. At a barrel elevation of 30 degrees, the *Bismarck* could hurl her 1,764-pound shells a distance of 38,700 yards—a distinct advantage over the *Hood*'s optimum range of 30,000 yards. *Bismarck*'s barrel elevation ranged from −8 degrees to +35 degrees; barrel endurance was designed for 180 shots. Each mounting had two hoists, one electric and one hand-operated, to expedite the 840 to 960 heavy shells that she carried in her hold. Fourteen-inch face armor and 8.7-inch side armor protected the 15-inch turrets.

Bismarck's secondary armament, intended for use against enemy destroyers, comprised twelve 6-inch guns, mounted in pairs, in turrets, three on each side of the upper deck. In theory, the well-tried 6-inch guns could fire eight shots per barrel per minute, but Lindemann would discover that the heavy work of hand-lifting its 95-pound shells reduced that rate to five shots. The heavy antiaircraft (flak) defense consisted first and foremost of sixteen 4-inch guns in double mountings. Designed to knock down high-flying hostile aircraft, these weapons could fire fifteen shots per minute and had a range of about 19,350 yards. It was heavy and dangerous work. The 33-pound shells were brought up to a central loading platform, from where they had to be hauled about 16 yards to each gun; final loading was done by hand. There was no protection for the flak's gunners—against the weather, hostile fire, or artillery splinters.

As well, the *Bismarck* mounted as medium flak sixteen semiautomatic 1.5-inch guns with a rate of fire of thirty to forty rounds per minute. To guard against low-flying aircraft, the battleship was given a light flak consisting of twenty .75-inch MG C/30 antiaircraft "pom-poms." The crews of both the 1.5-inch and the .75-inch flak were without protection of any kind. Designed to fight long-range artillery duels, the *Bismarck* carried no torpedo armament.

In line with the imperial navy's obsession with optimum armor, the *Bismarck* received a total weight of 17,569 tons of armor plate—about 25 percent more than the *Hood*. *Bismarck*'s armor plate made up 40 percent of her total weight. Her outer shell was covered by a Krupp Cementite and "Wotan hard" armor belt that measured between 5.5 and 12.6 inches and protected the vital turbines, boilers, and magazines. The upper deck was covered with 2-inch-thick armor, while the bridge, home to both Lindemann and Lütjens, was protected by 13.8-inch vertical armor and 8.7-inch roof plate. German designers, unlike their American and British counterparts, favored a wide distribution of armor over the hull, instead of concentrating armor over the vital spaces. The double-bottomed hull was constructed of steel and divided into twenty-two watertight compartments—numbered from Section I aft to Section XII forward—by a complex system of transverse and longitudinal bulkheads, 90 percent electrically welded. The *Bismarck* carried four single-engine, low-wing Arado 196 floatplanes, to be launched off either port or starboard by a double-ended 16-yard catapult athwartships. The planes were stored in a single hangar on either side of the funnel as well as a double hangar at the base of the mainmast. Pilots and mechanics came from the Luftwaffe. The two-seater Arados had a top speed of 199 miles per hour and a range of 665 miles.

With respect to range finding and fire control, *Bismarck*'s five high-resolution 11.5-yard optical range finders were mounted forward, aft, and in the foretop. Specifically, two of the Zeiss range finders (effective range of 9 miles, magnification of 50) were housed under rotating cupolas, the other three were installed in the turrets Bruno, Cäsar, and Dora. The first gunnery officer, Korvettenkapitän (Commander) Adalbert Schneider, directed the fire of *Bismarck*'s main armament from an artillery command post in the fore upper direction tower ("Vormars") high above the smoke of her guns. Range and bearing information supplied by the Zeiss range finders was fed down to the *Bismarck*'s two fire-control centers (or gunnery-computer rooms), where artillery officers and petty officers continuously translated them into precise ballistic data, which they then relayed to the artillery officers commanding each of the four 15-inch main turrets.

The *Bismarck* also carried three revolving-dome radar-detection (FuMO-23) sets. Dubbed "Seetakt," they measured range to target and operated on a frequency of 368 megahertz and a wavelength of 32 inches. The FuMO-23's effective range was about 27,340 yards. Their 2-by-4-yard mesh antennas were popularly referred to as "mattresses." But the Seetakt were extremely sensitive to shock caused by the recoil of the ship's heavy artillery—a full eight-barrel salvo of 24,490 pounds produced almost 60 million horsepower. Above all, they could only detect radar emissions, not calculate location and distance to enemy ships.

Bismarck's gunnery crew, serving under Commander Schneider, was trained to fire "bracketing groups." In other words, rather than firing test-shoot salvos in succession and awaiting the actual shell splashes, the *Bismarck* launched a bracketing group of three salvos separated by a uniform range (usually 440 yards) and loosed so rapidly that all shells were in flight at the same time. This allowed

Schneider—from the fore upper direction tower, with the aid of his Zeiss optical range finders—to "box" or "straddle" the target on the first fall of shot. The *Bismarck*'s broad beam made her a reliable gun platform.

Bismarck and her sister ship *Tirpitz* were the culmination, indeed the crowning glory, of German battleship building. For layman and naval professional alike, the *Bismarck*, with her clipper bow, cruiser stern, rakish superstructure, and cowled funnel, exuded elegance and power. At 263 yards long and with a beam of 39 yards, she was an imposing sight, putting to the test Germany's largest locks and docks. Her armament weighed 5,500 tons, and each 15-inch gun barrel was almost 19 yards long. At 30 knots, the *Bismarck* was 8 knots faster than imperial Germany's last class of battleships (the *Bayern* and the *Baden*), and her engines developed almost three times the horsepower of these vessels. In short, she was the state of the art, the most powerful battleship afloat in 1941, the terror of the seas. The fact that the *Bismarck* had been built in great secrecy added to her mystery. To be sure, Berlin had informed London of her specifications, as required under the Anglo-German Naval Agreement of 1935, but these had listed her at a mere 35,000 tons—a figure that Captain R. N. T. Troubridge, the British naval attaché to Germany, had accepted readily. The Swedish delegation that had visited the *Bismarck* in the summer of 1940 no doubt had passed on to London its observations concerning her true dimensions, size of power plant, and main armament, yet social visits did not translate into hard evidence. The *Bismarck*'s actual power and intended deployment remained open to speculation.

But the *Bismarck* was also already obsolete in some ways, and unfit for her projected mission—raids in the Atlantic Ocean—in others.[30] To be sure, due to the restrictions of the Treaty of Versailles of 1919, Germany had skipped almost a generation of naval architecture—between the *Baden* and *Bayern* of 1913–16 and the *Scharnhorst* and *Gneisenau* of 1933–36. Moreover, a lack of proper planning and a deep-rooted traditionalism dogged Berlin's naval leaders. Admiral Raeder designed his capital ships for ocean raiding in the Atlantic. This required long sea legs. To that end, the so-called Deutschland class of pocket battleships had each been given eight 9-cylinder diesel-powered engines, and thereby long legs (10,000 nautical miles range). Then, inexplicably, in 1934 diesels were abandoned in favor of traditional steam-turbine propulsion, a step that translated into 40 percent shorter range. Research and development lost out to tradition.

Armor also remained at the mercy of tradition. The *Bismarck*'s protective plates were designed to withstand the impact of a 15-inch shell fired from a range of 10 miles at right angles. But this failed to take into account the phenomenon of "plunging fire"—the arrival of shells at angles less than 20 degrees from the vertical, and especially from aircraft. A 1,100-pound bomb dropped from 4,900 yards could easily penetrate 6-inch armor plate. In July 1941, for example, a 1,000-pound bomb sliced through the *Scharnhorst*'s 7.5-inch horizontal armor plate.

With regard to main armament, Burckhardt, the *Bismarck*'s chief designer, opted for the traditional arrangement of two sets of twin turrets forward and aft. This allowed for a better field of fire and a more effective sequence of salvos. On the other hand, the secondary armament of twelve 6-inch guns was a bad compromise. A classic anti-destroyer weapon, the 6-inch gun fired six rounds per barrel per minute. But the Kriegsmarine used it as an antiaircraft weapon, designed to put up a long-range curtain of time-fused shrapnel shells to deter approaching bombers. Against high-flying fast bombers as well as torpedo bombers that skimmed the wave tops, the gun was useless—its rate of fire was too slow and its angle of elevation inadequate. In short, Raeder's designers had failed to appreciate the notion of a multipurpose flak gun.

Even the excellent 4-inch models had a potentially fatal flaw: designers in Berlin had overlooked the need to install fire directors individual to each gun, with the result that when the fire-direction instructions were relayed, the forward C31 gun fired at the target, while the aft C37 fired at a point behind the target. Finally, the

Bismarck was given a "grossly inferior" flak-direction center based on the revolving ring system. Its massive 40-ton revolving base, when engaged against hostile aircraft, tended to affect the ship's stability. Above all, the revolving base was extremely sensitive to underwater hits, and even the slightest damage could cause the ring to break, resulting in a total system breakdown.

As to radar, Germany had led the world in its development in the late 1930s with the "Freya" (.9-inch wave band) and the "Würzburg" (19.7-inch wave band). But thereafter, German radar industries fragmented, and a plethora of firms vied with one another, especially for Luftwaffe contracts. In short order, Germany lost the "radar race" to British centrimetric radar.[31] Publications that suggest that the *Bismarck* was already equipped with fire-control radar are in error, mistaking the FuMO-23 range finders for radar surveillance devices.

Finally, there was a major problem with any Atlantic sortie that had nothing to do with either the *Bismarck*'s design or Lindemann's skills: the lack of fleet air support. Time and again, both Raeder and Dönitz had pleaded with Hitler for a separate naval air arm. And while each time those pleas had found a sympathetic ear, eventually they foundered on the determined opposition of Field Marshal Hermann Göring. On 7 February 1941, for example, Admiral Dönitz held a lengthy discussion—or, in the terminology of the U-boat fleet commander, a "Jesuitical" discourse—with Göring regarding aerial surveillance. The chief of the air force declined to provide any air patrols west of 25 degrees latitude, arguing that he had constructed far-ranging aircraft only for bombing missions. After reminding Dönitz that Göring was "the number two man in the Reich," the field marshal brutally pressed his case: the navy could be assured that as long as Göring was alive and in office, "Grand Admiral Raeder would not be given a naval air force."[32] In short, Admiral Lütjens would have to provide his own aerial reconnaissance by way of the *Bismarck*'s Arado floatplanes.

In August and September 1940, Captain Lindemann had more immediate and pressing concerns. Hamburg was already a target for British night bombing raids, and whenever possible, the *Bismarck* added her flak to that of the city's antiaircraft batteries. The British had had "no success," Lindemann happily wrote in the war diary each time.[33] By day, Hamburg purveyors loaded mountains of equipment: charts, flags, signal books, code books, binoculars, typewriters, film, and medications. The *Bismarck*'s two canteens stowed away three hundred sides of beef and five hundred dressed hogs—enough to feed a city of 250,000 people for a day—as well as boxes of cigarettes, biscuits, chocolate, and almost a thousand 13-gallon barrels of beer (sold at 30 pfennigs per half liter).

At 2:20 P.M. on 15 September, in sunshine and still wind, the *Bismarck* eased out of the Blohm & Voss yards.[34] "Single up all lines," First Officer Oels, a native of Sande in the North Sea region of Oldenburg, barked out from the bridge. "Let go aft." As the hawsers were hauled in, Oels continued the routine. "Slow ahead port." The giant port screw churned the murky gray waters of the Elbe. Slowly the stern began to swing away from the dock. Deep-sea tugs strained to help. When the *Bismarck* stood 45 degrees off the jetty, the bowlines were cast off. "Slow astern both engines." Lindemann ordered that the third engine remain idle for the time being.

The battleship backed away from the Blohm & Voss pier. "Slow ahead starboard, port ten." The *Bismarck* swung her mighty bow into the Elbe. The tugs' screws thrashed the water as they pushed her farther into the river's deep channel. "Take in fenders, secure the upper deck. Half ahead both engines." No sooner had Oels issued the order than the *Bismarck* collided with the lead tug, *Atlantik*, which had not anticipated the increased speed. No damage, but an inauspicious beginning.[35]

Later that night, riding at anchor in Brunsbüttel Roads at the North Sea entrance into the Kiel Canal, the *Bismarck* fired 340 mainly .75-inch and 1.5-inch shells at attacking British aircraft.[36] Captain Lindemann immediately prepared for the worst: "Clear for action." He carefully watched as the ship's twenty-two watertight compartments were sealed. The next night Lindemann guided the battleship into the Kiel Canal. At 5:52 P.M. on 17 September the

Bismarck made fast in Scheer Harbor, Kiel. A week later the majestic vessel left Kiel and pointed east, arriving at Gotenhafen in the afternoon of 29 September. Ahead lay weeks of sea trials, personnel training, and gunnery practice in the Baltic Sea.

Lindemann was on edge. British aircraft droned overhead and dropped propaganda leaflets into the former Polish Corridor.[37] The presence of German capital ships in Danzig Bay was bound to attract their attention. Indeed, London had closely monitored the *Bismarck*'s progress toward operational readiness. The Admiralty knew her rough dimensions from RAF flyovers as well as from the leaked Swedish inspection report of the summer of 1940; its greatest fears were that the German super-battleship might join existing commerce raiders such as the pocket battleships and the two 11-inch battleships to attack transatlantic convoys. Prime Minister Winston S. Churchill instructed Bomber Command that the disabling of Germany's two super-battleships was "the greatest prize" open to it.[38] "Even a few months' delay in *Bismarck*," Churchill pleaded, "will affect the whole balance of sea-power to a serious degree." The spectacular British raid on the Italian naval base at Taranto during the night of 11–12 November 1940, wherein British torpedo planes damaged three battleships, two cruisers, and two fleet auxiliary vessels, only added to Captain Lindemann's consternation.

There was also a mechanical problem that demanded attention: Lindemann quickly discovered that the *Bismarck* was desperately reliant on her electric steering gear. Locking both rudders in the amidships position, Lindemann rotated the two outboard propellers in opposition at full power; he could maintain the *Bismarck* on course only with great difficulty.[39] As well, operating the manual steering gear required that the crews of both after turrets, thirty-two men, abandon their guns and rush to Section II of the upper platform deck. The pressure of the seawater against the rudders limited speed to less than 20 knots—hardly desirable under battle conditions. Continually Lindemann put the crew of the *Bismarck* through drills simulating a hit in the steering gear. Two or three compartments in the stern would be "flooded" and the men in them cut off. Rescue and repairs would be attempted. "But the chances of such a hit," the sailors were assured by their officers, "are a hundred thousand to one, practically nil."[40]

On 5 December 1940 the *Bismarck*, under a heavy war alert, shaped course for Kiel. In the Scheer Harbor, Ernst Lindemann cast his eyes on a brand-new heavy cruiser calibrating its guns and taking on ammunition. It was the *Prinz Eugen*, destined to be one of the scouts for Admiral Raeder's Atlantic task forces.

Work on "Cruiser J," contracted for 10,000 tons displacement and 8-inch main armament, had begun at Friedrich Krupp's Germania Shipyard at Kiel on 23 April 1936. After the Austrian *Anschluss* of 1938, it had been decided to honor the former Imperial and Royal Navy by christening the heavy cruiser *Tegetthoff*, in memory of Commodore Wilhelm von Tegetthoff, the Austrian fleet chief who had soundly defeated an Italian fleet off Lissa on 20 July 1866. Later, however, under the fear that the Rome-Berlin axis might not bear the strain of such a constant reminder of Italy's worst defeat ever at sea, it was decided to give the new ship the name *Prinz Eugen*, in honor of the greatest Habsburg soldier of all time.[41]

The *Prinz Eugen* was launched on 22 August 1938. Nicholaus and Magdalena Horthy de Nagybány christened her on 1 August 1940 at the Germania Shipyard at Kiel. Captain Horthy had commanded the Austro-Hungarian battleship *Prinz Eugen* from November 1917 until March 1918, at which time he had been promoted to rear admiral and appointed fleet chief. Hitler, who had accompanied Horthy to the christening ceremony, presented the crew with a contemporary portrait of Prince Eugene.

The heavy cruiser, Captain Lindemann acknowledged, was one of the most beautiful warships ever built. She displaced 19,000 tons fully loaded,[42] and mounted a main battery of eight 8-inch guns in twin turrets, capable of firing just over two shots per minute to a maximum range of 22 miles. The *Prinz Eugen* carried 960 heavy shells in her holds. The secondary armament consisted of twelve heavy flak 4-inch guns in six twin mountings, as well as twelve 1.5-inch guns and eight .75-inch C/30 machine guns. The *Prinz Eugen* also mounted twelve 21-inch torpedo tubes in triple mountings; each tube was armed with a single G7a "eel." Finally, in addition to the standard optical range finder mounted in the top foremast, the heavy cruiser possessed two FuMO-27 radar-detection systems, one each fore and aft.

Krupp belt armor ranged between 1.6 inches forward, 2.8 inches aft, and 3.1 inches citadel; the main armament had face armor of 6 inches. The cruiser's three-shaft Brown Boverie turbines each developed 44,000 horsepower for a top speed of 32.5 knots. The *Prinz Eugen* could bunker but 3,250 tons of fuel, giving her a limited range of 5,000 miles at 15 knots. For reconnaissance and antisubmarine operations, the heavy cruiser had been given three Arado 196 floatplanes and a catapult between funnel and deck-house.

Finally, *Prinz Eugen* carried a complement of 54 officers and 1,400 men. Her skipper, Captain Helmuth Brinkmann, was a graduate of the Crew of 1913, same as Ernst Lindemann. Born on 12 March 1895 at the Hanseatic city of Lübeck, Brinkmann had joined the imperial navy in April 1913 and seen service on battleships, cruisers, and torpedo boats during the First World War. In the postwar period, Brinkmann had commanded the dispatch boat *Grille*, after which he was posted to the Naval Defense Department. The popular officer had spent the period from October 1938 to June 1940 ashore as head of the Naval Defense Department. He received command of the *Prinz Eugen* on 1 August 1940. In December 1940 neither Brinkmann nor Lindemann could know that they were about to join forces for a dangerous sortie into the Atlantic.

After replenishing the *Bismarck*'s fuel supply at Kiel, Lindemann guided her back through the Kiel Canal. The *Bismarck* docked at Hamburg late on 9 December. Blohm & Voss engineers gave her the last finishing touches and undertook minor adjustments of the ship's machinery. Training, especially of the antiaircraft crews, continued day and night.

The war raged all around Hamburg and the *Bismarck*. Hostile aircraft sank several German ships in the Kiel Canal, blocking traffic in both directions. Steaming through the Skagerrak and the Danish Belts was ruled out as being too risky due to the danger of British mines.[43] The *Bismarck* spent Christmas at Hamburg. A heavy frost (23° Fahrenheit) brought icy winds down the stovepipes into the engine rooms, freezing critical pressure gauges and some of the sensitive electrical lines to the compensating tanks and ventilators.[44] An army of Blohm & Voss workers rerouted the air intakes and rewrapped many of the 5,000 miles of electrical lines on board ship that had snapped in the cold.

On 16 January 1941 Blohm & Voss pronounced the *Bismarck* cleared for action. Eight days later Lindemann reported that his command was ready to sail. No orders arrived. On 5 February he again radioed that his ship was seaworthy. No orders. Finally Naval Group Command North at Wilhelmshaven ordered him to steam out of Hamburg on 19 February. But the continued blockage of the Kiel Canal as well as unusually high water in the Elbe River frustrated these plans. Exasperated, Lindemann wrote in the war diary that his ship had "now been tied down at Hamburg for five weeks. . . . The precious training time at sea lost as a result cannot be made up, and a significant delay in the final war deployment of the ship thus is unavoidable."[45]

While readying his ship for front-line service, Lindemann had to host yet another foreign visitor. Captain Anders Forshell, the Swedish naval attaché to Berlin, had used his personal contacts with Raeder and his chief of staff, Captain Erich Schulte-Mönting, to gain permission to inspect the super-battleship. Lindemann was hardly pleased with this second interruption of the *Bismarck*'s final workup at Blohm & Voss, but once more there could be no question of disobeying Raeder's orders. And Captain Forshell was known to be pro-German. Obviously impressed by what he saw at Hamburg, Forshell sent a detailed technical report concerning the *Bismarck* to Swedish Combined Intelligence in Stockholm.[46] Captain Forshell's report constituted the first detailed description of the *Bismarck*. Until then, the Admiralty in London had had to piece together snippets of information it received from RAF spotters and from the earlier Swedish visit by Ericson and Kjølsen. But it lacked precise information concerning the ship's main armament, power plant, displacement, range, and top speed. The Naval Section of Swedish Intelligence could hardly believe the treasure it had been handed by Forshell—and immediately put its copy of the document in an unlocked desk drawer. Not surprisingly, given that Stockholm was awash in both Allied and German spies, each side sparing neither effort nor funds to secure up-to-date intelligence, the report soon found its way into the hands of the British naval attaché, Captain Henry Denham. He realized at once the critical content of Forshell's report and forwarded it to London by secure courier. Finally, Churchill and his naval planners knew what they would be up against: a 270-yard-long super-battleship of about 50,000 tons, powered by 150,000-horsepower steam turbines capable of best speed of about 30 knots, and with a main armament of eight 15-inch guns mounted on an extremely stable 40-yard-wide platform.

At dawn on 6 March Lindemann finally received the welcome news that the *Bismarck* was to proceed to Kiel. Several Messerschmitt 109 fighters, two armed merchantmen, and one icebreaker provided cover.[47] But problems continued to dog the *Bismarck*: at 8:45 A.M. on 8 March she ran aground on the southern shore of the Kiel Canal, though tugs pulled the ship free within the hour.[48] The following day, the *Bismarck* entered Dry Dock C in Kiel. She took on provisions, aligned her batteries, and received to hull and superstructure a special coat of dazzle paint designed to confuse visual observation. On 12 March enemy aircraft shelled both harbor and city.[49] Lindemann calmly bunkered ammunition, fuel, and more provisions, and stored two of the *Bismarck*'s allotted four Arado 196 aircraft on board.

Problems beset the floatplanes from the start. Neither the cranes, nor the catapult, nor the hangars permitted rapid deployment. The aircraft could be launched only one at a time, usually at twenty-five-minute intervals. The mobile hangars were difficult to operate, lacked proper lighting and heat to allow routine maintenance, and were flooded by surging seawater during "high-speed cruising and rising seas (the normal case)."[50] Still, on 17 March 1941 the old battleship *Schlesien* guided the *Bismarck* through the Baltic ice floes to Gotenhafen.

Two days later Captain Karl Topp, commander of the newly commissioned sister ship *Tirpitz*, surprised Lindemann with the news that Berlin had decided that the *Bismarck* was to be ready for operations by the end of April—that is, three to four weeks earlier than planned. Lindemann's remonstrance that his crew was not yet "100% battle ready" was ignored.[51] Rather, Raeder ordered him to speed up artillery training, to practice maneuvering with U-boats and cruisers, to fine-tune refueling at sea with the tanker *Bromberg*, to work up the air crews around the clock, and to drill them in reconnaissance.

Daily Lindemann drove his men on with a Spartan routine.[52] Reveille was at 6 A.M. Breakfast—coffee, butter, jam—was a half hour later, followed by cleaning decks at 7:15 A.M. and muster at 8 A.M. Instruction and practical work continued until the noon break—soup, potatoes or dumplings, meat—from 11:30 A.M. to 1:30 P.M., and then resumed until the evening meal—butter, cheese, sausage—was served at 5 P.M. The duty day ended at 6:30 P.M. after a final cleaning of the deck. The call to swing hammocks sounded around 10 P.M. All the while, Lindemann, a gunnery expert, personally supervised target practice. The gunners managed to fire the mammoth 15-inch shells at the rate of two per minute—that is, twenty-six seconds from loading to discharging the shells. With barrels elevated to 30 degrees, *Bismarck* could hurl her 1,764-pound shells 38,900 yards; weight of broadside was 29,500 pounds. Each shell could penetrate 20 inches of armor at 11,000 yards, and 14 inches at 21,900 yards.[53] Day by day, the men began to appreciate the Old Man's calm, dignified authority.

But the lack of proficient resupply facilities at Gotenhafen and Pillau slowed Lindemann's efforts. The open waters of Danzig Bay battered supply vessels and target barges alike. *Bismarck*'s starboard cranes broke down and required Blohm & Voss crews to rush to Gotenhafen to undertake the necessary repairs. The airplane catapults were damaged during a trial launch; on 30 March Lindemann requisitioned those designated for the *Tirpitz*. They, in turn, broke down on 4 April and required two weeks to repair. By steaming in a circle at 18 knots, Lindemann hoped to create a calm "duck's pond" on which to land the aircraft. But on 16 April an Arado 196 landed in heavy seas, and its propeller broke off and punctured both pontoons.[54] A patrol boat saved the crew; the aircraft sank. Lindemann was not pleased with his aircraft-launching ability. All the while, the *Bismarck* continued workup exercises off Danzig.

Lindemann's greatest frustration remained the absence of clear orders from Berlin. He had been informed that a major operation had been planned for early April 1941, but one day after another went by without further instructions. The *Bismarck*'s captain summarized his mounting disgust with the Navy Supreme Command during the first two weeks of April as follows: "The crew appears to have come to a first realization of the magnitude of the pending operation—which we still do not know but can hardly fail to surmise." After two weeks, there were still no further instructions from Berlin. Again, Lindemann vented his frustration in the ship's war diary for 16 to 30 March: "It becomes an increasingly heavy burden that the command receives no clear orders for the pending deployment—and that what instructions do come arrive so late as to prevent proper outfitting of the ship (for example, deployment in the tropics, stowing of prize crews, and the like) through normal channels."[55]

In fact, Grand Admiral Raeder's plan to sweep the Atlantic with a massive four-capital-ship task force (the *Bismarck* and the *Tirpitz* from Gotenhafen, the *Gneisenau* and the *Scharnhorst* from Brest) proceeded on course. On 2 April 1941 Raeder laid out the basic contours of what was to become Rhine Exercise to his fleet chief, the commander of U-boats, and Naval Commands West and North. As soon as the new *Bismarck*-class battleships and at least the *Gneisenau* were seaworthy, they were to raid the Atlantic sea-lanes, destroying escorts and merchantmen alike. The sudden appearance of two new battleships and the constant relocation of surface raids would "disperse" British warships to the point of ineffectiveness. In the process, the Kriegsmarine would be able "*gradually, methodically, and systematically*" to establish at least "local and temporary sea control."[56]

But these well-laid plans received a crushing blow on 6 April, when a Beaufort torpedo airplane of No. 22 Squadron, Coastal Command, torpedoed the *Gneisenau* in Brest harbor, wrecking its stern. A follow-up bombing raid six days later further damaged the *Gneisenau* while in dry dock. Raeder estimated repairs would last until early October. He was crestfallen. "Therewith, the Naval High Command's plans to conduct the Battle of the Atlantic with battleships has been dealt a crippling blow."[57] Raeder conceded that the enemy was pursuing the goal of destroying German battleships at Brest "with stubborn determination."[58] Any Atlantic operation incurring even minor damage, he noted with dismay in his war diary, might entail the ships returning to Trondheim rather than Brest. Moreover, such an operation would be without allies: on 10 April Vice Admiral Naokuni Nomura, head of the Japanese military mission, informed Berlin that Japan would not be ready "to attack the Anglo-Saxon powers before 1946."[59] In the meantime, the German army was finalizing its preparations to launch Operation Barbarossa, the invasion of the Soviet Union.

To make matters even worse for the navy, severe engine problems laid up the *Scharnhorst* at least until the end of June. Next, Raeder learned that the rush of new construction as well as a British air raid that destroyed many of the supply depots at Kiel would delay repairs not only to the *Admiral Scheer*, but also to the heavy cruiser *Admiral Hipper*; the former would not be seaworthy until the end of July, the latter not until 24 August.[60] Moreover, Raeder's staff now conceded that Germany's one aircraft carrier, the *Graf Zeppelin*, was still eight months from completion. Then on Good Friday, 11 April 1941, Raeder learned of President Franklin D. Roosevelt's decision of 9 April to "occupy" Greenland, "*without the knowledge of or permission by the Danish government*." There was no question in Raeder's mind that

"England/USA" had reached an agreement jointly to win "the Battle of the Atlantic." Coming on the heels of the destroyers-for-bases deal of September 1940, the Lend-Lease legislation as well as the American-British-Canadian "ABC-Staff Agreement" of March 1941, and the vast expansion of American armaments industries for Britain's rescue,[61] the Greenland decision was tantamount to a declaration of war against Germany.

More dark clouds gathered on the horizon: on 14 April German naval intelligence (B-Dienst) intercepted a message from the British naval attaché in Stockholm informing the Admiralty that he had installed a formidable news-gathering network in the Danish Belts, the narrow waters between Denmark and Sweden. Captain Denham promised to keep London abreast of the passage of any German warship through the Kattegat within twelve hours.[62] In fact, British cryptanalysts in Hut 8 at Bletchley Park throughout February, March, and April 1941 had intercepted and decrypted Admiral Lütjens' messages concerning his maneuvers in the Baltic Sea. Thus the Admiralty knew that some sort of an operation involving the *Bismarck* as well as other surface units was in the offing; time and place remained a mystery.

And then, the near-fatal blow. Placed in service on 25 February 1941, the *Tirpitz* was plagued by mechanical breakdowns and delays, which robbed her commander of precious weeks of workup exercises.[63] Although Captain Topp on 5 May bravely assured Lütjens (and Hitler) that his ship would be ready to participate in the Atlantic sortie, it became clear to the fleet chief that she would not be ready, as promised, by 20 May. Almost as if to mock these setbacks, the German army marched from victory to victory: Yugoslavia capitulated on 17 April and Athens on 27 April, the very day that the Afrika Korps invaded Egypt.

In a perverse way, the Wehrmacht's triumphs in the Balkans and in North Africa made Raeder even more determined to launch Rhine Exercise. Although bereft of the *Tirpitz*, the *Scharnhorst*, and the *Gneisenau*, the grand admiral rejected Lütjens' suggestion to await the completion of repairs to *Scharnhorst* or the placing in service of the *Tirpitz* before shaping course for the Atlantic. Instead, Raeder offered Lütjens the new heavy cruiser *Prinz Eugen*, Captain Brinkmann commanding. Lindemann was about to be reunited with his comrade from the Crew of 1913.

RHINE EXERCISE:

THE MARCH TO THE DENMARK STRAIT

CAPTAIN HELMUTH BRINKMANN SPENT the first few months of 1941 bringing the *Prinz Eugen* and her crew up to speed. Everything aboard had to be tested: the hydraulics, the electrical system, the guns, engines, rudder, and so on. There would be no time for routine workup; the heavy cruiser was scheduled to sortie at the end of April. And like the *Bismarck* before her, the *Prinz Eugen* was subjected to intensive enemy air attack. Shortly before midnight on 7 April 1941, while undergoing final fitting at the Deutsche Werke in Kiel, the heavy cruiser was bracketed by about two dozen high-explosive bombs and struck by three incendiary bombs. Captain Brinkmann reported that his inexperienced flak crews were hardly up to the task of warding off hostile aircraft.[1]

Continually, the *Prinz Eugen* practiced refueling at sea: on average, the crew managed to take on between 200 and 250 tons of oil per hour. Too slow. By 17 April, the heavy cruiser, now lying off Danzig, began maneuvers with the *Bismarck*. Two days later, an errant practice torpedo launched by the 24th U-Boat Flotilla damaged one of the cruiser's propeller blades. On 22 April the *Prinz Eugen* was ordered back to Kiel for repairs. More delays.

At 3 P.M. the next day, as the *Prinz Eugen* was making her way into the Kiel Bight, an explosion rocked her starboard side. The gauges on the turbines shattered. Lights went out. The optical range finder was ripped from its base; several Zeiss lenses cracked. Freshwater tanks ruptured. A generator tore loose. The forward gyrocompass and degaussing equipment fell out. Deck plates buckled. Foam from the fire extinguishers showered the crew. Captain Brinkmann recorded the event in detail in his war diary. "Mine detonation 15–20 m[eters] off her side. Strong convulsions throughout the ship. Ship immediately without power or steam." A preliminary examination by a team from the ship's damage-control center revealed "1 flotation chamber, 1 drinking water tank, 3 oil bunkers leaking. 1 turbine generator ripped off its bed. The bolts for the shaft housings loosened."[2] The *Prinz Eugen* most likely had struck a ground mine laid by the Royal Air Force. After fifteen minutes the engineers had restored essential power to the ship. At 3:45 P.M. Brinkmann took her into Kiel for a closer look. More delays.

Once in Dry Dock C, the *Prinz Eugen*'s chief engineer, Commander Graser, reported on the full extent of the damage: "Bilge keel torn open in several places and leaking. Tears in three places along the hull near the oil bunkers and flotation chambers." The outer plates were badly dented at the waterline along the starboard-side main deck. Several fuel bunkers were ruptured, and one turbo-generator had been ripped from its foundation. Most seriously, the coupling gear had been damaged. There was also a great deal of shock damage to the cruiser's fire-control and electrical systems. Rear Admiral Kurt Fricke in Berlin immediately agreed to shift men and resources from work on the heavy cruiser *Admiral Hipper* to the *Prinz Eugen*, but even so, the mine disaster "delayed operations for at least eight days."[3] Enemy aircraft, alerted to the cruiser's whereabouts, unsuccessfully tried to bomb her while she was in dry dock.

In Berlin, Grand Admiral Erich Raeder remained extremely anxious to launch Rhine Exercise during the new-moon period (26 April). An

Atlantic sortie would keep the Kriegsmarine's momentum going and possibly divert Royal Navy forces from the Mediterranean theater. But the *Prinz Eugen*'s woes gravely jeopardized his planning. The Naval High Command's diary tersely stated: "Operational delays of 12 days!"[4] Raeder was hamstrung. There seemed to be no end in sight to the string of setbacks that he had recently endured. And the Wehrmacht was getting closer to what was expected to be a campaign of at best nine weeks, and at worst seventeen, against the Red Army.

Raeder used the *Prinz Eugen*'s downtime to consult with his fleet chief. On 26 April he called Admiral Günther Lütjens to Berlin.[5] Several times Lütjens set out his reasons why Rhine Exercise should await either the *Scharnhorst* or the *Tirpitz,* why the Kriegsmarine should not squander its few available floating resources "teaspoon by teaspoon," and why the German fleet had to be extremely sensitive to British naval airpower. But, in the end, Lütjens agreed with Raeder's call for action. "The current tactical situation," Lütjens conceded, demanded that German surface units appear in the Atlantic. Moreover, the advancing season was bringing ever-shorter nights in the northern latitudes, thus increasing the difficulty of reaching the open waters of the Atlantic Ocean under cover of darkness. And the Americans were pushing their advanced naval forces forward from Newfoundland via Greenland to Iceland.

But Erich Raeder was also the consummate bureaucrat. Having just convinced his fleet chief of the need to sortie into the North Atlantic, he cautioned Lütjens: "It is imperative to operate cautiously and deliberately. One should not risk a major engagement for limited, and perhaps uncertain, goals."[6] In other words, Raeder ordered Lütjens to be bold and imaginative—yet concurrently to avoid major engagements with the enemy unless they could be undertaken with little risk and under the umbrella of the primary mission objective. Then Raeder further admonished his fleet chief that if battle was unavoidable, it should be conducted with full force, to the finish. In short, whatever happened, responsibility for the operation would lie squarely with Lütjens.

Unsurprisingly, Admiral Lütjens sought advice from several colleagues. First, he discussed the planned operation with Rear Admiral Fricke, Raeder's chief of operations. Fricke bluntly queried Lütjens what he would do, should major enemy forces confront him. The fleet chief's ready reply: "I would immediately head for home."[7] As far as Berlin was concerned, this was Lütjens' official policy.

Next, Lütjens looked up an old friend, Admiral Conrad Patzig, a fellow member of the Crew of 1907. Patzig suggested that Lütjens remain in port. There was no need, Patzig argued, to risk a fleet chief in a limited operation by a single capital ship. Lütjens concurred in theory but, fearing that such an action could lead to accusations of "cowardice," insisted on carrying out his assigned task. Admiral Lütjens' parting words to Patzig, which stood in direct opposition to what the fleet chief had told Admiral Fricke, were laced with pathos: "Given the uneven relation of forces [between Germany and Britain], I am of the opinion that I should have to sacrifice myself sooner or later. I have closed out my private life, and am determined to carry out the task assigned to me honorably, one way or another."[8] Lütjens also expressed similarly dour thoughts to the future Rear Admiral Hans Voss, who was then working at Raeder's headquarters. "Voss," Lütjens stated matter-of-factly, "I'd like to make my farewells; I'll never come back. Given the superiority of the British, survival is improbable."[9]

Finally Lütjens discussed the planned operation with the previous fleet chief, Admiral Wilhelm Marschall. The latter well remembered Erich Raeder's admonition of June 1940: "We must deploy the ships, even if it means the loss of one of the battleships—for if they are not sent into action, we will not get any more." Still, Marschall advised his successor not to stick too closely to Raeder's operational plan, as the situation in the Atlantic might change quickly and dramatically at any given moment. Lütjens would have none of it. "No, two fleet chiefs [Admirals Hermann Boehm and Marschall] have already been relieved of their commands for having raised the ire of the Naval Command. I do not want to be the third. I know what the Naval Command wants, and I will carry out their orders."[10] When he hoisted his white admiral's flag with the black cross on board the *Bismarck* in May 1940, Lütjens repeated his final decision to Admiral Marschall: "I will carry out their orders."[11] In short, Günther Lütjens would not be denied his rendezvous with destiny.

While Lütjens conferred with Raeder and the other admirals in Berlin, Captain Ernst Lindemann spent every available hour on workup exercises in the Baltic Sea with the *Bismarck* and (in the absence of the damaged *Prinz Eugen*) the pocket battleship *Lützow* (the former *Deutschland*), hoping that some sort of major task force was still being contemplated by Raeder. The ships were ordered to carry three months of provisions on board at all times. Lindemann accomplished this only by sending officers and ratings into the countryside and to army depots to commandeer what the navy was unable to supply.[12]

Most important, Commander Adalbert Schneider daily tested the *Bismarck*'s guns. First their crews had to familiarize themselves with the 11-yard-long stereoscopic naval range finders and Zeiss optics. Determining the range to a distant object by triangulation was no easy task.[13] As range increased, the angle being measured grew so minute that even minor changes resulted in major differences in range—at 33,000 yards, an error of only 0.02 degrees translated into an error of almost 1,100 yards in the range calibrated. Next came the task of gun laying, beginning with hydraulically rotating the ship's mammoth 1,100-ton turrets and ending by synchronizing the rotation of all four turrets to the same azimuth at the same time. Then Schneider drilled his crews in elevating the 100-ton 15-inch guns through an arc of up to 30 degrees. Out in the Baltic Sea, the roll and pitch of the ship called for frequent calibration of the guns. In theory, Schneider could quickly determine a shell's trajectory to the target by calculating the angle of gun elevation and the muzzle velocity of the projectile. But that formula was designed for a shell traveling in a perfect vacuum. In practice, air resistance, ambient temperatures, humidity, and wind affected the distance that a shell was fired and the angle at which it returned to the surface at the end of its flight. Slack in the turret's gear train introduced a further variable. Thus Schneider spent days and weeks developing gun tables for each type of gun.

Having mastered the basics of gun laying, the *Bismarck*'s gun crews then conducted firing tests at moving targets. Obviously, the aim was not to hit the place where a hostile vessel was first sighted, but rather where it would be when the shells actually landed. With a target moving at 30 knots and with a projectile flight time of about one minute at 33,000 yards, this required firing at a spot about 1,100 yards ahead of the adversary's initial sighting—if the ship did not undertake evasive action. And even then, hitting a moving target that measured less then 300 yards long and 40 yards wide at such great distances was no easy matter. Schneider quickly discovered that "straddling" a target at 33,000 yards with the first broadside was almost impossible; the fall of shot from the first salvo was usually a clean miss. At 27,000 yards the odds became reasonable; at 22,000 yards they were favorable. Once engaged by an enemy in the open waters of the Atlantic Ocean, the *Bismarck*'s fate would rest largely in Commander Schneider's skill in quickly identifying the target, judging its speed and course, anticipating its possible evasive maneuvers, calculating the firing solution, and firing at the appropriate time.

Concurrently, Captain Karl Topp conducted war games to test whether the *Tirpitz* could reach the Atlantic without first being detected and then confronted by major enemy units. In game after game, the results, in Topp's words, were "decimating": not even under the most favorable circumstances could a German capital ship reach the Atlantic without being sighted and attacked.[14] Topp shared his conclusions with Lindemann. It is highly unlikely that Lindemann would have failed to report Topp's findings to Admiral Lütjens.

Above all, Captain Lindemann was bitterly disappointed to hear of further delays (eight to twelve days) occasioned by the *Prinz Eugen*'s mine disaster. The crew obviously knew from the daily arrival of admiral's staff, prize crews, intelligence officers, and special engineers, as well as reporters and cameramen from the Ministry of Propaganda, that a major operation was in the offing. Lindemann did not inform them of the delays. "I fear a significant psychological blow to the morale of the crew," he wrote in his war diary, "in case of further delays in deployment."[15]

On the morning of 25 April, the very moment at which Raeder was discussing future operations with Lütjens in Berlin, Naval Group Command North handed Lindemann Operational Orders 16–18: Rhine Exercise, the "planned advance via Norway; breakout [into the Atlantic] between Iceland and the Faeroes." Target date: 28 April. Crews were to be on board by the 26th. Escort would be provided by the 6th Destroyer Flotilla. The *Prinz Eugen* alone was to accompany the *Bismarck*. Not only had the sortie now officially shrunk from four capital ships to one, but the *Prinz Eugen* was nowhere near ready for service.

As Captain Lindemann well knew, the *Prinz Eugen*, although a robust, well-built heavy cruiser, was a poor substitute for the *Gneisenau* or the *Scharnhorst*, much less for the *Tirpitz*. The cruiser's 8-inch guns were no match for the expected 15-inch naval artillery of the British Home Fleet. Above all, as even Admiral Raeder readily conceded, the *Prinz Eugen*'s modest bunkerage of 3,250 tons of fuel was woefully inadequate for operations in the Atlantic. For, at best speed (as during a chase or evasion of enemy units) her twelve boilers consumed 16,168 gallons of fuel per hour, reducing effective range to just over 2,000 nautical miles. Indeed, the *Prinz Eugen* would be heavily reliant on frequent refueling at sea during any oceanic operation. Still, might not an armada of tankers out at sea, Raeder argued, overcome this disadvantage?[16] Captain Lindemann was less than thrilled at the prospect of taking on the British Home Fleet (and possibly Force H at Gibraltar as well) with only a heavy cruiser as scout. He could only wonder what the naval planners at the Tirpitzufer in Berlin were thinking.

Still, orders were orders. At 7:05 P.M. on 28 April Lindemann undertook a final review of the *Bismarck*'s progress to date.[17] "Ship is fully operational in terms of personnel and material and provisioned for three months." The delays and breakdowns were a thing of the past. The *Bismarck*'s skipper proudly recorded that the "first phase" of the ship's life span, that is, the sea trials undertaken since commissioning on 24 August 1940, was now completed. "The goal was attained in eight months, with only 14 days delay due to the blockage of the Canal and the ice floes in Hamburg." Lindemann was well pleased. "The crew can be proud of these accomplishments. They were attained only because the desire to get at the enemy as soon as possible allowed me, without question, to make such superhuman demands of the men." Although the *Bismarck* was without battle experience, Lindemann expressed confidence that his men were "up to meeting any war tasks" assigned them. Both crew and equipment gave him confidence that "for the first time in a very long time, we can be a match for any possible adversary." Given the Royal Navy's numerical superiority of more than a dozen each battleships and heavy cruisers as well as eight aircraft carriers, Lindemann hoped to encounter only segments of the enemy fleet in Rhine Exercise. And while obviously disappointed at the delay, Lindemann felt sufficiently confident to give the men "more rest."

The men never enjoyed their promised rest. The next day Grand Admiral Raeder, as well as Naval Group Command West in Paris, ordered the *Bismarck* to make ready to advance through the Great Belt. Raeder assigned the *Bismarck* the code name "Eichenkranz," and *Prinz Eugen* "Meeresgott." Naval Group Command North was dubbed "Zwerghuhn," Naval Group Command West "Bilderbuch," and Fleet Command "Antilope."[18] On 5 May 1941, five days after having ordered the attack on the Soviet Union (Operation Barbarossa) for 22 June, Hitler visited the *Bismarck* and the *Tirpitz* at Gotenhafen. Grand Admiral Raeder remained in Berlin. He recorded not a word of the Führer's visit to Gotenhafen in his war diary.

At midnight on 12 May, Admiral Lütjens and Captain Lindemann received news via Radio Berlin that an apparently "delirious" Rudolf Hess, the Deputy Führer, had piloted his own aircraft from

Augsburg—to destination unknown.[19] Days later, the two naval commanders learned that Hess had landed in Scotland. Berlin was abuzz with rumors. As Deputy Führer, Hess was the number two man in the Third Reich. He had been at Hitler's side during the early struggles of the Nazi party in Munich during the 1920s, had transcribed Hitler's book *Mein Kampf*, and was widely believed to be the Führer's most intimate aide. Had Hitler known about the flight beforehand? Was it part of a planned operation whereby Britain's secret service hoped to promote a negotiated peace behind Prime Minister Winston S. Churchill's back? What was the true nature of Hess' contacts with the Marquess of Clydesdale (the future 14th Duke of Hamilton), whom he had known since the 1936 Olympics? And above all, what secrets had Hess carried with him? Perhaps the date set for the planned invasion of the Soviet Union? Or for Rhine Exercise?

More exercises in Danzig Bay. The port cranes and catapults broke down again, necessitating a return to the docks for repairs. Lindemann was without half of his air complement. Finally, good news: around suppertime on 13 May, the *Prinz Eugen* hove into sight off Gotenhafen Roads. Captain Lindemann immediately practiced refueling the heavy cruiser from his own ship at sea, and then had the *Prinz Eugen* tow the *Bismarck* in a further mock battle exercise.

Naval headquarters at Berlin that same day formally conceded that the *Scharnhorst* would not be seaworthy until the end of June, and the *Gneisenau* not before sometime in August.[20] Obviously, neither would be ready for Rhine Exercise. And when Hitler demanded concrete news concerning a service date for Germany's first aircraft carrier, Raeder confessed that the *Graf Zeppelin* required another eight months in dock, to be followed by one year of workup exercises.[21] That left the *Bismarck* and the *Prinz Eugen* as the only available vessels for Rhine Exercise. On 14 May Lindemann brought ashore the *Bismarck*'s war diary for the workup period.[22]

In Paris, Naval Group Command West drafted final orders for an armada of eighteen support ships for Rhine Exercise. The tankers *Belchen* (code-named "Dattelpalme"), *Esso-Hamburg* ("Opernhaus"),

Lothringen ("Dreschflegel"), and *Nordmeer* ("Känguruh"), as well as the supply ships *Ermland* ("Tigerfell") and *Spichern* ("Walzerkönig"), were declared seaworthy and, along with the scouts *Gonzenheim* ("Obstgarten") and *Kota Penang* ("Lebertran"), were to put out to sea between 17 and 18 May.[23] Concurrently, the commander of U-boats was instructed to place four U-boats along the Halifax (HX) convoy routes.

On 14 May Admiral Lütjens and Captain Lindemann received the code date for the top-secret Rhine Exercise: "Marburg 5724." By combining the first and last digits and dividing that number (54) by three, Lütjens and Lindemann learned that they were to pass through the Great Belt on the night of 18 May.[24] But the fleet chief refused to sortie without the *Bismarck*'s port cranes and catapults in working order. "Marburg" was postponed for at least three days. Delays undermined morale. By now, Lütjens feared, the entire eastern Baltic Sea region must have known the *Bismarck*'s whereabouts and her frantic preparations to sail.

Finally, at 10:33 P.M. on 16 May, Captain Lindemann reported that the repairs to the port aircraft facilities were complete. "17 May ready to sail evening." Thereupon, Naval Group Command North wired: "Marburg 5297"—the task force was to assemble in the Great Belt on the evening of 19 May.[25] Next came the latest intelligence report: Luftwaffe patrols flying over the Royal Navy's lair at Scapa Flow had sighted a small armada of about a dozen ships, including two battleships and an aircraft carrier, riding at anchor. Lütjens and Lindemann appreciated that they would somehow have to slip past these ships to reach their operations target, the convoys out in the mid-Atlantic.

Of course, the stepped-up aerial reconnaissance had not gone unnoticed by the enemy. Scapa Flow reported unusually heavy German air traffic. Intercepted Luftwaffe Enigma messages revealed that Focke-Wulf FW200 Condors had routinely patrolled the area between Jan Mayen Island and Greenland. And during the night of 17–18 May, Home Fleet received word that German patrols had overflown the waters northwest of Iceland.

Most alarming was an Enigma message from U-74 to Naval Group Command West in the early hours of 18 May. Late in the evening of 16 May, Lieutenant Eitel-Friedrich Kentrat, commanding U-74, was cruising on the surface of the North Atlantic on a smooth sea: "Good, clear visibility." Then, at 10:30 P.M., Kentrat spied what he believed to be three destroyers approaching in tight formation from the east about 1,000 miles south of the Denmark Straight. He immediately dove to periscope depth and watched the warships pass by at 1,600 yards. "They are American destroyers of the 'Dunlap' class, course southwest, speed 12 knots."[26] Soon the Americans were out of sight. But at 11:30 P.M. Kentrat sighted a battleship, also approaching from the east. Once more he allowed the stranger to pass by. Kentrat reported that it was of the *New York* class, and that it was also on a southwestern course. He watched the battleship's movements until it was two miles away, around midnight. Then U-74 surfaced. There was no doubt concerning the ships. "The battleship, which still has not set any lights, can be made out very well in the twilight at 7.5 miles."[27] For forty-five minutes U-74 shadowed the Americans. Then the destroyers set lights and communicated by searchlights. "Night exercises by the American task force," Kentrat noted in his war diary. When the lights were extinguished, he at once informed Vice Admiral Karl Dönitz of the sightings.

The commander of U-boats immediately grasped the significance of the report by U-74: a battleship of the *New York* class and three *Dunlap*-class destroyers were conducting night operations 900 nautical miles west of Ireland, the very waters in which the *Bismarck* and the *Prinz Eugen* were to operate. Admiral Dönitz passed the news by Enigma to Naval Group Command West, which, in turn, informed Admirals Raeder and Lütjens of Kentrat's sightings. Raeder was incensed at the obvious American display of support for Britain. "This news is alarming," he committed to his war diary, "since it means that the Americans have extended their Atlantic patrols even with battleships far beyond the middle of the Atlantic." Would the U.S. Navy interfere with the *Bismarck*'s planned operation? Or with the fleet of supply ships required to sustain Rhine

Exercise in the Atlantic? Raeder instructed Dönitz to order his "gray sharks" to attack darkened warships, even American ones, escorting convoys "as the situation demanded."[28] The German navy, if not its Führer, was steadfastly pointing for war with Washington.

Shore and ship commands now finalized the detailed tactical orders for Rhine Exercise.[29] The task force was quickly to close on the convoys, one ship bearing down on each side, and to cripple a few vessels, causing general panic. Only when no freighter remained within sight of the *Bismarck* and the *Prinz Eugen* were the warships to return to the grisly task of dispatching the crippled freighters. While the heavy cruiser deployed her torpedoes, the battleship was to close to about 300 yards and to fire single 15-inch shells at a freighter's waterline. If Allied ships with hull compartmentalization were encountered, "*all compartments are to be blown open. (The engine room is the largest compartment.)*" Just to be sure, Naval Group Command West instructed Captain Lindemann to riddle a freighter's superstructure with 1.5-inch shells, "so that air can escape through these [holes] as the compartments fill with sea water." No mercy was to be shown the enemy. "The work of destruction is not to be delayed by life-saving activities." Finally, Naval Group Command West noted, "Even if the breakthrough into the Atlantic is detected, the operation is to proceed."

Under the cumbersome German naval command structure, overall control of Rhine Exercise rested with Grand Admiral Raeder and his staff in Berlin. Generaladmiral (General Admiral) Rolf Carls, heading Naval Group Command North in Wilhelmshaven, would guide Rhine Exercise until the task force passed the line running between southern Greenland and northwestern Scotland, after which General Admiral Alfred Saalwächter, commanding Naval Group Command West in Paris, would take over. Admiral Lütjens had "a free hand" to direct tactical operations and all battle action from aboard the *Bismarck*.

Raeder and his staff ordered the task force to pass the Great Belts to Kristiansand by the third day of operations, and then, at high speed and under the protection of U-boats and destroyers, to steam along the deep coastal waters of Norway to the Korsfjord (now Krossfjord) near Bergen. There the *Bismarck* and the *Prinz Eugen* were to anchor on the fourth day of operations and to take on provisions from four supply ships as well as fuel oil from the tanker *Wollin*. Once resupplied, the task force was to steam at full speed to quadrant AF 8787 on the navy's grid map, dismiss its destroyer escort, change to a northerly course, and, weather permitting, quickly march through the Iceland-Faeroes passage, standing as far as possible off the ice-choked shores of Iceland. Air Fleet 5 was to provide cover over the North Sea, and a single FW200 Condor flying out of Bordeaux or Stavanger was to reconnoiter ice conditions off Iceland. A U-boat was to act as a weather ship in the North Atlantic; a French barque was to stand off Newfoundland for similar purposes; and four fishing boats (the *München*, the *Freese*, the *August Wriest*, and the *Lauenburg*) were put on standby alert in the North Sea and the Norwegian Sea. Raeder admonished Lütjens not to communicate with his own ships by wireless. The grand admiral's planners had timed every step of the route into the North Atlantic to the minute. Interestingly, neither Admiral Raeder nor his chief of operations, Rear Admiral Fricke, included a single word concerning either friendly or hostile radar capabilities in their operational orders.

No doubt the euphoria in Berlin that surrounded Rhine Exercise was in large measure driven by psychological considerations. The "taboo," first of revolt and then of scuttling by the High Sea Fleet in 1918–19, had to be overcome at all cost—as did the ignominious scuttling of the *Graf Spee* at Montevideo in 1939. Additionally, the surface units had to justify their expenditures—especially considering Dönitz's constant carping for more U-boats. As well, the Kriegsmarine desperately needed successes to allay the mounting feeling among Hitler and his paladins that the Wehrmacht and the Luftwaffe alone were carrying the burden of the war. Operation Barbarossa, the planned attack on the Soviet Union, was just a month away. Another quick victory on land, as expected, would do little for future naval funding. And there was always the chance that Hitler, deeply concerned about losing one of the big ships, would veto any sortie into the Atlantic. Rhine Exercise, Raeder and his staff concluded, had to proceed at once.

The Kriegsmarine quickly activated the vast supply force that had been put at Lütjens' disposal. The tanker *Belchen* was ordered to proceed to quadrant AJ 26 (120 nautical miles south of Cape Farewell, Greenland); the *Lothringen* to quadrant AJ 27 (200 miles south of Cape Farewell); the *Esso-Hamburg* to CD 32 (450 miles northwest of Fayal Island in the Azores); the *Friedrich Breme* ("Laubfrosch") to DF 96 (700 miles southwest of Fayal); the tenders *Ermland* to DR 16 (between the Azores and the Lesser Antilles) and *Spichern* to CD 64 (400 miles west of Fayal). Just for good measure, the tanker *Gedania* ("Maikäfer") was added to the list. In case inclement weather delayed the task force's speedy passage through the Iceland-Faeroes gap, the tanker *Weissenburg* ("Ruhekissen") was dispatched to the Norwegian Sea and the *Heide* ("Puderdose") to Trondheim.[30] In fact, the first tanker, the *Belchen*, had already put out to sea from La Pallice on 10 May, followed by the *Lothringen* one day later. Both vessels were now directed to quadrants AJ 25 and AJ 16, southwest of Greenland.[31] The tanker *Spichern* headed into the Atlantic on 19 May, followed by the *Esso-Hamburg* and *Friedrich Breme* two days later. Six U-boats also shaped course for the North Atlantic.

Finally, German naval intelligence, the B-Dienst, informed Admiral Lütjens that he could expect to meet various combinations of powerful British units from Scapa Flow (the battleships HMS *Prince of Wales*, *Nelson*, and *Rodney*, as well as the light cruiser HMS *Sheffield* and ten light cruisers), out in the North Atlantic (the battleships HMS *King George V*, *Revenge*, *Ramillies*, and *Royal Sovereign*), and from Gibraltar (the battleship HMS *Queen Elizabeth*, the battle cruisers HMS *Renown* and *Repulse*, and the aircraft carriers HMS *Ark Royal*, *Furious*, and *Argus*, as well as three cruisers and sixteen destroyers). Most likely, several of the battleships would be escorting Halifax convoys, while the *Queen Elizabeth* and *Resolution* were in dock undergoing repairs. But Lütjens knew that German maritime intelligence was notoriously unreliable due to a lack of reconnaissance aircraft. As late as 20 May, the B-Dienst still was not certain whether the *Prince of Wales* or the *King George V* rode at anchor off Gibraltar.[32] Obviously, Lütjens had to be prepared to meet any possible combinations of Royal Navy heavy units.

At 10:00 A.M. on 18 May, Admiral Lütjens, after formally inspecting the *Prinz Eugen*, called a final commanders' conference on board the *Bismarck* to review Rhine Exercise. Lütjens and his chief of staff, Captain Harald Netzbandt, informed Captains Lindemann and Brinkmann that Grand Admiral Raeder, in conjunction with General Admiral Saalwächter of Naval Group Command West, had assigned Rhine Exercise a straightforward task: "Attack on enemy traffic in the Atlantic north of the equator."[33] Specifically, the task force was to pass unnoticed between Iceland and the Faeroe Islands and ruthlessly to attack all traffic on the Halifax convoy route, doing "the greatest possible damage by destroying the enemy's merchant ships, if possible, en route *to* England." Lütjens instructed his two commanders that they did not have to "respect American neutrality zone any longer during this operation."[34] Since destruction of enemy merchant shipping had top priority, Lütjens reminded Lindemann and Brinkmann of the need "to preserve the seaworthiness of our own ships. Therefore, battle with equally powerful enemy forces is to be avoided." Given that the finicky aircraft on board the *Bismarck* were hardly likely to function in the North Atlantic, the *Prinz Eugen* was to act as scout. And then Lütjens relayed another one of Raeder's seemingly confusing orders: "Even if the breakout is discovered, the task at hand [operations against convoys in the Atlantic] remains." But, the fleet chief went on, in case "major repairs are called for, or in case of a major change in plans," the task force was "to head home, if at all possible." Clear as mud.

There could be no doubt in the minds of Lütjens and Netzbandt, Lindemann and Brinkmann, that the operation was predicated on a number of iffy suppositions and contradictory propositions. As the weaker side, the Germans relied heavily on the element of surprise. While not a sine qua non for the sortie, concealment (at least until attacking the first convoy) nevertheless was Raeder's top priority. As experienced commanders, Lütjens and his captains were all too aware that enemy agents in Sweden and Denmark, as well as the prying eyes of Baltic Sea and North Sea fishermen, would be on the task force, as would those of Coastal Command's aircraft.

Raeder's orders that Lütjens strive "*gradually, methodically, and systematically*" to establish "local and temporary" command of the North Atlantic must have raised an eyebrow or two on board the *Bismarck* that 18 May. After all, the Royal Navy maintained superior surface forces in each of three theaters: Scapa Flow, the North Atlantic, and Gibraltar. And what were Lütjens and his commanders to do with the battery of seemingly conflicting orders? Avoid battle with superior forces; but if this proved unavoidable, assume battle with full might. Reach the open ocean undetected; but if this proved impossible, proceed with the primary mission. If need be, put into one of the occupied French ports; but if damaged, return via Norway. At all times maintain contact with shore commands at Berlin, Wilhelmshaven, and Paris; but out at sea, operate silently and independently.[35]

Admiral Lütjens ended the briefing on the morning of Sunday, 18 May by informing Lindemann and Brinkmann that he had altered several key aspects of Rhine Exercise.[36] Instead of putting in to the Korsfjord as ordered, Lütjens now planned to press on and rendezvous with the tanker *Weissenburg* in the Norwegian Sea. A rupture in one of the *Bismarck*'s fuel lines had allowed Lindemann to take on only 6,000 tons of oil; Lütjens planned to top up to 8,000 out at sea. Additionally, the fleet chief decided not to steam through the 255-mile-wide Iceland-Faeroes passage, as ordered by Raeder and Naval Group Command North; rather, he intended to head through the 180-mile-wide Denmark Strait. In doing so, he ignored Naval Group Command North's admonition that the British could better monitor the relatively narrow and possibly ice-choked strait and that time and fuel could be saved by taking the more southerly route.

As was his custom, Lütjens offered no reason for changing the operational orders. Perhaps what he termed the ever-present "ice fog" in the waters between Iceland and Greenland would accord the task force better cover. After all, this had been Lütjens' experience aboard the *Gneisenau* in February. The ships' crews were to be told only that they were heading for "the Norwegian Sea." The fleet chief informed his captains that he was prepared to attack any enemy cruisers or auxiliary cruisers encountered in the Denmark Strait. Finally, Lütjens distributed the special "battleship key" for Enigma ciphers; it was to be used for the first time.

At 11:12 A.M. on 18 May the *Prinz Eugen* eased away from her berth at Gotenhafen, followed a few minutes later by the *Bismarck*. The battleship had on board 2,221 officers and ratings, including an admiral's staff of nearly sixty-five and a prize crew of eighty to crew any merchantmen seized in the Atlantic. Most of the ratings were former Hitler Youth boys, now in their late teens or early twenties. The band assembled on the battleship's upper deck and played "Muß i denn, muß i denn zum Städtele hinaus"—a song of parting and grief, of long absences. But then Lütjens ordered both warships to anchor in Gotenhafen Roads. Later that afternoon he conducted routine exercises in the Baltic Sea. Then he returned and dropped anchor off Gotenhafen. The men were confused. Spotters on shore likewise wondered what the enigmatic Lütjens was up to.

Well after the onset of night, at 2:00 A.M. on 19 May, *Bismarck* weighed anchor and pointed for the Danish Belts. The first officer, Commander Hans Oels, supervised the departure from the bridge. "Coxswain, shape course for Point Green 03." It was a clear night, with occasional clouds. A slight east-northeast wind blew steadily. The men were issued duffel coats lined with sheep's wool; obviously, the *Bismarck* was not heading for the tropics. Captain Lindemann at last apprised his officers of the *Bismarck*'s mission to raid British trade in the North Atlantic.

The *Prinz Eugen*, having already left Gotenhafen at 9:18 P.M. on 18 May, at first steered a separate course. She then rejoined the *Bismarck* off Cape Arkona, the northern tip of Rügen Island, at 11:25 A.M. on 19 May. Captain Brinkmann assembled the band and a naval chorus on the upper deck to greet Admiral Lütjens with the "Prinz Eugen Lied"—a march composed after Prince Eugene's capture of the town and fortress of Belgrade in 1717. All German maritime traffic had been suspended in the Belts for the night of 19–20 May.

Around noon on 20 May, Captain Lindemann decided to inform the *Bismarck*'s crew of Rhine Exercise. He addressed the men over the ship's loudspeakers:

> The day that we have longed for so eagerly has at last arrived: the moment when we can lead our proud ship against the enemy. Our objective is commerce raiding in the Atlantic, imperiling England's existence. Let us hope for great success. I know that it has been, and will continue to be, the crew's sincerest desire to participate directly in Germany's final victory. I give you the hunter's toast: Good hunting and a good bag![37]

Commander Oels pointed the *Bismarck* due west. "Coxswain, shape course for Point Red 05." A light rain offered welcome cover for the task force and its three-destroyer escort as it approached the Great Belt at 10:34 P.M. Oels ordered a course correction to Point Red 20.

The next morning, 20 May, brought clear skies and bright sunshine. From high up on the *Bismarck*'s bridge, Lütjens and Lindemann spotted a host of Swedish, Danish, and Norwegian fishing trawlers as well as some coastal freighters in the distance. Lütjens recalled Raeder's assurance to him as late as 18 May: "Danish fishing boats constitute *no* danger of espionage."[38]

The sortie's first air alert was stillborn: the craft spotted were German fighters, whose mission had not been reported to Lütjens. Naval Group Command North relayed the latest weather conditions at 11:56 A.M. Strangely, the German task force around noon failed to notice ten or twelve Swedish aircraft flying a routine reconnaissance mission some 20 nautical miles west of Vinga. The Swedish flyers at once reported their sighting to naval headquarters in Stockholm.

Then, at 1 P.M., Lindemann, who just that January had received the Swedish Grand Cross of the Order of Swords, Second Class, spotted the 4,775-ton Swedish flight-deck cruiser *Gotland*.[39] The 6-inch *Flygplankryssare*, built in 1933, had been designed to act as an advance scout in case of war with the Soviet Union. Already obsolescent, she carried eight S9 Hawker Osprey floatplanes. Apparently on a routine training cruise, the *Gotland* for two hours ran on a parallel course through the Kattegat, hugging the Swedish coast off Bohuslän. Nils-Hugo Lilja, an apprentice radio signalman, was at his command post in cabin D on the upper bridge.[40] Over his 20-watt UK radio receiver he heard a voice in German issuing sets of two or three numbers. Kommedör Isaac A. Cassel, a squadron commander aboard the *Gotland*, immediately recognized them as instructions to the *Bismarck*'s advance escort screen.

On the German battleship, Admiral Lütjens at 5:37 P.M. informed Naval Group Command North of the intruder: "Thus we can assume that the task force will be reported." But Admiral Carls was not concerned: "Because of the strictly neutral conduct of Sweden, I do not think the danger of being compromised by the Swedish warship is any greater than from the already present, systematic enemy surveillance of the entrance to the Baltic."[41] There was no question in Captain Lindemann's mind that the element of surprise—key to the entire operation—had been forfeited. Why had the task force not been routed through the Kiel Canal and into the North Sea, far from the prying eyes of Swedish and Danish mariners and coastal lookouts?

Stockholm was a hornets' nest of rumor and intrigue in May 1941. For weeks on end now, small Swedish "BV" coastal tankers, on lease to Denmark, had plied the waters off Gotenhafen in the service of the Kriegsmarine. Their skippers had kept the Swedish Defense Staff informed of the *Bismarck*'s every move. As well, the Swedes had noted a steady German buildup of men, ships, and supplies at the Baltic port of Swinemünde. And through their military attaché at Helsinki, Lieutenant Colonel Curt Kempff, who had been tipped off by the German naval attaché, Rear Admiral Reimar von Bonin, the Swedes learned of the pending Operation Barbarossa. Rumors ran wild not only in diplomatic and military circles, but also in the press and on radio concerning a major action in the Baltic region by the Germans. There was talk of intelligence leaks at all levels of the Swedish government—especially the Swedish navy. In short, the atmosphere at Stockholm already was electric and highly charged when a coded radio message arrived from the *Gotland*'s skipper, Captain Knut G. Ågren, informing the Swedish Admiralty of the sighting of the *Bismarck* and the *Prinz Eugen*. Were the ships en route to the Atlantic? Or were they about to land German troops to secure the delivery of vital Swedish iron ore to Germany? And could the pro-German Ågren be trusted?

The intelligence community in Stockholm got little rest that 20 May. All vital threads of information to be exchanged ran through Colonel Alfred Roscher Lund, the Norwegian government-in-exile's military attaché in Stockholm. In March 1941 Roscher Lund had established an exchange of information arrangement with both the British Legation and Swedish Intelligence, whereby the Norwegian routinely reported on fuel supplies, coastal defenses, and troop movement in German-occupied Norway. In return, Major Carl Petersén ("P"), of Swedish Secret Military Intelligence, who until 1943 played both sides, shared his office's delicate information with Roscher Lund.

The key to the arrangement was that the British were not to contact the Swedes directly. And since Captain Henry Denham, Britain's naval attaché to Stockholm, spoke neither Swedish nor Norwegian, Roscher Lund used Denham's assistant, Acting Lieutenant Dan Harris, as a conduit of information. The twenty-five-year-old Harris spoke Swedish, largely thanks to a young Swedish girl at the Naval College whom he was dating (and whom he would later marry). Moreover, Roscher Lund was leery of Denham, who in the 1930s had been seen regularly at the Kiel Regatta in the company of Admiral Erich Raeder and who routinely exchanged Christmas cards with German admirals.[42]

Around 7 P.M. on 20 May Roscher Lund went to the British Legation in Stockholm and requested a special meeting with Denham and Harris. The two naval officers were at separate dinners. Contacted by telephone, both realized immediately the urgency of the moment. Denham and Harris raced on bicycles back to the Legation. Harris arrived in time to see Denham sign a green report form. The naval attaché allowed that Roscher Lund had just received reliable information from his contact at Swedish Secret Military Intelligence that the *Bismarck* and the *Prinz Eugen* were at that moment steaming northward through the Kattegat.[43]

Captain Denham could hardly believe Roscher Lund's news and wanted to know whether the information could be verified.[44] The Norwegian colonel shook his head. Still, the news was too precious to delay. With the cables between Sweden and Britain cut, Denham raised the Admiralty in London at 8:58 P.M. by way of a ciphered telegram via Gothenburg radio:

> *Most Immediate.* Kattegat today 20th May. At 1500 two large warships escorted by three destroyers, five escort craft, ten or twelve aircraft passed Marstrand course northwest 2058/20th May/1941. B-3 repeat B-3.[45]

"B-3" was a modest intelligence grading, for Denham could not verify Roscher Lund's information.[46] Neither Roscher Lund nor Denham knew that Captain Ågren's communication from the *Gotland* formed the basis of this incredible piece of intelligence. And in one of the many ironies of Rhine Exercise, the Germans at Stockholm, who had broken the Swedish codes, intercepted and deciphered Denham's radiogram to the Admiralty. But their own relay of this vital piece of information to Berlin somehow ended up at the bottom of the Naval High Command's "in" basket. It would rest there until Rhine Exercise had ended.[47]

Denham's sensational communiqué, combined with numerous reports of German aircraft sighted over Scapa Flow, Iceland, and Jan Mayen Island, left no doubt at the "much excited" British Admiralty that a major sortie by German warships was in the offing. Moreover, British cryptanalysts at Bletchley Park, who were then reading about twenty messages per day of the intercepted German naval Enigma—albeit with three to seven days' delay—reported that the *Bismarck* and the *Prinz Eugen* had taken on prize crews before exercising in the Baltic and that the *Bismarck* had requested sea charts from Berlin for those prize crews. It became clear that the German ships intended to raid the Atlantic convoy routes.[48] But how many ships were there? Would the two German battleships at Brest join them? And what was their ultimate destination? To answer these questions, the Admiralty at once ordered two Supermarine Spitfire fighters up from Wick to reconnoiter the Norwegian coast. The hunt for the *Bismarck* was on.

Shortly after sighting the *Gotland*, Admiral Lütjens gave the order not to pass through the cleared opening in the Skagerrak mine barrier out of fear that British submarines might be lurking just beyond. Instead, he ordered Lieutenant Commander Rudolf Lell of the 5th Minesweeping Flotilla to open a new passage through the field. It was a time-consuming operation—compounded by the unexpected appearance of more than a dozen German freighters. But perhaps they were a godsend, as they might confound British agents and Admiralty alike as to the task force's true intent.

At 4 P.M. on 20 May Captain Lindemann shaped course for 300 degrees through the new opening in the minefield. The *Bismarck* was making 17 knots, steaming on a zigzag course. Lindemann marveled at the austere beauty of the black Norwegian mountains set against the red glow of the setting sun. By 10 P.M., the squadron, now making 27 knots and pointing due west, passed the Kristiansand minefield: the three destroyers Z-10, Z-16, and Z-23 ahead, then the *Bismarck* and the *Prinz Eugen*, in line-ahead. On shore, Viggo Axelssen and several colleagues in the Norwegian underground spotted the German warships and immediately radioed London: "20.30, a battleship, probably German, westerly course." The report reached Colonel J. S. Wilson, chief of the British Intelligence Service for Scandinavia, who at once passed it on to the Admiralty. London now had confirmation of Captain Denham's B-3 report of two hours earlier.[49]

Half an hour after Axelssen sighted the task force, Professor Edvard K. Barth, an ornithologist researching the gulls of Heröya Island, southwest of Kristansand, was completely surprised by the sight of three destroyers and two large warships gingerly passing through the Kristiansand minefield at 10 knots. Axelssen immediately attached a telephoto lens to his camera and snapped what turned out to be the last picture of the task force taken from shore.[50]

At 12:58 A.M. on 21 May Lütjens and Lindemann received word from Naval Group Command North that German aircraft the day before had spotted "1 aircraft carrier, 3 battleships (one of them probably 'Hood'), 6 light cruisers, 2 submarines, 4 destroyers, 6 freighters, 2 tankers, 33 smaller ships" at Scapa Flow.[51] Was the information reliable? And current? Two hours later Lütjens ordered: "Action Stations!" Best to test the men while still in friendly waters. For two hours, the crews of the *Bismarck* and the *Prinz Eugen* went through their night drills.

At 6:45 A.M. the *Bismarck*'s intelligence officer, Lieutenant Commander Kurt-Werner Reichard, received an urgent message from the B-Dienst: "English air wireless station orders: aircraft search for 2 battleships and 3 destroyers reported on a northerly course."[52] Had British and neutral agents in Sweden or Denmark mistaken the *Prinz Eugen* for the *Tirpitz?* Whatever the case, this was the first *official* indication that Rhine Exercise was no longer a secret. Twenty minutes later, spotters from the *Prinz Eugen* sighted four aircraft, "nationality unknown,"[53] aglow in the dawn's first light. Just as quickly, the intruders disappeared. Could the aircraft have been anything other than British? A second indication that the task force had been detected.

Lütjens saw no cause for alarm and shaped course north. Messerschmitt 109 and 110 fighters provided cover for the task force. But in Berlin Raeder and his staff finally became alarmed. There was no question now that the enemy had detected the task force. But what had prompted the search for the *Bismarck?* Enemy agents in Sweden? Or in Norway? Danish fishing boats? Or pure chance? After consulting with Admiral Carls at Wilhelmshaven, Raeder concluded: "*Enemy agents in the Great Belt* are responsible."[54] The Kriegsmarine had forfeited the operation's one possible advantage: stealth. Raeder opted not to recall the task force.

At 11:15 A.M. Fleet Chief Lütjens informed Berlin of his next step. "Tonight continue march north."[55] Admiral Lütjens now faced his first critical decision. Should he proceed to the southern perimeter of the Arctic Ocean, refuel from the tanker *Weissenburg*, and pass through the Denmark Strait, as he had announced to Captains Lindemann and Brinkmann back at Gotenhafen on 18 May? Or should he, per Raeder's instructions, put into the Grimstadfjord and top up the *Bismarck*'s fuel bunkers, which had not been fully filled at Gotenhafen? The task force needed to refuel somewhere, for the *Prinz Eugen*'s last report showed that she was down to 2,457 tons of fuel—which meant a cruising range of only 1,000 nautical miles at full speed. Alone (or with the *Tirpitz*), Lütjens could have headed for the Denmark Strait.

Around noon, the task force dropped anchor—the *Bismarck* in the Grimstadfjord south of Bergen, and the *Prinz Eugen* in Kalvanes Bay to the north. The three destroyer escorts were sent into Bergen. The Germans enjoyed their first sight in brilliant sunshine of Norway's rugged, barren mountains, dotted with picturesque wooden houses. German occupation forces rushed to the shore to get their first glimpse of the mammoth *Bismarck*.

Lütjens, stoic as always, informed neither Lindemann nor Brinkmann of the change in plans from the commanders' meeting on 18 May. Hundreds of Norwegians gathered along the shores of the Grimstadfjord to gaze at the *Bismarck*. As well, Bergen was the Norwegian harbor closest to British air bases. A more northern port, such as Trondheim or Narvik, not only would have been practically beyond the range of British land-based aircraft, but also much closer to the eastern exit of the Denmark Strait. The layover at Bergen cost Lütjens one precious day. He almost seemed to be daring the British to find him.

Next, a debate ensued whether to lay freighters closely alongside the ships to guard against possible torpedo attacks. "Admiral Norway" rejected the suggestion "due to reasons of maintaining secrecy." Naval Group Command North at Wilhelmshaven, while it rated the possibility of keeping the sortie secret remote, nevertheless agreed because the merchant ships possessed insufficient draft to protect the warships.[56] As the Luftwaffe flew cover, both ships painted over their camouflage with the Kriegsmarine's standard outboard gray—which resembled the Royal Navy's own battleship gray. The *Prinz Eugen* took on 764 tons of fuel from the tanker *Wollin*.[57] Strangely, the *Bismarck*, which had left Gotenhafen 200 tons short of fuel and which had burned about 1,000 tons of fuel since leaving Gotenhafen, simply rode at anchor. Lütjens, as customary, offered no explanation for not refueling. The day continued bright and clear.

At 1:15 P.M. Flying Officer Michael Suckling of British Coastal Command banked his Spitfire for a final turn at 25,000 feet above the Grimstadfjord—and discovered "two large German warships." Suckling immediately headed home. Special couriers rushed his film to London for development. All Royal Navy commands received a terse but urgent message: "One *Bismarck* and one *Prinz Eugen* class reported by reconnaissance at Bergen on 21 May. It is evident that these ships intend to carry out a raid on trade routes." Burkard von Müllenheim-Rechberg, the *Bismarck*'s fourth gunnery officer, would learn of Suckling's coup while reading *The Globe & Mail* in the summer of 1943 at a prisoner-of-war camp in Bowmanville, Ontario.[58]

Meanwhile, the junior officers and ratings on board the *Bismarck* and the *Prinz Eugen* caught up on gossip. Whether on the mess decks or up on the smoke deck, there was consensus that the enemy knew about the planned sortie, that the task force had been discovered. Some of the men talked openly about the ship's sighting by the *Gotland*. Others grumbled about the Norwegians presently watching them in the fjord; still others about the Swedish and Danish fishing trawlers that had seen the *Bismarck* as she steamed through the Baltic Sea and into the Kattegat.[59] Surely, the argument went, one of those vessels must have radioed the battleship's whereabouts to neutral or even hostile parties.

Captain Lindemann was also on edge. Reichard's message from B-Dienst in Germany made it perfectly clear that the enemy was aware of the presence of the task force in Norwegian waters. Dr. Otto Schneider, a medical officer who had briefly come aboard the *Bismarck* off Bergen, later recorded his impression of the captain's state of mind: "I believe that at this moment Lindemann was well aware of the great dangers that the *Bismarck* faced."[60] The *Bismarck* could hide in the Greenland Sea until the danger was past or refuel from the *Weissenburg* and head home; or the ships could lay over in Bergen or Trondheim. But Lindemann understood that any change to Rhine Exercise could be made only by the task force commander. And Lütjens had not shown any inclination to discuss his course of action with either Lindemann or Brinkmann.

At 7:30 P.M. the *Bismarck* weighed anchor, rejoined the *Prinz Eugen*, and, escorted by the three destroyers, steamed through the Hjeltefjord at 20 knots. The task force exited the fjord at Fedjeosen seventeen minutes later. Admiral Lütjens dropped the Norwegian pilot. Suddenly white, yellow, and red lights flickered through the intermittent clouds that engulfed the Norwegian mainland. Five British aircraft had dropped flares and bombs over Kalvanes Bay in search of the *Bismarck*.

The weather finally turned favorable for the forthcoming breakthrough into the Atlantic. The sky became overcast and a southerly moderate breeze drove heavy rain clouds before it; haze hung in the fjords.

Lütjens, like his predecessor Admiral Reinhard Scheer in May 1916 on his way into the Skagerrak, was without hard intelligence concerning the enemy. In contrast, Admiral Sir John Tovey, commander in chief of the Home Fleet and a veteran of the Battle of Jutland, was alert to the German task force's actions. By combining Denham's reports from Stockholm, the Norwegian visual sightings, and the Enigma intercepts with Royal Air Force reports concerning increased Luftwaffe surveillance flights over Iceland, Tovey concluded that the Germans were either mounting an invasion of Iceland or a major surface raid into the Atlantic.

At this critical moment, at 6:28 P.M. on 21 May, Special Intelligence (ULTRA) delivered the last missing piece of the puzzle. An Enigma intercept dated 24 April from the tugs serving the *Bismarck* in the Baltic Sea revealed that five prize crews had been detached to serve with the battleship.[61] This could mean only one thing: "a raid on trade routes." At midnight Admiral Tovey ordered Vice Admiral Lancelot E. Holland to refuel and then take his Battle Cruiser Force, consisting of the battle cruiser *Hood* and the battleship *Prince of Wales,* screened by six destroyers, to patrol the Iceland-Faeroes passage north of 62 degrees latitude. The recently completed *Prince of Wales* had the latest Type 284 long-range search radar on board. Tovey remained at Scapa Flow with the battleship *King George V* and the aircraft carrier *Victorious,* awaiting further intelligence from Coastal Command concerning the German task force. The heavy cruiser HMS *Suffolk*, Captain R. M. Ellis commanding, was to be relieved by HMS *Norfolk*, Captain A. J. L. Phillips commanding, on surveillance in the Denmark Strait.

Admiral Lütjens, alone with the burden of command on the *Bismarck*'s bridge, of course was unaware of these countermeasures. His job was to carry out the Naval High Command's orders as best he could. At 4:20 A.M. on 22 May Lütjens dismissed the escort provided by 5th Destroyer Flotilla in the latitude of Trondheim. Ever the loner, Lütjens offered not a word concerning his intentions to the escort's chief, Commander Alfred Schulze-Hinrichs. At Naval Group Command North, Admiral Carls vented his displeasure at the lack of communication. Lütjens' silence seemed to indicate to Carls that the fleet chief had not yet made a final decision whether to take the southern Iceland-Faeroes passage or to head for the more northerly Denmark Strait. Carls recorded in the official war diary his certainty that the British would notice any German attempt to pass the Denmark Strait: "If the Fleet Commander still had a choice between the Denmark Strait and a southern passage, the latter appeared preferable to me because it would be shorter and quicker."[62] Just to be on the safe side, Naval Group Command North ordered the tanker *Weissenburg* in the Norwegian Sea to prepare to transfer fuel to the *Bismarck*.

Perhaps Lütjens simply saw no need to inform a subordinate destroyer leader of his decision of 18 May to pass through the Denmark Strait. Whatever the case, the admiral routinely ordered the task force's clocks to be set back one hour at 1 P.M. the next day.[63] The *Bismarck* and the *Prinz Eugen* were now on their own.

Shortly after 9 A.M. Lütjens received welcome intelligence from the B-Dienst: "Nothing special to report from enemy radio intercepts. No operational signals. No discernible reaction to the task force's departure or to the English order to search for the battleships."[64] The Royal Air Force bombing raid on Kalvanes Bay indicated that the British were searching for the task force far to the south of its actual location. Captain Brinkmann uttered a sigh of relief aboard the *Prinz Eugen*: "According to all available radio messages," he recorded in his war diary, "the task force seems to have advanced undetected."[65]

At 10:59 A.M. Admiral Carls at Wilhelmshaven informed Lütjens that German paratroopers had landed at Crete. The news could not have been more fortuitous for Rhine Exercise: "Force H [from Gibraltar] out to sea, likely en route to Crete."[66] It appeared as though the Royal Navy was concentrating all its efforts on repelling the German invasion of Crete.

By noon on 22 May Admiral Lütjens' task force, steaming at 24 knots in hazy weather, stood 200 miles off the Norwegian coast, in the latitude Iceland-Norway. Lütjens ordered hostile submarine and aircraft drills to keep the men on battle alert. At 12:15 P.M. he finally shared his intentions with Captains Lindemann and Brinkmann: "Proceed, if current favorable weather holds, via quadrant AF 1675, 1155, AE 3313, 2257."[67] The dice were thrown: north to 69 degrees latitude and then west to the Denmark Strait. Given the fact that the Swedish cruiser *Gotland* had spotted him in the Kattegat, perhaps the German commander chose this longer way hoping to elude British spotters off the Faeroe, Shetland, and Orkney Islands. Later that afternoon, Lütjens ordered the *Bismarck* and the *Prinz Eugen* to paint over the aerial recognition markings on the tops of their gun turrets and nationality marks on fo'c'sle and quarterdeck.

By 6 P.M. rain set in. A gentle breeze blew steadily at 10 miles per hour from the southwest, scattering whitecaps as the crests of the wavelets began to break. Visibility was down to between 200 and 400 yards. Patches of fog appeared. Lütjens, fearing that he might lose sight of the heavy cruiser, ordered the *Prinz Eugen* to close up. Brinkmann no longer could make out the *Bismarck* in the thick soup and merely followed in her wake. Occasionally he tried to hail the lookouts on the battleship with dimmed search lights. At 9:16 P.M. he noted in his war diary: "The weather seems to have been made for the breakthrough."[68] Twice on 22 May Naval Group Command North radioed assurances that the enemy had not discerned the task force's whereabouts.

In fact, the dark clouds were moving faster than the *Bismarck* was. The ship's meteorologist, Dr. Heinz Externbrink, suggested to Lütjens that he increase speed from the present 24 knots to keep up with the cloud cover. The fleet chief declined—as usual, without comment. By his calculations, the *Prinz Eugen* already was down to about 2,600 tons of fuel; he dared not consume fuel at a greater rate. And the forecast for the Denmark Strait remained favorable for the next two days: fresh to strong breeze, mostly cloudy with light rain, moderate to poor visibility. Externbrink demurred, informing Lütjens that there was a possibility of "unpleasantly good visibility in the Denmark Strait." Again, Lütjens brushed aside his meteorologist's prognosis. Exasperated, Externbrink poured out his frustration to the *Bismarck*'s fourth gunnery officer, Müllenheim-Rechberg: "But he won't budge. He simply rejects the idea without giving any reaons."[69] After a decent interval, Lütjens ordered both ships to increase speed to 27 knots.

As Lütjens made his final preparations to break out into the Atlantic through the Denmark Strait, Admiral Tovey at Scapa Flow was desperate for further information on the *Bismarck* and the *Prinz Eugen*. He did not have long to wait. In the afternoon of 22 May an American long-range, twin-engine Glenn Martin Maryland bomber of No. 771 Squadron left the Fleet Air Arm station at Hatston in the Orkney Islands and, braving the inclement weather, flew over

Bergen. At 7:39 P.M. its pilot, Lieutenant Noel Goddard, reported that the German warships had left the area. At 10 P.M. Tovey received this vital information. He immediately put out to sea with the flagship *King George V* and the carrier *Victorious*. He also ordered the battle cruiser *Repulse* up from Clyde to join his squadron at Lewis Island, and assigned four cruisers and seven destroyers the task of screening his armada. Next, Tovey instructed the heavy cruiser *Suffolk*, which had just received the latest Type 284 search radar, to return at once and, in tandem with the *Norfolk*, to patrol the Denmark Strait. HMS *Arethusa* was ordered to reinforce two other cruisers, the *Manchester* and the *Birmingham*, on patrol in the waters between Iceland and the Faeroes. Coastal Command was requested to conduct air searches over all three possible routes that were available to the Germans. Finally, Tovey ordered Vice Admiral Holland, en route to the Hvalfjördur in Iceland, to steer instead to a position of 62 degrees North and guard the cruisers; the Home Fleet would cover those south of 62 degrees North.

Prime Minister Winston S. Churchill cabled President Franklin D. Roosevelt: "We have reason to believe a formidable Atlantic raid is intended." In case the Royal Navy failed to detect the planned breakout of the *Bismarck* and the *Prinz Eugen*, Churchill requested that the neutral U.S. Navy "mark them down for us . . . Give us the news and we will finish the job."[70] Churchill would have liked nothing better than to get the U.S. Navy involved in the Battle of the Atlantic. The hunt for the *Bismarck* was moving into high gear.

By midnight on 22 May, Admiral Lütjens had received a series of critical messages from Naval Group Command North. First, at 8:15 P.M. Admiral Carls reported yet again that aerial reconnaissance over Scapa Flow around noon had brought no change: "4 battleships, one perhaps an aircraft carrier, apparently 6 light cruisers, numerous destroyers. Assumption that breakout has not yet been detected by the enemy reconfirmed."[71] Even if Admiral Tovey now charged out of Scapa Flow with all available units and headed for Cape Farewell at the southern exit of the Denmark Strait, according to German projections the two task forces would be equidistant (1,200 nautical miles) from the southern tip of

Greenland; the advantage would lie with Lütjens, who would dictate the precise line of advance.[72] This would be the last Luftwaffe report before the task force entered the Denmark Strait, owing to increasingly foul weather and the first snow showers.

The second and more important message Lütjens received was from Carls, who reassured Lütjens that he still enjoyed the crucial element of surprise: "Advance through *Norwegian Narrows* undetected." Then, shortly after 11 P.M., Naval Group Command North sent another positive report: "Until now, no operational deployment of hostile naval forces." A final radio message four minutes past midnight informed Lütjens that the Royal Navy maintained one battleship and four cruisers in Plymouth harbor. There was great relief at German naval headquarters. "Confirms anew our hypothesis that the enemy up to now still has not discovered the breakthrough."

In fact, the flood of radiograms from the B-Dienst was encouraging. At 10:34 P.M. Admiral Carls had passed on stirring news concerning potential targets for Rhine Exercise: "U-111 reports sighting enemy convoy in quadrant AK 1245, steaming north at slow speed."[73] Due west of Cape Çort Adalaer, near the lower tip of Greenland, this convoy was heading straight into Lütjens' designated area of operations. Next, Carls informed Lütjens that the German assault on Crete was "advancing according to plan," and that four British cruisers had been destroyed off the island. "Appearance of [our] fleet in the Atlantic as soon as possible promises to inflict new and serious damage to Britain's maritime position."[74]

Unbeknown to Admiral Lütjens, Naval Group Command West at Paris received information from the U-boats that they had spotted an "American coast guard vessel" about 240 nautical miles southwest of Cape Farewell, Greenland.[75] Not only was that the intended operations area for the *Bismarck* and the *Prinz Eugen*, but the task force's supply ships and tankers were now only 120 miles from the intruder—which, in fact, was the U.S. Coast Guard cutter *Modoc*. The support vessels would have to be moved to a more remote part of the Atlantic.

At 11:22 P.M. on 22 May Admiral Lütjens announced his final

decision to Captains Lindemann and Brinkmann: "Shape course for 266°."[76] The *Bismarck* and the *Prinz Eugen* pointed almost due west. Ahead of them through the fog and the snow showers lay the Denmark Strait. It was a gutsy call: Lütjens had decided to take advantage of the favorable weather and to forgo time-consuming refueling from the *Weissenburg*.

Erich Raeder spent 22 May 1941 at the Berghof, Hitler's retreat on the Obersalzberg, high above Berchtesgaden in the Bavarian Alps. The grand admiral took up his Führer's time with a long series of reports dealing with U-boat successes and losses, the death of U-boat ace Lieutenant Commander Günther Prien commanding U-47 in the North Atlantic on 7 March, cruiser warfare in foreign waters, successful blockade runners, prize ships arriving in German and other friendly ports—and only then slipped in a brief reference to the fact that the *Bismarck* and the *Prinz Eugen* at that very moment were planning to break out of the Norwegian Sea to conduct "trade war in north and central Atlantic."[77] Raeder chose not to inform Hitler that he had received no news from Lütjens concerning the task force's probable route of advance. Or that the *Bismarck* had been spotted by a Swedish warship in the Baltic Sea. Or that he had no news from the supply ships as to their present position. Or that the British had detected the task force in Norwegian waters.

Adolf Hitler was not amused. He disliked having such a momentous decision sprung on him, and reminded Raeder that earlier, in his official capacity as commander in chief of German armed forces, he had raised serious objections to Atlantic sorties, given Britain's numerical and especially naval air superiority.[78] Politically, Hitler was concerned that Rhine Exercise could embroil the Kriegsmarine in "hot" confrontations with the officially neutral U.S. Navy on the high seas. Over and over, the Führer had counseled restraint in the navy's dealings with the neutral United States. Thus he had raised no objection in October 1939 when Washington had proclaimed a 300- to 1,000-mile pan-American "safety belt" around the states south of Canada. In February 1940 Hitler had vetoed Raeder's proposal to send submarines to the waters off Halifax, Canada, fearing that this might adversely affect German-American relations. Three months later he had refused Raeder's request to shell oil refineries on Aruba in the Lesser Antilles, as these were owned by the American company Standard Oil. And when the German navy established a war zone around the British Isles in August 1940, Hitler made certain that this corresponded precisely to the area in which the United States had forbidden its citizens and ships to sail. Above all, the Führer wished to avoid any confrontation with American naval forces in the Atlantic until after the successful completion of Operation Barbarossa.

Raeder handed his Führer a lengthy treatise dealing with what the admiral termed "problem U.S.A.," as well as the text for a mock, staged discussion of the matter in the press. The first document fell just short of asking Hitler to declare war against the United States. Given the United States' overt support of British maritime and naval shipping in the Atlantic, Raeder sought to have the entire North Atlantic, from the coast of Canada to Britain above 45 degrees latitude, declared a war zone. The United States, Raeder informed Hitler, had abandoned its policy of neutrality on the Atlantic. Roosevelt had extended the U.S. Navy's zone of activity to 38 degrees west, that is, to the middle of the Atlantic. He had instructed American warships to warn convoys of sighted U-boat patrols. He was converting merchant ships under construction into escort aircraft carriers to hunt down U-boats in future. He was finalizing plans to base American aircraft on Newfoundland, Greenland, and Iceland for convoy protection; similar plans were being discussed with regard to the Azores, Cape Verdes, and Dakar. And Roosevelt was even formulating plans to have American warships formally escort Atlantic convoys to Britain. The admiral demanded that Hitler immediately expand the war zone around Great Britain to 38 degress west, that is, to the edge of American naval patrols, and that the Führer declare the entire North Atlantic, from the shores of eastern Canada down to a line running from southern

Argentina to the Cape of Good Hope at the tip of Africa, a German war zone wherein surface vessels and U-boats were free to destroy hostile as well as neutral shipping at will.

Hitler lectured Raeder that President Roosevelt was still "wavering" on the issue of war or peace. Moreover, in the third-person vernacular of the "Führer Conferences on Naval Affairs," Hitler "wishes under no circumstances to provoke the entry of the USA into war through incidents right now," given that the planned invasion of the Soviet Union was precisely a month away.[79] Finally, Hitler queried Raeder whether it was still possible to break off Rhine Exercise: "Herr Grossadmiral, if at all possible, I would like to recall the ships." Raeder stood his ground. He informed Hitler that the planning of Rhine Exercise had already gone too far to recall the ships, and that no one in the Kriegsmarine would understand a sudden recall at this late date. He declined to inform Hitler that Admiral Lütjens had already been given the green light to ignore the American neutrality zone. The discussion ended with the Führer, whose mind was now fully concentrated on the final preparations for the pending invasion of the Soviet Union, in an uncharacteristically indecisive mood. "Well, perhaps now you have to leave things the way they are, but I have a very bad feeling." Raeder refused to include Hitler's final words in the official war diary; they were recorded only by the Führer's naval adjutant, Commander Karl Jesko von Puttkamer.[80]

Grand Admiral Raeder returned to Berlin fully aware that both his career and the future of the surface fleet rested with Rhine Exercise. On 5 May at Gotenhafen, Raeder had purposely chosen not to be present for Hitler's discussion with Admiral Lütjens for fear of having to reveal the precise nature of the planned sortie. On 22 May at Berchtesgaden, Raeder brazenly confronted Hitler with a fait accompli. The Kriegsmarine's future rested with Admiral Lütjens.

THE KING'S SHIPS, BUT TOVEY'S MEN

SCAPA FLOW, ORKNEY ISLANDS, 21 May 1941. As the *Bismarck* was anchoring in the quiet waters of Grimstadfjord, near Bergen, Norway, HMS *King George V* lay at anchor near the island of Flotta in Scapa Flow. The *King George V* was the newest battleship in the Royal Navy. Laid down in 1937 and completed in 1940, "*KGV*," as she was known throughout the fleet, had been built to conform as closely as possible to the London Naval Treaty of 1935, which imposed a maximum battleship displacement of roughly 35,000 tons. She was the first of four of her class; her sister ship the *Prince of Wales*, newly launched with sea trials just completed, lay at anchor a few hundred yards away. With an actual displacement of 38,000 tons (44,800 fully loaded for war), *KGV* mounted ten 14-inch guns as her main armament and was capable of 29 knots. She was barely in the same league as the *Bismarck*, but she was the most up-to-date, fully operational battleship in the Royal Navy. She had been chosen as the flagship of Vice Admiral Sir John Tovey, commander in chief of the Home Fleet.

Scapa Flow is in the southernmost part of the Orkneys, about ten miles from the north coast of Scotland. The harbor, some 15 miles east to west and 8 miles north to south, is formed by five islands—Mainland to the north, Hoy to the southwest, Flotta in the south, and Burrey and South Ronaldsay to the southeast. In World War I it had been selected as the base for the Royal Navy's Grand Fleet because it was ideally located to support the navy's blockade of shipping to and from Germany via the North Sea. It was also thought to be far enough away from the German coast to give protection from attack by surface ships or submarines.

Scapa, and the Orkneys that surrounded it, had a long history of accommodating ships of war and a checkered past as far as the Royal Navy was concerned. First used as a naval base by the Viking King Haokon in the thirteenth century, the Royal Navy had considered basing ships there during the Napoleonic wars. Shortly after the start of World War I, a German submarine penetrated into the Flow, forcing the British to sink blockships at strategic openings to the basin and place an antisubmarine net across the main harbor entrance. The precautions rendered the harbor itself safe against attack, but the British minister of war, Lord H. H. Kitchener, was killed in the Orkneys in June 1916 when the *Hampshire,* carrying him to visit Russia, struck a mine and sank just off the Orkney coast. When the war ended, seventy-four ships of the German High Sea Fleet were interned at the Flow. Manned by skeleton crews, the German fleet lay at anchor until 21 June 1919, when its officers scuttled it rather than see it handed over to the Allies.

When World War II began, the Royal Navy intended once again to blockade the North Sea, and once again Scapa Flow was selected as the base for the Home Fleet, the successor to the Grand Fleet of the previous war. Once again the Germans succeeded in sending a submarine into the Flow, this time with disastrous results. On the night of 13 October 1939, U-47, commanded by Lieutenant Günther Prien, edged its way into the Flow on the surface of Home Sound, with but a few feet to spare under its keel, and torpedoed the battleship *Royal Oak* as she lay at anchor in Scapa Bay. Prien escaped and was feted as a hero at home; the *Royal Oak* went to the bottom in 13 minutes with 833 officers and men. For the next three years, construction gangs worked hard to build causeways, sink more blockships, and make the harbor as impregnable as possible.

John Cronyn Tovey had gone to sea just before his fifteenth birthday. Now fifty-six, he had spent his entire adult life in the service of His Majesty and had demonstrated quick intelligence, courage, and character from the beginning. He was twenty-nine at the start of World War I and second in command of the light cruiser HMS *Amphion*. She became one of the very first ships of the Royal Navy to engage in a surface action when, on the second day of the war, she sank the German minelayer *Königin Luise*. But Tovey was also one of the first Royal Navy officers in the war to lose his ship when, on the very next day, the *Amphion* struck a mine that the *Königin Luise* had previously laid. War always brings opportunities for rapid promotion to those who distinguish themselves at the butcher's trade, and Tovey was no exception. In early 1915, still shy of his thirtieth birthday, he was given command of the destroyer HMS *Jackal*; fifteen months later he took command of HMS *Onslow*, a fleet destroyer attached to Vice Admiral Sir David Beatty's battle cruiser squadron based at Rosyth.

It was on the *Onslow*, and at the Battle of Jutland in particular, that Tovey first demonstrated the personal courage, decisiveness, aggressiveness, and verve that marked the rest of his career. At one point in that day's action Beatty retired north at high speed to lure the main German fleet toward Admiral Sir John Jellicoe's battleships. The *Onslow*, with the destroyer *Moresby* under command, was assigned to stay back to cover the seaplane tender *Engadine* as she hoisted her aircraft aboard. With each passing moment Beatty's ships raced to the north with the German High Seas Fleet hot on their heels; the *Onslow*, the *Moresby*, and the *Engadine* were caught in the middle. As soon as the *Engadine* finished her task, Tovey turned the *Onslow* north and raced at 30 knots to join Beatty. For a split second, however, he realized that nothing lay between him and the German heavy ships speeding to cross Beatty's bow at about 18,000 yards. "I was unable to see any enemy light cruisers or destroyers ahead of their battle-cruisers," he later reported. "It seemed a favourable opportunity to deliver an attack with torpedoes," so he did. With Tovey in the lead, the two lightly armed and barely armored destroyers swung to close the Germans at high speed. With spray breaking over her bow, the *Onslow* vibrated to the rhythm of the straining turbines as the two British destroyers and the German battle cruisers raced toward each other at a closing speed of more than 50 knots. On the *Onslow*'s open bridge, Tovey grimly hung on to the captain's chair as someone called off the range: "Nine thousand yards . . . eight thousand five hundred . . . eight thousand." Still Tovey waited. He had to get closer to launch his torpedoes to make this mad dash count. Suddenly four German light cruisers raced quickly ahead of the battle cruisers. Within seconds they "opened heavy and accurate fire on both the *Onslow* and *Moresby*." Hit repeatedly, the *Onslow* shuddered under the blows. Within moments she was badly damaged, and Tovey was forced to turn away. When the two destroyers cleared the battle area, the *Moresby* took the *Onslow* in tow and brought her to Aberdeen, Scotland for repairs.[1] Tovey was awarded the Distinguished Service Order for this daring attack and, at the end of June 1916, received a special expedited promotion to commander—an incredible achievement for a man of only thirty-one.

In 1923 Tovey was promoted to captain and command of a destroyer flotilla. After seven years alternating between sea and shore duty, Tovey went to the Admiralty as naval assistant to the second sea lord, a senior staff appointment. In 1932 he took command of HMS *Rodney*, then one of Britain's newest battleships. He achieved flag rank in 1935 and three years later the demanding Sir Andrew Browne Cunningham, commander in chief of the Mediterranean Fleet based at Alexandria, Egypt, brought Tovey to the Mediterranean. Tovey became Cunningham's rear admiral in charge of destroyers.

When war broke out in September 1939, the Royal Navy's overall strategy was to concentrate its ships in home waters and leave the job of securing the Mediterranean to the smaller but generally newer French fleet based principally at Toulon in France and at Oran and Mers-el-Kebir in Algeria. On 10 June 1940 Italy declared war on Britain and France, adding to Britain's problems. The Italian fleet was not large compared to the Royal Navy, but it was both concentrated in Italian waters and modern; suddenly the naval odds in this important theater of war were not so favorable to the Allied cause. Eleven days later the odds shifted even more toward the Axis when Marshal Henri-Philippe Pétain took power in France and announced that his government would seek an armistice with Germany. Suddenly Cunningham's small and mostly aging fleet faced the Germans and Italians alone in the Mediterranean.

"ABC," as Cunningham was known in the service, was an exacting and demanding commander; He insisted that his captains make up in aggressiveness what they lacked in numbers and firepower.[2] Tovey did not disappoint. Given command of all Cunningham's cruisers, as well as destroyers at the start of July 1940, he put to sea from Alexandria on 7 July with six light cruisers (armed with 6-inch guns) to help Cunningham meet two convoys evacuating British women and children eastward from Malta. Cunningham was certain the Italian fleet would strike at the convoys. As his ships sailed westward on the 8th, Italian bombers attacked them; HMS *Gloucester*, one of Tovey's cruisers, was hit, and her captain and seventeen others were killed. Later that day Royal Navy reconnaissance aircraft flying from the carrier *Eagle* spotted an Italian force of three modern battleships, six heavy cruisers (armed with 8-inch guns), and seven destroyers about 100 miles northwest of Benghazi, Libya, steering northwest. Cunningham directed his entire force, led by the battleships *Warspite* (newly modernized), *Royal Sovereign*, and *Malaya* and the carrier *Eagle* to race to interpose themselves between the Italian ships and Italy. The Italians would have to fight, which Cunningham knew they might not do even though they had the superior force.

By noon on 9 July the fleets were about 90 miles apart; three hours later the light cruiser *Neptune* was the first to sight the enemy off the Calabrian coast. Tovey's cruisers were fast, but they were outranged by the Italians and could fire only about half the weight of broadside of the enemy's heavy cruisers. Tovey never hesitated. At 3:48 P.M. he gave the order to close and engage. Battle pennants flying from yardarms, the Seventh Cruiser Squadron raced into the van. They quickly outpaced the slower British battleships as they dashed to close the range as quickly as possible. Only at short ranges could their 6-inch guns do real damage to the Italian ships, while their thin deck armor was most vulnerable to heavy armor-piercing shells at long range, when those shells would be almost vertical as they plunged toward their targets.

This was the first day since the Napoleonic Wars that a British warship had signaled her consorts "enemy battle fleet in sight." Sea warfare and the preparations for it had changed a great deal since the days of Admiral Horatio Nelson. In each of Tovey's light cruisers, it all began with the ringing of the "action stations" bell.

Until that moment, a third of the ships' companies were on cruising watch, tending to the normal duties that keep a ship moving and sailors fed. They worked in the engine room, or in the cook's shack, or on radar watch. They were on watch four hours out of every twelve on a rotating basis. Those not on watch were either sleeping as best they could in their swaying hammocks, strung in their mess decks, or eating, writing letters, playing cards, or just soaking up the sun on an upperworks or the main deck. Sleeping arrangements on British warships were the same irespective of ship. Sailors slept in hammocks, or 'micks, in their particular mess, which was also the place they ate and whiled away their off hours. Stokers slept in the stokers' mess, gunners in the gunners' mess, and so on. Officers had their own cabins with bunks, usually shared and never large. The captain had his sea cabin near the bridge, little more than a place to sleep at sea. In port, he lived and worked in his day cabin, usually somewhere just under the rear quarterdeck and much larger and more comfortable. All officers stood specifically assigned watches except the captain. He had no special watch, but he was on the bridge when leaving or entering harbor, and at times of danger.

When the action stations bell rang, the entire ship's company rushed to their assigned battle positions. They manned the guns and the torpedoes, climbed into their lookout positions, tended the engines, and took their places on the bridge or other control stations throughout the ship. The coxswain, the ship's senior noncommissioned officer, took the wheel, and the captain took the bridge. The executive officer, called the first lieutenant in smaller Royal Navy warships and first lieutenant commander in larger ones, went aft, usually to the damage-control station near the auxiliary steering station somewhere by the stern. When all stations were reported to the bridge as ready, the ship was thought to be "closed up," or watertight and prepared for battle. The men were ready and tense at their stations. Some might see or hear signs of impending battle, but those below, especially in the loud and hot confines of the boiler room or engine room, would not see or hear anything. On the bridge, someone was always peering intently through his binoculars at the flagship, watching for signal flags to flutter up the yardarm. A flag going up was a sign that an order to execute was about to be given, usually to increase speed or turn in a certain direction. As soon as the flag snapped down the flagship's yardarm, all ships of the flotilla were expected to obey instantly. Thus maneuvering could be done while maintaining radio silence.

For a time after the ship closed up, there was an air of expectancy. The bow sliced through the sea, the gulls cried above, the sun shone or the rain fell, the water swished along the hull, the faint funnel gases vented through the funnel. The gunners, in flash protection gear and helmets, waited in their turrets, ready to lay and fire the main guns. The men at the antiaircraft stations peered intently into the sky. Those on radar or sonar watch stared at flickering screens or concentrated on the noises in their earphones. The captain quietly gave steering directions or requests for speed to the coxswain or to the ratings standing by the two bridge telegraphs, one for each screw. It was always quiet in the moments before the gun bell rang and the main guns opened fire or the whizzing sound of incoming shells was heard and fountains of water erupted alongside.

In rushing straight at the enemy, Tovey's captains were breaking one of the fundamental conventions of sea battle; they could fire their forward guns at the Italians, but their rear turrets could not be brought to bear. In naval parlance, their A arcs were closed. This was supposed to be the least advantageous position from which to fight a gun battle at sea. For example, since most of Tovey's light cruisers had four turrets—two in front of the superstructure and two to the rear—they could bring only half their firepower to bear when doing so. The Italians, broadside to them, could use all their main armament. Never a man to just follow the rules, Tovey believed that losing the use of the after turrets was more than compensated by the advantages of presenting the enemy with the smallest possible target, closing at the highest possible speed. And since rear turrets were going to be useless anyway at most angles of approach to an enemy, why not just go straight at them?

It took a little more than ten minutes before Tovey's squadron was in range of the Italian main force. Although the *Warspite,* some 6,000 yards to the southwest of Tovey's cruisers, was rushing to his support (she was about 5 knots faster than the other battleships), the Italian heavy cruisers opened fire before she got within range. The western horizon was alive with gun flashes; 8-inch shells, each weighing about 500 pounds, began to fall among Tovey's four-ship flotilla. Large columns of water rose above the onrushing cruisers. Tovey continued to turn toward the enemy. Then, at about 3:53 P.M., the *Warspite* opened fire. The tremendous booms from her eight 15-inch guns rolled across the water. Far to the north, 26,000 yards distant, huge columns of ocean climbed into the sky alongside the Italian battleship *Cesare.* Then a hit. No real explosion, but a faint glow on the Italian ship's superstructure as a 2,000-pound armor-piercing shell from the *Warspite* buried itself in the ship's vitals before blowing up. Oily black smoke belched from the open wound. The Italians turned away to retire northward at high speed. Tovey's cruisers scored no hits, but Tovey earned high praise from Cunningham. "Our cruisers were outnumbered and at times under a very heavy fire," Cunningham wrote in his report of the action. "They were superbly handled by Vice-Admiral Tovey, who, by his skillful maneuvering, managed to maintain a position in the van and to hold the enemy cruiser squadrons."[3]

In the fall of 1940, Prime Minister Winston Churchill fired the commander in chief of the Home Fleet, Sir Charles Forbes. Forbes was not wanting as a naval commander; he was just in the wrong place at the wrong time. Like many a good Allied commander at the outbreak of war, he was short on resources working with a peacetime force that had to suddenly adapt to war. Forbes' Home Fleet, like the rest of the Royal Navy, was stretched beyond capacity; he paid the price for years of government negligence and apathy. Churchill demanded aggressiveness from his commanders, and although Forbes did his best to seek out and destroy the enemy, he was on the defensive much of the time. In October 1940 Tovey learned he had been chosen to replace Forbes.

As commander in chief of the Home Fleet, Tovey took upon his shoulders the heavy responsibility for the defense of the United Kingdom's home waters. He was, by that time, one of the three or four best commanders in the Royal Navy. Married for twenty-five years, he and his wife, Aida, had no children. The navy was his life. Though small in stature, Tovey kept himself very fit. His facial features were sharply defined; he would have been thought of as looking very English. He had blue eyes and delicate hands. He dressed well, he loved good food and wine, and he had a strong sense of humor. He was deeply religious and strongly believed that the British race, as Churchill called them, had a special mission to bring law and culture to the world. He also believed that the Royal Navy was the chief instrument of that mission. He sought relaxation in quiet moments standing in hip waders, casting flies for salmon or trout in cold Scottish streams or on a golf course, where he consistently shot in the seventies.

Tovey's ready twinkle, love of good living, and easy personal style masked his strong drive, his abiding self-confidence, and his absolute refusal to settle for anything but the best effort of the men under him. Some thought him arrogant, but he was not so much conceited as definite in his carefully arrived-at views and unwavering in his well-thought-out convictions. When John Tovey thought himself right, he would bend for no man, not even Churchill. After his first interview with the prime minister on his appointment as commander in chief of the Home Fleet, he wrote Cunningham: "You will understand how I loved him almost at first, but he made some astounding statements about naval warfare. . . . I still don't know if he was wanting to find out if I was prepared to applaud everything he said or whether he really believes half of what he said." When Tovey had been captain of the *Rodney* in the early 1930s, an admiral had written of him: "[He] shares one characteristic with me. In myself I would call it tenacity of purpose. In Tovey I can only call it sheer bloody obstinacy." When he left the Mediterranean, Cunningham, always sparing in his praise, expressed his appreciation of Tovey's "advice, outspoken criticism, loyal support, cheerful optimism and imperturbability."[4]

As commander in chief of the Home Fleet, Tovey abandoned the blue skies and temperate waters of the Mediterranean and the bustle and exoticism of Alexandria for his old home base of the First World War, Scapa Flow.

Scapa Flow may have been well suited as a base from a strategic point of view, but it was as far as the moon from the portside pubs, the dockside bustle, and the warm ladies of Portsmouth or Plymouth. The sailors hated the place. A few small fishing villages sat along the shore of the Flow, and there were Norse ruins and puffins aplenty for those few who hiked the low scrub- and heather-covered hills of the Orkneys. But it was cold the year round, and wet, and when the wind came howling across the open sea it drove spume and sleet so hard, it pitted a man's face. Isolated, inhospitable, and far from home, with almost no shoreside amenities, Scapa Flow ranked with the Falkland Islands in the South Atlantic, the Faeroes in the North Sea, and Hvalfjord on the south coast of Iceland as one of the worst places a British sailor would ever have to endure.

On the graying morning of 21 May 1941, the welfare of his

sailors and the wretchedness of Scapa Flow's weather were far from Tovey's mind as he looked to the distant hills through the scuttle of his spacious admiral's cabin near *KGV*'s stern. The fair weather that had brought sunny skies to the Orkneys over the last few days was already ending. To the northwest of the British Isles an intense low-pressure system that had stalled over Iceland was now on the move toward the Faeroes. The morning's weather chart, lying on Tovey's desk, forecast that the low would soon cross the Irish coast, bringing rain and heavy cloud over Scotland and the North Sea. There would be no reliable aerial reconnaissance over the Danish Belts, the North Sea, or the Norwegian coast for several days; it was the perfect time for the *Bismarck* to begin its run.

Royal Air Force and Royal Navy reconnaissance aircraft had been keeping watch over the *Bismarck* from the time her keel had been laid down. They watched even more closely after she had been launched, when her superstructure rose daily and huge dockside cranes lifted her armament aboard. As early as late March 1940, nine high-ranking officers of the Royal Navy and Royal Air Force met at the Admiralty to discuss the ship's progress (and that of the aircraft carrier *Graf Zeppelin*) and to think of possible ways of attacking her before she could sortie. The government of Neville Chamberlain was still reluctant to order long-range air attacks on German population centers, and since the *Bismarck* was still in the Blohm & Voss shipyard in Hamburg, the British officers spent little time discussing that option. But they agreed to maintain constant aerial reconnaissance over German shipyards as long as the *Bismarck*—and her sister ship, the *Tirpitz*, building at Wilhelmshaven—was under construction, and to try to keep track of them when sea trials commenced. Only then, when the *Bismarck* was in open water, was there even a remote possibility of an attack by torpedo bombers, though the costs would be high and the odds of success long due to Luftwaffe strength.[5]

Tovey had no real idea of the *Bismarck*'s status, but German aerial reconnaissance had increased in the last few days. That could mean some sort of breakout by heavy warships from the Baltic was imminent. On 14 May Tovey had asked the flag officer in charge, Iceland, for a report on ice conditions around Jan Mayen Island. The pack ice was still extensive, so Tovey concluded that German warships trying to break into the North Atlantic would most likely head for the Denmark Strait. That was what the 11-inch battleships *Gneisenau* and *Scharnhorst* had done when they had broken into the Atlantic at the beginning of February. Admiral Günther Lütjens, whom naval intelligence had fingered as the prospective fleet commander of any German task force built around the *Bismarck*, had commanded those two ships. Tovey knew Lütjens well; earlier that year the German fleet commander had led him a merry chase.

On 23 January 1941 Tovey had barely settled into his new command when naval intelligence had alerted him to an imminent sortie by the *Scharnhorst* and the *Gneisenau*. Aboard the *Nelson*, then his flagship, Tovey had directed the hunt. He had left Scapa Flow with the *Nelson*, its sister ship *Rodney*, the battle cruiser *Repulse*, eight cruisers, and eleven destroyers, and positioned his entire fleet 120 miles south of Iceland to intercept the two German warships no matter which passage they took into the Atlantic. He ordered intensified air patrols between the Faeroes and Iceland. But Tovey soon concluded that he had moved too fast and concentrated too much force in one spot. He had no backup. If a chase developed after several days of patrolling, his capital ships might run dangerously low on fuel. He sent the *Rodney* and a number of cruisers and destroyers back to Scapa to refuel. In the meantime, he and his fleet prowled the waters south of Iceland. It was midwinter and extremely cold. For days lookouts strained through their glasses while ice fog, mist, and snow squalls obscured their vision. The ships rolled in the heavy winter swells. Sea spray froze as soon as it hit metal surfaces, making the ships top-heavy; it was absolutely vital that every available man be on deck picking and smashing away at the ice. Then, on 28 January, one of the men on Tovey's northernmost cruiser, the *Naiad*, steaming eastward from Iceland, caught a fleeting glimpse of Lütjens' flotilla. The German ships were very hard to see at extreme range. They were there as low gray shapes one moment, gone the next. Lütjens' sailors had spotted the British masts, and Lütjens guessed he was steaming into a trap. He ordered speed increased and rudders hard over; the two German battleships raced back north. Tovey lost them; after searching in vain for several hours, always conscious of his fuel, he called the mission off and returned to Scapa.[6] Lütjens refueled from a waiting tanker, turned about, and steamed south through the Denmark Strait as close as possible to the icepack that extended some 80 miles eastward from the Greenland coast. The two German ships slipped into the North Atlantic on 4 February 1941 and began a two-month voyage of destruction that ranged from a few hundred miles east of Newfoundland to the waters off West Africa. They sank or captured twenty-two merchant ships for a total bag of some 115,600 tons. The destruction itself was not great, considering the massive resources the Germans had employed. But the strain on the Royal Navy, and the Home Fleet in particular, was out of proportion to the actual threat Lütjens' little flotilla had posed. Tovey knew better than anyone that if he had caught Lütjens at the very start of the episode, the tremendous draw on Royal Navy resources could have been avoided.[7]

The breakout of the *Gneisenau* and the *Scharnhorst* on 4 February was only one of many successful German passages into the Atlantic. By spring 1941 it began to seem as if the Germans had smooth sailing anytime they chose. Warships, tankers, weather ships, and raiders disguised as merchant ships slipped through on a regular basis. The weather was often too bad for these passages to be detected by air patrols, and the expedient of sending a cruiser out from Iceland to search for German ships whenever a transit was suspected was obviously not enough. Tovey's fleet was inadequate for all the tasks assigned to it—distant blockade of the North Sea, convoy protection, home defense, and augmentation of other Royal Navy commands such as Force H, the task force based at Gibraltar. At the same time most of his ships desperately needed modernization, while all his ships required regular prolonged maintenance and repair after months at sea. For several days in

March 1941 he had only a single major warship to spare. Nonetheless, it was his responsibility—and a major one—to stop these breakouts. In mid-April 1941 he had decided to mount standing patrols at the northern end of the Denmark Strait and across the Iceland-Faeroes gap. The task of watching over the Denmark Strait was given to Rear Admiral William F. Wake-Walker and his First Cruiser Squadron, consisting of the county-class heavy cruisers *Norfolk* and *Suffolk*.

On 18 May Tovey signaled Wake-Walker, whose flag was on the *Norfolk*, to step up his patrols. If the *Bismarck* sortied, Tovey wanted the *Norfolk* and the *Suffolk* at sea at the same time. The *Suffolk* would be especially valuable, since her brand-new Type 284 centimetric radar could detect an enemy warship at night, or in bad weather, as far out as 15 miles and also give accurate ranges for gunnery in all weather. In light of Lütjens' previous passage through the strait along the edge of the pack ice, Tovey cautioned the *Suffolk*'s commanding officer, Captain R. M. Ellis, to pay special attention to the open water close to the ice on the Greenland side of the strait. When Wake-Walker received Tovey's instructions, the *Norfolk* was refueling in Hvalfjord, Iceland, but sailed on the 19th to relieve the *Suffolk*; the *Suffolk* then steamed to Hvalfjord to refuel and to wait for further instructions. If needed for a long vigil, her bunkers would be full and her crew rested.[8]

Two days of fair weather over the North Sea and the Danish Belts momentarily pushed thoughts of the *Bismarck* from the center of Tovey's mind. There were ten convoys at sea in the North Atlantic, six inbound to the United Kingdom and four outbound. Another, the five-ship troop transport convoy WS8B (*WS* stood for "Winston Special") was about to depart the Clyde estuary on the 22nd, bound for the Middle East, escorted by two cruisers, eight destroyers, the battle cruiser *Repulse*, and the new aircraft carrier *Victorious*. The *Victorious* was carrying dozens of crated Hurricane fighters to Gibraltar; she had room for nine obsolescent Swordfish torpedo bombers and six almost-as-obsolete Fairey Fulmar fighters for her own air operations. The battleship *Rodney* was due to escort the passenger ship *Britannic* to Boston. She would then stay several months for a long-overdue refit. Captain J. C. Leach reported the *Prince of Wales* fit for sea duty on 19 May, but Tovey and his staff had strong doubts about how ready she really was.[9]

The meteorological reports on the night of the 20th and the one made up at 7:00 A.M. on the 21st brought Tovey's thoughts back to the *Bismarck*. As he sipped his tea that morning and pondered the high cloud gathering over the Flow, there was a sharp knock on the slightly open watertight door between his cabin and the office of his secretary, Paymaster-Captain A. W. Pafford. It was a message from the Admiralty containing Captain Henry Denham's report from Stockholm: "Most immediate: Kattegat today 20 May. (a) This afternoon eleven German merchant ships passed Lenker North; (b) at 1500 two large warships escorted by three destroyers, five escort vessels, [and] ten or twelve aircraft, passed Marstrand course north-west."[10] As he read and reread the note, he wondered how reliable the information was. Operational Intelligence Centre had rated it a mere B-3, about as unreliable as could be. Could he send his ships to sea on a note like that?

Tovey immediately phoned the Admiralty and spoke to Rear Admiral Sir John Godfrey, director of naval intelligence, and to Admiral Sir Tom Phillips, vice chief of the Naval Staff. He learned that Coastal Command was making preparations to send two high-altitude reconnaissance Spitfires to survey the Norwegian coast sometime after noon. Everyone was desperate to prove or disprove the news from Stockholm. If true, however, no one could figure what connection if any, "escort vessels" might have with the warships. If the warships were about to break into the Atlantic for commerce raiding, as the Admiralty believed, the presence of the merchant ships was puzzling; Tovey knew that German commerce raiders would have had their tankers and supply ships already prepositioned at sea. What did Grand Admiral Erich Raeder intend?

Tovey was still on the phone to London when his chief of staff, Commodore E. J. P. Brind, and his staff officer (operations) came into the cabin. They too had the Admiralty's message. They too wondered if it was accurate and if so, what the "escort vessels" were doing in company with the warships. Personally, Tovey was convinced that the *Bismarck* was starting its run and that Lütjens was going to try a second time what he had successfully pulled off in February. But he needed more to go on. Not a ship would sail until he knew for sure that *Bismarck* was coming out.

Tovey's staff stayed. They lit the first of what would be a dozen or so packs of cigarettes, called for coffee and tea, and settled in. For the next several hours they discussed every possible enemy intention they could think of. They called for charts and weather maps. They were briefed by the weathermen. They spoke to naval intelligence in London. They assessed the readiness of the Home Fleet, focusing on which ships were at sea and when they could be detached to rejoin the Home Fleet. They evaluated the state of the *Victorious* and her virtually green aircrew. They evaluated the *Prince of Wales*; was she really ready for sea, let alone a long sea voyage ending in a heavy gun battle? She had only recently completed sea trials to ensure that her engines and maneuvering gear performed properly, but hundreds of vital systems remained untested and her 14-inch guns and turrets, the same design as those on the *King George V*, were full of manufacturers' defects. Gunnery experts from Vickers, which had built the guns, were still aboard. If she sortied with the *Hood*, there would be no time to put these civilians ashore; worse, there was no assurance that her guns would perform.

Even the *Hood* was a question mark. The "mighty *Hood*," as she was referred to throughout the fleet and around the British Empire, was the pride of the navy and the symbol of British sea power. Launched on 22 August 1918, she first made her reputation in a round-the-world cruise in 1922, accompanied by the *Repulse* and several other ships. At just over 48,000 tons displacement loaded for war, the *Hood* was the largest warship afloat until the advent of the *Bismarck*. She was also thought to be the most beautiful by those who find beauty in warships. She was very long and had a low freeboard (the height from the sea to the main deck). In profile she looked lean, fast, uncluttered, and ready for action. She was the empire's ultimate symbol of sea power in the interwar years. After Admiral Raeder rebuilt the Kriegsmarine, German sailors almost always envisaged the *Hood* steaming against them when they practiced war games. She was the nemesis of all who would oppose the Union Jack.

The *Hood* was also a badly flawed ship with deck armor too thin to resist the plunging fire of armor-piercing shells fired by battleship-sized naval guns. Like all battle cruisers, she had been a design compromise. She was larger than any true battleship afloat, 860 feet long compared to the *Prince of Wales*' 745 feet and the *Rodney*'s 710. Her eight 15-inch guns, mounted two apiece in four turrets, two forward and two aft, were the match of any battleship. But in reality, she was nothing more than a large cruiser, fast but unable to survive a slugging match with any modern, well-armored battle wagon. The Royal Navy had discovered the awful vulnerability of battle cruisers in 1916, when three of them literally blew up at the Battle of Jutland, all the victims of German armor-piercing shells plunging into their magazines and exploding the tons of cordite stored there. The *Queen Mary, Invincible,* and *Indefatigable* were gone in a flash with virtually all their companies. Constantly scheduled for major reconstruction to enhance her deck armor in the interwar years, the *Hood* was needed too much at sea to undergo the expensive and time-consuming modifications. As it was, the addition of modern antiaircraft guns, new radar and electronics, and other updated add-ons at the outbreak of the war had made her about 6,000 tons heavier than her original design weight. This lowered her freeboard even more and degraded her performance in a heavy sea. The additions also put extra force on her spine, which was already stressed by a long keel with two heavy turrets at both ends.[11]

The morning of 20 May passed into afternoon. The small boats and motor launches that tended to the moored warships of the Home Fleet went about their business on the waters of the Flow. The gulls cried overhead. The men in the warships cleaned or rested or mended. They waited for the liberty boats or came back from liberty. They had no idea what was transpiring in the admiral's cabin. To them, it was just another boring day spent in the brisk air of the Home Fleet's remote anchorage. But in Tovey's cabin, the commander in chief slowly developed a series of suppositions as to who the enemy likely was, what he was most likely to do, and how the Home Fleet ought to be deployed to meet him. The plan that began to take shape, even as they waited anxiously for news from the Coastal Command Spitfires, was really the outcome of a process of elimination based on deciding which enemy initiatives posed the greatest danger to Britain and, therefore, should be guarded against first.

Then, in late afternoon, Tovey learned the results of Coastal Command's reconnaissance flights over the Norwegian coast. They confirmed what Tovey already suspected—the *Bismarck*, in consort with a heavy cruiser that was, without doubt, the *Prinz Eugen*, was coming out. Tovey wondered why she had anchored in a Norwegian fjord. If Lütjens was going commerce raiding, he should have been hell-bent for the Norwegian Sea as soon as he passed through the Danish Belts.

Now Tovey made the key decisions. He would essentially ignore, as not relevant, the information that the *Bismarck* and the cruiser had passed the Kattegat with eleven merchantmen, and even that she and her consort had stopped near Bergen. He knew the greatest danger the *Bismarck* posed to the British war effort was in the Atlantic convoy lanes. Not only could she destroy dozens of ships and seriously disrupt traffic—she would force the Royal Navy to spread its meager heavy-ship resources over thousands of square miles of ocean to keep watch and to destroy her if possible. That was the threat Tovey had to take most seriously. The only question, then, was how to meet that threat.

Lütjens might pick the Iceland-Faeroes gap to enter the North Atlantic, but he had taken the Denmark Strait successfully the last time. Besides, if Lütjens could hide his ships from aerial reconnaissance under the deteriorating weather for only a day or so, he could emerge from the Denmark Strait not far from Newfoundland, right near the eastern terminus of the most heavily traveled convoy tracks. When the U-boats had started sailing from Biscay ports a year before, the Admiralty had shifted the main North Atlantic convoy track far to the north. Now, when convoys left the Canadian east coast, they sailed through the Strait of Belle Isle, or around Cape Race, then across the Davis Strait to a point east of Cape Farewell at the southern tip of Greenland, then across the Denmark Strait to pass a hundred miles or so south of Iceland.

Tovey decided to deploy the bulk of his ships south of Iceland, enabling him to intercept the *Bismarck* whichever route it took. But he also decided to keep the heaviest ships nearer the Denmark Strait. He would not concentrate his fleet, as he had done in February, but split it into two forces close enough to reinforce each other, though far enough apart to cover more ocean and make it harder for Lütjens to slip around them. The first force, the battle cruiser squadron under Vice Admiral Lancelot Holland, consisted of the *Hood* and the *Prince of Wales,* accompanied by six destroyers. Tovey wanted Holland to sortie as soon as possible and steam for Hvalfjord to refuel. If the *Bismarck* was still lying at anchor near Bergen, Holland's force would deploy to the Denmark Strait with full bunkers; if the *Bismarck* had already left Bergen and was on its way to the Denmark Strait, Holland could go straight to back up Wake-Walker's ships. The ships that remained with Tovey at Scapa, plus any others the Admiralty could spare from current or expected duties, would make up the follow-up force. They'd stay at Scapa as long as possible to preserve fuel, but Tovey ordered his captains to bring their ships to short notice, so as to be able to sortie no more than two hours after receiving the order. And he took further steps to keep his options open. He sent the light cruisers *Birmingham* and *Manchester,* patrolling the Iceland-Faeroes gap, to proceed immediately to Iceland to refuel, then to resume their patrols. He also ordered Captain Alex C. Chapman, of the light cruiser *Arethusa*, en route to Hvalfjord on another mission, to place his ship under Wake-Walker's command. In the meantime, the Admiralty detached the *Victorious* and the battle cruiser *Repulse* from the troop convoy WS8B, due to sail from the Clyde, and placed them at Tovey's disposal. The *Victorious* was already at Scapa; the *Rodney* would join Tovey's force at sea.

There was still a solid band of twilight in the northwestern sky as Holland's ships prepared to depart. Last messages were exchanged over landlines; last mail was transferred to small boats. Machinery was checked and gear stowed. The boilers were brought up to pressure. The Jacob's ladders that climbed along the ship's sides from the water to the ship's main decks were raised. The special sea duty men who would raise the anchors and take the ships out of harbor were called to their stations. Then over the loudspeakers came the call: "Hands to station for leaving harbor. Close all watertight doors and scuttles. Stand by anchors." The huge steam-driven winches that pulled the massive anchors of the two large warships from the thick mud of the harbor bottom began to haul in the heavy chain links as men hosed off the mud. The chains rumbled down into the cavernous chain lockers on the foredecks of the *Hood* and the *Prince of Wales*. In the engine room of each ship the massive turbines spun while the engine room artificers, as the Royal Navy called the men who worked there, stood by to throw the ships' transmissions into gear. On the bridge of the *Hood*, Holland stood quietly just back of her commanding officer, Captain Ralph Kerr, as Kerr orchestrated the movements that would bring the warship from her moorings through the harbor gates and into the North Sea. "Slow back, both," Kerr said. The ratings on the bridge telegraphs rang out the order. Moments later the engine room responded. The huge screws began to turn in reverse as the *Hood* backed from her mooring. When she had moved back a hundred or so yards, Kerr uttered, "Slow ahead both, port ten." Again the orders were rung up on the bridge telegraphs, again the engine room responded. The screws slowed, stopped, then began to turn in the opposite direction as the coxswain swung the wheel to turn *Hood* 10 degrees to the left, so as to clear the mooring. Then the coxswain called, "Ten of port wheel on, sir." The *Hood* began to move forward. When Kerr was satisfied she was heading for the harbor mouth, he called, "Midships," and the coxswain straightened the ship. Ahead the boom boats opened the massive antisubmarine nets strung across the mouth of the Flow, and the six destroyers squeezed through to take up station ahead of the warships following in their wake. The flotilla moved through the harbor mouth in stately procession. The black waters of the Flow eddied behind them, then were still. It was midnight.

The man who now bore the chief responsibility for hunting the German ships, Vice Admiral Lancelot Ernest Holland, had been born in 1887. Like many of his peers, he had gone to sea in his early teens. Unlike Tovey, however, he had gained no appreciable command experience in World War I and had spent most of the interwar years in a variety of nonoperational posts. He was one of the very few of the Royal Navy's senior commanders who did not hold the Distinguished Service Order (DSO), an award that almost always went to a commanding officer whose unit distinguished itself in action on land, at sea, or in the air. In 1930 he went to Athens as head of the British naval mission to Greece. He served at the Admiralty as assistant chief of the naval staff in 1937 and 1938 before assuming command of the Second Battle Squadron in 1939. He was a gunnery specialist. Of medium height but very fit and trim, Holland skied and played polo. He was intensely ambitious. He once told a colleague that he might become first sea lord someday. He kept to himself much of the time. He and his wife, Phyllis, had suffered a deep personal tragedy in 1936 when their only son died of polio.

Holland's first real test as an operational commander had come in a clash between an Italian task force and several units of the Mediterranean Fleet under Vice Admiral Sir James Somerville off Cape Spartivento, Sardinia, on 27 November 1940. On that day Somerville's Force H—divided into two task groups, Force B under Somerville and Force F under Holland—had been shepherding a convoy eastward to a point where it would hand off its charges to a detachment of Cunningham's fleet based at Alexandria.[12] The convoy was midway between Cape Spartivento and North Africa when an air search from the carrier *Ark Royal* detected a strong force of Italian warships coming down from the north. When the sighting report came in, Somerville's ships—the *Ark Royal*, the battle cruiser *Renown*, the light cruiser *Sheffield*, and a number of destroyers—were steaming about 25 miles to the northwest of the convoy and parallel to it. Holland's ships—the light cruisers *Manchester* (Holland's flagship) and *Southampton*, a destroyer, four corvettes, and three transports—were close to the convoy. Each of his cruisers was crowded with some 700 Royal Air Force and army personnel, in addition to their ship's companies, and the transports were loaded with motor vehicles. Another British task group, Force D, was steaming toward the convoy from the east. It consisted of the old battleship *Ramillies*, the light cruisers *Newcastle*, *Coventry*, and *Berwich*, and five destroyers. The Italians were making about 18 knots and were far enough away when first detected to allow Somerville to get a good fix on their task force; it included two battleships, a number of heavy cruisers, and at least fifteen destroyers. One of the Italian battleships was the World War I–era *Conte di Cavour*. Displacing 29,000 tons, she had been modernized in the late 1930s. She mounted ten 12.6-inch guns as main armament and was capable of 28 knots. But the other was the brand-new *Vittorio Veneto*, displacing 45,000 tons. She had a top speed of 30 knots and mounted nine 15-inch guns.

Somerville's force stayed with the convoy as it closed on Force D. Then he ordered the convoy to turn to the southeast while he turned north to pursue the Italians. He ordered the *Ramillies* from Force D to join him. He detached the *Sheffield* from his own group and ordered it, along with the *Newcastle* and the *Berwick*, to join Holland's cruisers, now closed up for action and steaming ahead of the main body to engage the Italian warships. A torpedo attack by aircraft from the *Ark Royal* left the Italians undamaged. Holland's five cruisers, in a rather loose line-abreast formation, raced toward the Italian fleet. A few minutes past noon the Italians came into view on the northern horizon. Holland decided not to order his cruisers to concentrate their fire at a single target, nor to stay in close formation, because he believed the ships had had too little experience fighting as a unit.[13]

The gun action commenced, with the Italian heavy cruisers opening fire on Holland's ships just moments later. The British cruisers were outgunned and outranged. They scored some hits but had little direct impact on the Italians, who decided, in any case, to withdraw toward their battleships and the cover of their land-based aircraft. If they also lured Holland into range of the heavy guns of their capital ships, so much the better. Somerville knew that the *Ramillies*, with a top speed of only 21 knots, could not stay with his force in a high-speed chase. That meant any encounter would pit the *Renown*, with the thinly armored decks of a battle cruiser, against the two Italian battleships—a recipe for disaster. He also had to think about the convoy and the possibility that the Italians might try a high-speed end run to get at it.[14] He decided to disengage. The action ended at 1:30 P.M.

Andrew Browne Cunningham was as tough and aggressive a commander as the Royal Navy possessed. He was no doubt correct to break off the action and thought little of it. But his superiors at the Admiralty, driven by the relentless prime minister and minister of defense, Sir Winston Churchill, mounted a full-fledged investigation of Cunningham's actions. Thus Holland too came under scrutiny. Holland had fought his cruisers under two major handicaps; the extra personnel in the *Manchester* and the *Southampton* impeded the fighting efficiency of those two ships, while the five cruisers that raced toward the Italians were strangers to each other. In his report of the action, Somerville discussed Holland's actions and specifically his decision not to fight his ships as a unit and concentrate his fire. The official battle summary recorded Somerville's view "that . . . in many important respects the standard of fighting efficiency obtained in peace considerably exceeds that reached in war." Somerville chalked this up "to lack of systematic practices and exercises" and pointed to "the reluctance of Vice-Admiral Holland to attempt a concentration of fire by the . . . cruisers of his squadron."[15] Was that a criticism? Or was it merely Cunningham's explanation for why Holland fought his ships as he did? One of the main tenets of Royal Navy tactical doctrine for a surface action, embodied in the Admiralty's fighting instructions, was concentration of fire. Another tenet was to fight ships in division, or close formation, whenever possible. Holland had done neither and had been singled out for not going by the book, even if only for illustration.

In April 1941, after transfer to the Home Fleet, Holland had led a small force of cruisers and destroyers that seized the German weather ship *München* with important German cipher materials aboard. To his fellow officers, any stain his career might have suffered because of Cape Spartivento was erased by the time he had assumed command of the battle cruiser squadron on 10 May 1941. But no one can ever know how Holland himself had responded to Somerville's comments. If he had taken them even as mild criticism, he no doubt recalled, as the *Hood* sortied from Scapa Flow, the last time he had commanded ships that were not at peak fighting efficiency. If he had to fight the *Bismarck* with a thinly armored battle cruiser and an untried *Prince of Wales,* would he keep his consort close, fight his two ships as a division, and concentrate their fire, as he had not done at Cape Spartivento?

As the *Hood* and her consorts steamed eastward, Tovey asked the Admiralty for an additional first-light reconnaissance of the Norwegian coast; he badly needed to know if the *Bismarck* was still there. Tovey and his staff then waited anxiously through the early evening for news of a planned RAF attack on the Grimstadfjord. As they waited, a motley group of twin-engine RAF bombers struggled through turbulent air and heavy cloud over the North Sea in their vain effort to find and bomb the *Bismarck* and her consorts.

The night dragged into the cold gray dawn of 22 May; Tovey's anxiety grew by the moment. Two of his most powerful ships were already on the high seas steaming for Iceland. The rest of the Home Fleet was prepared to weigh anchor at two hours' notice. He was ready, his ships and his men were ready, but all he really knew was that the *Bismarck* had been in a Norwegian fjord some twenty hours earlier. If she had sailed soon after Suckling's Spitfire had flown over, she could have covered more than 500 miles by now. At this very moment, Lütjens might be rounding the Faeroes to steam past Iceland into the Atlantic. Worse, the British cruisers out there might be minutes away from destruction by the *Bismarck*'s plunging shell-fire. If he did not find out within the next eighteen hours, at the latest, whether the *Bismarck* had sailed, it would be too late to do anything except hope for blind luck and a chance encounter with one of his scouts. Or he might hear of a scattered convoy, dozens of ships sunk, hundreds of sailors dead, and tons of cargo lost anywhere from Newfoundland to the South Atlantic. It had happened before.

There was another factor feeding Tovey's growing desperation for news. In the days before nuclear-powered ships, the fuel capacity and fuel consumption of a warship—how much fuel it could carry and how quickly that fuel was used up—was a crucial factor in its deployment. Fuel capacity varied from ship to ship, but in every case fuel consumption increased dramatically during high-speed chases, or in sea fights, when high-speed maneuvering was needed to avoid enemy bombs, shells, or torpedoes. Tovey's two newest battleships, the *King George V* and the *Prince of Wales*, were "short-legged," in naval parlance, because of their relatively small bunker capacity of 4,000 tons of fuel. At a leisurely pace of 18 knots, this might allow them to steam as far as 4,750 nautical miles before refueling. But at high speeds, their range was about half that. It was not nearly enough to chase an elusive quarry for many days at high speed. The German fleet was designed for long-range commerce raiding. The *Bismarck* and the *Tirpitz* could steam 8,525 nautical miles at 19 knots; for smaller-fuel-capacity ships such as the *Prinz Eugen*, the Kriegsmarine prepositioned tankers at possible refueling points.

The United States Navy, with its ships built for long voyages across the Pacific and with few naval bases outside the continental United States and Hawaii, had long ago developed a substantial fleet train of fast transports and fleet tankers to accompany their task forces. They perfected the science of refueling at sea from these tankers and even from other warships. This lessened their dependency on bases. The Royal Navy, on the other hand, had virtually no fleet train and no fleet tankers; it was highly base-dependent. One of the main objectives of British diplomacy in the nineteenth century was the securing of naval bases to resupply and repair Royal Navy ships virtually around the globe. As Britain began to build a global empire after 1885 or so, some of these small bases and coaling stations were expanded into major facilities with dry docks and all the major repair and reprovisioning facilities the Royal Navy could ever need. At the start of World War II, then, Britain's navy was still base-minded.[16] One solution might have been to do what the Kriegsmarine had done and preposition tankers at sea. But the danger of U-boats attacking those tankers, and the uncertainty of where a chase might lead, made that resolution impractical. Another answer was to build the fleet train and quickly acquire the means to refuel from other warships at sea. That was eventually done, but on 22 May 1941 that ability was still years in the future. Tovey's only real solution was to keep his tanks as full as possible, sortie the main Home Fleet only on solid news of the *Bismarck*, and close in on the enemy by the most direct route.

The fuel situation was not the only limitation on the Royal Navy's ability to hunt the *Bismarck*. Britannia may have ruled the waves in Napoleon's day, or even on the day in 1916 when the German High Sea Fleet retreated to base after the Battle of Jutland. But in the spring of 1941 the Royal Navy was not the overwhelming force it had once been. Twenty years of peacetime neglect had taken its toll on ships and men, and even though the Royal Navy was the equal of any modern navy in some important areas such as radar development, it lagged behind in engineering, gunnery, and naval aviation, while most of its capital ships were outmoded and incapable of slugging it out with a modern opponent.

In the years after World War I, Britain's political leaders should have remembered the words of King Charles II in the "Preamble to the Articles of War" he sent to the British Parliament in the early 1630s: "It is upon the navy under the Providence of God that the safety, honour, and welfare of this realm do chiefly depend." Charles II put the navy front and center in the government's consideration as the one instrument of war and foreign policy that could literally decide the fate of the nation. He made the navy "royal" and spent lavishly on rejuvenating and modernizing it as the guardian of the independence, the commerce, and the overall welfare of the British Isles. From his day forward, the Royal Navy was Britain's senior service. Until the November 1918 armistice, no British government could afford to let the Royal Navy languish. There would have been no British Empire without the Royal Navy. British greatness depended on many factors, but the Royal Navy underlay all of them.

At the apex of the Royal Navy was the Admiralty. The Admiralty was both an administrative and operational headquarters. Like the War Ministry or the Air Ministry, it oversaw production, recruitment, training, long-range planning, provisioning, staffing, and promotion of ships and men. It gathered and evaluated intelligence, distributed resources among its many fleets as well as ships from theater to theater during operations, and generally did what was necessary to support its seagoing commanders. The Admiralty was the link between the civilian ministers who directed broad policy and the naval commanders responsible for the strategic execution of those policies. But although fleet commanders such as Tovey, or Cunningham in the Mediterranean, were supposed to have daily control over all aspects of their fleets' operations, the Admiralty reserved the right to issue orders not only to fleet commanders, but also to task force commanders and even to individual ships' captains. This interference posed the constant danger of dual control of operations at sea, command from the Admiralty as well as from the fleet commander, with all the risks of confusion and contradiction inherent to that situation.

It was most unfortunate for the fortunes of the Royal Navy in the spring of 1941 that the man who held the top post, the first sea lord and chief of the naval staff, was Admiral of the Fleet Sir Alfred Dudley P. R. Pound. Appointed to this exalted position in the summer of 1939, Pound was sixty-four and not in the best of health when the *Bismarck* made its breakout. He suffered from slowly advancing brain cancer and very painful arthritis in one hip. He rarely enjoyed a decent night's sleep and often catnapped during the day, sometimes in important meetings of the naval staff. One colleague who saw him just after the start of the war noticed "with horror" that Pound "had become a worn-out old man. His hair was snow white and wispy, his face seamed and ashen, [and] there was a noticeable distortion of one eye."[17]

Pound had had a long and distinguished career, going to sea as a youth of fourteen and serving as a flag captain during the Battle of Jutland. Like most naval officers of his generation, he had spent the interwar years in a variety of positions ashore and at sea. In 1936 he had been placed in command of the all-important Mediterranean Fleet, but he had already started to show his age and was not expected to move beyond that post before retirement. He had neither the brilliance nor the grasp of larger issues that was imperative in a man who commanded the entire Royal Navy. One senior admiral wrote of him in 1936: "He is too pig-headed; too unwilling to recognize that there may be another side." In Tovey's view, Pound "was neither a great tactician or [*sic*] strategist, [but] unfortunately he firmly believed he was."[18] Death and illness removed all the likelier candidates for first sea lord by June 1939, however, and Pound virtually inherited the mantle. He was, in effect, a stopgap and, as such, the weak link atop the chain of command.[19]

Pound had two overriding drawbacks as first sea lord. He was a centralizer and a meddler. He was too willing to second-guess his subordinates at sea, too eager to run important shows from the Admiralty, too involved in daily operations for a man at his level of command. They knew better than he what lay over the horizon and should have been allowed to fight their fleets as they saw fit. Pound agreed somewhat with that concept, but at one point in 1940 he also told one of his admirals: "Naturally, I reserve the right to butt in if I consider it necessary."[20] Pound's other major shortcoming was that he bowed too easily to his first wartime chief, Winston Churchill, who became first lord of the Admiralty when Britain declared war on Germany on 3 September 1939 and prime minister on 10 May 1940.

While Pound had shortcomings, it was not his job to sketch out the Royal Navy's strategic approach to the war. His obligation was to give his political masters his best advice, and to take the strategic aims transmitted to him by the first lord of the Admiralty and put them into effect.[21] Pound might have had considerable leeway with a more passive man as his boss, but he was blessed, or cursed, with Churchill. This already famous and much revered man was determined to take the offensive against the Germans before the Royal Navy was truly ready, and he had little patience for those who appeared to show less aggressive spirit than he believed warranted by the times.

Winston Spencer Churchill had first been named first lord of the Admiralty in 1911, when he was but thirty-seven. Energetic, brash, brilliant, Churchill had run afoul of the lords who ran the navy after the outbreak of war and clashed occasionally with first lord of the Admiralty Sir John A. "Jackie" Fisher, father of the modern dreadnought battleship. Churchill was one of the few British war leaders of the day who thought about strategic alternatives to the stalemate on the Western Front; the Gallipoli landings of 1915, aimed to knock Turkey out of the war and open a third front against the Central Powers, were one result. But that campaign came to a disastrous conclusion, largely because of the Royal Navy's lukewarm support, and Churchill had been forced to resign his post. When he returned to the Admiralty on 3 September 1939, he was determined that he would run the navy, subject only to the higher authority of Prime Minister Chamberlain and the War Cabinet, and not the other way around. Churchill's aim as first sea lord was not only to direct the Royal Navy in the performance of its defensive duties—keeping the empire's commerce flowing—but also to take the war to Germany. Given that the war was primarily a land war and that the Battle of the Atlantic, as it was being waged in the first year of the war, was a desultory affair fought in fits and starts in response to German initiatives, Churchill searched for ways to recover the initiative. Taking the offensive would energize the navy, he believed, and imbue it from top to bottom with aggressive spirit.

Churchill was a man of restless intelligence with a sweeping understanding of the ebb and flow of history. He was capable of great bursts of energy. He was unsparing in his criticism of those who did not meet his sometimes unreasonable expectations. To some in the Admiralty, he seemed convinced that the Royal Navy was too soft, too flabby, too reticent to fight a war. Rear Admiral Sir John Godfrey, director of naval intelligence, would write after the war:

> I have sometimes wondered if Mr. Churchill's long years in opposition to all governments left him with a feeling that, during his early days at the Admiralty, we all shared the delinquencies of those politicians that he had so consistently bastinadoed [*sic*] in public. Certainly his written words gave the impression that he thought we all needed a good shake up.[22]

Churchill threw himself into his job with all the strength he could muster. His last meeting of the day at the Admiralty was usually held around midnight, and he often slept there overnight. He quickly developed the practice of firing out memos late every night, each beginning with the phrase "Pray tell me," "Pray inform me," or words to that effect, wherein he asked detailed questions about operations, often demanding answers by the end of the day. The staff began to call these notes "Churchill's prayers." When the staff arrived first thing in the morning, Churchill's "prayers" lay on their desks. The wording of these memos was always "insistent," Godfrey recalled. They were "frequently harsh . . . they put one on the defensive and added greatly to the strain of those early months."[23] Though many of the people working at the Admiralty no doubt felt greatly invigorated by Churchill's presence, many others were irritated beyond reason by his aggressive and gruff manner. Churchill also found it almost impossible to resist meddling directly in operations. During the Battle of the River Plate in December 1939, Pound barely restrained him from sending Commodore Henry Harwood instructions as to how to conduct the fight.

Churchill then hatched a number of schemes for action in the Baltic Sea (Operation Catherine) that would most certainly have foundered for lack of air cover, while his overall direction of, and periodic direct intervention in, the Norwegian campaign of March 1940 was a disaster.[24]

If Churchill was overbearing as first lord of the Admiralty, he was far more so as prime minister. When King George VI appointed him to that post, Churchill named himself minister of defense as well. In the words of one historian, he "became virtually a military dictator."[25] He ran the War Cabinet as prime minister. As minister of defense, he ran the Chiefs of Staff Committee, which consisted of the chief of the air staff, first sea lord, chief of the imperial general staff (army), and chief of staff of combined operations. The chiefs of staff Committee ran Britain's war. In his dual position, Churchill almost always imposed his will on these men. That was well enough, but he also continued to micromanage the war, especially the war at sea.

When Churchill relinquished his post at the Admiralty, his successor as first lord was a nominee of the Labour party, A. V. Alexander, surely one of the least-known leaders of the British war effort. Alexander served the entire five years from May 1940 to the end of the war in Churchill's shadow, rarely heard from and usually after the fact. In his missives to U.S. president Franklin D. Roosevelt, Churchill took the nickname "former naval person," as if to signal his proprietary interest in that service. It was a brief walk from 10 Downing Street across Horse Guards Parade to the Admiralty and not much farther to the underground Cabinet War Rooms, and Churchill strolled to the Admiralty often to check the progress of the war at sea. Pound stood up to Churchill during the Battle of the River Plate in December 1939 but hardly ever afterward. In one of his first actions as prime minister, Churchill ordered the destruction of the French fleet at Mers-el-Kebir on 3 July 1940 because he feared it might fall under German control. Pound and virtually every Royal Navy officer serving in the Mediterranean had strongly opposed Churchill at that time, but the man at the top had his way.

One of the senior Royal Navy commanders who thought Mers-el-Kebir would be a grave error was Sir James Somerville. At fifty-nine, Somerville stood out among senior Royal Navy commanders for his energy, his outspokenness, his salty language, and his great good humor. He was a big man, energetic, a natural leader. He had an instinctive grasp of technical matters and was a first-class tactician. Somerville's promising career in the navy was almost cut short in the Far East when he was invalided out with pulmonary tuberculosis in 1938. But as soon as the war broke out, he was back at the Admiralty as a civilian advisor on radar and high-frequency direction finding. In May 1940 he volunteered to help with the Dunkirk evacuation; he returned from Calais in the last British ship to clear that port. He was recalled to active service the following month and given command of Force H, that part of the Mediterranean Fleet based at Gibraltar. It was then that he was ordered to destroy the French fleet at Mers-el-Kebir. He was convinced there was no need for the slaughter and that Anglo-French relations would long suffer from it. He was right. Churchill never forgot his opposition.

Churchill almost put an end to Somerville's career after the action at Cape Spartivento. When Somerville returned to Gibraltar after the clash, he was shocked to learn that the Admiralty had ordered a board of inquiry into his decision not to chase the Italian task group. Given Churchill's virtually complete control over the naval high command, it is inconceivable that the board could have sat without Churchill's permission and probable that it sat at his direction. Everyone at Gibraltar knew it was the proverbial shot across the bow of one of the Royal Navy's most exalted commanders from a prime minister who wanted action. It was widely resented throughout the fleet.[26] According to Somerville's biographer, "the wardrooms of the fleet were seething with indignation at the insult." Admiral Cunningham wrote Somerville: "I don't believe [Dudley Pound] is at the bottom of it but he allows himself to be talked into these things, by W[inston] C[hurchill] and others."[27]

The Board of Inquiry completely exonerated Somerville, though he was insulted by the very insinuation that he had acted improperly.[28] No doubt Churchill intended the inquiry as a symbolic repetition of the hanging of Admiral John Byng on the quarterdeck of his own flagship in 1756 for insufficient aggressiveness in the face of the enemy—*pour encourager les autres,* in the caustic words of Voltaire. After the board of inquiry, every commander and every captain in the Royal Navy, no matter how exalted or accomplished, knew that his command decisions at sea would be second-guessed by the prime minister himself. From then on, Churchill's brooding presence, ever distant but easily discernible between the lines of Admiralty messages, was the éminence grise in every admiral's cabin. That presence was ignored at the cost of distinguished careers, as Admiral Sir Charles Forbes had found when forced to retire in October 1940.

The Royal Navy's troubles did not stem solely, or even primarily, from a weak and less-than-capable man as first sea lord who answered to a micromanaging prime minister. They were, for the most part, the result of a series of interwar naval treaties that badly handicapped the Royal Navy in its efforts to meet the challenges of advancing naval technology. The first of the treaties was the Washington Naval Treaty of 1922; the last was the Anglo-German Naval Agreement of 1935. Those treaties grew out of both Britain's postwar economic weakness and the widespread popularity of pacifist views among the British people; most could not face the prospect of yet another world war and did not want to spend on the military. The naval treaties limited the number and size of ships of the navies of the principal sea powers. That in itself was no bad thing overall. But because the Royal Navy was the world's largest and, arguably, most technologically advanced by 1921, it gave up major comparative advantages throughout the interwar period and allowed the navies of other nations to catch up to or surpass it. The navy that effectively won the Battle of Jutland in 1916 was the best in the world; the navy that sought the *Bismarck* was not.

The interwar naval treaties grew out of American ambition and British bankruptcy. Though neutral until 1917, the United States had embarked on an unparalleled fleet construction program in

1916; at the end of the war, the Americans decided to keep building. Britain could not afford to. Though Britain and the United States were allies, British leaders believed prestige and British diplomatic leverage would erode if the U.S. Navy outstripped the Royal Navy. Britain, therefore, agreed to participate in the 1921 Washington Naval Conference and sign the treaty that emerged from it. The treaty put the U.S. Navy on par with the Royal Navy and set limits on the number of capital ships in the British, American, Japanese, French, and Italian fleets in the ratio of 5:5:3:1.75: 1.75, respectively. It also placed an upper limit of some 35,000 tons on any capital ship and banned new construction for ten years. Britain was allowed to build the *Nelson* and the *Rodney* in truncated form to abide by treaty limitations. The subsequent treaties followed the pattern—except for the 1935 agreement between Britain and Germany in which Germany was allowed to build a navy that was 35 percent the size of the combined Royal and Dominion Navies.

The treaties had a stultifying effect on the Royal Navy's shipbuilding program. Naval shipyards were closed; naval architects found other work; skilled technicians in electronics and communication, fire control, hull and turret design, and other essential naval skills disappeared from the labor pool. Naval strategy was neglected while tactics were studied primarily to discern how the Royal Navy might better fight a new, future Battle of Jutland. Other, smaller navies built newer and more powerful ships, but the Royal Navy had to scrap ships and could only hope to modernize existing ones. The treaties seemed fair at first blush, but the Royal Navy had a global mission to protect its home waters, its Atlantic supply routes, the shipping lanes from Gibraltar to Suez to India, and the British colonies and Dominions in the Far East and the South Pacific. Ships badly in need of modernization, such as the *Hood*, could not be removed from service for long periods. So a treaty that gave Germany "only" 35 percent of British naval tonnage was actually of significant advantage to Germany, which had nothing like the Royal Navy's obligations and duties.

The Royal Navy went to war in September 1939 with a very old fleet. By 21 May 1941 that had not significantly changed. The *King George V* was brand-new, and the *Prince of Wales* had just completed her manufacturers' trials. Both ships displaced 44,800 tons with a full war load and mounted ten 14-inch guns. The ships' companies totaled 1,650 officers and men. Their top speed was just under 30 knots. They were both equipped with the latest Type 284 search and gunnery radar. Their belt, or side armor was as much as 16 inches thick; main deck armor was 6 inches. Smaller and slower than the *Bismarck*, they were nevertheless perfectly adequate for modern war. The rest of the British battleship fleet was vintage World War I: five battleships of the *Queen Elizabeth* class (ordered in 1912), and five of the subsequent *Royal Sovereign* class. Although most of the old battleships had been updated to some extent, they were still much slower, smaller, more vulnerable, and packed considerably less punch, than the *Bismarck* or other modern rivals such as the Italian *Vittorio Veneto*–class or the French *Richelieu*–class battleships.

The balance of the Royal Navy's battleship fleet was made up of the two *Nelson*-class battleships *Rodney* and *Nelson*, completed in 1927. Each had a company of 1,640 men, displaced 38,000 tons, and mounted nine 16-inch guns in a unique three-forward-turret arrangement. Heavily protected, these two battleships boasted side armor of up to 14 inches and main deck armor of just over 6 inches. But with their three main turrets forward of the superstructure, gun laying was complex and difficult. These ships were slow, with top speeds of just 24 knots. Aside from fourteen true battleships, the Royal Navy also included three World War I–era battle cruisers: the *Repulse*, the *Renown*, and the *Hood*. None of those should have been forced to face the heavy guns of the *Bismarck*, but all were indispensable to the ship-strapped fleet.

All warship designs result from engineering and design compromises, but none more than the dreadnoughts, the all-big-gun, one-caliber ships—battleships or battle cruisers—that first appeared in Britain and the United States shortly after the turn of the twentieth century. In the five decades from about 1895 to 1945, these ships epitomized naval power. In each case basic ship design was initially determined by how much money a navy had to spend and, flowing from that factor, the ship's maximum size, measured as displacement. Maximum displacement determined the other major design factors—how much weight would be devoted to armor, guns, fuel load, engines, and crew accommodations. If the navy wanted a ship that was heavily armored, for example, there would be less weight available to accommodate guns, engines, and so on. Battle cruisers were as large as battleships and carried heavy guns of the same caliber, but were designed to be much faster. That meant their armor was much thinner than that of battleships and they were more vulnerable. Everyone knew that, but naval strategists believed that a battle cruiser's very speed was its main protection. Battle cruisers such as the *Hood* were never intended to go toe-to-toe with a battleship; if such ships were ever in a position where they might face that eventuality, their speed was supposed to allow them to race out of danger.

The formula that determined the speed, power, range, and overall design of heavy ships was simple: overall displacement = weight of ordnance + weight of accommodation + weight of armor + weight of fuel. It could be made to yield different and better results only by improvements in technology. Engines could be made smaller but more powerful by improvements in turbine design, for example, or armor might be improved with a lighter but stronger steel alloy. Building new fleets in the interwar years, the Germans, the Italians, the Americans, and even the French took advantage of improvements in warship design and technology to build ships that stayed within treaty limits but were much improved over World War I designs. The British, for the most part, did not.

That was especially true of Royal Navy guns and gunnery. The large naval rifles of 14- to 16-inch bore that were the main hitting power of ships such as the *Bismarck* or the *King George V* were heavy and complex. A barrel alone, without breech mechanism, might weigh 130 tons. Shells ranged in weight from an average of about 1,500 pounds for a single 14-inch shell to over a ton for a 16-inch shell. Since the whole point of a gun action at sea was to plunge as many tons of armor-piercing steel as possible into the enemy's vitals as fast as possible, a ship's guns had to be loaded, trained, and fired in coordination precisely and efficiently. That was not easily done because the guns were mounted in three or four turrets with two to four guns per turret. Modern high-speed naval warfare necessitated the very best of long-range optical sights (until the advent of gunlaying radar) mainly in one central location, which was usually at the top of the superstructure. The information from the sights was then hand-fed into a complex central mechanical computing device, which came up with the firing solution and relayed the gun-laying information to the individual turrets. That was difficult in practice, and doubly difficult in a sea battle where both protagonists were steaming and maneuvering hard at ranges up to 20 miles.

A shell exploded out of a gun muzzle only after a succession of tasks had been performed quickly and efficiently. The mechanical computers had to provide the gunners with moment-by-moment updates on how much to elevate their guns, where to train the turrets, and how much propellant, or charge, to load into the breeches. The propellant was contained in silk bags (from one to four) shoved into the breech separately from the shell. The more charge, the greater the range of the shell. The extremely explosive propellant bags had to be stored in armored magazines deep in the ship. A whole assembly line of electrically operated grapples, hoists, pulleys, and plungers had to operate flawlessly to bring the heavy shells from their storage areas and the propellant bags from the magazines to the breech of the gun quickly and with no interruption. There were over sixty-five different mechanisms of this type to load and train the 14-inch guns of the *King George V*; each of these mechanisms consisted of dozens, even hundreds, of interworking parts. All of this machinery, as well as the guns, were encased in heavy armored turrets, which had to turn smoothly and quickly to follow the movement of the target. Most of the turret, like most of an iceberg, could not be seen; it lay far below the main deck. Dozens of crewmen worked inside each of these turrets. Anything could go wrong in the firing sequence, and in the Royal Navy in the first years of World War II, it often did.

Whether it was the effect of the naval limitation treaties or the post–World War I atmosphere of "never again a war," the Royal Navy seemed to go to sleep after 1920. Fighting efficiency took second place to spotless tropical whites, shining brass, polished teak decks, and fresh paint. The brand-new 16-inch guns mounted on the *Nelson* and the *Rodney*, for example, began to malfunction almost immediately after they were installed in 1926. Problems with shell-handling machinery, the mechanisms that rotated the turrets, the recoil mechanisms of the guns, and the turret power systems plagued both ships for the next decade. When war broke out in 1939, these guns were as good as they were going to get, but they were still not completely reliable. Similarly, it took more than five years of postlaunch fixing and tinkering to get the 8-inch guns on the new county-class cruisers into decent working order, and even then gun failure on these ships was endemic. The attitude in the Royal Navy was that a gun turret and everything in it was such a complex piece of equipment, subject to tremendous forces whenever the guns were trained and fired, that "teething troubles" were to be expected even after launch. But when a quarter inch of burr left on a casting might jam a shell hoist or cause a recoil slide to malfunction in the middle of a gun action, such laxness was inexcusable. German warships put to sea with main guns in full working order; Royal Navy warships went to sea with guns that might not elevate or fire, or turrets that might not train.[29]

The British also lagged in propulsion systems. The new engines in German and American heavy ships were smaller, lighter, and more powerful than the engines in most British capital ships at the beginning of World War II. The key to better performance was greater useable steam pressure and improved means of delivering propulsion power from the engines themselves to the turbines and thence through the transmissions to the propeller shafts. The net result was that the Germans (and the Italians, for the most part) had a much faster fleet than the British. In virtually any given encounter, a Royal Navy captain could invariably count on his ship being slower than his German antagonists and had to shape course and determine tactics accordingly.[30]

The relatively slow speed and the greater unreliability of the guns on British warships might not have mattered so much if the Royal Navy had kept the decided lead it had had in naval aviation at the end of World War I. But here too it lost its advantage in the interwar years. When the Royal Air Force was created from the Royal Flying Corps and the Royal Naval Air Service in 1918, British naval aviation came under the dual control of the Royal Navy and the Royal Air Force until May 1939. The split in responsibility seemed simple at first; the navy built and operated the carriers, the air force supplied the aircraft and the trained crews. In fact, an aircraft carrier and the aircraft that are its main fighting component are an integral unit. Since the Royal Air Force was dominated by airpower advocates who believed an air force existed primarily to bomb the enemy's heartland, carrier aviation took a backseat to the RAF's other priorities. British carrier aircraft design languished far behind that of the Americans and Japanese. Britain's main naval strike aircraft at the outbreak of war, and for several years after, was the Fairey Swordfish, a single-engine, two-seater biplane with an open cockpit and fixed landing gear. The Swordfish was very slow, with a top speed of only 138 miles per hour. To extend its inadequate range of 546 miles, a removable fuel tank replaced the observer/gunner in the rear seat. That made longer missions possible, but constant exposure over several hours to wind, cold, rain, and engine noise bore heavily on Swordfish pilots. The aircraft was a typical product of British interwar naval aviation: starved for funds and low on the RAF's priority list, the Fleet Air Arm ordered the Swordfish as a combined reconnaissance/torpedo bomber/dive-bomber aircraft. The United States and Japanese navies, by contrast, had dedicated aircraft for dive-bombing and torpedo bombing.

Although the Royal Navy had pioneered carriers, and some of the most basic components of carrier aviation such as catapults and arrester gear, the British carriers in use, or just about to come off the ways in 1941, were slower and smaller than their U.S. or Japanese counterparts. In part that was because the British insisted on building carriers with armored flight decks, thus sacrificing speed and carrying capacity. But it was also due to British naval aviation doctrine. It is not true that the Royal Navy did not realize the potential of the aircraft carrier, but it is true that the navy did not foresee the aircraft carrier taking over from the fleet's heavy gunships as the prime means of its striking power. British carrier aircraft were designed for two main purposes—to find and follow the enemy fleet and, if possible, to slow it up by making torpedo attacks on it so that the main battle fleet might catch it and blow it out of the water with gunfire. In essence, the carrier and its aircraft were going to be a better way of winning the next Battle of Jutland. That was why Tovey did not have a single fast carrier equipped with modern, long-range naval strike aircraft to sortie against the *Bismarck* and the *Prinz Eugen*.[31]

In intelligence gathering, too, the Royal Navy suffered from the lethargy of the interwar years. When World War I ended, there seemed to be no more need to maintain an efficient and modern intelligence-gathering operation than there had been to improve naval airpower or to design and build turbines that were more up-to-date. As Admiral J. H. Godfrey, director of naval intelligence from the outbreak of war until 1943, later wrote: "The Navy and Army of Germany had disappeared, never was it supposed to rise again, and the idea of watching those of Allied or friendly powers did not seem worth while."[32] The Naval Intelligence Division (NID) ceased to function effectively, as resources were drastically reduced and staff cut back. In 1922 the NID's code-breaking section was closed and all responsibility for deciphering foreign nations' codes was transferred to the Foreign Office. When the still distant rumble of war was heard again in the early 1930s, the Royal Navy had virtually no operational intelligence capability. That had not improved much by the outbreak of war. The German naval intelligence service (B-Dienst), by contrast, readily deciphered Royal Navy radio traffic and easily tracked most Royal Navy ship movements when radios were used. Although the British scientists at Bletchley Park worked hard to build the equipment and find the formulae to break the German Enigma codes, the Kriegsmarine code largely eluded them until the summer of 1941. When the *Bismarck* sortied, it still took the cryptanalysts at Bletchley Park up to seven days to break the code.

The continuing drought of reliable intelligence on the *Bismarck*'s planned operation was Admiral Tovey's biggest concern as he awoke from a fitful sleep on the morning of 22 May. The meteorological report showed the weather across the Norwegian Sea deteriorating rapidly, with thick cloud down to 200 feet above the sea surface. That was good for the *Bismarck*, bad for Coastal Command. Scapa was already socked in. Winds of as much as 30 miles per hour, blowing counterclockwise around the low in the Denmark Strait, were pushing the ocean surface between the United Kingdom and Iceland into 6-foot whitecaps. The Beaufort Wind Scale called this a "strong breeze." Neither wind nor wave posed a danger to the warships already out there, but when those ships were headed straight into this stuff, the sea spray washing over turret range finders would make gunnery more difficult.

At midmorning Tovey was handed the latest information from Coastal Command. Their aircraft had taken off at first light and flown out to the Norwegian coast, but the crews saw nothing below a rolling plain of thick cloud. Pilot Officer Suckling's report was now almost twenty hours old. If the *Bismarck* had sortied in midafternoon the previous day, she could be anywhere along an expanding semicircle of ocean some 500 nautical miles from Grimstadfjord, and that circle was expanding by 25 to 30 nautical miles every hour. No one knew that better than Captain H. L. St. J. Francourt, the commander of Naval Air Station Hatston, a few miles to the north of Tovey on the main Orkney Island. He had sent his only operational squadron, No. 828, consisting of old Albacore torpedo planes, north to the Shetland islands in case they might be needed for a strike against the *Bismarck*; now he had only training planes and a twin-engine Martin Maryland, normally used for target towing, at his disposal. But he was determined to try to help Tovey by finding out exactly what lay under the cloud cover along the Norwegian coast. He managed to scrounge a volunteer crew to fly the Maryland and recruited Commander G. A. Rotherham, a longtime Fleet Air Arm observer, to do the spotting. After obtaining permission from Coastal Command, the Maryland lumbered down the main Hatston runway and into the thick cloud of the North Sea at about 4:40 P.M. With Rotherham stretched out on the floor at the front of the bomber, peering intently through the forward Perspex bubble, they ran in under the clouds as low as they dared, then pulled up into clear air. The pilot headed for a point on the Norwegian coast south of their intended search area. His idea was to somehow spot the coast, then turn north and search for the fjord. After two hours of blind flying, holes opened in the cloud and they saw the coastline sliding beneath them. A hard bank left, then down, through the cloud. There! The fjord. Empty! Then the sky exploded with black puffs of smoke—flak, tracer, heavy and light machine-gun fire, Bofors guns, a storm of shot and shell. But no *Bismarck*. Rotherham was quite sure of that. She was gone. He scribbled a note and handed it up to the pilot, who gave it to the radio operator. At about 8 P.M. the message reached Tovey as he and his staff were sitting down to dinner. The *Bismarck* had sortied.[33]

No one knew where she was at that moment, nor her actual destination or mission. But John Tovey had gone against Günther Lütjens before, and he had known since the previous day what he would do and where he would head when he left Scapa. Quickly the signals went out. The light cruiser *Arethusa* was to sail immediately to join the *Manchester* and the *Birmingham*, patrolling the Iceland-Faeroes gap. Vice Admiral Holland was to head for the northern entrance of the Denmark Strait to patrol north of 62 degrees latitude; Tovey would bring the Home Fleet to cover the ocean south of 62 degrees. Captain Wilfrid R. Patterson, commanding the *King George V*, was told to make ready for sea with all dispatch, as were the other fleet captains. The *Suffolk* was sent back to the Denmark Strait to rejoin the *Norfolk*. The *Repulse*, with her three destroyers, was ordered to rendezvous with Tovey's force off the Butt of Lewis in the late morning of the following day. Coastal Command was asked to increase air reconnaissance across all possible passages from the Norwegian Sea into the North Atlantic.[34]

The ships of the Home Fleet still in Scapa had been on short notice for about a day and a half. But now these dozen or so warships began to prepare for immediate departure. Boats raced across the harbor, bringing aboard the last men or last-minute messages from shore. There were dozens of tasks, large and small, to be carried out before they weighed anchor. Scuttles were closed. Watertight doors were sealed. Personal gear was stored. Ships were darkened completely. The last few tons of fuel oil were pumped into bunkers. Stokers and engine room artificers watched their instruments as they checked boiler steam pressures and turbine rotation. Final checks were made on the communications systems and on the damage-control system. Last loads of food were stowed. The special sea duty men manned their posts. The cable that connected the telephone in Tovey's office with the mainland and the Admiralty was kept in place until the last possible minute. There was to be complete radio silence. Once that cable was uncoupled, Tovey would be cut off from the Admiralty for hours at least, possibly days.

As loudspeakers barked orders and bosuns' pipes whistled, Tovey slipped on his thick beige duffle coat, put on his sea boots, donned his cap, and made his way to the bridge, where Captain Patterson and the rest of the bridge crew were already at their stations. At about 10:40 P.M. the sound of anchor chains being hoisted in ships all across the harbor resonated to the hills and back across the water. The destroyers moved first and headed silently for the boom. The boom ships slowly and silently pulled back the antisubmarine nets to let the fleet pass. When the *Prince of Wales* began to move toward the harbor mouth at last, the order was given: "Hands to station for leaving harbour." Dozens of men not occupied with the business of taking the warships to sea, raced to stand at attention in long rows on the main deck, their bibs blowing in the breeze, their hands behind their backs. Within minutes, the entire fleet was moving in line-astern through the entrance. The screening destroyers were out first; the *King George V* and the *Victorious* followed. It was 10:45 P.M. but not completely dark at this northern latitude. To any fisherman who might have been outside the harbor, the departure of the Home Fleet would have been an inspiring sight as, one by one, the ships slipped silently through the harbor mouth and headed for the open sea. Behind them, the boom ships closed the net. Ahead of them, a rising sea awaited in a cold, dark night. Tovey ordered the fleet to increase speed; course was set at 280 degrees. Every man knew the German behemoth had to be found as quickly as possible.

DEADLY ENCOUNTER

THE *Bismarck* AND THE *Prinz Eugen* carefully picked their way through the first ice floes with the aid of several merchant marine captains who had plied these waters in peacetime and who had been taken on board as prize skippers. The Germans knew that the Royal Navy had mined the Denmark Strait but, obviously, were unaware of the whereabouts of those minefields. Around 8 A.M. the wind shifted from south-southwest to north-northeast, thus blowing from astern at 30 miles per hour, a near gale.

Around noon on 23 May Admiral Günther Lütjens, suspecting British lookouts in the Denmark Strait, put his task force on battle alert. Just before 2 P.M., the *Bismarck* and the *Prinz Eugen*, on a course of 250 degrees, undertook a radical turn to avoid the solid ice off Greenland. Naval Group Command North reported around 3 P.M. that the current fog and rain as well as an approaching Atlantic low would prevent the Luftwaffe from flying ice reconnaissance missions over the strait in the next two or three days. But that was all. Lütjens lacked the essential knowledge about the enemy that was vital to his mission: the disposition of the Home Fleet and possible enemy sighting of his task force.

On full alert, the German ships steamed down a 3-nautical-mile-wide channel of clear green water. By 4 P.M. the fog had lifted somewhat. Captain Ernst Lindemann could spot fields of bluish white pack ice from Greenland drifting off the *Bismarck*'s starboard side; to port, a heavy haze at times obscured Iceland. It was bleak and desolate, yet also grimly beautiful, Lindemann mused, this jagged, white-streaked northwest coast of Iceland. At times, brief but heavy snow showers enshrouded the two raiders. At 6:30 P.M. Admiral Lütjens ordered the ships to switch on their FuMO radar-detection gear. The task force was making 27 knots. Quadrant AD 29 of the German sea chart.

"Alarm from fleet!" Sirens pierced the air on board the *Bismarck* and the *Prinz Eugen* at precisely 7:11 P.M. "Ships off to starboard. Course 240°."[1] Admiral Lütjens barked a sharp command: "Hard a-port." Nerves were on edge. Gun crews raced to their stations. Eyes strained to make out the gray shadow looming in the distant fog: an iceberg. Fog and haze again wrapped themselves around the German vessels. Both ships tacked a zigzag course through the heavy pack ice hard off the coast of Greenland. The men in the bowels of the great battleship were subjected to a constant cacophony of cracking and crunching sounds as the *Bismarck*'s bow sliced through the ice.

"Alarm!" It was now 7:22 P.M. "A shadow at 340°," a lookout roared above the wind. "Distance 14,000 yards."[2] Lütjens and Lindemann, on the *Bismarck*'s bridge, could barely make out through the haze a dark gray outline. On the *Prinz Eugen*, Captain Helmuth Brinkmann could only discern the hazy outlines of a raised stern. Was it an auxiliary cruiser on patrol in the Denmark Strait? The shadow disappeared into a dense fog bank, then briefly reappeared. Now lookouts on the German ships could make out "a massive superstructure and three stacks"—the silhouette of a heavy cruiser. Brinkmann's chief wireless officer, Lieutenant Hans-Henning von Schultz, and his eleven-man cryptographic team quickly picked up and deciphered the shadower's radio signal: "One battleship, one cruiser in sight at 20°. Range seven nautical miles, course 240°."[3] Then Brinkmann's B-Dienst team deciphered the intruder's code name as belonging to the Royal Navy heavy cruiser HMS *Suffolk*. Brinkmann at once apprised his crew of this turn of events: "To all stations. The shadow off to port was a British heavy cruiser, which is now shadowing us. He has recognized us and reported our position by wireless." Admiral Lütjens immediately signaled "JOTDORA," giving permission to fire. But Brinkmann could not make out his target. Moreover, the skipper of the *Prinz Eugen* declined to open fire on the *Suffolk* out of operational considerations. "I remind you that our task is not to destroy British cruisers," he informed his 1,400 sailors. "Our goal is and remains warfare against Atlantic convoys. Over and out."[4]

Refueled and reprovisioned, HMS *Suffolk* had slipped anchor in the Hvalfjord early that morning and shaped course to join Rear Admiral William F. Wake-Walker on the *Norfolk* in the harbor at Isafjördur, on the northwest coast of Iceland at about 10:00 A.M. Across the Denmark Strait, along the Greenland coast, the pack ice jutted some 80 miles eastward into the strait. On the eastern side of the strait, off Cap Nord, the Royal Navy had sown a minefield that stretched from the shore about 40 miles to the west. Wake-Walker, flåg officer commanding the First Cruiser Squadron, knew the minefield was not especially dense and no real obstacle to a determined attempt to sweep it. But he also knew that if the Germans were coming this way, they would be moving fast, with no time to spare, and no minesweepers accompanying them. That left from 25 to 40 miles of open water between the minefield and the Greenland ice pack. Anywhere but here, that would pose little problem to scouting cruisers. On 23 May, however, a powerful low-pressure system centered just to the west of the Faeroes had brought low-hanging clouds, heavy fog, and intermittent rain and snow showers to the eastern side of the strait. Over the Greenland icepack, and for about three miles into the strait, the sky was clear. Wake-Walker directed

Captain R. M. Ellis, commanding the *Suffolk*, to patrol from northeast to southwest off the icepack, to keep watch over the icepack edge. The *Suffolk*'s new radar could detect a ship about 13 miles distant; if that ship was the *Bismarck*, she could report the sighting, then duck into the bad weather on the Iceland side of the strait. The *Norfolk*'s much inferior radar, with a considerably shorter range, would not allow her to track the *Bismarck* from inside the fog and rain squalls. If either cruiser found itself within effective gun range of the *Bismarck* for more than a minute or so, disaster would be swift.

With the *Suffolk* on the western side of the strait and the *Norfolk* some fifteen miles to the south, off the *Suffolk*'s port beam, Rear Admiral Wake-Walker stood beside Captain A. J. L. Phillips, commanding the *Norfolk*, in the cruiser's cruelly open bridge and waited. Hour after hour the cruiser rose and fell on a moderate sea while it pushed southwestward through the fog and rain. Small ice pans, large floating chunks of ice, and thin patches of sea ice were shoved aside by the bow and brushed along the *Norfolk*'s sides. The *Norfolk* was equipped with Type 286M fixed-aerial radar, a combined aircraft and surface warning radar that swept only ahead of the ship and could only detect large objects a few miles away. The *Suffolk*, out in the clear weather on the other side of the strait, had two much better radars, an air-warning Type 279 and a 50-centimeter Type 284 with a rotating antenna mounted on the main armament director abaft the bridge. When switched on, the main radar covered about 270 degrees of arc to the front and sides of the ship but left a blind spot of about 90 degrees of arc to the stern. For fear of damage to the equipment from continuous use, Ellis ordered the radar not to be used all the time.[5]

At 7:22 P.M. Able Seaman Newell, his binoculars watching the *Suffolk*'s starboard quarter, shouted: "Ship, bearing green one four oh!" A moment later: "Two ships bearing green one four oh!" There they were, emerging out of the mist like charging behemoths, about seven miles behind the *Suffolk* but quickly overtaking her. The *Suffolk* was dangerously close to the massive 15-inch guns on the *Bismarck*'s two forward turrets, Anton and Bruno. A quick shiver of fear ran through Ellis. He'd hoped, even expected, to spot her first. He had no plans to become her first victim. "Full ahead both, hard a-port." The chief engineer fed full power to her screws as the *Suffolk* heeled to the right, making for the edge of the fog bank. Barely a moment later, as the *Suffolk* speeded to safety, Ellis shouted: "Make to Admiralty, repeat to C in C Home Fleet: Emergency. One battleship and one cruiser sited [*sic*] . . . send our position." Then, before the *Bismarck* had a chance to fire, the mist swirled around the *Suffolk*.

Ellis waited in the fog for the *Bismarck* to pass to his north. With the radar now powered up, he intended to mark time until the *Bismarck* was some 13 miles ahead, then swing in behind her. At that distance his radar could follow the *Bismarck* through rain and mist, but he would still have time to run, or hide, if the *Bismarck* swung about to attack. The *Suffolk* emerged from the fog bank to find that the *Bismarck* had indeed passed by on a course of 240 degrees but was still close enough to blast the *Suffolk* out of the water. Ellis sent off a second sighting report, then returned to the safety of the mist. Whether it was the strange atmospherics, a failure of radio equipment, or something else, his signals never reached Admiral Sir John Tovey on board HMS *King George V*, then about 600 miles to the southeast. But they were picked up by the *Bismarck* and by Rear Admiral Wake-Walker, and eventually by the Admiralty, which relayed them to the fleet. On board the *Norfolk*, Wake-Walker and Phillips made a rough guess as to the *Bismarck*'s position and steamed hard to take up the trail alongside the *Suffolk*. That was a mistake. Steaming at high speed through the fog and clouds, with inadequate radar, they had no way of knowing how far they were from the *Bismarck*'s guns, or precisely when they would emerge from cover to face them.

They came out at about 8:30 P.M. Captain Lindemann saw them himself almost immediately. He at once ordered, "Full speed ahead!" Then Lindemann informed his crew over the ship's loudspeakers: "Enemy in sight to port, our ship accepts battle."[6] Admiral Lütjens barked out: "Fire!" Five times the *Bismarck*'s great guns belched out fire and smoke. Three of the five salvoes from the *Bismarck*'s aft turrets, Cäsar and Dora, straddled the *Norfolk*, sending up 200-feet-high columns of water. One shell ricocheted across the water and over her bridge. Some large splinters landed on board the *Norfolk*, but she managed to make good her escape by laying down smoke and retreating into the fog banks off Iceland. Then, silence.

Admiral Lütjens briefly informed shore commands in Paris and Wilhelmshaven of the chance encounter: "My position is quadrant AD 29. One heavy cruiser." There was no cause for alarm. While Naval Group Command West at last conceded that the element of surprise had been lost, it nevertheless reassured Lütjens that the sudden sighting "posed no great danger for the task force." After all, the enemy's heavy units were still in port.[7] German naval planners at Paris remained troubled only about "the reported USA coast guard cruiser" south of Iceland, and ordered the supply ships for Rhine Exercise to reposition themselves 180 miles to the south and to stay 60 miles apart.[8]

For many of the *Bismarck*'s crew, the action with the unidentified "intruder" came as a nasty shock. Few had expected to man their battle stations before breaking out into the Atlantic—and then against cruisers or destroyers guarding convoys. The general feeling on the battleship was that they had been lured into a trap. As one sailor wrote in his diary, "The British must have noticed what we wanted to do. They had laid a trap for us, into which we would have fallen had not our ship had such high speed; it would have fared ill with us."[9]

Steaming in the *Bismarck*'s wake, Captain Brinkmann reported that the *Prinz Eugen* had been fired on from an unidentified "heavy cruiser" well astern of her. At first, Brinkmann had feared that the battleship HMS *King George V* was bearing down on him. Admiral Lütjens reacted immediately: "Full speed ahead!" Upon learning that the deafening roar and jolts of the 15-inch guns had knocked out the *Bismarck*'s forward FuMO-23 radar-detection set, Lütjens ordered, "Number Change!" The heavy cruiser, with her FuMO-27 "Seetakt" intact, was to take up station ahead as scout. Also, the *Bismarck* with her heavier guns could better monitor the shadowers astern. Then, a near disaster. As the *Prinz Eugen* pulled out of the line, increased speed, and came abeam, the *Bismarck*'s electric push-button wheel jammed, and the great battleship heeled to starboard—straight toward the *Prinz Eugen*. But Brinkmann was on his toes. He immediately ordered, "40° Hard a-starboard," a dangerous evolution even at less than full speed. Heeling over hard, the *Prinz Eugen* veered away from the *Bismarck*.[10]

As the two German warships passed by one another, Lütjens hailed Captain Brinkmann and complimented him on his "wonderful ship." Brinkmann thereupon asked Captain Lindemann what he had made of the last messages from Naval Group Command West concerning the enemy's whereabouts (Scapa Flow). The *Bismarck*'s skipper was thunderstruck: he had received none. Nor had the admiral. A hasty review of the *Prinz Eugen*'s radio traffic with Paris brought the task force commander up to speed. "Command decisions taken to date," Lütjens laconically signaled Brinkmann, "are absolutely correct even after perusing the messages not received" by the *Bismarck*.[11]

Still, the sudden and unexpected contact with the two British cruisers had been a most disturbing development. Rhine Exercise depended on stealth, on both ships breaking out into the Atlantic undetected. Naval Groups North and West repeatedly had assured the task force that it had not been detected—neither in Norwegian waters nor in the Denmark Strait. Moreover, they had said that the British heavy naval units remained anchored at Scapa Flow, and that the neutral Swedish government could be counted upon not to reveal the *Gotland*'s sighting of the *Bismarck* and the *Prinz Eugen* in the Kattegat. But somehow the British had been able to sight the task force between Iceland and Greenland.

After the gun action, the *Norfolk*'s damage-control parties assessed the result. A few rivets were popped, nothing more. At 8:32 P.M. Captain Phillips sent out another sighting report: "One battleship and one cruiser sighted 330°, 6 miles distant . . . course 240." The *Bismarck* was on the same course as when she had first been spotted more than an hour earlier. In fact, the ship stuck to that base course throughout the night, always coming back to 240 degrees.[12] Then the *Norfolk* took up station on the *Bismarck*'s port quarter, while the *Suffolk* trailed the German vessel from the starboard quarter. It was a fast chase, 30 knots or so into gathering snow showers, through the ice-dappled sea, into the high Arctic twilight. As they steamed to the southwest at high speed, the weather deteriorated. They plowed through a surrealistic seascape. The dark green waters of the strait were almost calm but strewn with ice chunks as far as the eye could see. The half-light, the ice, and the rain and snow squalls created a miragelike effect. The lookouts on the two cruisers were never quite sure what those faraway dots were doing, continuing on course or swinging about to destroy their pursuers.

On board HMS *Suffolk*, the strange Arctic half-light played tricks on the men manning her bridge. Around 10 P.M. the *Suffolk*'s lookouts reported that the *Bismarck* was making a right about turn and bearing down on them. But then, just as suddenly, the *Bismarck* disappeared from view. In fact, Lütjens, growing tired of the constant shadowing, had ordered Lindemann to execute a 180-degree battle turn.[13] Taking advantage of the cover provided by a momentary squall, the admiral had hoped to surprise the *Suffolk* by running straight at her out of the rain and snow showers. The *Suffolk*'s 8-inch guns would be no match for the *Bismarck*'s 15-inch barrels. But for the Germans it proved to be a game of blind man's buff: the *Suffolk*'s radar had picked up Lütjens' clever maneuver, and further rain qualls soon shielded both vessels from each other. Meanwhile, the *Norfolk* and the *Suffolk* signaled their position and the position, course, and speed of the enemy warships. The *Norfolk* lost contact five times through the night, the *Suffolk* at least once, but each time they regained contact, the *Bismarck* was back on the same heading.

Try as he might, Lütjens could not shake his pursuers, the *Suffolk* to starboard and the *Norfolk* to port. Time and again German spotters could make out one or both enemy ships through the fog. Always the tips of their masts were visible on the distant horizon. Lieutenant Hans-Henning von Schultz on the *Prinz Eugen* became convinced that the British must have some form of new shipboard radar. But naval headquarters had assured him at Kiel that the British were far behind the Germans in this area of research. For hours the two enemies charged down the long, jagged tube of the Denmark Strait, in and out of fog banks, rain squalls, and snow showers, through the eerie half-light of the Arctic night, and always at 30 knots, course south-southwest. The *Prinz Eugen* remained in the lead. The British cruisers remained at all times 10 to 14 miles astern of the *Bismarck*, the *Suffolk* to starboard, the *Norfolk* to port. Steel decks vibrated. Glass and pottery smashed against walls and floors. Rest was impossible. The ships' screws thrashed the mushy ice, throwing up great plumes of water. Brinkmann and Lindemann passed out soup and coffee to their crews.

Just before midnight Lütjens ordered smoke to be laid down, to no avail. The hostile cruisers kept dogging the task force. The *Bismarck*'s radio operators picked up the *Suffolk*'s steady stream of radio messages detailing the battleship's precise position, speed, and course. Admiral Lütjens was fast coming to the same conclusion as the *Prinz Eugen*'s chief wireless officer, namely, that the British cruisers were in possession of a new type of radar unknown in Germany. The enemy plotted his movements minute by minute. On the *Prinz Eugen*, Captain Brinkmann calculated that the British could range in on the German task force at a distance of 18 nautical miles.

"Attention! Aircraft off the port beam!" A PBY Catalina flying boat, most likely from Iceland, banked over the *Bismarck* in the distance, then disappeared as quickly as it had appeared. Shortly after midnight Lütjens once more ordered the battleship's 150,000-horsepower plant up to full power, and the *Bismarck*'s 50,500 tons sliced through the snow showers at 30 knots. Then a most welcome piece of intelligence came through from Naval Group Command North at Wilhelmshaven: "Until now, no discernible deployment of enemy naval forces."[14] The admiral as well as his two captains breathed a sigh of relief. Brinkmann noted in his war log, "The breakthrough out of the Denmark Strait has succeeded."[15] Finally, the

Naval High Command in Berlin suggested to Lütjens that he pay no heed to suspected British radar ("Dete") gear; in the ice-cold waters of the Denmark Strait, normal hydrophones could pick up the noise from the task force's propellers.

The very early hours of Saturday, 24 May broke clear and cold. Seas were moderate, and a light wind blew from the northwest. The German task force had successfully raced through the narrowest passage of the Denmark Strait. Ahead lay the open waters of the Atlantic. Just to be on the safe side, Admiral Lütjens kept his crews at battle stations. The *Prinz Eugen*'s second gunnery officer, Lieutenant Paul Schmalenbach, had taken up his duty watch on the bridge at 5 A.M. The task force, with the *Bismarck* 1,750 yards dead astern the heavy cruiser, was steaming on a southwesterly course, making 28 knots. At 5:07 A.M. Lieutenant Karlotto Flindt, one of the *Prinz Eugen*'s hydrophone operators, alerted the bridge: "Noise of two fast-moving turbine ships at 280° relative bearing!"[16] Range: 20 miles. Schmalenbach could discern nothing from the bridge. Just then, the *Bismarck*'s aft radar-detection set went out of commission.

The *Norfolk*'s first contact report reached the Admiralty's Operations Center at 9:03 P.M. Prime Minister Winston Churchill and First Lord of the Admiralty A. V. Alexander were immediately notified, as were First Sea Lord Sir Dudley Pound, Vice Admiral Sir Thomas Phillips, and other key strategists and analysts gathered near the large wall-mounted situation map. There were eleven convoys at sea, some perilously close to the Denmark Strait exit that the *Bismarck* and her consort were heading toward at 30 knots. Middle East troop convoy WS8B, which had sailed for Gibraltar on 22 May, had already been stripped of the battle cruiser *Repulse*, which was sent to join Admiral Tovey. The convoy would need immediate protection. There was no choice but to move Vice Admiral Sir James Somerville's Force H from Gibraltar into the Atlantic to meet the convoy off the coast of the Iberian Peninsula. Just before 11 P.M. on 23 May Somerville was handed a message from the Admiralty in his day cabin in the battle cruiser *Renown*, riding at anchor in Gibraltar harbor: "Raise steam for full speed." The message was quickly relayed to the rest of Somerville's force. Then, two hours later, Somerville received his final instructions before departure. He was to "proceed when ready" to join the troop convoy west of Brest after dawn on the 26th. He would be informed if the *Scharnhorst* or the *Gneisenau* sortied from Brest. And he could decide to keep his destroyers with him or send them back to Gibraltar, depending on their state.[17]

From ancient times Gibraltar had been the key to the Mediterranean. The famous Rock loomed above the small peninsula that jutted southward into the Mediterranean 10 miles from Spain's most southerly point. Crammed into that peninsula was the British Crown Colony with its narrow streets, climbing pathways, and the airstrip that stretched into the Bay of Algeciras. Since the start of the war, galleries and gun caves had been carved out of the rock itself, while antiaircraft guns and searchlights ringed the peninsula. Every night it was blacked out, but the sailors from Somerville's ships still managed to find their way through the dark to the bars on Main Street and the whorehouses in La Linea de la Concepción, just across the border in Spain. Liquor and women had been in great demand since the outbreak of the war. Warships, mostly destroyers and corvettes, came and went virtually by the hour. Merchant ships about to form into convoys to Crete or the eastern Mediterranean anchored in the roadstead. The bay shimmered deep blue in the clear, warm days of midspring while the lights of the Spanish city of Algeciras twinkled across the water from Gibraltar in the soft, subtropical night.

The late evening of 23 May was cool but clear, with a light breeze from the northwest as Vice Admiral Somerville's ships rode at anchor below the Rock. The message from the Admiralty sparked off hurried preparations for sea. Some of the ships' companies were already aboard, working up steam, stowing gear, and checking out the fire-control and damage-control systems, but many others had to be rousted out of dozens of shoreside establishments and brought out to the ships by barge and motor launch. Like

Admiral Tovey's Home Fleet, Force H was a motley collection of leftovers from World War I and more-modern warships. The *Renown* was a much-revamped battle cruiser originally launched to fight in the kaiser's war. Her main armament consisted of six 15-inch guns in three double turrets. She was capable of 32 knots, but her horizontal deck armor, like that of the *Hood*, would not survive the *Bismarck*'s plunging fire within the German vessel's effective range. The aircraft carrier *Ark Royal*, launched in 1937, displaced about 28,000 tons and could make 31 knots. But like other British carriers of the period, she carried far fewer aircraft than comparably-sized American or Japanese carriers (sixty aircraft in all), and her main striking power was the obsolescent Fairey Swordfish.

The remaining major ships of Force H were the light cruiser *Sheffield* and the heavy cruiser *Dorsetshire*. The *Sheffield* lay at anchor with the *Renown* and the *Ark Royal*, but the *Dorsetshire* was, at that moment, on convoy duty in the eastern Atlantic. Somerville and his staff oversaw the final provisioning and bunkering of this small force and the loading of aviation gas and torpedoes onto the *Ark Royal*. He had little doubt that German spies, crossing easily among the crowds of workers who daily entered Gibraltar from Spain, were watching and listening. As the clock struck 2:00 A.M., Somerville's destroyers began to move south, past Algeciras to port and the Rock of Gibraltar to starboard, to the mouth of the bay to take up station for the larger ships to follow. Then the *Renown* began to move, followed by the *Ark Royal* and the *Sheffield*. One by one they exited the bay, then shaped course southwest, past the town of Tarifa, at the tip of Spain, and into the Strait of Gibraltar. Next they formed line-ahead with the *Sheffield* in the lead and the *Renown* at the end of the line, and altered course northwest into the gray Atlantic. The sailors had no idea where they were headed, but they knew from the cold-weather gear that had been broken out that their days in the tropics were over for now.

Until the *Norfolk*'s first contact report at 8:32 P.M. on the 23rd, the main body of Admiral Tovey's Home Fleet had steamed faithfully westward in company with the *King George V*, unaware of what lay ahead. Tovey's force maintained strict radio silence, and Tovey knew that Vice Admiral Lancelot Holland and Rear Admiral Wake-Walker would do the same until the *Bismarck* was actually spotted. As his ships drove westward, through the center of the low-pressure system that hung over the Faeroes, their bows crashed into rising seas, with a gusty wind coming from the northwest. Low clouds added to the sullen seascape. The signalmen stood by their receivers all day but heard nothing from the Admiralty except the usual routine radio traffic. Radar swept the horizon and lookouts peered intently through their glasses, but nothing was seen or heard that would indicate a contact. At 7:03 P.M. the radio sprang to life, and the Admiral Commanding Western Approaches at Liverpool sent out the bad news to all the ships at sea searching for the *Bismarck*: "Denmark Straits reconnaissance was not—repeat not flown—cause weather." Tovey knew the *Bismarck* might already be emerging from the Denmark Strait, ready to take on her first convoy. Then, precisely ninety minutes later, his chief yeoman of signals handed him the *Norfolk*'s first contact report. The *Bismarck* was some 600 miles to the northwest of the Home Fleet. Tovey ordered a course change to 280 degrees to intercept, and the fleet increased speed to 27 knots.

Vice Admiral Lancelot Holland's task group was steaming past the southwest coast of Iceland when the *Hood*'s radio operators picked up a sighting report from the *Suffolk* a few minutes past 8:00 P.M. on the 23rd. Holland realized that *Bismarck* was a mere 300 miles away, just a bit east of due north from the *Hood*'s position, running southwest at high speed. He knew the two British cruisers were hot on the *Bismarck*'s trail and, like beaters pushing the prey toward the hunters in the bush, would push the *Bismarck* right to him if he positioned his force correctly. He could alter course to proceed due westward at reduced speed to set up an ambush right in the *Bismarck*'s path. The odds for success were in his favor. He knew where the *Bismarck* was, he knew her course and speed, and he knew her intentions. They knew nothing of his presence. He was far ahead of the German task force, and they were blindly closing in on his position at a rapid rate. If need be, he could patrol back and forth until they came in sight. This way he could keep his ships to the south of the Germans, and they would come upon him at about 6:00 A.M. the next morning, silhouetted against the northeastern dawn. They would be steaming straight toward him, but the *Hood* and the *Prince of Wales* would be broadside to them. Holland already held a two-to-one superiority over Lütjens in both numbers of ships (two capital ships to one, two heavy cruisers to one) and firepower (eighteen heavy guns against eight). But if he positioned his ships across their path and they came upon him from the north, he would "cross the T" on Lütjens; he would present his broadsides to the *Bismarck*'s bow. He would have eighteen heavy guns bearing on the Germans and they would have only the four forward heavy guns from turrets Anton and Bruno with which to defend themselves. In addition, the *Hood* had a combat-experienced crew, while the *Bismarck*'s Hitler Youth had never been engaged in fleet action. From Swedish naval officer Anders Forshell's report on the *Bismarck* to Swedish Naval Intelligence, Holland knew all he needed to know about the *Bismarck*'s size, power, and capabilities. Holland also knew that Tovey and the Home Fleet were approaching fast, and it was a fair assumption that they had picked up the same radio signals that he had, or would intercept one of the many signals that the *Suffolk* and the *Norfolk* now began to transmit. Who could doubt that the commander in chief would bring the *King George V* and the rest of his fleet to support the *Hood* and the *Prince of Wales* as quickly as possible?

Had Tovey been on the *Hood*'s bridge, he might well have realized that the greatest danger was that *Bismarck* would somehow work around the *Hood* and the *Prince of Wales*, lose the shadowing cruisers, and escape into the Atlantic. The most prudent course to avert that danger would have been to continue west at slow speed, rest his ships' companies overnight, set up a morning ambush, and wait for the first wisps of the *Bismarck*'s funnel gases to appear on the northern horizon. But Holland was not Tovey. He did not share Tovey's self-confidence. He was unwilling to face Churchill's wrath by not showing the aggressiveness that Churchill perpetually demanded of his commanders. He was also ambitious. Fate and circumstances had placed him in a moment in time when he might become the greatest British naval hero since Horatio Nelson. Holland's very own Battle of Jutland was within his grasp—except this time the Royal Navy would score a complete victory and he alone would bask in the glory of that victory. He most probably cast his mind back to Cape Spartivento, when he had been in command of ships that had not fought together before, and when Somerville, and by implication he, had in effect been accused by Churchill and Pound of dereliction of duty. These very personal factors likely weighed heavily on him as he decided how to proceed.

At 9:00 P.M. Holland made the decision from which all subsequent action would flow: he ordered the *Hood* and the *Prince of Wales* to change course, head 295 degrees northwest, and increase speed to 27 knots. Two of the six destroyers were sent to Iceland to refuel; the other four were told to make their best speed. It was not easy. A fresh breeze was blowing from the north at Force 5, about 20 miles an hour. These were not high winds, but at 27 knots the British ships threw up huge clouds of sea spray, drenching the men in open positions and making it difficult for lookouts to see to the north. The *Hood* was a wet ship in any case, weighed down by the additional guns installed at the start of the war, and her bow crashed into the waves with a heavy pounding. The gun crews in her forward turrets could see nothing through their stereoscopic sighting gear. Holland insisted that all radar sets be turned off so that the German ships would not pick up the impulses.

Once the turn had been executed and the speed increased, Holland's and Lütjens' ships began to close at about 60 knots. Holland was gambling the outcome of the Battle of the Atlantic on his ability to pinpoint exactly where the *Bismarck* would be at any point in the next several hours and thus make an interception that would put the Germans at a decided disadvantage. But by charging at the *Bismarck*, instead of waiting for her, Holland was making that job very, very difficult. He was like a fielder in baseball opting to charge a ball hit shallow into the outfield instead of taking the ball on the bounce. By deciding to charge the ball on the run, he was obliged to scoop it up and throw it quickly and accurately to the correct infielder in time to make the out. If he stumbled, miscalculated, threw wildly while off balance, or, worse, allowed the ball to get behind him, disaster would ensue. But if he made it, he would have pulled off the play of the week.

At 10 P.M. Holland instituted preparations for battle and called for Action Stations. Before leaving Scapa Flow, he had told Captain J. C. Leach, commanding the *Prince of Wales*, how he intended to fight an action should the *Bismarck* be found. He would concentrate the fire of his two capital ships, as he had not done at Cape Spartivento; he would use flank marking, a technique in which each ship spotted and reported the other's fall of shot; and he would use the *Prince of Wales*' Walrus seaplane to spot for the battleship's guns. Now he flashed the signal to Leach confirming what he had told him in safe harbor the night before, adding that he would call the *Norfolk* and the *Suffolk* into the fray to take on the *Prinz Eugen* while the *Hood* and the *Prince of Wales* went after the *Bismarck*.[18] That was good thinking—to divide the German firepower and concentrate the four capital ships under his command to overwhelm the Germans. It would also have been good thinking to keep his destroyers with him, to screen him, and to attack the *Bismarck* and her consort with torpedoes. He might also have taken a page from the latest Royal Navy tactical doctrine, which suggested that British warship captains use utmost flexibility when attacking an enemy with two or more ships, dividing the enemy's fire as Commodore Sir Henry Harwood had so successfully done in the Battle of the River Plate in December 1939.[19] By skillfully maneuvering the three outgunned cruisers under his command to fight the German pocket battleship *Graf Spee* from two flanks at once, Harwood had got the *Graf Spee* on the run and inflicted severe damage on her, though his own ships were badly shot up. The *Graf Spee* had sought refuge in Montevideo Harbor, where she had been trapped and eventually scuttled.

But Holland did almost none of the above. He failed to signal his intentions, even his presence, to the two shadowing cruisers. Rear Admiral Wake-Walker learned that Holland was close by only when the *Norfolk* intercepted a radio transmission from HMS *Icarus*, one of Holland's destroyers, at 4:45 A.M. the next morning. Holland loosed his destroyers to screen ahead of him at 11:18 P.M. on the 23rd, but when he turned to the southwest later in the night, he told them to continue on track to the north. He refused to allow either of his capital ships to use their search radar and he delayed permission for the Walrus to be launched from the *Prince of Wales*. For most of the night, the aircraft sat uselessly on her launcher, though she might easily have spotted the *Bismarck* or the *Prinz Eugen* in the half-light of the Arctic night. Then, when it was almost too late to make any use of the aircraft, the crew discovered that its fuel had become contaminated by seawater. It could not be flown until refueled with uncontaminated aviation gas.[20]

Holland's worst decision was that he would allow Captain Leach no leeway in how he would fight the *Prince of Wales*. Despite his initial intentions to allow the two ships some freedom to maneuver independently, he gave strict instructions to Leach to stay about a half mile off the *Hood*'s starboard beam and follow the *Hood*'s every move with the precision of a dance partner. To compound the problem, he also decided that the *Hood*, with her thin deck armor, would lead the charge once the *Bismarck* was spotted. The *Hood* was dreadfully vulnerable to plunging fire, even if a green crew manned the *Prince of Wales* and her guns were still plagued by mechanical problems. If the *Hood* was in the lead, however, the Germans were sure to fire at her first, because it was instinctive in most warship captains to fire at the enemy's lead ship when engaging two or more that posed equal dangers. That decision led Tovey to declare later, after the *Hood*'s encounter with the *Bismarck*, that he had had serious reservations about the *Hood* leading the attack but that he "did not feel . . . interference with so senior an officer justified."[21]

As the *Hood* and the *Prince of Wales* raced to their destiny, the ships' companies prepared for heavy gun action. Vice Admiral Holland's command to move to Action Stations transformed both ships into beehives of frenetic activity. The men from Vickers-Armstrong helped the gunners aboard the *Prince of Wales* elevate and train the guns, as well as check the ammunition hoists. Sailors donned white antiflash hoods and gloves to protect against burns, and clean socks and underwear, according to Royal Navy tradition, to prevent infection should they be wounded. Elsewhere, communications were tested, watertight doors closed, and pressure as well as temperature gauges monitored closely. Cooks dampened down the galley fires. Everything loose either on deck or below was battened down. In the wardroom and sick bay, doctors and their assistants sterilized instruments, laid out bandages and gauze, and checked the supply of morphine and anesthetics. Men kept close watch from every possible vantage point. Gun crews stood expectantly by their weapons. There was small talk, but tension and fear dominated the atmosphere in both ships. The *Hood*'s company had seen at Mers-el-Kebir what a heavy armor-piercing shell could do to thick armor, or to human flesh. No one was lulled into a false sense of security by the immense size of the *Hood* and the *Prince of Wales*, or their armor or heavy guns.

Shortly after midnight Holland ordered the battle ensigns hoisted and changed course to 000 degrees or due north; eight minutes later he reduced speed to 25 knots. Then a report from the *Suffolk*: she had lost radar contact with the two German ships. If the *Hood* and the *Prince of Wales* continued on their present course and speed, and if the shadowing cruisers did not regain contact, the *Bismarck* might slip by. Here was the first difficulty arising out of Holland's hasty decision to turn north; by the time the *Bismarck* was spotted again, she might be south of Holland's ships, heading into the Atlantic. He'd never catch Lütjens in a high-speed chase, even if he did not run out of fuel first. Holland signaled Leach that if contact with the *Bismarck* was not regained by about 2:00 A.M., he intended to reverse course and head south to make sure he stayed ahead of the enemy. The *Hood*'s company was allowed some rest at their posts, since the imminence of action had abated somewhat. At three minutes past two Holland swung both heavy ships through an arc of 110 degrees to settle on a new course of 200 degrees, or just south of west, and released his destroyers to continue to search to the north. Forty minutes later the *Suffolk* regained radar contact;

Holland stayed his course. At 3:40 A.M. Holland executed a 40-degree turn to port and increased speed to 28 knots. At 4:00 A.M. he calculated that the German battle fleet was some 20 miles to the northwest, but he still refused permission for the *Prince of Wales* to switch on her Type 284 radar.

At 5:35 A.M. a reedy voice from the *Prince of Wales'* crow's nest drifted down to the bridge: "*Enemy in sight! Enemy in sight!*"[22] The battleship's range finder, director tower, and finally 14-inch guns began to turn to the northwest, where the enemy's funnel gases had been spotted. Captain Leach peered through his binoculars. Within moments he could make out the tops of two masts on the horizon. Next came the superstructures. Then he spied the black and sinister ships themselves. Range: about 30,000 yards, too far for accurate fire. It was also hard at that distance to tell which German ship was which, especially since their profiles were similar; no one noticed that the *Prinz Eugen* was in the lead. The two German warships were charging southwest on a course of 220 degrees. But instead of catching the Germans from ahead, the *Hood* and the *Prince of Wales* were now on the Germans' port beam, slightly ahead but on a gradually converging course. If Holland stayed this course, he would soon have to go broadside to broadside with Lütjens' ships. He would still have the advantage of eighteen to eight heavy guns, but the *Hood*'s vulnerability and the *Prince of Wales*' gun problems and the greenness of her company might very well cancel out that advantage.

At the southern end of the Denmark Strait, visibility improved slightly as the first pale golden rays of sunshine broke over the horizon. By 5:27 A.M. Lieutenant Schmalenbach could make out "two targets" on the distant horizon. Two minutes later the cruiser's forward gunnery control station confirmed two smoke smudges: "The smoke plumes are close together and rise almost perpendicular into the sky, slightly off to our right." Schmalenbach wasted no time: "Alarm!"[23]

The first gunnery officer, Commander Paul Jasper, reached the bridge at 5:35 A.M. He quickly confirmed the sightings and judged the "targets" to be cruisers, most likely of the *Exeter*, *Birmingham*, or *Fiji* class. Captain Brinkmann now joined his gunnery officers on the bridge and, after a brief report from Jasper, informed Admiral Lütjens of the presence of hostile craft, "presumably light cruisers," 20 degrees off the port bow.[24] Lütjens ordered a 45-degree turn to starboard, coming to a course of 265 degrees. He needed time to think. Should he avoid action? His mission was to destroy commerce, but he had been determined since the moment he had received his sailing orders not to join the growing ranks of Kriegsmarine commanders in chief who had failed to deal aggressively with the enemy. He had the most powerful battleship in the world under his command. He had known from the start what he would do. At 5:47 A.M. Brinkmann again reported "smoke plumes on the horizon to port." The smoke plumes quickly grew bigger.[25] Obviously, enemy warships, probably cruisers, were approaching at a high rate of speed. The tips of the masts of the approaching ships pierced the horizon. But heavy gray smoke billowing from their four funnels obstructed a clear view of the enemy silhouettes. Brinkmann estimated range at 33,000 yards (18 miles).

"Alarm!" The *Prinz Eugen*'s captain and first gunnery officer, believing that they were dealing with 10,000-ton cruisers, ordered the gunners to load high-explosive shells and impact fuses. The cheek of British cruisers wishing to engage the *Bismarck* flabbergasted Brinkmann.[26] But which ships were they? A lively debate ensued on the bridge of the *Prinz Eugen*. While Captain Brinkmann and Commander Jasper maintained that they were dealing with cruisers, others voted for a mix of cruisers and destroyers. The lone dissenter was the *Prinz Eugen*'s second gunnery officer. The lead enemy ship on the right mounted a menacing tripod mast and was throwing such a "high and wide bow wave" that Lieutenant Schmalenbach became "suspicious." There was no doubt in his mind: "It's a battleship!"

Commander Jasper rejected the suggestion. The enemy was closing at too high a rate of speed to be a battleship.[27] And the Royal Navy possessed only two modern battleships with twin funnels—

HMS *King George V* and HMS *Prince of Wales*. But the latest B-Dienst intelligence indicated that the *Prince of Wales* was still fitting out. Captain Brinkmann agreed, and noted that the Luftwaffe had reported as late as 22 May that the *King George V* still rode at anchor in Scapa Flow. Further, Naval Group Command North had radioed the task force just four hours earlier that nothing had changed since that report. Of the Royal Navy's three 15-inch battle cruisers, HMS *Renown* was known to be at Gibraltar. Perhaps the two intruders were the *Hood* and the *Repulse*?[28] Or were they two additional heavy cruisers sent to reinforce the *Suffolk* and the *Norfolk* as the eyes of the Home Fleet? The hostiles' approach was still at such a fine angle that it precluded positive identification. Lieutenant Schmalenbach left the bridge for his post in the forward fire-control station convinced that the task force was about to engage a battleship of the *Emerald* class.[29]

Admiral Lütjens, deprived of accurate intelligence by the Naval High Command, could only guess at the composition of the naval force he was facing. He was like a fighter about to enter a title bout with one hand tied behind his back. The task force commander informed the crew of the approaching smoke plumes over the loudspeakers. The moment for decision had arrived. Lütjens quickly recalled his last conversation in Berlin with Grand Admiral Erich Raeder: operate cautiously and deliberately, but if battle should prove unavoidable, conduct it with full force to the finish. Adolf Hitler had berated the Kriegsmarine for the scuttling of the *Graf Spee* off the River Plate. German warships, Raeder had decreed, were to fight to the last shell and, if necessary, to go down with flag flying. There was no thought of running for the open waters of the Atlantic.

At 5:47 A.M. Lütjens ordered: "General Quarters!" From his foretop fire-control station about 90 feet above the waterline, Commander Schneider also took the rapidly approaching ships to be heavy cruisers and quickly calculated targeting range on the lead ship. It would be a difficult shoot: the *Bismarck*'s forward turrets would be at their maximum limits for traversing toward the rear. With the

15-inch guns loaded, Schneider trained the battleship's turrets on the nearest target. The two adversaries were now closing nearly bow-on at a relative approach rate of just under 35 knots. Range was down to 27,000 yards.

Bundled up against the wind in his beige duffle coat, his helmet square upon his head, Vice Admiral Holland focused his glasses tightly on the two German ships. The *Hood* was plunging forward at 28 knots, and everything on the ship was being knocked about. The turbines were screaming. He could hear the whine of the huge electric motors straining to train his turrets toward the enemy. He could hear the background chatter on the bridge and the range to target being called out every few seconds. The range was closing at about a fifth of a mile every minute. Though both the *Hood* and the *Prince of Wales* could shoot as far as 30,000 yards, the chances of scoring hits at that distance were slim. If he continued on his current course, Holland knew, he would not be within effective gun range for at least fifteen more minutes. At any point in that quarter hour, the *Bismarck* could open fire and plunge its shells through the *Hood*'s thin deck armor. Or—and this was a distinct possibility, given the German tendency so far in the war to run away from British capital ships—the *Bismarck* might alter course to the west and try to run past him. More than three thousand British sailors' fates hinged upon his decision; so possibly did the outcome of the Battle of the Atlantic. Standing beside him, the *Hood*'s Captain Ralph Kerr waited. A half mile away on his starboard beam, Captain Leach waited. The ships pounded on as the range closed. It was really only a few seconds, but it seemed like hours before Holland spoke. "Make to *Prince of Wales*; on my signal alter course forty degrees to starboard." A Blue Four Pennant was quickly raised to the top of the yardarm. On the *Prince of Wales*, Leach waited for the pennant to come down. That was when he would make his turn in concert with the *Hood*. Then Holland told Kerr, "Starboard 40." The message was relayed to the coxswain, who replied, "Forty degrees of starboard wheel on sir." At 5:37 A.M. the *Hood* heeled over in a high-speed turn, the *Prince of Wales* nailed to her beam. The two ships settled on a new course of 280 degrees; the *Bismarck* would be in effective gun range within five minutes.[30]

Vice Admiral Holland had gambled again. The new 35-degree angle of convergence increased the rate of closure, but it put the German task force at a bearing of only 20° from the two British ships. Did Holland decide in these few moments to follow Admiral Tovey's advice to charge straight at the Germans? In doing so, he made it impossible to bring the rear turrets of his two ships to bear. The angle on the bow was too fine. But he still had six forward heavy guns on the *Prince of Wales* and four on the *Hood* to the *Bismarck's* eight in total. With the *Hood* in the lead, this diagonal approach would most certainly expose her vulnerable main deck to the *Bismarck's* plunging fire, but at a high closing rate, the greatest moment of vulnerability would pass quickly. An unhappy trade-off at best.

Aboard the *Hood*, Captain Kerr's gunners raised their 15-inch barrels to an elevation of 22 degrees, with estimated time of shell flight to target at fifty seconds. The shells from the *Prince of Wales'* 14-inch guns would reach the enemy five seconds quicker. At 5:49 A.M. Holland signaled another course change, starboard to 300 degrees to increase the closing rate and reduce the *Hood's* period of greatest vulnerability. He signaled Leach to stay close and follow his every move. Almost immediately he gave another order: "Stand by to open fire. Target left-hand ship."[31] The left-hand ship was the *Prinz Eugen*, which posed no real threat to the British ships. Aboard the *Prince of Wales*, Captain Leach immediately recognized the error and corrected the order. His guns would fire at the *Bismarck*, even if the *Hood's* did not. The tremendous advantage Holland had enjoyed the night before had now vanished. Across the gap between the two racing British ships, Vice Admiral Holland turned to Captain Kerr: "Execute." Kerr at once ordered: "Open fire."[32] The senior gunnery officer shouted into the sound-powered telephone, "Shoot!" Then came the always incongruous tinkle, tinkle of the ready bells in the gun-director tower that preceded the great roar of the main guns and the thick clouds of bitter brown cordite smoke that spewed from them. Four 15-inch shells, each weighing about 1,600 pounds, flew out of the *Hood's* barrels in the direction of the

Prinz Eugen. At some point in the next few moments, Holland recognized his mistake and tried to get his gunners to shift to the right-hand ship. A few seconds after the *Hood* opened fire, the *Prince of Wales*' heavy guns roared at the *Bismarck*. One of the battleship's 14-inch guns promptly went out of action, and now Lütjens had eight heavy guns to Holland's five, with no telling when the next *Prince of Wales* gun might fail.

Almost simultaneously, Admiral Lütjens, from high on the *Bismarck*'s admiral's bridge, ordered his chief yeoman to hoist the signal for the *Prinz Eugen* to open fire on the lead enemy ship. Captain Brinkmann responded at once: "Commander to Artillery: Heavy; clearance to fire!" Eight shells thundered out of their guns at the *Hood* from a distance of 24,000 yards. Within minutes Brinkmann's gunners scored a hit on the *Hood*'s starboard side with their fifth salvo. The shell crashed into the base of the foremast, setting off some antiaircraft rockets, which in turn set afire one of the ammunition lockers amidships on the upper deck. A raging fire "burning with a pink glow shrouded in dense fog" ensued. While not fatal, the shot from the *Prinz Eugen* nevertheless informed the British that they were in for a tough fight.

From the *Bismarck*'s fire-control station in the Vormars, Commander Schneider pleaded with Lütjens over the telephone: "Request permission to fire." No reply. The *Bismarck*'s first gunnery officer had been taught to take advantage of superior German artillery training and at all times to fire first. Schneider grew more anxious with every second that passed. He next telephoned the bridge: "Enemy has opened fire." No reply. The enemy fired his third, then his fourth salvo. "Enemy's salvos well grouped," Schneider screamed into the telephone. But there was still no order to reply from Lütjens. Was the admiral determined to stick to the strict letter of his instructions and avoid battle with heavy enemy units at all costs to concentrate on the primary mission of commerce raiding? In that case, the time was at hand to order a change of course and to bring the task force up to full speed.

"Request permission to fire," Schneider repeated. Not a word from the phlegmatic Lütjens. The *Bismarck* remained steady on course 220 degrees, making 28 knots. An experienced task force commander and artillery specialist, Lütjens obviously calculated his chances of straddling the hostile "cruisers" with the first salvo at slim to none. Distance to targets remained about 15.5 miles. The enemy vessels, approaching at a bearing of about 35 degrees abaft his port beam, offered only a slender target. Moreover, they were at the outer limit of traverse for his forward guns. Nor could Lütjens afford to waste precious ammunition registering his heavy guns.

Deep down in the *Bismarck*'s cavernous compartments, several sailors recorded what they believed to be a first hit. Ordinary Seaman Georg Herzog encountered a wounded chief petty officer just moments before the *Bismarck* opened fire. Machinist Petty Officer Adolf Eich was even more precise: "All of a sudden there was a great bang. The ship was shaken in a way different than the firing of her SA [heavy artillery]. Then we received permission to fire." Fellow Petty Officer Walter Lorenzen recalled that the *Bismarck* received a hit in the foreship at about the same time as she opened fire.[33] The battleship's officers, high up on her bridge, registered no enemy hits.

Finally, Lütjens sprang into action. He ordered, "Hard turn port 170°," to gain a more favorable firing position, and then steadied his task force on a new course of 200 degrees. This brilliant maneuver placed the German ships on a course that was almost perpendicular to that of Holland's task force. Lütjens was in a position to "cross the T" of the British. He had gained the tactical advantage: while he could bring to bear his ships' full broadsides, the British were limited to their forward turrets. All the while, the two enemy forces closed range at about 1,100 yards per minute.[34]

Vice Admiral Holland now realized his precarious position. At 5:55 A.M. he abandoned his previous course and decided to change tactics in the middle of the fight. He would no longer rush at the enemy in Tovey style, but slug it out broadside to broadside. He made the signal for a Blue Pendant turn of two points (20 degrees) to port to open his A arcs (naval terminology for bringing his full broadsides into play). But it was too late to fix things with a quick patch job. In turning, Holland revealed the silhouettes of both his ships to the Germans, and he was now steaming on a diagonal course across the enemy's line of fire. This maneuver exposed his ships to the greatest probability of a salvo hit. The *Prince of Wales*' fire was especially erratic: her first salvo was over, and she did not straddle the *Bismarck* until her sixth.

On the bridge of the *Prinz Eugen*, Captain Brinkmann finally determined the enemy to be HMS *Hood* and HMS *King George V*, though Commander Schneider, high up in the *Bismarck*'s forward upper direction tower, continued to believe that he was dealing with British cruisers. But the *Bismarck*'s second gunnery officer, Commander Helmut Albrecht, at once recognized the extremely long fo'c'sle and two heavy turrets of the lead ship. "Herr Schneider," he pleaded from his post in the lower forward direction tower, "observe the superstructure, you know well which ship in the British fleet has that superstructure. That is no other than the battle-cruiser 'Hood'!"[35] In the aft fire-control station, the fourth gunnery officer, Burkard von Müllenheim-Rechberg, heard Albrecht scream over the ship's telephone, "The *Hood*—it's the *Hood!*"[36]

The atmosphere on the *Bismarck* was tense: the *Hood* had been the ship's paper adversary during many training exercises in the Baltic Sea, but now she was menacingly real. A sailor standing with Schneider and Albrecht in the forward direction tower could hardly believe what he was hearing. "Who of us ever thought," he wrote in his diary later that day, "we should be engaged in a sea battle! We had merely thought of commerce raiding and sunning ourselves on deck."[37] Admiral Lütjens was less charitable: the sight of what he believed to be the battleship *King George V* and the battle cruiser *Hood*, the two most powerful ships in the Royal Navy, was most disturbing. German intelligence had reported both to be still in port. Their appearance off the Denmark Strait could mean only one thing: the sortie had long been discovered. This was no chance meeting.

The *Hood*'s first shells splashed into the ocean 100 to 330 yards forward and 55 yards to port of the *Prinz Eugen*, raising 200-foot columns of water. The next salvo fell 100 to 160 yards from the heavy cruiser. One shell landed 55 yards ahead of the *Prinz Eugen* and doused her forecastle with seawater. Yet a fourth salvo landed squarely in her wake. Why, Captains Brinkmann and Lindemann wondered, were the British targeting the smaller ship? But there was no time for mental gymnastics. Captain Lindemann was becoming anxious for the safety of his ship. One of the *Bismarck*'s crew recalled that Lindemann muttered, "I will not let my ship be shot out from under my ass." He demanded Permission to Fire from Lütjens, high up on the admiral's bridge.[38] At 5:55 A.M., two minutes after the British opened fire, the *Bismarck*'s 15-inch guns returned fire on the *Hood*. Commander Schneider fired a bracket of four 15-inch shells to register the big guns. The roar of the artillery duel could be heard as far away as Reykjavik, Iceland.

On board the *Bismarck* all eyes were riveted on the flight of the first salvo toward the *Hood*. Commander Schneider quickly ran the vital figures through his head: at a range of 24,000 yards, with a gun elevation of 13 degrees and muzzle velocity of 875 yards per second, the battleship's 1,764-pound shells should reach their target in thirty-four seconds. They did not. "Short!" The wind blew the *Bismarck*'s black smoke southward toward the British ships, making target observation difficult. Still, Schneider immediately adjusted the range and deflection: the *Bismarck*'s second salvo splashed into the sea between the two enemy ships. He again adjusted range and deflection and ordered a 440-yard bracket to be fired at the adversary, well placed off the *Bismarck*'s beam. Thirty-two seconds later Schneider observed the long salvo to be clearly over the target, the short a direct straddle. The *Bismarck* had zeroed in on the target. There was no time to lose. "Full salvos good rapid," Schneider barked from the foretop fire-control station.[39] "Attention, fall!" Concurrently he directed the battleship's 6-inch secondary armament on the port side to target the *Prince of Wales*.

At 5:55 A.M. Captain Brinkmann from the bridge of the *Prinz Eugen* screamed at the cruiser's first gunnery officer, Commander Jasper: "Fire four! Four-hectometer straddling group!"[40] Two minutes later Brinkmann spotted two shells exploding near the *Hood*'s aft mast and second funnel. A rapidly spreading red-orange fire followed by black and yellow smoke on the port side led him to believe that his gunners (or those of the *Bismarck*) had struck either some gasoline tanks or the floatplane hangar.[41] In fact, the *Prinz Eugen*'s salvo had struck the *Hood* near the port after 4-inch gun, probably in a ready-use locker for that gun or in a locker for a new type of unguided antiaircraft rockets. From the *Prince of Wales*, men could see the fire burning with a clear reddish flame. It flared up quickly, then appeared to die down. From near the hit, Able Bodied Seaman R. E. Tilburn heard sporadic explosions from within the fire, like the noises of a string of Chinese firecrackers, and concluded that the ready-use ammunition was going off.

The British task force was desperate to close with the Germans. However, not only had Holland allowed Lütjens to "cross the T," but his ships were now crashing at high speed into rough seas and into the face of a 10-mile-per-hour breeze blowing out of the northeast. Both the *Hood* and the *Prince of Wales* were notoriously "wet" ships: their low forecastles, a design error, allowed great mountains of green water to crash over the fore turrets, blinding the range finders in the process. In fact, the *Hood*'s 42-foot main range finder was not mounted in the foretop, but rather at the back of B turret, and the Atlantic salt spray continued to blind its crew. Similarly, heavy ocean spray forced the *Prince of Wales* to rely on her 15-foot range finder in the director control tower. Worse yet, the *Prince of Wales*' modern Type 284 radar had been kept switched off until the very last moment as a precaution against early detection by the enemy. It now could give no range.[42] Captain Leach could only continue to fire by guesstimate. And he still could not bring his after turrets to bear on the enemy. Holland ordered another turn, "Port 20," and the blue pennant shot up the yardarm, ready for the order to execute. Leach warned his coxswain to stay with the flagship.

At 5:59 A.M. Admiral Lütjens, not wishing to leave the *Prince of Wales* unengaged and afraid that his ships' gunners might not be able to separate the fall of shell from their separate guns, ordered:

"Target the enemy furthest left." The *Prinz Eugen*, which had just fired its sixth salvo at the *Hood*, shifted sights onto the *Prince of Wales*. The German ships were now shooting across one another's line of fire. Lütjens did not for a moment contemplate withdrawing the heavy cruiser to the lee of the fire—that is, to the *Bismarck*'s disengaged side, as stipulated in the German Tactical Regulations—but rather kept her in the line.[43] Within minutes of concentrating on the *Prince of Wales*, Commander Jasper noted two detonations and a "small fire" on the enemy battleship.[44] Next Lütjens ordered the *Prinz Eugen* to drop back, off the *Bismarck*'s starboard side. There she could train her FuMO-27 radar detectors on the British cruisers *Suffolk* and *Norfolk*, still trailing the German task force ten to twelve nautical miles off to the east.

At 6:00 A.M. Commander Schneider loosed a fifth broadside from the *Bismarck* against the *Hood*, just as the battle cruiser was completing her second 20-degree turn to port. Range: 19,700 yards. Speed: 28 knots. "Straddling," boomed a voice over the loudspeaker. Then, "Attention! Hit!" The *Bismarck*'s salvo had indeed straddled the *Hood*. Two shells landed in the water close off the battle cruiser, but one or more armor-piercing shells seemingly had ripped through her thin deck armor—apparently without effect. Schneider was perplexed: "Good grief! Was that a dud? That really bit into him." It was no dud; the *Bismarck*'s shells had penetrated deep into the *Hood*'s magazine, setting off 112 tons of cordite propellant. Suddenly Schneider screamed over the loudspeaker: "He is sinking!"[45]

HOT PURSUIT

HAD VICE ADMIRAL LANCELOT Holland's gamble worked, the "mighty *Hood*" might today be berthed somewhere in a British port, a tourist mecca and a memorial to the Royal Navy's dead of World War II. Instead, what is left of the pride of the Royal Navy lies on the sea floor, 15,000 feet below the gray Atlantic, at the northern end of the Newfoundland-Labrador basin. In the months after the disaster, the Admiralty conducted two formal investigations, but no one can be completely sure of what happened. Perhaps one day the wreck will be found and examined, as the *Bismarck*'s was in June 1989, but until then, speculation will continue on how a ship of this power and majesty could have been eliminated with one sudden stroke.

What is almost certain about the *Hood*'s fate is that at least one of the *Bismarck*'s massive 15-inch shells, plunging seaward with a velocity of 2,700 feet per second, sliced through the *Hood*'s thinly armored main deck or drove through her side, buried itself in one of her magazines, and then exploded. The blast broke the *Hood*'s back, already strained by so many years of rough oceans, high-speed practice maneuvers, and practice firing of her main guns. HMS *Hood* simply split in two somewhere between the main mast and the after funnel. Her forward section continued to surge ahead at 28 knots for a few moments, then quickly lost way, slewing to the left as tons of seawater surged into the hundreds of ripped-open compartments and companionways at the rear of her doomed front half. As this half ship filled from the rear with seawater, the bow lifted at a sharp angle. Then the entire section slid backward into the sea. Incredibly, at the very moment of her doom, the *Hood*'s forward turrets managed to fire a last salvo, a funeral salute to a once great ship.

The after section of the *Hood* was shrouded in a veil of dense black smoke as it skidded to a stop, taking giant quantities of seawater in at the broken-off front. Like ants, men scrambled over the wreck trying to save themselves, but the inrushing seawater quickly tilted the section forward, raising the stern completely out of the water and exposing screws and rudder. In less than a minute, it too slipped beneath the waves. A massive cloud of black smoke drifted away to leeward. Debris littered the sea: streams of fuel oil, Carley floats, clothes, human remains. Tons of fuel oil burned brightly on the ocean surface.

Ordinary Signalman A. E. Briggs had been on the *Hood*'s compass platform since the ship had gone to action stations. He saw little of the approach of the two enemy fleets, but he could hear desperate snatches of conversation as the *Hood*'s great guns boomed and huge columns of water from *Bismarck*'s 15-inch shells rose on every side. Just before 6:00 A.M. Briggs heard the senior gunnery officer report to Captain Ralph Kerr: "She has been hit on the boat deck and there is a fire in the R.U. lockers." Vice Admiral Holland could spare no time for the fire: "Leave it until the ammunition is gone!" Just then the superstructure vibrated as if struck by a giant hammer. There was almost no noise, but Briggs heard someone yell, "Compass has gone!" Midshipman W. J. Dundas was midshipman of the watch high on the upper bridge as the *Bismarck*'s shells struck home. Like

Briggs, he was in a closed-in position and saw very little. He tried to keep count of the incoming German salvos and of the *Hood*'s outgoing fire as he worked at the chart table. Suddenly everyone on the bridge was thrown off their feet and wreckage started to come down. Dundas managed to regain his footing and saw a mass of brown smoke drifting to leeward on the port side. The *Hood* was listing heavily to port, and Dundas scrambled uphill and started climbing through one of the bridge windows. He saw the officer of the watch climbing through another window. When he was halfway out, seawater came up underneath him and he found himself swimming. He managed to look backward and saw the bow of the ship looming above the water at a 45-degree angle, then sliding back into the sea.

Able Bodied Seaman R. E. Tilburn had been preoccupied with the burning ready-use ammunition near the *Hood*'s port 4-inch gun mount when he heard a noise as if the *Hood*'s guns had fired, then dead silence. A massive wall of flames rose between the control tower and B turret above the forecastle deck. Then Tilburn, too, was in the water. The shock was tremendous. He saw debris and bodies scattered over the *Hood*'s deck, then lost sight of the wreck. As he swam away, he saw long steel tubes sealed at both ends floating in the water. He couldn't make out what they were. In fact, they were the crushing tubes that protected the side bulges of the *Hood*'s hull. Her innards were spewing out onto the water as she began her final plunge.[1]

Eight hundred yards away, Lieutenant Esmond Knight, RNVR, watched from his antiaircraft fire-control station on the battleship *Prince of Wales*. He saw the *Hood*'s two forward turrets fire; then he heard a great "rushing sound" that just as suddenly ceased.

> As I looked, a great spouting explosion issued from the centre of the *Hood*, enormous reaching tongues of pale-red flame shot into the air, while dense clouds of whitish-yellow smoke burst upwards, gigantic pieces of brightly burning debris being hurled hundreds of feet in the air. I just did not believe what I saw—*Hood* had literally been blown to pieces.[2]

Captain Helmuth Brinkmann from the bridge of the heavy cruiser *Prinz Eugen* probably had the best view of the engagement between the *Bismarck* and the *Hood*. "An extremely loud detonation on the 'Hood.' High columns with pieces of iron can be seen. A heavy, black cloud of smoke envelops the ship, which is rapidly sinking by the stern while it makes a 180° turn."[3]

On board the *Bismarck*, there were shouts of "She's blowing up!" and "'Hood' has exploded and is sinking!" The *Bismarck*'s fourth gunnery officer, Lieutenant Burkard von Müllenheim-Rechberg, briefly abandoned his task of scouting the horizon astern for the possible appearance of the heavy cruisers *Suffolk* and *Norfolk* and went to the port gunnery-direction station.

> The sight I then saw is something I shall never forget. At first the *Hood* was nowhere to be seen; in her place was a colossal pillar of black smoke reaching into the sky. Gradually, at the foot of the pillar, I made out the bow of the battle cruiser projecting upwards at an angle, a sure sign that she had broken in two.[4]

In the *Bismarck*'s charthouse, an assistant to her navigator, Commander Wolf Neuendorff, rushed to the forward conning tower.

> Suddenly, the *Hood* split in two, and thousands of tons of steel were hurled into the air. . . . Although the range was still about 19,700 yards, the fireball that developed where the *Hood* still was seemed near enough to touch. It was so close that I shut my eyes but curiosity made me open them again a second or two later. It was like being in a hurricane.[5]

Other spotters on the *Bismarck*'s deck noted "a mountain of flame and a yellowish-white fireball" bursting 220 to 330 yards high in the air between the *Hood*'s masts. Still others observed pieces of metal—shattered structural members, high-explosive shells, an entire 15-inch turret, and other equipment—shooting out of the mushroom cloud and black smoke that followed the initial flame.

On the bridges of the two German ships, many officers recalled the similar destruction of the British battle cruisers *Indefatigable*, *Queen Mary*, and *Invincible* during the Battle of Jutland in May 1916. Commander Hans Oels, the *Bismarck*'s first officer, was beside himself with joy. "A triple *Sieg Heil* to our *Bismarck*!"[6] In the bowels of the battleship, Ordinary Seaman Otto Höntzsch heard a voice coming over the loudspeaker: "Enemy burning!" And shortly thereafter, "Enemy exploding!" Machinist Petty Officer Walter Lorenzen and Ordinary Seaman Otto Maus recalled a follow-up announcement from the bridge: "An English battleship, probably the 'Hood,' has just been destroyed by an explosion. The other battleship has received two hits and is turning away." Three loud hurrahs greeted the news.[7] The jubilation was such that the *Bismarck*'s officers brought the men back to their stations only with great difficulty.

Date: Saturday, 24 May 1941. Position: 63° 20' N, 31° 50' W. Quadrant AD 73 on the German sea chart. Ninety-five officers, including Vice Admiral Lancelot Holland and Captain Ralph Kerr, went down with the *Hood*, as did 1,416 sailors. There were only three survivors: Midshipman W. J. Dundas, Able Bodied Seaman R. E. Tilburn, and Ordinary Signalman A. E. Briggs. A destroyer fished them out of the cold Atlantic waters and took them to Reykjavik. Rear Admiral William F. Wake-Walker, flag officer commanding the First Cruiser Squadron, watched the devastation from the bridge of his flagship, the heavy cruiser HMS *Norfolk*. Then, at 6:15 A.M., he laconically signaled the Admiralty: "*HOOD* blown up in position 63° 21' N., 31° 50' W."

There was no time on either side to mourn, to celebrate, or to reflect. The *Prince of Wales* had been steaming about 1,000 yards behind the *Hood* when the battle cruiser went down. Captain John C. Leach immediately put his wheel over, hard a-starboard, to avoid plowing into the wreckage. In doing so, he again closed the arc of his aft turrets so that they could not bear on the enemy. The *Prince of Wales* was thus in a highly dangerous position. By 6:02 A.M. the *Bismarck* and the *Prinz Eugen* were concentrating their fire on what they still believed to be the "K3G," that is, HMS *King George V*. Distance to target was the same as that at which the *Hood* had been annihilated, and Commander Schneider only had to rotate his guns through the 1 or 2 degrees of bearing that had separated the *Hood* from the *Prince of Wales*. Schneider's first salvo straddled the *Prince of Wales*.

Once safely cleared of the remains of the *Hood*, Captain Leach laid down heavy black smoke and shaped a course of 260 degrees, which allowed him to bring the battleship's full broadside to bear. Both battleships were on a converging course in a moderate sea and easterly winds. Range quickly fell to 15,000 yards as the *Bismarck* and the *Prinz Eugen* hounded their game. Then, at 6:03 A.M., Captain Brinkmann spied a chance to bring the *Prinz Eugen*'s G7a torpedo outfit into action. He had been most anxious to do so, given that the task force's General Orders for the Atlantic Operation stipulated the heavy cruiser's torpedo outfit to be her "*primary*" armament.[8] Moreover, since the German task force was without destroyers, the *Prinz Eugen* alone had torpedo-firing capability. As the heavy cruiser's torpedo officer calmly calibrated distance to target to be 14,000 yards, the *Prinz Eugen*'s skipper was suddenly roused by shrill cries from the sounding room: "Torpedo noises off to port!" Brinkmann ordered a violent turn to starboard. At that moment, a broadside from the *Prince of Wales* splashed into the cruiser's old wake. Brinkmann could only watch helplessly as the tracks of two torpedoes approached his ship. In fact, not two but three "kippers" missed their intended mark. Since the *Prince of Wales* mounted no torpedo tubes, the *Prinz Eugen*'s captain concluded that the *Hood* must have fired the torpedoes shortly before she went down.[9]

Brinkmann's hard a-starboard had placed the *Bismarck* to starboard, astern of the heavy cruiser. The officers on the *Prinz Eugen*'s bridge marveled at the sight of the great battleship slicing through the water at 27 knots, her turrets menacingly trained hard a-port and spewing out their deadly heavy artillery fire every fifteen seconds. Admiral Günther Lütjens ordered both ships to steer a similar course, 3,300 yards apart, after the *Prince of Wales*. Gunners from the *Bismarck* and the *Prinz Eugen* poured a withering fire of armor-piercing shells into the fleeing foe, which could only reply with her rear turrets.

On the *Prinz Eugen*, the second gunnery officer, Paul Schmalenbach, detected an unending "crescendo of barrel flashes and shell detonations,"[10] mixed with dense black smoke and sea spray. All the while, her first gunnery officer, Paul Jasper, roared, "Full salvos good rapid!" to the cruiser's fore and aft fire-control stations. The *Prinz Eugen*'s 8-inch turrets fired a salvo every 27 to 28 seconds. It was a modern-day mêlée fight in the best Nelsonian tradition. All of a sudden, several light shells landed about 4,400 yards astern the German task force: the pesky *Norfolk* had almost caught up, but her 8-inch artillery remained well out of range. At 6:10 A.M. the *Prinz Eugen* sounded the aircraft alert; a PBY Catalina flying boat was quickly chased away by the task force's antiaircraft batteries.[11]

By now, range to the *Prince of Wales* had stabilized at 15,000 yards, and the *Bismarck*'s heavy shells took just 20 seconds to reach their target. A 15-inch shell from the *Bismarck* sent up a towering wall of water close by the *Prince of Wales*. Six-inch shells from the *Bismarck*'s secondary armament and 8-inch shells from the *Prinz Eugen* splashed all around Captain Leach's ship every ten to fifteen seconds. The din of battle was frightful. The crash of the enemy's shells mixed with the great roar and banging of the *Prince of Wales*' heavy and medium guns. Walls of water rose as high as the masthead and then showered the ship's decks whenever one of the *Bismarck*'s 15-inch shells landed close at hand.

In a sea fight with heavy guns, the men manning the antiaircraft guns have little to do but watch and worry. Esmond Knight had seen the *Hood* explode, had watched her disappear, had heard the great roar of the *Prince of Wales*' own guns. Then, once again, he heard a great rushing noise, like the approach of a cyclone. For a moment Lieutenant Knight thought he was in Hyde Park, listening to a band. No, it wasn't a band; it was a loud ringing noise in his head. Then he regained consciousness:

> I had the sensation that I was dying. It was a strange feeling, and one that made me feel rather sad—no more. There was a lot of water swishing about—I was lying on my side with a great weight on top

> of me. . . . I remember being able to raise enough breath to let out a squeaky, "Georgie, old boy, can you get me out?" Strong hands lifted the dead men off of me; there was a horrible smell of blood, and the uncanny noise that men make when they are dying.

The shell that almost killed Esmond Knight had knocked out the *Prince of Wales'* two forward antiaircraft directors and turned the bridge into a mass of smoking, twisted, bloody wreckage. In the upper plot below the bridge, blood ran down the voice-pipe from the carnage above; someone caught the drips in a half-empty jug of cacao. Almost everyone on the bridge was dead save Captain Leach and the chief yeoman of signals. Moments later a second 15-inch shell from the *Bismarck* slammed into the superstructure supporting the fore secondary-armament directors. A third glanced off the aircraft crane, blowing both wings off the plane and forcing the catapult officer to push the gasoline-laden fuselage into the sea. A fourth penetrated the *Prince of Wales'* hull beneath the waterline but failed to explode, coming to rest beside the ship's diesel generator. Two 8-inch shells from the *Prinz Eugen* struck the *Prince of Wales* at the waterline in the stern, piercing her hull and causing her to take on 400 tons of seawater. A third 8-inch shell penetrated an ammunition-handling room for the medium artillery, where it whizzed around several times before coming to rest—without exploding or touching a man. One of the crew calmly carried the shell to the railing and tossed it into the sea.

Throughout the terrible pounding, Captain Leach's gunners heroically struggled with their cranky heavy guns and scored three hits on the *Bismarck*. Shortly after 6:05 A.M. the first of the 14-inch shells crashed through the *Bismarck's* forecastle above the waterline but below the bow wave. A machinist petty officer vividly recalled the hit as being distinct from the recoil of the *Bismarck's* great guns: "Suddenly we sensed a different jolt, a different tremor through the body of our ship: a hit, the first hit!"[12] Lieutenant Karl-Ludwig Richter, second engineer officer at the damage-control center, immediately rushed forward. As he clambered down to Section

XXI, Richter found himself in more than a 3 feet of water lapping over the battery deck. The bulkheads between Sections XX and XXI and between Sections XXI and XXII were severely damaged. A gaping hole about a yard and a half in diameter had been blasted into the ship's starboard hull. As Richter turned to the port side, he detected another hole, this one about a yard in diameter. The *Prince of Wales*' shell had gone clean through Section XXI from port to starboard. En route, it had ruptured two fuel tanks and flooded the salvage pump room. The *Bismarck* soon had 2,000 (and eventually 4,000) tons of seawater in her fo'c'sle; she was down 3 degrees by the bow, with a 9-degree list to port. Richter at once rushed all available salvage pumps forward and began the laborious task of trying to pump the water out of the bow sections. Up above on the main deck, another crew from the damage-control center slipped the ship's mangled port bow anchor cable.[13]

Shortly thereafter, a second shell from the *Prince of Wales*' aft turrets struck the *Bismarck*'s portside armored belt below the waterline near Sections XIII and XIV. The 14-inch shell did not penetrate the ship's side, but exploded against the torpedo bulkhead. As emergency crews managed to start the salvage pumps and to pump Section XIV dry, they noted that the forward port turbo-generator room and the auxiliary boiler room had sustained serious damage. Five sailors had been scalded by steam gushing forth from a burst pipe. Floor plates were buckled and gauges shattered. The lights were out. Water now entered Section XII, and it had to be evacuated. Upon further inspection, the damage-control center discovered that the shell had ripped open several fuel storage tanks in the ship's double bottom. The *Bismarck* was now leaving a wide, telltale streak of oil in her wake. The third 14-inch shell from the *Prince of Wales* merely blew away the forepost of the commandant's service boat abaft the funnel. Thereafter, it passed through the floatplane catapult-launching apparatus and fell into the sea off the starboard side without exploding.[14]

On board the *Prince of Wales*, Captain Leach realized that, with the death of Vice Admiral Holland, Rear Admiral Wake-Walker of the

First Cruiser Squadron automatically became the senior officer present. But Wake-Walker's flagship, the *Norfolk*, was well astern the German task force, and Leach bore full responsibility for his ship. He quickly evaluated his situation. One forward 14-inch gun had been put out of commission at the start of the battle. Two of the aft 14-inch guns malfunctioned with alarming regularity. An average salvo consisted of but three guns. The battleship's bridge was a shambles. And her two fire-control directors were out of commission. Despite the hits scored on the *Bismarck*, the *Prince of Wales* was definitely getting by far the worst of the exchange of gunfire. Could Leach afford to continue a seemingly hopeless fight with the two German warships? Could he risk another deadly hit, like the one that had destroyed the *Hood?* Or had the time come to cut British losses that 24 May 1941?

At 6:13 A.M. Captain Leach made his decision. With only two 14-inch guns still firing at the *Bismarck*, he turned the *Prince of Wales*' wheel over a second time, falling away 160 degrees behind a heavy smoke screen. As the mighty ship swung to the southeast, the shell ring on which the aft Y quadruple turret rested slid over on its rollers and jammed—a final insult. As well, the black smoke that the *Prince of Wales* laid down blinded the gunners in the two rear turrets. Leach had made the only decision possible. There was no need to continue a hopeless struggle and possibly lose his ship.

Out in the cold, gray expanse of the Atlantic that 24 May 1941, as HMS *Prince of Wales* fell away under a dense cloud of smoke, the *Prinz Eugen* continued to dog her with its 8-inch guns. The German cruiser tacked a zigzag course. Then at 6:09 A.M. the *Prinz Eugen* briefly tucked in behind the *Bismarck*. Captain Brinkmann immediately instructed his gunners, "Do not overshoot *Bismarck*!" Shortly thereafter he ordered, "Cease Fire!"[15] The Battle of Iceland was over.

Prime Minister Winston Churchill was at Chequers, his country estate, when he first received news of the *Hood*'s destruction and Captain Leach's decision to withdraw. His guest that weekend was Averell Harriman, U.S. president Franklin Delano Roosevelt's special envoy to the United Kingdom. The United States had been doing all it could as a supposedly neutral country to help Britain fight the Battle of the Atlantic, and Harriman was deeply interested in the Royal Navy's efforts to bring the *Bismarck* to heel. Churchill broke the news of the sea battle to Harriman early on Saturday morning. Harriman thought him strangely calm, almost distant as he told Harriman that the *Hood* was lost. But Churchill was, in fact, bitterly disappointed by his navy's performance and furious that Leach had broken off the action. Over the next few days, he thundered his anger at Captain Leach, at the first sea lord, Admiral Sir Dudley Pound, and at anyone else he thought responsible. He accused Leach of "the worst thing since [Admiral Ernest] Troubridge turned away from the *Goeben* in 1914."[16] That had taken place soon after the outbreak of World War I in the eastern Mediterranean, when Troubridge had not demonstrated sufficient offensive spirit in action against the German battle cruiser and her escort, the light cruiser *Breslau*. The two ships escaped to haunt the Royal Navy for the duration of the war. Much later, when *Bismarck* had been hunted down, Admiral Pound (no doubt at Churchill's urging) threatened to court-martial Leach and Wake-Walker for not pursuing the *Bismarck*. But Admiral Tovey threatened to resign if he did, and that ended the matter.[17]

According to the testimony of survivors, a heated debate ensued on the bridge of the *Bismarck*. Captain Ernst Lindemann, his large blue eyes sparkling with anticipation, demanded what every battleship commander in his place would have: to hunt down the crippled *Prince of Wales* and sink her. His ship had dispatched the "mighty *Hood*" in less than six minutes; surely the *Prince of Wales* could not escape a similar fate. A master naval gunner, Lindemann knew that he had the heavily damaged battleship within reach. A chase of perhaps two or three hours to the southeast would suffice. Lindemann could smell another kill.

Admiral Lütjens brusquely rejected Lindemann's request—as usual, without a word of explanation. But the *Bismarck*'s skipper, nervously chain-smoking cigarettes, again pressed his point: how could the task force commander deny him an almost certain second victory? Even if Admiral Tovey's squadron had left Scapa Flow the day before, which Lindemann did not know for sure, it would still be some 500 nautical miles to the east, halfway between Scapa Flow and the *Bismarck*. And even if the chase after the *Prince of Wales* consumed three hours, Tovey would still be at least 300 nautical miles away.

Admiral Lütjens remained unmoved. The man with the "iron mask" of a face once again declined to share his innermost thoughts. What is certain is that the *Bismarck*'s crew stood with their captain in demanding that the *Prince of Wales* be hunted down and destroyed. Of course, there was never any doubt as to the outcome of the short, formal, cold debate that took place on the *Bismarck*'s bridge. Lindemann, in the rank of captain, was in no position to force his views on the task force commander and fleet chief, in the grade of admiral. Lütjens ordered Lindemann to shape a course for 220 degrees, almost due southwest.[18] Great disappointment and downright grumbling were heard throughout the *Bismarck* as she headed for the open waters of the Atlantic.

The clash between the two senior German officers reflected their separate and distinct command functions.[19] Captain Lindemann, as commander of a single warship, operated first and foremost at the tactical level. For him, there was no question but that the immediate objective was to destroy the crippled *Prince of Wales*. He had spent his professional career preparing for this moment, and he had pressed his case as hard and as far as he dared. Surely neither Adolf Hitler nor Grand Admiral Erich Raeder would chastise an officer who aborted a chancy operation to return to port flying two pennants from his topmast, one for the *Hood* and the other for the *Prince of Wales*.

Admiral Lütjens, in his dual capacity as fleet chief and task force commander, operated at the strategic and operational levels. His orders were clear, up to a point: the primary mission was to operate in the Atlantic against enemy convoys. Grand Admiral Raeder had admonished his fleet chief not to "risk a major engagement for limited, and perhaps uncertain, goals," and to avoid engagements with the enemy unless these could be undertaken with little risk or under the umbrella of the primary mission objective. And yet Raeder had also ordered Lütjens to be bold and imaginative; to accept battle, if battle proved unavoidable, and to conduct it vigorously, to the finish. Before leaving Germany, Lütjens had informed Admiral Conrad Patzig, a fellow member of the Crew of 1907, and Admiral Wilhelm Marschall, his predecessor as fleet chief, that he would adhere to Raeder's directives. "I know what the Naval Command wants," Lütjens had averred, "and I will carry out their orders." He was not about to become the third fleet chief to be relieved of command for crossing the commander in chief of the Kriegsmarine. Nor was he about to discuss a command decision with a subordinate officer. The mission was commerce raiding, the area of operations the Atlantic Ocean.

At 6:32 A.M. Lütjens had reported to Naval Group Command North: "Battle cruiser, probably 'Hood' sunk. Another battleship, 'King George V' or 'Renown,' turned away damaged. Two heavy cruisers maintain contact." When Wilhelmshaven failed to acknowledge the signal, apparently due to poor atmospheric conditions off Greenland, Lütjens ordered it repeated continually until acknowledged. Additionally, he signaled Naval Group Command West in Paris: "'Hood' destroyed within five minutes in artillery duel at 0600 this morning. 'King George' turned away after hits. My speed reduced. Bow down due to hit in foreship." Then at 7:05 A.M. he once again signaled Naval Group Command North: "Have sunk a battleship at approximately 63° 10' North, 32° 00' West."[20] By now, the entire enemy naval community in Greenland, Iceland, and Britain must have been alerted to the Battle of Iceland. Shore commands at Wilhelmshaven and Berlin would receive Lütjens' signal only at 1:26 P.M. and 1:40 P.M., respectively.

On the *Prinz Eugen*, Captain Brinkmann registered his grievous concerns about this inordinate amount of radio traffic in the ship's war diary. "The constant use of radio signals constitutes a special danger. Practically speaking, everything can be decrypted, given today's technology." Brinkmann lamented the fact that Lütjens, since departing Gotenhafen, had apprised German shore commands of every intent to alter course, and then had confirmed this by another radio signal, "Execute!" For his part, Brinkmann had abandoned that practice back in the Denmark Strait. "A linguistically well trained intelligence service," he percipiently noted in the *Kriegstagebuch*, or war diary, "can gain valuable information even from fragments of radio signals."[21]

At 8:01 A.M. Admiral Lütjens, without consulting either Lindemann or Brinkmann, signaled the Naval High Command his damage report, and then almost as an afterthought informed Berlin: "Denmark Strait 50 nautical miles wide, floating mines, enemy two radars . . . Intention: to proceed to St. Nazaire, *Prinz Eugen* [to conduct] cruiser warfare."[22] The admiral had once more reached a critical decision without consultation—and without knowing the full extent of the damage to the *Bismarck* or the nature of the repairs required.

The news struck Berlin, Wilhelmshaven, and Paris like a bolt from the blue. A flurry of urgent telephone calls concerning Lütjens' intentions and his reasons for this dramatic change in Rhine Exercise rattled across German-occupied Europe. In Berlin, Grand Admiral Raeder immediately rang up his chief of staff, Admiral Otto Schniewind; thereafter, both men discussed the fleet chief's strange signal with General Admiral Alfred Saalwächter of Naval Group Command West in Paris and General Admiral Rolf Carls of Naval Group Command North in Wilhelmshaven. Without precise information as to the physical state of the task force or of the extent of damages inflicted on the *Prince of Wales*, none of the admirals ashore was prepared to issue direct orders to Lütjens. All command posts on the Continent merely assumed that the task force commander would continue into the open Atlantic, as prescribed by the operational orders previously issued for Rhine Exercise.[23] Carls simply informed Lütjens of the whereabouts of the nearest supply ships and tankers: the *Belchen* in quadrant AJ 25, the *Lothringen* in AJ 16, the *Gonzenheim* in AJ 58, the *Kota Penang* in BC 35, the *Spichern* in BD 94, the *Esso-Hamburg* in BE 74, and the *Friedrich Breme* in BE 94.

Last but not least, Raeder telephoned Hitler at the Oberzalzberg in the Bavarian Alps. The Führer received the news of the sinking of the *Hood* stoically, with no joy and none of the usual triumphalism. Undoubtedly his nagging fears concerning the vulnerability of the big ships to airpower surfaced yet again.[24] After hearing Raeder's report, Hitler turned to his retinue and expressed his personal thoughts:

> If now these British cruisers are maintaining contact and Lütjens has sunk the *Hood* and nearly crippled the other, which was brand new and having trouble with her guns during the action, why didn't he sink her too? Why hasn't he tried to get out of there or why hasn't he turned around?[25]

Once more, Hitler, who seemed to demand either that the *Prince of Wales* be finished off or that the task force return home, put the navy on alert.

Admiral Lütjens, having reached his second fateful decision in two days, awaited his captains' after-action reports. Lindemann stated that the *Bismarck* had fired but 93 15-inch shells during the course of the battle.[26] Brinkmann noted an expenditure of 179 8-inch shells for the *Prinz Eugen*. Next came the damage reports. While Brinkmann happily informed the admiral that his ship had received not a single direct hit, Lindemann's report was a sobering document. He apprised Lütjens of the three hits that the *Bismarck* had taken, and then turned to the current damage-control report.

Since receiving the first hit in the forecastle, the *Bismarck*'s six damage-control parties, each with twenty-six men, had been at work without stop to repair the damage. Given that the tips of the starboard propeller could be seen out of the water, Lindemann had ordered Warrant Officer Wilhelm Schmidt, in charge of damage-control team no. 1, to flood Sections II and III astern to restore the ship's trim. Next, he had sent Lieutenant Richter and several divers into the fo'c'sle with instructions to connect the forward fuel tanks, holding 1,000 tons of precious fuel, first directly to the fuel tanks near the boiler room and then to the rear fuel tanks by way of a provisional line run over the ship's upper deck. When both of those maneuvers failed, Lindemann requested permission to slow down and to heel the *Bismarck* first to one side and then the other to allow the holes in the forward hull to be patched temporarily by welding plates against them from the inside. But Lütjens refused permission to reduce speed—again without comment. Eventually, the admiral had to agree to reduce speed to 22 knots so that collision matting and hammocks could be stuffed into the holes in the no. 2 boiler room and the auxiliary boiler room at least to slow the growing intake of seawater. But this maneuver also failed. Richter, standing in the no. 2 boiler room in seawater up to his chest, abandoned the pumps; the boiler had to be shut down. The *Bismarck* continued, bow down by 3 degrees, with best speed reduced to 28 knots. In the wardroom, the *Bismarck*'s officers gathered to offer a champagne toast to Commander Schneider for his superb artillery work against the *Hood*. The ship's crew was given an abundant issue of chocolate, sausage, and cigarettes that evening.

Given the loss of the *Bismarck*'s war diary, one can only conjecture what prompted Admiral Lütjens to abandon Rhine Exercise. Less than two hours earlier, he had refused to break off the operation and to pursue the fleeing *Prince of Wales*. The fleet chief's motives were probably a mix of pressing considerations, all of which added up to abandoning Rhine Exercise. First, the element of surprise, a sine qua non for the operation, had definitely been lost. Second, the task force continued to be shadowed by the heavy cruisers *Suffolk* and *Norfolk*, and around noon even by the *Prince of Wales*; two of its pursuers mounted state-of-the-art Type 284 radar sets. Lütjens' special mention of "enemy two radars" in his terse signal to Naval High Command that morning underlined his continuing fears that the enemy had developed a special electronic detection system unknown to the Germans. His own forward radar-detection set had been out of order since the clash with HMS *Norfolk* in the Denmark Strait. Third, the *Bismarck* was running dangerously low on fuel. A thousand tons of fuel remained inaccessible in the forward storage tanks. The fact that Lütjens had insisted on leaving Gotenhafen before the ship's tanks had been fully filled, that he had refused to top up in the Grimstadfjord in Norway, and that he had eschewed refueling from the tankers *Weissenburg* or *Wollin* in the Norwegian Sea before entering the Denmark Strait now became relevant. Fourth, Lütjens continued to believe that the heavy ship shadowing him was the efficient *King George V*. Might it not try to lure him onto Admiral Tovey's Home Fleet, which was sure to have steamed out of Scapa Flow upon receiving first news of the *Hood*'s fate? Fifth, the *Bismarck*, with two holes in her bow and 2,000 tons of water in her fo'c'sle, had lost 2 knots of critical speed. Add to that the loss of some electric power, a steady leakage of fuel, and the possibility that two boilers contaminated with seawater might also have to be shut down soon, and Lütjens' decision to abort Rhine Exercise made eminent sense.

But why head for St. Nazaire, 2,000 nautical miles to the south and within reach of Vice Admiral Sir James Somerville's powerful Force H, based on Gibraltar? A first observation: Brest, which was closer than St. Nazaire, was out of the question, as it lay within ready range of the Royal Air Force and as it already berthed the 11-inch battleships *Scharnhorst* and *Gneisenau*, undergoing repairs. That left three other possible avenues of return by way of Norway: back through the Denmark Strait to Trondheim (1,400 nautical miles), through the waters south of Iceland to Trondheim (1,300), or via the same course to Bergen (1,150).[27] Most likely Lütjens decided against the passage south of Iceland, the shortest, because it would force him to pass by the Faeroes and Shetlands and thus expose his task force to the greatest concentration of hostile air, sea, and coastal forces. That left the return passage through the Denmark Strait. There the admiral could count on the rain and fog to hide his movements through the ice pack, hostile aircraft were likely to be kept down because of the customary inclement weather, and the *Bismarck* was least likely to encounter heavy British naval units, as the Home Fleet out of Scapa Flow most likely had rushed out to the scene of the *Hood*'s demise.

This should have been the route of choice, but Admiral Lütjens instead chose to head to St. Nazaire. Three considerations probably motivated him. First, his fear of superior British radar militated against another dash through the narrow channel of the Denmark Strait, where earlier he hadn't been able to shake the *Suffolk* or the *Norfolk*. German intelligence would be of no help: the B-Dienst in the recent past had assured him not only that the task force's dash through the North Sea and the Denmark Strait had gone undetected, but also that the *Hood* still stood off West Africa. Lütjens' references in the same signal to Naval High Command in Berlin concerning "floating mines" and the strait being but "50 nautical miles wide" indicate his hesitancy in retracing his earlier route. Second, there was the nagging matter of the primary mission. St. Nazaire was on a southerly route, which translated into more hours of darkness to make good his escape. It possessed a dry dock large enough for the *Bismarck* to repair her punctured hull. And, most important, it provided a convenient point of departure for a resumption of Rhine Exercise.[28] In fact, the *Bismarck* was soon rife with rumors that the fleet chief intended to resume the Atlantic mission as soon as the necessary repairs had been undertaken in St. Nazaire.[29] Augmented by the *Scharnhorst* and the *Gneisenau*, once repaired and seaworthy again, the *Bismarck* could also rejoin the *Prinz Eugen* and thus confront the British with a formidable task force along the Atlantic's busy convoy routes. Third, the 400-nautical-mile-longer run to St. Nazaire might also deplete the fuel reserves of his notoriously short-legged pursuers. Obviously, the admiral could not know that the British cruisers had replenished their fuel supply at Iceland.

According to *Bismarck* survivors who had been on the bridge that day, there had taken place yet another terse exchange between Lütjens and Lindemann. The *Bismarck*'s skipper had recommended that the ship return at once to Bergen. The *Bismarck*, in Lindemann's view, was "too fine a ship to be risked in further unequal engagements." According to these survivors, what they termed the "friction" between Lütjens and Lindemann extended to their respective staffs and officers.[30] Once more the task force commander simply overruled the flagship's captain.

Having lost the argument, at 9:50 A.M. Lindemann signaled his damage report to Captain Brinkmann by flag.

> I have received 2 heavy hits. One in Sections XIII–XIV. Thereby loss of electrical station 4; port boiler room is taking on water, which we can control. Second hit Sect. XX–XXI in forecastle. Shell entered port, exited starboard above armored deck. Third hit on a boat, of no concern. Otherwise I am well. 5 lightly wounded.[31]

Twenty minutes later Lütjens ordered the *Prinz Eugen* to fall astern the *Bismarck* to confirm the oil slick. Brinkmann reported to Lindemann, his classmate at the Navy School, that the men on board the heavy cruiser could not only see but also smell "broad streams of oil on both sides of [the *Bismarck*'s] wake."[32] Mission accomplished, Admiral Lütjens returned the *Prinz Eugen* to a position ahead of the battleship to take advantage of her forward FuMO radar detector. Already a short Sunderland flying boat out of Iceland had reported the *Bismarck*'s oil slick to HMS *Suffolk*. That very moment, at 11 A.M., the weather took a turn for the better as far as Lütjens' designs were concerned. Haze turned to fog, and rain squalls alternated with brief breaks of sunshine. Meanwhile, German radio intelligence aboard both ships reported that the British shadowers managed to maintain contact at 33,000 yards.

After Captain Leach had broken off the action, the *Prince of Wales* waited for the heavy cruisers *Norfolk* and *Suffolk* to come up. Rear Admiral Wake-Walker took command, then assessed the damage to the *Prince of Wales*. The battleship was in rough shape. Only three of her ten main guns would fire, her Y turret would not rotate, her bridge was a smoking ruin, she had 400 tons of seawater in her stern compartments, and her best speed had been reduced to 27 knots. Wake-Walker quickly decided that Leach had made the right call and that there was nothing to be done for the moment but to resume trailing the German task force. He ordered Leach to the rear while the men aboard the *Prince of Wales* cleared the wreckage of her bridge and tried to get the guns back in working order. The *Suffolk* and the *Norfolk* each took the same flank they had taken before the battle. Just after 11:00 A.M. the visibility began to decrease as all five ships ran under a weather front. At noon, the *Bismarck* and the *Prinz Eugen* disappeared into the rain and mist. The *Suffolk*'s radar kept watch.

Emotions ran high among the men and women at the wall chart in the Admiralty's Operations Centre. The *Hood* had been more than just another large warship, and her destruction had come at an especially bad time. German forces were pressing the British and their Commonwealth allies hard on Crete, the Battle of the Atlantic was going badly, and there were now growing signs of unrest in the Pacific. What had seemed twenty-four hours before to be a more or less sure thing had turned into disaster. Admiral Pound and the others had had every right to think they would bag the *Bismarck*, but now the *Hood* was gone, in a literal flash, just like that—an institution of the British Empire broken by German shells in less than ten minutes of battle. What now?

There were two dominant thoughts. First, all available resources had to be brought up from wherever they were and concentrated to hunt down the *Bismarck*. Second, why was Rear Admiral Wake-Walker hanging back and seemingly avoiding battle? Admiral Tovey and the main body of the Home Fleet were about 360 miles to the east of Wake-Walker, but given the fate of the *Hood*, Tovey alone could not be counted on. There was too much at stake to risk all on a single intercept at sea, as Vice Admiral Holland had tried and failed. So to both sides of the Atlantic the call went out to virtually every heavy British warship at sea to join the hunt. The light cruisers HMS *Manchester*, HMS *Birmingham*, and HMS *Arethusa* were ordered back to patrol the Iceland-Faeroes gap in the event that Admiral Lütjens broke back to the Norwegian coast. The battleship HMS *Rodney*, to the southeast of Wake-Walker, escorting the *Britannic* to the U.S. East Coast and itself due for repairs in the Boston Navy Yard, was told to divert to join Tovey's force. Another battleship, HMS *Ramillies*, some 900 miles to the south of the *Bismarck*'s position, was ordered to leave convoy HX 127 and take a position west of the German battleship. HMS *Revenge*, a third battleship, riding at anchor in Halifax Harbor, was told to leave immediately and shape course to intercept. The light cruiser *Edinburgh* was to join Wake-Walker and share shadowing duties.

In the early afternoon Admiral Pound tried to hurry Wake-Walker to engage the *Bismarck* once again. He radioed a long message to the *Norfolk* to ask for information about how much ammunition the *Bismarck* might have expended, how much damage she had suffered, and why she had made numerous minor course changes. The first sea lord also wanted to know what Wake-Walker's intentions were to reengage. Rear Admiral Wake-Walker was no fool; he knew his career depended on his answers, and he was very cautious in his replies. He radioed the Admiralty that he thought the *Bismarck* was in excellent shape and had expended only about a hundred rounds of main-gun shells. He could not account for the *Bismarck*'s course changes except to suggest that she might be trying to shake her followers. More to the point, he emphasized the *Prince of Wales*' very poor condition and told Pound that he did not think the *Prince of Wales* should engage at all unless in company with other heavy ships. Pound did not reply, and Wake-Walker got the message. At 5:11 P.M. he ordered the *Prince of Wales*—now with nine out of ten guns working again—to move ahead of the *Norfolk* should any chance present itself to attack the *Bismarck* from astern.[33]

Just before 2 P.M., steaming in quadrant AK 11, some 240 miles east of Cape Farewell, the southern tip of Greenland, Admiral Lütjens ordered Captain Lindemann to shape a course of 180 degrees, due south for France. At the same time he signaled Paris, which had taken over control of Rhine Exercise from Wilhelmshaven, "'King George' and a cruiser maintaining contact. Intention: if no action, to attempt to lose them after dark." Next, Lütjens sent a radio message to the commander in chief of U-boats, requesting that the U-boats stationed between Newfoundland and Greenland to assist in Rhine Exercise instead be positioned in quadrant AJ 68, that is, across his intended path to St. Nazaire. Perhaps they could pick off one of the heavy cruisers, or even the slowed *Prince of Wales*.

Then, at 2:20 P.M., Admiral Lütjens dashed off a final Olympian command to Captain Brinkmann:

> Intend to shake off contact [with the enemy] as follows: *Bismarck* will turn away on a westerly course during rainsqualls. *Prinz Eugen* to maintain course and speed unless forced to turn away or 3 hours after *Bismarck* has turned away. Thereafter, release to refuel from [tankers] *Belchen* or *Lothringen*. Then conduct independent cruiser warfare. Execute on signal "Hood." Fleet.[34]

No prior discussions had been undertaken with Brinkmann or with Lindemann. No reasons were given for the decision.

As Lütjens contacted Paris concerning his intentions and requests, a Royal Air Force Catalina flying boat approached the *Bismarck* from astern. Lieutenant Karl Gellert's antiaircraft batteries managed to drive the intruder off, but not before it radioed the battleship's presence and dropped star shell in her wake to light up the battleship. At 3:15 P.M. German naval intelligence signaled the fleet chief about the presence of the U.S. Coast Guard cutter *Modoc* in quadrant AJ 3829, not far from the *Bismarck*. Later that night Vice Admiral Karl Dönitz confirmed the *Modoc*'s presence in quadrant AJ 3920.[35] Mere happenstance, or an overtly hostile action by a neutral power?

On 24 May 1941 the North Atlantic lived up to its reputation for nasty weather. Early in the day fog banks of ever-changing density and size engulfed the *Bismarck* and the *Prinz Eugen*, running on a course of 230 degrees south of Cape Farewell, Greenland. Later in the day rain showers sliced holes into the fog. A gentle to moderate breeze from the east kicked up large wavelets and scattered white-caps. Both ships had changed to a southerly course of 180 degrees, making 24 knots. The *Bismarck* remained 3 degrees down by the bow due to the hit she had taken in her forecastle. One hostile heavy cruiser, HMS *Suffolk*, as well as a battleship, which the Germans still believed to be "K3G," that is, HMS *King George V*, were shadowing the task force from a distance of about 11 miles. The two Kriegsmarine ships darted in and out of heavy rain squalls, making optical identification nearly impossible.

At precisely 3:40 P.M. Admiral Lütjens signaled the *Prinz Eugen*: "Execute *Hood*." The *Bismarck* immediately increased speed to 28 knots and veered off to starboard in a westerly direction. The *Prinz Eugen* again rang aircraft alert—and then spied the *Bismarck* coming up from astern out of the rainy haze. Captain Lindemann's ship had run into one of its British shadowers and therefore abandoned its westerly course. Lütjens sent a short signal to Brinkmann at 3:59 P.M.: "A heavy cruiser stands off to starboard!"[36] The *Prinz Eugen*'s captain now was certain that the two ships would remain together.

Fog banks returned by 6 P.M. For a second time Admiral Lütjens signaled Brinkmann: "Execute *Hood*." Again the *Bismarck* veered off to starboard, first on a westerly course and then on a northerly one. The *Prinz Eugen*'s second gunnery officer, Lieutenant Schmalenbach, poignantly recorded the parting of the two ships: "As the *Bismarck* turns away sharply, for the second time, the sea calms. Rain squalls hang like heavy curtains from low-flying clouds." The officers on the bridge of the heavy cruiser were almost overcome with melancholy. Suddenly the *Bismarck* reappeared out of the rain, and bright flashes of light tinged with brown powder smoke painted the sea as her heavy guns roared out in anger at HMS *Suffolk* once more. "Then the curtain of rain squalls closes for the last time. The 'big brother' disappears."[37]

For the first time since departing Gotenhafen in the early hours of 19 May, the *Bismarck* and the *Prinz Eugen* steamed on separate courses. While the battleship set out to shake off her British pursuers, the heavy cruiser acted as a decoy, continuing on a course due south at 24 knots. With a heavy heart, Captain Brinkmann left the bridge of the *Prinz Eugen* to update the ship's war diary. Twice Brinkmann wrote the sentence: "Unfortunately, I was not allowed to know the fleet [chief's] intentions."[38]

Left to his own devices, Captain Brinkmann considered his

options. "Refueling is of critical importance to my ship." Proceeding north to the tanker *Belchen* in quadrant AJ 25 was fraught with danger. First, the enemy would probably surmise that the *Prinz Eugen* was running low on fuel and that it might head for a tanker stationed off Greenland. Second, he would have to count on fighting an engagement off Greenland, should he head in that direction, as he had been dogged since morning "by a USA-aircraft." To the north and west, he would encounter more "American aircraft on patrol." And then there was the "American coast guard vessel [*Modoc*] in Quadrant AJ 3920." The intentions of the Americans were obvious: "They will certainly report me [to the British]."[39]

Next Brinkmann evaluated his chances if he continued on a southerly course. The broad stretches of the Atlantic offered greater opportunities to shake off possible pursuers. With every degree of latitude, the nights would get longer and thus reduce the chance of detection. And there would be less likelihood of being shadowed by American flyers. "Late in the evening of 24 May I was again detected twice by a USA-flying boat."[40] But where would the tankers *Esso-Hamburg* and *Spichern* be? Brinkmann decided to leave the decision with Naval Group Command West. He did not have long to wait: Paris replied almost immediately that the *Spichern* would be in quadrant BD 78 by 2 P.M. the next day and the *Esso-Hamburg* in quadrant CD by the 26th. "Therewith my decision to head south is final." At 11:43 P.M. Brinkmann recorded yet another contact made by hostile air. "Apparently we are dealing with an American machine."[41] Naval Group Command West reported that Grand Admiral Raeder was about to release a communiqué in Berlin to the effect that "American patrols, American convoys," and "darkened neutral warships" would be met with "German political intervention."[42] Raeder was ready to let the world know that he no longer considered the United States to be neutral.

The *Prinz Eugen* was a lucky ship. Not only had she escaped the encounter with the *Hood* and the *Prince of Wales* without a scratch, but also she was now free and clear in the Atlantic. At 6:06 A.M. on 26 May Captain Brinkmann spied the tanker *Spichern*. He could

Tribal class destroyer HMS *Cossack*, flotilla leader under command of Capt. Philip Vian RN.
(Courtesy of H.M.C.S. *Haida* Naval Museum, Toronto, Ontario)

Swordfish torpedo bombers on deck of HMS *Victorious* during the *Bismarck* chase. (Source: www.world-war.co.uk)

Reconditioned Fairey Swordfish torpedo bomber with 18-inch torpedo. (Courtesy of Gordon Bain, *Silver Wings*)

Battleship *Bismarck* down in the bow after three hits from HMS *Prince of Wales* during the Battle of Iceland. (Courtesy of Bundesarchiv-Koblenz)

Bismarck firing a broadside at HMS *Prince of Wales* during the Battle of Iceland.

(Courtesy of Bundesarchiv-Koblenz)

Bismarck firing a broadside during the Battle of Iceland, as observed from the *Prinz Eugen*.

(Courtesy of Bundesarchiv-Koblenz)

Battleship *Bismarck* in dazzle paint in Norwegian waters, May 21, 1941. (Courtesy of Bundesarchiv-Koblenz)

Battleship *Bismarck* easing out of the Blohm & Voss yards into the Elbe River at Hamburg. (Courtesy of Bundesarchiv-Koblenz)

U556 lying next to *Bismarck* in Hamburg. (Courtesy of Bundesarchiv-Koblenz)

Bismarck's twin rudders, her Achilles heel. (Courtesy of Bundesarchiv-Koblenz)

Hitler inspects *Bismarck* at Gotenhafen, May 5, 1941. (Courtesy of Bibliothek für Zeitgeschichte)

Right: Capt. Ernst Lindemann displaying rescue gear aboard the *Bismarck*.
(Courtesy of Bundesarchiv-Koblenz)

Below: Adm. Günther Lütjens visits the heavy cruiser *Hipper*.
(Courtesy of Bundesarchiv-Koblenz)

Above: First Officer Capt. Hans Oels on battleship *Bismarck*.

(Courtesy of Bundesarchiv-Koblenz)

Right: Adm. Erich Raeder congratulating Hitler on his 51st birthday.

(Courtesy of Bibliothek für Zeitgeschichte)

Left: Capt. Helmuth Brinkmann inspects his cruiser *Prinz Eugen*.

(Courtesy of Bundesarchiv-Koblenz)

Below: Watercolor by Edward Tufnell RN (Retired), depicting British battle cruiser *Renown*, battleship *Malaya*, and aircraft carrier *Ark Royal* operating together as force H in 1941.

(Courtesy of the U.S. Navy Art Collection, Washington, D.C. Donation of Melvin Conant, 1969. Photograph courtesy of U.S. Naval Historical Center)

HMS *Repulse* (British battle cruiser) firing her 15-inch guns during maneuvers off Portland, England, during the 1920s. HMS *Renown* is next astern. Photographed from HMS *Hood*.

(Courtesy of U.S. Naval Historical Center)

USS *New York* (BB-34) off North Africa, November 10, 1942, just after the Battle of Casablanca.
(Courtesy of U.S. Naval Historical Center)

HMS *King George V* (British battleship) at sea in company with U.S. Third Fleet ships, August 16, 1945. Photographed from USS *Bon Homme Richard* (CV-31). Just beyond *King George V* is USS *Missouri* (BB-63) with a British destroyer alongside. (Courtesy of U.S. Naval Historical Center)

Painting by J. C. Schmitz-Westerholt depicting the destruction of HMS *Hood*, May 24, 1941. HMS *Prince of Wales* is in the foreground. (Courtesy of U.S. Naval Historical Center)

HMS *Hood* in American waters, summer 1924. (Courtesy of U.S. Naval Historical Center)

HMS *Prince of Wales* lowering a Supermarine "Walrus" amphibian over the side in 1941.
(Courtesy of U.S. Naval Historical Center)

The Atlantic Charter summit. *Left to right*: Harry Hopkins, Averell Harriman, Adm. Ernest J. King, President Franklin D. Roosevelt, Gen. George C. Marshall, Prime Minister Winston Churchill, Field Marshal Sir John Dill, Adm. Harold R. Stark, and Adm. Dudley Pound. Photograph taken during church services aboard HMS *Prince of Wales*, off Newfoundland, August 10, 1941.

(Courtesy of U.S. Naval Historical Center)

Heavy cruiser *Prinz Eugen* in dazzle paint. (Courtesy of Bibliothek für Zeitgeschichte)

Swedish light cruiser *Gotland*. (Courtesy of Bibliothek für Zeitgeschichte)

scarcely conceal his joy: "We have made it!" The heavy cruiser was down to 250 tons of fuel. Brinkmann had avoided his worst nightmare: "to stop dead in the water with a fully intact ship."[43] From 8:30 A.M. to 10 P.M. the *Prinz Eugen* took on 2,815 tons of fuel from the *Spichern*.[44] Not a single hostile sighted her. Two days later, Brinkmann took on another 680 tons of fuel as well as 10 tons of fresh water and 8-inch shells from the *Esso-Hamburg* in quadrant CD 36 before smoke on the horizon forced him to break off the refueling. He was now ready to raid the target-rich environment of the Halifax (HX) convoys.

The heavy artillery from the *Bismarck* that Lieutenant Schmalenbach had observed from the *Prinz Eugen* had been directed at the battleship's old nemesis, HMS *Suffolk*. Admiral Lütjens had turned on his pursuer, guns blazing, to create a diversion that would allow the *Prinz Eugen* to escape undetected. The gambit worked. But no sooner had the *Suffolk* been driven off after laying down a thick cloud of smoke than another old acquaintance, HMS *Prince of Wales*, opened fire on the *Bismarck* at 6:47 P.M. Lütjens at once ordered a return to a southerly course. Both ships ceased firing as the distance between them grew to 17 miles. Neither side registered a hit. Unknown to Lütjens, two guns of the *Prince of Wales'* A turret had broken down. At 7:14 P.M. Lütjens briefly reported the encounter: "Short action with *King George V* without result. *Prinz Eugen* released to fuel. Enemy maintains contact."[45] On board the *Bismarck*, the feeling that the ship was now alone finally sank in. As did the knowledge that the British would activate every warship available to hunt her down.

On the admiral's bridge, Lütjens assessed his situation. His task force was now down to one ship, the *Bismarck*. Her hull had been holed, with the result that she was down by the bow and listing to port, with best speed reduced to 28 knots. Her forward radar-detection gear was out of order, and 1,000 tons of fuel remained inaccessible in the flooded forward compartments. There was no hope of reinforcement: the *Tirpitz* was still in the Baltic Sea undergoing final workup, and both the *Scharnhorst* and the *Gneisenau* remained in dock at Brest undergoing repairs. The *Bismarck* was beyond the range of Luftwaffe aircraft based in France. The enemy continued to shadow him from astern. There was no doubt in Lütjens' mind that Churchill would put every ship out to sea to find and sink the *Bismarck*. Indeed, at 5:22 P.M. Naval Group Command West passed on to the task force commander a message it had received from the Spanish Intelligence Service: "*Renown, Ark Royal*, and a *Sheffield*-class cruiser left Gibraltar during the night of 24 May, course unknown."[46]

CHAPTER 6

ROOSEVELT'S DILEMMA

AS WARSHIPS WENT, the United States Coast Guard cutter *Modoc* was as frail and weak as the *Bismarck* was mighty. In fact, the *Modoc* was no warship at all. She was an old and slow cutter now used primarily to ferry supplies from the United States to Greenland, to watch the outer perimeter of the U.S.-proclaimed neutrality zone, and to report on icebergs. Built in 1921, the *Modoc* displaced 1,780 tons, which made her about the size of a small destroyer, but unlike a destroyer, her turbo-electric motors could drive her no faster than 15 knots or so; she was armed with a handful of depth charges, two old 5-inch guns, and a number of machine guns. Her normal crew was 140 officers and men. Based at Wilmington, North Carolina, the *Modoc* had left the Boston Navy Yard at midmorning on 12 May and steamed directly to St. John's, Newfoundland, where she had moored on 16 May.[1] At 10:30 P.M. the night before she left Boston, Richard L. Davies, a highly placed Washington, D.C., civilian, slipped aboard. His ostensive purpose for taking this long and dangerous cruise into North Atlantic waters was to help the United

States Coast Guard ensure the continued operation of a small but vital cryolite mine at Ivigtut, on the south western coast of Greenland.[2]

A rare mineral composed of sodium and aluminum fluoride, cryolite was used principally as a flux in the smelting of aluminum. In World War II aluminum was the primary metal used in the production of aircraft skin; the United States had a number of important deposits of bauxite, from which aluminum is made, and British Guiana and Canada had even more. But none of these countries had cryolite, most of which came from the small mine at Ivigtut. This was one reason why the United States had assumed responsibility for the defense of Greenland from the government of occupied Denmark on 9 April 1941. There were two other reasons, both of which may have been connected to the Davies mission: to set up military bases in Greenland to counter German use of Greenland to strike at U.S. bases in Newfoundland or the northeast coast of the United States, or to build airfields that might be used both to patrol the North Atlantic for U-boats and to allow Canada and the United States to ferry short-range aircraft from North America to the United Kingdom.[3]

By the fall of 1940, evidence had started to mount that Germany was intensely interested in Greenland. Not only was Greenland an important step from Europe to North America, but the southern tip of Greenland, Cape Farewell, jutted almost into the main North Atlantic convoy routes, while the massive ice sheet that covered the island was a key factor influencing weather over the European continent. Throughout the war, Germany slipped agents into the remote Greenland fjords to set up clandestine weather stations or to establish listening posts to spy on Allied radio transmissions. Sometimes the Germans used Norwegian or Danish vessels and hired their crews to serve the Reich's purposes. Reports of German landings and even of German aircraft flying over remote Greenland islands or German patrol boats nosing up Greenland fjords reached the Americans and the British. In late summer 1940 a mixed British–Free Norwegian commando force attacked and destroyed a number of German weather and radio stations on the eastern shore of Greenland and took a number of heavily armed Danish "hunters" into custody. Both Britain and Canada had warned the United States that Greenland had to be occupied by an ally to forestall German intentions. That eventually forced the Americans' hand on 9 April 1941.

The *Modoc* started out from St. John's on 17 May 1941 and headed for the south coast of Greenland for a rendezvous at sea with the Coast Guard cutter *Northland*. The *Northland* was a few years newer than the *Modoc*, but larger and heavier, with a hull designed for icebreaking operations. The *Modoc*'s mission was to relieve the *Northland*, assume command of the Greenland Patrol from the *Northland*'s skipper, and arrange the safe transfer of a U.S. Army reconnaissance team from the *Northland* to the Greenland motor ship *Ternen*.[4] Almost as soon as the *Modoc* cleared the narrow harbor mouth of St. John's, she was being swept by heavy seas driven by that same low-pressure system that would bring wind, rain, and heavy cloud to the North Sea when Admiral Sir John Tovey's Home Fleet sortied from Scapa Flow several days later. In the late afternoon of 20 May, the *Modoc* and the *Northland* began to prepare for their meeting at sea about 200 miles northeast of the northern entrance to the Strait of Belle Isle. The wind blew from the northwest at 30 miles an hour, pushing waves 6 feet high ahead of it. It wasn't much of a swell for a battle wagon, but it was rough for a cutter of the *Modoc*'s size. Slowly and with great difficulty, her commanding officer, Coast Guard Lieutenant Commander H. G. Belford, brought the *Modoc* close to the *Northland*. Then, as soon as mail, movies, and vital documents were transferred by motor launch, the *Northland* shaped course for Boston; the *Modoc* resumed her trip due north to southern Greenland.[5]

As the *Northland* and the *Modoc* split up, convoy HX 126 was being slaughtered about 400 miles to the northeast. Outbound from Halifax with fuel and food for Britain, U-94 had spotted the convoy late the previous evening. There was only one inadequate escort, an auxiliary cruiser. U-boats this far west were still rare at that point in the war, which was why the nearest British destroyers and corvettes were moored in Hvalfjord, Iceland. In the early-morning hours of 20 May, however, Lieutenant Herbert Kuppisch's U-94 attacked, sinking three merchantmen in short order. The ether was filled with the Morse code signal "SSS," the international distress call of ships torpedoed, and the night sky was white with distress rockets as the submariners struck. Torpedoes thundered into ships' sides or exploded under their keels; survivors scrambled for the life boats, the Carley floats, or any piece of junk that might keep them afloat. The water temperature was 45 degrees Fahrenheit; anyone not in a lifeboat or on a raft would be dead within an hour. But distress calls were not the only radio signals going out in the dark hours of 20 May; U-94 radioed the convoy's speed, position and direction to Admiral Karl Dönitz' other gray sharks in the vicinity. They came quickly, chewing their way through the remnants of HX 126; seven more ships went down. Kuppisch, unknowingly, was about to become embroiled in the *Bismarck* saga. The convoy scattered to the wind over a thousand square miles of ocean. The Royal Navy's Escort Group 12 steamed westward from Iceland at high speed; the *Modoc* and the *Northland* were ordered to search eastward for survivors in mounting seas.[6]

The two American vessels steered toward Iceland, directly into the war zone. As ostensive neutrals, they broadcast hourly reports in the clear announcing who they were, where they were, and what their mission was. They kept their lights on after dark, flew large U.S. flags from their jackstaffs, and kept two even larger flags ready to spread on their decks, fore and aft, if approached by air. As they steamed slowly eastward they found wreckage, oil slicks, and empty rafts and lifeboats, some with rations half eaten. They saw corpses in life jackets, rising and falling on the six- to seven-foot waves, staring sightlessly at the sodden sky. They saw the detritus of the Battle of the Atlantic, but they found no living being. Then, on the afternoon of 22 May, the *Northland* spotted a stricken British tanker. As the cutter nosed nearer in the heavy seas, they made her out to be the 8,470-ton *British Security*. She was abandoned, "wallowing in the swell, her decks awash," the *Northland*'s skipper, Commander E. H. "Iceberg" Smith, later reported. There was "a large gaping hole just forward of her bridge," and she was "completely burned from the results of the ensuing fire. The boat falls were still hanging in the water, eloquent testimony to the rapid departure of those who were able to escape." The *Northland* stayed near the ghostly tanker all night. Sometimes when the wind died down a bit the Coast Guardsmen could hear banging metal or hollow groans from the old wreck across the water. She was still there at dawn, stubbornly refusing to succumb to her attackers and to the scavenger sea that demanded the last of her remains. The *Northland* pushed off.[7]

All that day and into the next, the *Modoc* and the *Northland* followed the current eastward along the main convoy track. They made occasional radio contact with ships that had survived the slaughter and saw and signaled British escorts trying to round up and reform the scattered convoy. All day the wind blew hard from the northwest. With the seas running high and the small ships tossed about, it was nearly impossible to search for rafts or small boats in the storm. Visibility deteriorated to less than a mile, especially when snow showers racing across the seascape enveloped them. Still they ran across wreckage. Once they spotted a group of empty, drifting lifeboats they had seen the day before, giving them confidence that they had correctly calculated the effect of wind and current on anything still floating. Then, on the afternoon of 23 May, the *Northland* caught a glimpse of the Royal Navy rescue trawler *Northern Wave* struggling eastward in the heavy swell. Signals were exchanged, and the two ships effected a rendezvous. The trawler captain told Smith that 120 men had been pulled from the sea but that 140 were still unaccounted for. He also informed him that the *Bismarck* was believed to be about 100 miles to the east.[8] "Iceberg" Smith passed the information to Lieutenant Commander Belford.

Several miles to the southeast of the *Northland*, the *Modoc* struggled through a box search pattern all day of the 23rd and into the 24th. At 4 A.M. she hove to alongside a large abandoned lifeboat. The boat contained life preservers, canned water, a boat box with flares and emergency rations, and a gas mask, but no people. There were no marks indicating which ship it was from.[9] They cast it adrift and continued to search. At 2:00 P.M. the off-duty watch gathered in the mess to watch a musical acquired from the *Northland* on the 20th. The sea ran high and the wind increased. Belford slowed the *Modoc* to about 6 knots, barely enough to keep her stem into the wind, then hove to about 5:30 P.M. The *Modoc* was about 300 miles southeast of Cape Farewell.

The Americans heard the Swordfish torpedo bomber about an hour later, before they caught sight of it struggling through broken cloud at about 1,500 feet. The Royal Navy aircraft was the first of nine of No. 825 Squadron, led by Acting Lieutenant Commander Eugene Esmonde, launched from the HMS *Victorious* about an hour earlier. Several hours before that, Admiral Tovey had ordered the *Victorious* and four cruisers to detach themselves from the main body of the Home Fleet and race to within about 100 miles of the *Bismarck*'s position to launch an air strike. In appalling conditions of high foaming seas and low scudding cloud, her flight deck pitching wildly, the carrier had drawn to 120 miles from the *Bismarck*, then reduced speed from 28 to 15 knots and turned ponderously into the wind. The old, slow torpedo bombers, flown mostly by neophyte pilots, struggled airborne. Each waited until the *Victorious* had pitched her stem down toward the sea, then gunned their engines. The Swordfish gathered speed as the flight deck rolled up, then launched themselves into the storm. They formed up as best they could and turned southwest, making just 85 knots into the teeth of the gale heading for Rear Admiral W. F. Wake-Walker's ships. Esmonde intended to use the ships to take a bead on the *Bismarck*, about 15 miles farther on from the heavy cruiser the HMS *Suffolk*. Newly equipped with an early version of the airborne ASV (air-to-surface-vessel) search radar, the Swordfish were Tovey's last hope of striking a blow to the *Bismarck* before total darkness.[10]

Aboard the *Modoc*, Lieutenant (jg) Dick Bacchus saw the Swordfish first. He had just come from a tour of duty near the U.S. Naval

Air Station at Norfolk, Virginia. "Hey, there's an airplane," he shouted, peering at the growing shape. Then, quickly, "Hey, that's a land plane," and as the Swordfish bore down, "My God, that *is* a land plane."[11] The torpedo bomber flew down the starboard side of the *Modoc*, banked, then flew back up, flashing recognition signals at the *Modoc*'s bridge. The *Modoc* answered, and the Swordfish flew off to the northwest. Every eye on deck followed the biplane as she flew just below the cloud bottoms toward the horizon. Then they saw an astonishing sight, about six miles away and broadside on: "A large battleship on the horizon dead ahead," Davies later wrote his wife.[12] The *Modoc* log entry was more prosaic: "1837 [6:37 P.M.] observed large unidentified man-of-war bearing 310T [north-northwest] approximately 10 miles distant proceeding course about 250°T [west-southwest]."[13] The *Bismarck* was still heading to the west after the gun action with the *Prince of Wales*.

Quickly someone manned the new and powerful signal light recently installed on the *Modoc*'s bridge. The signaler's hand banged down on the shutter lever as he blinked out "What ship?" and gave the *Modoc*'s name and nationality. Davies was standing right beside him: "We got no reply, until a little later, when we saw the flash of the battleship's guns, but not at us." Rushing past, the *Bismarck* did not deign to reply to the *Modoc*. The German vessel began to pull away rapidly when more Swordfish flew toward the *Modoc*. "Then we saw eight biplanes," Davies later wrote, "carrying torpedoes, wheeling around us. Then heading for the *Bismarck*."[14] Lieutenant Commander Belford ordered the U.S. flags spread on deck. It was 6:45 P.M. The sky above the rapidly receding *Bismarck* lit up with antiaircraft fire as the Swordfish flew toward the German battleship. Belford ordered flank speed. The *Modoc* could barely make 15 knots in good weather, but she scuttled away from the battle as quickly as the heaving seas would allow, an unwitting witness to the Royal Navy's first effort to hit the *Bismarck* from the air.

After takeoff from the *Victorious*, Lieutenant Commander Esmonde's squadron had divided into three subflights of three aircraft each, then droned through the heavy weather, straining to catch a glimpse at the seascape. About an hour after launch, Esmonde's radar picked up a ship about 16 miles off his port bow. Then, through a rapidly closing gap in the clouds, he saw the *Bismarck*'s massive bulk, foaming bow wave, and long curving wake. Then the *Bismarck* was gone, lost in the overcast. Esmonde's planes altered course to the northeast. The light was fading fast. Where was she? Two blips on the radar screen, one to port, the other to starboard. The Swordfish let down through the low clouds, almost to mast height, and spotted Rear Admiral Wake-Walker's three gray warships hurrying along about 15 miles back of the *Bismarck*. Esmonde circled the *Norfolk*, and his observer blinked out a message. Where was the *Bismarck*? There, 14 miles, almost due south. The British aviators climbed back to 1,500 feet and banked away. They flew on through low cloud, hoping to maneuver to a position where they could swoop down out of the overcast on both of the *Bismarck*'s beams, deliver a swift attack, then climb back into the cloud. Esmonde's radar picked up another vessel, and he descended to begin his torpedo run. But it was not the *Bismarck*. It was the *Modoc*, hove to in the heavy swell. The *Bismarck* was another 6 miles away.

Very few of Esmonde's pilots had ever delivered a torpedo attack, much less taken off from a pitching carrier and, later, found their way back in the dark for a night landing. A torpedo attack was no easy thing, even in practice. The standard Royal Navy 18-inch aerial torpedo was smaller than the submarine or destroyer-borne version, but it still weighed 1,610 pounds and had enough explosive packed into its warhead to sink a 10,000-ton freighter. Royal Navy torpedo bomber pilots were taught to approach the target from a steep dive of 180 knots or more. With an open cockpit, it was like standing on the rudder bar with the tops of their faces fully exposed to the wind and the prop wash. Ideally, they would begin their pullout still a mile or so from the target, reduce speed to 90 knots, then hold steady at 60 feet above the water; no more and no less. Few Swordfish were equipped with blind-flying instrument panels at that stage of the war, so the pilots had to estimate their height as they bore in to the target. Aiming was done with a crude, Rube Goldberg–like device that used light bulbs mounted on a horizontal bar fastened to the top of the fuselage ahead of the cockpit that gave a pilot his true aiming point ahead of his target. From then on, he had to hold course and speed until the drop point while every small-, medium-, and even large-caliber gun mounted on the target fired at him. At the same time the enemy coxswain spun his wheel and the heavy ship twisted and turned at high speed to throw off the torpedo bomber's aim. If the Swordfish reached the drop point, the pilot had to hold the aircraft absolutely steady in a slight nose-up position so that the torpedo would enter the water at the correct angle and run true. If the Swordfish's nose was too high or too low, the torpedo would dive and "porpoise."[15]

Esmonde's eight aircraft (one aircraft had lost its way in the cloud) turned toward the *Bismarck*. They dove to 100 or so feet above the sea surface, split up, and began their attack runs. It was just after 11:30 P.M.

"Alarm! 240 degrees! 5, 3 aircraft approaching!"[16] Aboard the *Bismarck*, Seaman Apprentice Georg Herzog of the port third 1.5-inch antiaircraft (flak) mount spotted several pair of double-winged aircraft coming at the *Bismarck* on the port bow at 11:33 P.M. The hostiles were flying low out of the northeast, torpedoes menacingly hanging from their fuselages. In an instant, the *Bismarck* was transformed into a mountain of fire. The sixteen 4-inch heavy antiaircraft batteries leapt into action, followed immediately by an equal number of medium 1.5-inch flak, and then twenty .75-inch light flak "pom-poms." Barrels fired until they were red-hot. Paint blistered. A fire hose was turned on a gun to cool it down. Some of the lighter flak guns' breech mechanisms jammed. Smoke poured across the battleship's decks and superstructure. First Gunnery Officer Adalbert Schneider also joined in the mêlée. Schneider ordered the great 15-inch guns as well as the secondary armament's 6-inch barrels to their lowest possible elevation (–8°) and fired round after round into the ocean ahead of the approaching aircraft. Giant columns of water rose ahead of the *Bismarck* as the shells splashed into the sea, but they failed to bring down any of the hostile aircraft. Closer and closer the planes came. Some seemed barely to skim along the top of the Atlantic swells.

On the open bridge, Captain Ernst Lindemann roared, "Hard a-port!" Barely had the coxswain, Seaman Hans Hansen, executed the order than Lindemann roared again, "Hard a-starboard!" Lindemann increased speed to 27 knots and began to zigzag sharply to avoid the incoming torpedoes. Over and over, Lindemann repeated the orders to turn hard to port and then hard to starboard. After a few minutes Hansen could no longer keep up with the captain's commands and simply kept heeling the ship from port to starboard as quickly as he could. The *Bismarck*'s violent zizags ripped the matting that had just been placed over the holes in her hull, causing great amounts of water to rush into her forecastle. The ship was now even more deeply down by the bows. Vibrations from the firing of the main artillery ripped open the already damaged bulkhead between the no. 2 boiler room and the adjacent electric power station, flooding the boiler room and causing it to be closed down.

The attackers held course as the *Bismarck* twisted and turned at high speed to avoid the torpedoes that had been set to run at 31 feet below the sea surface. The slow biplanes came on, three abreast pounding toward the *Bismarck*'s port beam, another three abreast at her port bow. Another flew across her bow and banked sharply right to launch at the *Bismarck*'s starboard. An eighth flew ahead of the others to launch at her port beam.[17] The German pom-poms and Oerlikon guns blasted away as the Swordfish bore in. As the bombers droned toward their release points, the huge 15-inch shells of the *Bismarck*'s main guns threw up massive columns of seawater in front of them. Flying into one of those columns would mean instant destruction.

One of the attacking aircraft was Swordfish C of Lieutenant Commander Esmonde's subflight. Acting Sub-Lieutenant J. C. Thompson, RN, flew the aircraft. He and his two crewmen were as green as grass. They had crawled into the air at 10:15 P.M., formed up on Esmonde, and then followed him southwest as he flew toward

Wake-Walker's ships. After an hour they had sighted the three gray Royal Navy warships pounding into the swell. The heavy cruiser HMS *Norfolk* flashed a signal at them. The *Bismarck* was 14 miles off on the starboard bow. They circled the British ships, then headed for the *Bismarck*, but first flew over "a small vessel that appeared to be stationary." This was the *Modoc*. They circled the *Modoc* before once again heading for the German battleship. They spotted her through gaps in the cloud. The *Bismarck* opened fire "almost at once, bursts appearing very close to the squadron." Esmonde's aircraft was hit. He climbed into the cloud and Thompson lost sight of him. For a split second Thompson caught sight of Swordfish B, flown by Acting Lieutenant N. G. Maclean, RN. Then Maclean disappeared too, and Thompson was on his own.

He pushed the stick forward, lower and lower, miraculously evading the antiaircraft fire. He tried to work his aircraft around to the starboard side of the weaving battleship. No dice. The *Bismarck* lurched to port in a sharp turn. Thompson pulled back on the stick and zoomed up into the clouds again to avoid the streams of tracer and the exploding shells. Then he pushed the stick sharply forward and dove steeply toward the water and the *Bismarck*'s port beam. He pulled out of the dive about half a mile from the side of the fast-looming battleship. He could see no other aircraft. At 90 knots the Swordfish bore in, buffeted by the wind and bounced by the shellfire. Thompson cleared his mind of any thought of sudden destruction and focused on the lighted bar. He remembered that for each five knots of target speed, he was to count one bulb to the left or right of his aiming point, but he was so close now that he could see men running this way and that on deck, and every gun mounted above that massive dark gray hull seemed to be firing at him. At 500 yards he pushed the button on the throttle that released the torpedo. The Swordfish bucked up as soon as the weight was clear. Thompson zoomed over the *Bismarck*, kicking rudder frantically as he zigzagged the Swordfish over the water for two miles before beginning his pullout. His gunner and observer saw a large column of smoke rising from the *Bismarck*'s side, but no sign of a hit from their own torpedo.[18] The torpedo that Thompson's two crew members saw strike the *Bismarck* on the port side was the only one to hit home. In the confusion of the attack, none of Esmonde's pilots were sure who had launched it, but most noticed a large puff of thick black smoke that belched from the *Bismarck*'s funnel when it struck.

Suddenly the *Bismarck* shuddered. A column of water rose off the starboard side amidships as high as Commander Schneider's gunnery-control station in the Vormars. A torpedo hit. The combination of waterspout and blast concussion from the 300-pound warhead hurled Chief Petty Officer Kurt Kirchberg, who was bringing ammunition up to the deck, against the aircraft catapult. Kirchberg became the *Bismarck*'s first battle casualty. His body was sewn into sailcloth and laid into a boat. To head off any panic among the crew, Lindemann announced over the loudspeaker: "The torpedo hit is harmless, just a few paint scratches!"[19]

The kipper launched by the second wave of Swordfish torpedo bombers had exploded against the *Bismarck*'s citadel armor belt starboardside between Sections VIII and X, thrusting the ship sideways and causing her to list to port. Lights went out in the command and damage-control centers. Five seamen suffered broken bones. Then, as quickly as it had begun, the attack was over. Lindemann reduced speed to 16 knots so that the damage-control teams could replace the matting in the holes in the forward hull. Gun crews exchanged wild stories about the number of aircraft that had attacked and been shot down—at least five, perhaps eight, and possibly twenty-seven. According to *Bismarck* survivors, Lindemann informed the crew that of the twenty-seven attacking planes, only one had managed to return to its carrier.[20] Of course, neither Lütjens nor Lindemann knew that the carrier was HMS *Victorious*, part of Admiral Tovey's task force out of Scapa Flow. At 11:38 P.M. Lütjens dispatched one of his customary terse radio signals: "Aircraft attack quadrant AK 19."[21]

Shortly after the fight with the *Victorious*' torpedo bombers, the *Bismarck* exchanged two or three salvos with the *Prince of Wales*, which, along with the heavy cruisers *Suffolk* and *Norfolk*, continued to shadow the German off the port quarter at a distance of 9 miles. The task force commander immediately apprised Paris of the action. "Short battle with 'King George' without result. Released 'Prinz Eugen' to refuel. Enemy maintains contact."[22] Then Lütjens ordered Lindemann to shape course for St. Nazaire. Finally, he sent off a flurry of radio signals to Naval Group West about the encounter with the Swordfish torpedo bombers. At 12:28 A.M.: "Attack by aircraft carrier planes. Torpedo hit starboard side." At 12:37 A.M.: "Expect further attacks." And at 1:53 A.M.: "Torpedo hit immaterial."[23]

The *Modoc* had a front-row seat for the torpedo bomber attack and for the short gun battle between Rear Admiral Wake-Walker's ships and the *Bismarck* that followed. But had she truly been an unwitting witness, as British and American records have attested? Or had she helped Esmonde's attackers pinpoint the *Bismarck*'s position in the low cloud and scudding rain? The official British version of the torpedo bomber attack, as recorded in "The Chase and Sinking of the 'Bismarck,' the Naval Staff History, Second World War Battle Summary No. 5," barely mentions the *Modoc*. It says only that when Esmonde's aircraft headed for the *Bismarck* after circling the *Norfolk* to get their bearings, they picked up a vessel on radar and descended through the clouds to find themselves flying over the *Modoc*. Then the *Bismarck* opened fire from six miles away, and they commenced their attack. Was Esmonde's radar so poor in quality that, as he neared the *Bismarck*, he could not differentiate between the 53,000-ton *Bismarck*, making south at over 25 knots, and the 1,700-ton *Modoc*, stationary, just 6 miles away? If he had not picked up the smaller *Modoc* on his radar and was surprised to see it there when he set down through the cloud cover, did he just fly directly to the *Bismarck* without any exchange of signals, as the first Swordfish had done about fifteen minutes earlier? Had no one in his squadron or on the *Victorious* picked up a report from the first Swordfish? Perhaps no report was made to preserve radio silence.

The *Modoc*'s log adds to the mystery of the role she played in the attack: "1845 [6:45 P.M.] observed squadron of 8 torpedo planes approaching from NE which circle *Modoc* and disappear to the westward. Noted anti-aircraft fire above aforementioned man of war."[24] So Esmonde's planes had circled the *Modoc*. That was Davies' recollection: "Then we saw eight biplanes, carrying torpedoes, wheeling around us. Then heading for the *Bismarck*."[25] Although neither account, written at a time when the United States was still officially neutral, mentions the *Modoc* helping the Swordfish, an account written thirty-nine years later offers a different view. In 1980 T. R. Sargent, the *Modoc*'s engineering officer, and B. M. Chiswell, her communications officer, wrote: "Suddenly seven [*sic*] British swordfisher torpedo planes were using us as a point of departure flying low over our masthead, waggling their wingtips, and heading for that distant gray shadow."[26] They concluded their recollections this way: "No doubt, *Modoc* played a vital role in the discovery of the *Bismarck*. . . . Certainly history has not given full due to the saga of the USCGC *Modoc*."

But then, why should history have recorded the *Modoc*'s role in the 24 May torpedo bomber attack on the *Bismarck*? The attack failed. The *Modoc* was no doubt in the middle of a major sea battle purely by coincidence, but the *Modoc* was also under orders, as every U.S. Navy and Coast Guard vessel was by the third week of May 1941, to help the British fight the Battle of the Atlantic, particularly by reporting German warships and submarines to the Royal Navy. The order had come from the President himself. It had capped off a growing operational relationship between the Royal Navy and the United States Navy that had started in earnest in the fall of 1940. On the evening of 24 May, when the British torpedo bombers circled over the *Modoc* and then headed straight for the *Bismarck*, United States Navy patrol bombers flying from Argentia, Newfoundland, were already heading out to help keep track of the *Bismarck* at the express instructions of Admiral Ernest J. King, commander in chief of the United States Atlantic Fleet.[27] This American aid was strictly off the record. At one point in the spring of 1941, for example, King landed at the U.S. Naval Air Station in Bermuda and asked—for the record—whether all help had been given to a recent British request to help locate a Vichy French naval vessel at sea. In the presence of others, two pilots told King that they had done what they could but that written orders limited them to flights no farther than 50 miles from Bermuda. Later, when the pilots were alone with King, they affirmed that they had flown five times that far in search of the Vichy warship.[28] The British were no more eager than the Americans to talk about U.S. aid. As one British chronicler of the *Bismarck* chase wrote many years after the war: "In a major naval operation of this kind, the British would have been loath to admit that they had needed 'outside' help."[29] No one is ever likely to know for sure what role the *Modoc* played in the 24 May torpedo bomber attack on the *Bismarck*, but it is a good bet that when Esmonde's Swordfish circled the *Modoc*, he asked where the *Bismarck* was, and was told.

The *Modoc*'s help in the search for the *Bismarck* was but the tip of the iceberg of U.S. involvement in the pursuit of the German battleship. At the moment the *Modoc* encountered the *Bismarck*, two United States Navy battleship task groups were also at sea in the Atlantic. The old USS *Texas*, accompanied by the brand-new *Benson*-class destroyers *Benson*, *Gleaves*, and *Mayo*, was then about 450 miles southwest of Cape Race. She was inbound to her home port at Newport, Rhode Island, after a patrol that had taken her to 250 miles southeast of where the *Modoc* lay hove to when Esmonde's Swordfish circled her. At that same moment, the *Texas*' sister ship, USS *New York*, accompanied by the *Sims*-class destroyers *Hughes*, *O'Brien*, and *Russell*, was 250 miles east of Montauk Point outbound from Norfolk, Virginia. The *New York*'s orders were to proceed to approximately the same spot as the *Texas*, some 300 miles south of the Denmark Strait's southern entrance, and, as the *Texas* had done, conduct training and maneuvers as she went.[30] At midnight on 24 May the *Bismarck* was heading directly for that very spot. Given Grand Admiral Erich Raeder's order to Admiral Lütjens concerning how to treat American naval vessels he encountered, and Lütjens' own growing contempt for the United States' very pro-British "neutrality," an encounter at sea between the *Bismarck* and either of the two U.S.

battleships would have probably resulted in the loss of the *Texas* or the *New York*, the deaths of many hundreds of U.S. seamen, and the entry of the United States into World War II.

Franklin Delano Roosevelt, thirty-third president of the United States, was fifty-seven when war broke out in September 1939. He was a bit more than one year shy of completing his second term and was still very popular among American voters. He had served as President Woodrow Wilson's assistant secretary of the navy during World War I and had run unsuccessfully for vice president on the Democratic Party ticket in 1924. Handsome, self-confident, educated at the best schools, Roosevelt exuded charm and charisma. His early political ambitions had appeared to suffer a severe blow when he was stricken with polio soon after his vice presidential run. After the disease had run its course, he was wheelchair-bound. He could walk only with severe difficulty and not without heavy braces, crutches, or assistance. But Roosevelt had another quality that served him well in life: a dogged determination to get where he wanted to be no matter what. In 1928 he was elected governor of New York; four years later he offered the American people action in the face of the despair of the depression and was elected president by a landslide. In March 1933 FDR was inaugurated, and he and his advisors, backed by a solidly Democratic Congress, immediately went to work trying to put Americans back to work. Roosevelt no doubt also took notice of the rise to power across the Atlantic of a younger man who had also promised his people that he would tackle their severe economic problems through vigorous action: Adolf Hitler.

The United States had sunk into isolationism in the early 1920s. Roosevelt had watched as the U.S. Senate rejected American membership in the League of Nations, dealing a severe blow to those like himself who believed that American security and prosperity depended strongly on American engagement. From his uncle, Theodore Roosevelt, president from 1901 to 1909, FDR had inherited a strong belief in internationalism, a love of the navy, and an understanding of sea power. He was an upstate New York patrician from a powerful and wealthy family, but he had the instincts of a democrat. He was strongly anti-imperialist and equally strongly antifascist. He deplored everything Hitler stood for, and he recognized, earlier than many Americans, the danger Hitler posed to world order, to peace, and to democracy. But Roosevelt had also seen at first hand how Wilson's internationalism had been shattered by post–World War I U.S. isolationism, and he was determined never to get ahead of public opinion when dealing with the fascists. He always tried to ensure that he had congressional support for everything he did. He was not about to risk his program of domestic reform, or divide his nation, by an overly activist foreign policy.

President Roosevelt and Prime Minister Winston Churchill had some things in common but were very different war leaders. The two men had abiding interests in their nation's navies. Churchill, of course, had been first lord of the Admiralty in World War I, while Roosevelt had been assistant secretary of the navy. FDR sometimes referred to the U.S. Navy as "my navy" and showed a deep interest in all aspects of naval life. He closely followed the U.S. Navy's naval reconstruction program, and he loved to hobnob with high-ranking naval officers. But unlike Churchill, he did not fancy himself as a strategist and, with rare exceptions, did not try to micromanage America's war. After the fall of France in June 1940 and Churchill's accession to the prime ministership, however, the greatest difference between the two men was that one was leading a nation on the verge of losing a war while the other was leading a neutral. Throughout their wartime relationship as heads of state of the two western Allies, Churchill was the supplicant.

When war broke out, Roosevelt had unhesitatingly signed a series of neutrality acts passed by Congress. He did not ask the American people to be neutral in thought and deed, as Wilson had done in 1914, because he himself felt no such neutrality and he knew the vast majority of the American people were no friends of Nazism. But the outbreak of war called forth a strong and growing neutrality movement, which enlisted many prominent Americans and many powerful members of Congress. This movement represented a widespread feeling in the United States that even if the Nazis were inimical to the "American way of life," the United States must stay out of the war. Most Americans also believed, as did the president, that Britain and France would handle Hitler and there would be no need for the United States to get involved. Besides, U.S. defense planners had for years believed that the United States' greatest potential enemy was Japan; that was why the great bulk of the U.S. fleet was based in the Pacific and why most U.S. war plans fingered Japan and not Germany.

The United States was neutral, but Roosevelt went as far as he thought he could go to help the Allies within the limits of his own presidential authority. On 5 September 1939 he established the Neutrality Patrol using mostly World War I–vintage ships that the United States could deploy off the Atlantic coast to keep warring nations out of a neutrality zone that stretched 300 miles seaward from the east coast of the Americas (except for Canada, which was at war). He authorized low-level secret staff talks between the United States Navy and the Royal Navy, aimed at sharing basic defense plans and establishing an ongoing liaison. But there was little else he could do until the fall of France in June 1940. That catastrophe galvanized FDR and his interventionist supporters into action, just as it swayed U.S. public opinion toward Britain. Roosevelt was greatly worried about the prospect of the Royal Navy passing to Germany after a possible British defeat. He worked through the prime minister of Canada, William Lyon Mackenzie King, to ensure that Churchill would not allow that to happen. In early August 1940 Canada and the United States concluded a continental defense pact.

In the summer of 1940, the president and his key military and foreign policy advisors, Secretary of the Navy Frank Knox, Secretary of War Henry Stimson, Chief of Naval Operations Admiral Harold R. "Betty" Stark, U.S. Army Chief of Staff George C. Marshall, and Secretary of State Cordell Hull, began to face the new reality of this war. The U-boats were already moving to former French naval bases along the Biscay coast, bringing them much closer to their mid-Atlantic hunting grounds. Convoy losses began to mount alarmingly. Britain barely hung on through the late summer of 1940, during the Battle of Britain and the London Blitz. If Britain fell, as the American ambassador to the United Kingdom, Joseph P. Kennedy, forecast it would, whatever equipment the United States had given the United Kingdom would have been wasted. Worse, the United States would have to live between a Hitler-dominated Europe and North Atlantic and a Japanese-dominated Pacific. The only option for FDR was to consider Britain America's first line of defense. The United States had to help in any way it could without declaring war on Germany. FDR told the nation in July 1940 that U.S. policy henceforth would be "all aid to [Britain] short of war." Discussions began between Britain and the United States aimed at transferring forty-four old U.S. "four-piper" destroyers to the Royal Navy and six to the Royal Canadian Navy in exchange for ninety-nine-year U.S. leases on bases of British territory from Newfoundland to the Caribbean. The "destroyers-for-bases" deal was announced in August 1940, and the transfers of the destroyers began in Halifax Harbor the following month.

Here was Roosevelt's dilemma: he knew the United States had no choice but to help Britain—that it was only a matter of time before the United States was also in the war. But he also knew that the neutrality movement in the United States was still powerful, especially in Congress. To compound this dilemma, or maybe to resolve it, he had also decided to run for an unprecedented third term as president in the upcoming November 1940 election. FDR, therefore, proceeded cautiously, fending off Churchill's regular beseechments for more aid, dragging his heels, seeming to assent to more help—or a more activist role—one day, only to ignore his commitments the next. Roosevelt conducted his foreign policy in the same way he had run his domestic programs; building consensus, trying not to get too far ahead of popular opinion, holding out to the last moment when necessary to avoid undue controversy, waiting until the solution to a problem was obvious, even to the dimmest of his political opponents, before he acted. All that was for public consumption, but beginning in July 1940, at Roosevelt's behest, the

United States Navy and the Royal Navy began to construct a close working relationship of the sort wartime allies might have had. The United States was not yet at war and no one knew when it might be, but as far as Roosevelt, Knox, and Stark were concerned, the time to plan for a war at sea was now.

In early August 1940 three men in business suits carrying briefcases stuffed with confidential military papers boarded a train at Washington's Union Station. Three hours later they were in New York, met in Manhattan by men who drove them to the Marine Air Terminal near Floyd Bennett Field in Brooklyn. The three men from Washington were no doubt happy to escape the oppressive heat and humidity of the capital in August. New York was not much better, but they weren't staying in New York. Toward evening they boarded the Pan-American clipper for a thirteen-hour flight to Lisbon with refueling stops in Bermuda and the Azores. In Lisbon they walked past neutral, Allied, and Axis passenger planes to board a KLM DC-3 bound for London. Officially, the three travelers constituted the Standardization of Arms Committee, sent from the United States to the United Kingdom to discuss the technical aspects of weapons standardization between the two countries.[31] In fact, however, they were a secret delegation of United States officers, chosen by Roosevelt to initiate high-level staff discussions between the two nations' military forces.

The head of the delegation was Rear Admiral Robert Lee Ghormley, fifty-six, assistant chief of naval operations and one of the finest planners in the U.S. Navy. Born in Portland, Oregon, Ghormley had graduated twelfth in his class at Annapolis and made his reputation as a consummate naval staff officer. His two colleagues were Brigadier General George V. Strong, deputy chief of the army's General Staff, and General Delos C. Emmons, commanding general, General Headquarters Air Force. Their visit was intended by Roosevelt, Knox, and Stimson, to be the first step in planning for eventual U.S. involvement in the current war. When the United States had joined the war against Germany in 1917, no real preparation had been made for the deployment of U.S. ground and naval forces;

months of confusion had undermined the initial U.S. effort, delaying effective U.S. involvement. Roosevelt and his senior military advisors were determined not to allow this to happen a second time. Although Strong and Emmons returned to the United States after a month or so in London, Ghormley set up shop in the U.S. embassy and stayed on as special naval observer. He did so not only because he was the head of the mission, but also because the U.S. Navy was already involved in the war at sea by virtue of enforcing Roosevelt's neutrality zone, and because the protection of the growing shipping traffic from the United States to the United Kingdom was a real consideration, not just a planning exercise. With FDR's Lend-Lease program due to begin in early 1941, U.S. naval involvement in the Battle of the Atlantic was certain to expand rapidly.

Ghormley was the highest-ranking U.S. Navy observer ever sent abroad on such a mission. The British and American press described him as a "mystery man," as a man who "kept his eyes open and his mouth shut," as if Ghormley was in London only to watch and learn. At least one historical account of Ghormley's mission describes him as being "in close, but still one way, liaison with the Admiralty," pleading in vain with his superiors in Washington to "permit full mutual discussions of common strategic problems."[32] In fact, Ghormley acted as Harold Stark's personal representative in dealing with the Admiralty. He took part in full discussions at the Admiralty on a wide range of issues and worked with Admiral Sir Dudley Pound, the first sea lord, and other high-ranking Royal Navy officers on the operational steps required to bring the U.S. Navy more fully into the Battle of the Atlantic. He and his British counterparts explored the sharing of intelligence, the allocation of escort resources, and the setting up of zones of responsibility. Ghormley was the ultimate source of a Stark memo to the president in mid-November 1940 explaining why U.S. naval involvement in the war was inevitable. Of greatest long-term importance, Ghormley secured a commitment from the British that in the event Japan and the United States went to war in the Pacific, the Royal Navy would "safeguard all mutual interests in the Atlantic" so that the

U.S. fleet would "be free to operate in the Pacific."[33] This British commitment to "prevent any naval aggression in the Western Atlantic against the Western Hemisphere by the Axis Powers" was repeated often in the ensuing months.[34] Ghormley took it as an unwavering commitment.

November 1940 was a difficult time in London. German bombers came every night. Residents heard the drone of aircraft engines, saw the swaying searchlights; the heavy "ack-ack" guns firing from Regent's Park or Hyde Park lit the sky in intermittent flashes. Through the night the whistle of the incendiaries and the powerful blasts of the parachute mines intermingled with the bells of the emergency vehicles and the loud cries of air raid wardens and volunteers. Each night men, women, and children died beneath the bombs. Dawn revealed smoking wreckage where blocks of flats or stores had once existed, huge craters, water flowing in the streets from the previous night's fire hoses or broken water mains, brick and tile and glass on sidewalks, and traffic routed around still-buried, unexploded bombs. The small American community in London was divided between those like Joseph Kennedy, who saw around them the wreckage of a decaying imperial power about to be supplanted by a younger and more vigorous Germany, and those like Edward R. Murrow, the CBS radio newsman who chronicled the heroic struggle of the British people to fight on alone. Ghormley believed that the United States was duty bound for both moral and political reasons to help the United Kingdom in any way it could. Each morning as he was driven through the rubble-strewn streets from the U.S. embassy to the Admiralty, his determination to help grew stronger.

One of his most important meetings took place on 22 November 1940 when, accompanied by Captain Alan G. Kirk, USN, and Lieutenant Commander B. L. Austin, USN, he met Admiral Sir Sidney Bailey and four representatives of the British Chiefs of Staff Committee. They discussed possible plans of action in the event the United States became involved in a war with both Germany and Japan and agreed, again, that the United States might devote the bulk of its navy to the Pacific war while the Royal Navy assumed the chief responsibility for keeping the Atlantic convoy routes open. But they did more than that; in effect they took inventory of both fleets—what ships were where—and made a preliminary allocation of whose ships should fight where in the event of war. They also determined how much of an American force was required in the Atlantic, and when it might be needed, to supplement the Royal Navy's ongoing program of convoy escort.

In view of the dangers posed by German surface raiders, the British sought the active participation of at least five American battleships.[35] The Americans did not have five battleships for the sea war in the Atlantic, but they did have three old and slow battleships due to enter dry dock for modernization and especially to have their guns and turrets rebuilt so as to increase their maximum main gun elevation from 15 degrees to 30 degrees. This modification would improve the current maximum range of their main guns to about 25,000 yards. The three battleships were the *New York*, the *Texas*, and the *Arkansas*; the *New York* and the *Texas* were due to enter dry dock at Norfolk Navy Yard in mid-March 1941 and would be unavailable until early February 1942.[36] Toward the end of November 1940, the director of war plans for the U.S. Navy wrote Admiral Stark to urge that the modification program for the two battleships be postponed indefinitely. Since most of the heavy-gun action in the war to date had been at distances of 24,000 yards or less, he did not see what real difference the increased gun elevation would make at that particular time. What it would most certainly do, however, was to take these battleships out of action for almost a year when they might be sorely needed. "The present state of world affairs," he wrote, "is such that this Division considers it unwise to have these battleships unavailable."[37] Stark agreed. On 7 December 1940 he deferred the proposed modifications "until some future date when the services of these ships can be spared for the required length of time."[38] The *Texas* and the *New York* were free to operate in the North Atlantic indefinitely.

In early January 1941 Ghormley prepared to return to the United

States for several months, where he was to play the key role in a new round of staff talks in Washington beginning at the end of that month. In the half year that he had been in London, Ghormley had come to know the Royal Navy's high command well, and had also received considerable attention from Churchill. From virtually the moment of his arrival, Churchill had wooed Ghormley at dinners at No. 10 Downing Street and in trips to see the ravaged English countryside. At the height of the invasion scare the previous fall, Churchill had taken Ghormley and U.S. naval attaché Commander Raymond Lee to Kent to see British defensive preparations. Ghormley had felt privileged and had written Churchill: "To me this is an occasion which will never be forgotten, not only for the enjoyable trip, but because a man loaded with responsibility can at the same time be the genial host which you were."[39] On 2 January 1941, when Ghormley and Admiral Pound met for lunch, the first sea lord reviewed the war at sea at that point, then added, almost as an afterthought, that the new German battleship *Bismarck* was almost ready for her sea trials.

There was shrewd calculation behind Churchill's ongoing efforts to win important Americans over. And it worked more often than not, as Harry Hopkins and Averell Harriman soon discovered. Both men followed Ghormley to London in short order, Hopkins in early January 1941 and Harriman in March. Hopkins' visit was intended to give Roosevelt an unembellished view of the British military situation. Originally a professional social worker, Hopkins had been a close policy advisor to the president since the earliest days of the New Deal. Churchill originally thought that Hopkins was coming to the United Kingdom to discuss British wartime social policy, but at dinner the first Saturday night Hopkins was in the United Kingdom, Hopkins told Churchill: "I came here to see how we can beat that fellow Hitler."[40] The next few days were devoted to ways and means to shore up the British war effort and especially to expedite Roosevelt's newly announced Lend-Lease program. Hopkins came back to Washington more convinced than ever that Britain must be helped as much as possible and without delay.

Lend-Lease was Roosevelt's single largest step toward active U.S. belligerence. Signed into law on 11 March 1941, the Lend-Lease Act gave the president authority to "exchange, lease, lend or otherwise dispose of" defense articles to be used by a foreign government acting in a manner the president deemed "vital to the defense of the United States." The original act specified the United Kingdom only, but at various times in the war it was extended to other Allied nations. This act made the U.S. the chief foreign supplier of war matériel to Britain and put aside the question of payment because, quite simply, Britain could no longer afford to buy it. Lend-Lease made it imperative that the U.S. Navy take upon itself much greater responsibility to ensure that cargo completed the journey from the United States to the United Kingdom, because if it did not, much of the Lend-Lease cargo would end up on the sea floor. At that point in the war, Roosevelt refused to countenance U.S. ships actually escorting convoys of non-U.S. vessels to the United Kingdom, but after Hopkins' return, and with Lend-Lease anticipated, a series of steps was taken to shore up the Royal Navy's escort capability and its effectiveness against the U-boats.

For much of the interwar period, the United States fleet, based at Pearl Harbor, Hawaii, had had only a token presence in the Atlantic. The American military's first priority was to prevent war with Japan by maintaining a strong presence in the Pacific. But with Nazi Germany's invasion of Poland in September 1939, the Atlantic theater grew in importance and danger. By the fall of 1939, the U.S. Navy's Atlantic Squadron had been beefed up and now included the old battleships *New York*, *Texas*, *Arkansas*, and *Wyoming*; the heavy cruisers *San Francisco*, *Tuscaloosa*, *Quincy*, and *Vincennes*; the aircraft carrier *Ranger*; and Destroyer Squadron 10. In February 1941 the U.S. fleet was divided into Atlantic, Pacific, and Asiatic fleets. The Atlantic Fleet, renamed Support Force Atlantic Fleet, was augmented by three destroyer squadrons under Admiral Arthur L. Bristol Jr.[41] Ernest J. King, sixty-two, was appointed CINCLANT (naval parlance for commander in chief, Atlantic Fleet) with a mandate to actively increase the U.S. Navy's presence in the neutrality zone and help the Royal Navy.

From a professional point of view, King's appointment was fitting. Though some might have thought him too old for the command, he had had a long, active, and varied career in the navy, mostly at sea. King knew the navy from the smallest harbor craft to the largest battleship and had served in many of them. In the spring of 1927, when he had initially been assigned to command the carrier USS *Wright*, he insisted on getting his aviator's wings, though he was already forty-eight. He was not a natural flier, but he made up for his lack of natural ability through hard work and dogged determination.

But King was a difficult man to work with in a post that would challenge the diplomatic abilities of even the most affable. Tall, well-built, and sure of himself, he was a gruff, outspoken, hard-drinking, poker-playing man who swore with the best of them. He was tough on his staff. He found it very difficult to delegate authority. When he had commanded the USS *Lexington* in the early 1930s, King had tried to run the entire ship from his bridge. He hated formality, palaver, and, most of all, delay. It was soon no secret in Washington that Stimson hated him. King fought with United States Army Air Force chief H. A. P. Arnold and with Marshall. His impatience was always on display, especially to the British, who grew to dislike him as much as he did them. One of King's biographers described him as a "dispassionate warrior who held his own political system in contempt and spurned all civilian authority except that of his commander in chief—the President. The Axis powers happened to be the enemy that he had to destroy." In fact, just before the war, King had considered Great Britain among the Republic's "greatest potential enemies and we may assume he would have fought the British as ruthlessly as he had Japan and Germany."[42] His antipathy for all things British was, at times, a real hindrance to the Allied war effort, as when he dragged his heels in early 1943 when ordered by the president to make very-long-range (VLR) antisubmarine Liberator patrol bombers available to the British and Canadian navies.

Shortly after his appointment, King shifted his flag from USS

Texas to the new heavy cruiser *Augusta* and set up his headquarters near the U.S. Naval War College in Newport, Rhode Island. He then flew to every major East Coast base in the U.S. Navy inventory and to the new bases in Bermuda and at Argentia, Newfoundland, that the United States had acquired in the destroyers-for-bases deal. Located in the southeast corner of Placentia Bay, at the southern tip of Newfoundland, Argentia was a typical sleepy Newfoundland outport until the Americans began to arrive in late 1940. It was well located for sea and air patrols far into the North Atlantic, but communications to the outside world were virtually nonexistent except for the weekly boat to the capital at St. John's. The U.S. Navy would soon change all that. The surveyors arrived first, laying out an airfield just back of the harbor and a sprawling base of 10,000 acres. Then the dredging and construction equipment arrived, and the harbor resonated to the sounds of hammers and saws, bulldozers and diesel generators day and night as the base sprang out of the rocky Newfoundland soil. Eventually some twenty thousand personnel would call Argentia home. The navy provided all the creature comforts it could to the lonely men and women stationed there: clubs and gymnasiums, baseball diamonds, handball courts, a radio station, and a post exchange stocked with duty-free cigarettes and cheap Canadian whiskey. But to American sailors, especially those from mild climes, Argentia was the U.S. equivalent of Scapa Flow, cold, windy, and isolated. All the clubs and all the duty-free cigarettes and Canadian whiskey could not make up for Argentia's miserable weather and unending loneliness.

Admiral King initially stationed thirty destroyers of the new American support force at Argentia, backed by a dozen navy PBY Catalina flying boats at the Argentia Naval Air Station. The Catalinas were twin-engine patrol bombers with a range of 3,100 miles and an endurance of more than ten hours in the air. They were excellent reconnaissance aircraft, as the Royal Navy also knew. At the same time as the dark blue U.S. Navy Catalinas with the white star on their wings and fuselages began to arrive at Argentia, light blue Catalinas with the Royal Air Force roundel began to arrive in the

United Kingdom. More than a dozen United States Navy fliers secretly went to the United Kingdom with them, ostensibly to train the RAF's Coastal Command how to fly them, but, in fact, flying them themselves, some even on combat missions.

Rear Admiral Bristol commanded most of the United States Navy destroyers that began to moor in Argentia's harbor in the early spring of 1941. These were the escorts King had scrabbled together for his new Support Force Atlantic Fleet. The ships ranged from World War I–era four-stackers, such as the USS *Reuben James*, to the brand-new 1,800-ton destroyers of the *Benson* class. The USS *Niblack* was typical of these modern warships. Laid down in 1938 at the Bath Iron Works in Maine, she was launched 18 May 1940 and commissioned two and half months later. The *Niblack* was a thoroughly modern destroyer. She displaced 1,625 tons, carried 250 officers and men, and had a top speed of 37 knots. To detect submarines, she carried the latest sonar and radar. With her speed, armament of four 5-inch guns, amidships multiple torpedo tube mount, antiaircraft guns, and depth charge throwers, in addition to her stern depth-charge racks, she was a formidable opponent for any enemy submarine.

The base at Argentia and the destroyers of rear Admiral Bristol's Support Force Atlantic Fleet greatly strengthened the American presence in the western Atlantic. U.S. involvement also increased on 3 April 1941, when Roosevelt announced that the United States would repair, or refit, Royal Navy warships in U.S. naval shipyards. This was a tremendous boost for the heavily overburdened Royal Navy, which quickly sent the battleship HMS *Malaya*, torpedoed in action in the Atlantic, followed by the carrier HMS *Illustrious*, damaged by air attack in the Mediterranean, to the United States for revamping. Other capital ships were scheduled to follow the *Malaya*, including the HMS *Rodney*, due to depart for the U.S. East Coast in the third week of May.

By early April 1941, the United States was almost as far from being neutral in the Battle of the Atlantic as a nonbelligerent could be. Admiral King was still not certain what his fleet's specific task was, and he was constantly frustrated by Roosevelt's vagueness. American warships patrolled the neutrality zone, mostly to keep German surface raiders away. But what else were they supposed to do? FDR wanted them to help the Royal Navy protect cargoes bound for Britain, but he would not allow them to escort convoys. Admiral Stark tried to get Roosevelt to make firm commitments, to give simple-to-understand instructions, but FDR refused to be pinned down, even after he handily won the presidential election in November 1940 and was inaugurated for an unprecedented third term in March 1941. Stark complained to a friend in July 1941, "To some of my very pointed questions . . . which all of us would like to have answered, I get a smile or a 'Betty, please don't ask me that!' Policy seems something never fixed, always fluid and changing."[43] In the absence of specific instructions as to what his fleet should do, Admiral King established his own rules of engagement. In early April he warned his superiors that in view of the growing seriousness of the U-boat situation, it was necessary to take "strong measures."[44] The world saw what King had in mind on 10 April 1941.

Just after dawn on 10 April the USS *Niblack*, skippered by Lieutenant Commander Edward R. Durgin, approached the southwest coast of Iceland, steaming from Argentia across the southern end of the Denmark Strait. On board the *Niblack* that day was Commander D. L. Ryan, commander of Destroyer Division 13. The *Niblack* was far to the east of the eastern boundary of the neutrality zone on a mission to reconnoiter the sea approaches to Iceland. Hitler had announced several weeks earlier that his U-boats would now hunt far to the west of Iceland, right up to the 3-mile territorial limit of Greenland. Roosevelt had responded by extending American protection to Greenland on 9 April, and the *Niblack* was at sea the following day to begin preparation for the next U.S. move into the Battle of the Atlantic: the occupation of Iceland.

Durgin and the *Niblack* were not alone in the waters to the southwest of Iceland on 10 April. Lieutenant Otto Salmann, commanding U-52, was there also. Salmann's boat, a 700-ton Type VIIB, along with U-73 and U-123, had run past Iceland to pioneer U-boat operations in waters south of the Denmark Strait, farther west than any preauthorized war patrol to that date. They had arrived in their patrol area six days earlier but had spotted little steamer traffic. On the night of 9–10 April, however, Salmann and his crew spotted and tracked the 6,600-ton Dutch freighter *Saleir*, outward bound from the United Kingdom in ballast as part of convoy OB 306. Salmann hoped the Dutch ship might lead him to a convoy, but when it became apparent after a few hours that she was just a straggler, he finished her off in short order and watched as the survivors scrambled into three lifeboats. He was about to surface to head over to the lifeboats to question the sailors when his soundman picked up the noise of approaching screws. Through his periscope, Salmann could make out the faint trace of funnel gases, then the masts, and finally the low-slung superstructure of a destroyer. After a rapid flip through the well-worn pages of *Jane's Fighting Ships*, the lieutenant identified the warship as one of the new U.S. *Benson*-class destroyers. He decided to watch from a distance.

On the bridge of the *Niblack*, the three lifeboats could be seen in the distance rising and falling on a moderate swell. The men in the lifeboats had spotted the destroyer and were trying to row toward her with as much strength as they could muster. It was bitterly cold, and the long night in the open boats after the shock of the explosions and the scramble to abandon ship had left them exhausted. Durgin maneuvered the *Niblack* gingerly, bringing her alongside each of the frail lifeboats, stopping the ship long enough for his bluejackets to throw down scrambling nets. The survivors struggled aboard, cold, wet, and hungry. They were wrapped in blankets and taken below for hot food, coffee, and sleep. As the rescue was being carried out, the lookouts scanned the horizon, the radar antenna at the topmast revolved, and a sonar beam swept the water around the ship. The division commander joined Durgin on the bridge. Then, from the sonar room: "Sonar contact!" The bridge repeater speaker was turned on; they could all hear the double ping indicating that something was down there. Suddenly the seconds between the outgoing pings and the incoming echoes grew shorter. Whatever was down there was taking a run at the *Niblack*.

No one can know Lieutenant Salmann's intentions. By that stage in the war, the U-boat captains were itching to fling a few torpedoes at the Americans. They resented the help the U.S. Navy was giving to the Royal Navy under the guise of Roosevelt's so-called hemispheric defense. The Americans were obviously on Britain's side, but they did not have the guts to make a real shooting war of it. Everyone was talking about how silly this all was, that Hitler was so scared of the Americans he had ordered Grand Admiral Raeder to avoid armed confrontation under virtually any circumstances. Maybe Salmann was just trying to make the *Niblack* nervous; maybe he wanted to be the first U-boat commander to notch an American. He bore in.

"General Quarters, General Quarters!" The klaxon sounded throughout the *Niblack* as men scrambled to their posts, grabbed their helmets, and manned their positions. Lieutenant Commander Durgin waited until the last survivor was hauled aboard, then called for flank speed. The *Niblack's* stern dug into the sea as her screws began to churn faster and faster. "Stand by depth charges!" Durgin turned to Ryan. This was Ryan's call. Attack or run? With the U-boat's top underwater speed of perhaps 6 knots, the *Niblack* could make an easy getaway. So far there were no sounds of torpedoes coming at them. What was it to be? Commander Ryan remembered Admiral King's words; he was as anxious to get at the U-boats as Salmann was to get at the Americans. The *Niblack* had just taken aboard three wretched boatloads of sailors who had lost everything. And Ryan knew there were more men out there on the Atlantic—American merchant seamen among them, dead or barely alive and waiting to die. He gave Durgin the go-ahead. The *Niblack* swung quickly around and headed for the sound contact. The depth-charge crews cranked in the settings, which would determine how deep the 250-pound barrel-shaped charges would sink before exploding. If one blew within 30 feet of the U-boat's hull, the submarine was a goner. The men at the four throwers awaited the order to fire; those at the stern racks hung on to the levers that would drop the charges into the water. The *Niblack* picked up speed. The sonar beam echoed off the U-boat's hull as the destroyer's bow sliced through the water. Then, as they approached the underwater contact, contact was lost. That always happened in a high-speed attack run. There was nothing to do but estimate where the U-boat was from the last contact, calculate the destroyer's speed, then guess where to make the drops. Two depth charges were dropped from the stern rails, four were fired from the amidships throwers, and two more were dropped from the stern. The destroyer sped on. Then huge domes of water erupted in the destroyer's wake, and the escaping gases of the underwater explosions burst through the domes and rose 60 or so feet into the air. The *Niblack* slowed, her sonar beam searching, but there was nothing. Salmann and U-52 had slipped away, but the *Niblack* had delivered the very first U.S. Navy attack of the war and, in so doing, had signaled Berlin that henceforth there would be little difference between a U.S. warship and a British warship in the high drama of the Atlantic campaign.[45]

The growing U.S. involvement in the Battle of the Atlantic reflected the increasingly close, but still secret, operational relationship between the United States Navy and the Royal Navy at the very highest levels of command. That close relationship was pursued on both sides of the Atlantic, in London and Washington, at the same time that Admiral King was building up the U.S. Atlantic fleet at sea. The president's man in London that spring was Averell William Harriman, scion of one of the United States' most important railroad families. Tall, handsome, self-assured, with a ready smile and a firm handshake, Averell Harriman was the son of Edward Henry Harriman, a scruffy little man with a genius for re-organizing money-losing railroads. Born in New York City in 1891, Averell Harriman had attended Yale University before joining his father's business empire in the 1920s. He had worked in railroads, shipping, and banking before joining the Roosevelt team in 1934. Though exceedingly wealthy, Harriman was a Democrat and one of the very few of his class or station to support the president's New Deal. Harriman was to serve Roosevelt faithfully in a number of capacities until the end of FDR's life.

On 10 March 1941 Harriman embarked on the Pan-American clipper to Lisbon and then flew on to London as Roosevelt's special representative, with the rank of minister. Churchill welcomed Harriman with open arms, especially because Harriman's real mission was to find out what Britain needed from the United States and cut through the red tape to get it there as quickly as possible. He found offices for his mission on the second floor of No. 3 Grosvenor Square, a building adjacent to the U.S. embassy in London. As work crews broke through the wall to join the mission to the embassy, Harriman and his staff got down to work. One of their earlier successes was to arrange the transfer to the United Kingdom of a million tons of mothballed U.S. merchant ships of World War I vintage.[46] Churchill wined and dined Harriman repeatedly and gave him access to all levels of the British government with a special office in the Admiralty. Harriman was too busy to use that office much, but Commander Lee, assigned to the Harriman mission by Admiral Stark to attend to naval and ship repair matters, went there every day.[47]

Harriman's arrival in the United Kingdom coincided with the ending of the secret Washington staff discussions between the United States and Britain (Canada occasionally took part in these talks due to the already deep involvement of the Royal Canadian navy in the Battle of the Atlantic) led by Admiral Ghormley. The men engaged in those discussions decided that if Japan and the United States both entered the war, the chief focus of the United States and Britain ought to be Germany. Germany was the most important of the Axis powers. A victory over the Third Reich would deprive the Axis of any real chance for victory, but a victory over Japan would leave Germany in substantial control of Europe. The Atlantic Ocean and Europe were the keys to victory. They also decided that victory would depend heavily on U.S.-British cooperation; the two nations should fight not as totally independent allies, but as coalition partners sharing key strategic decisions, resources, and major theater commands.

The British were especially happy about the outcome of the naval part of these discussions. Although the U.S. Navy was not then in a position to substantially increase the number of warships it could deploy in the Atlantic, it did promise to assume more responsibility for protecting merchant shipping as soon as it was able to do so. Both sides agreed that a special effort needed to be made to "prevent [surface] raiders from passing from Europe [into] the North Atlantic." If no more raiders slipped through, "heavy striking forces further south [in the Atlantic] would become unnecessary and the work there could be done with merchant cruisers." The way to stop the raiders was to establish a defense in depth, beginning as far north as possible, and to ensure that all arrangements between the two navies be based on strict "collaboration."[48] The meaning was plain and simple: The interests and objectives of the United States Navy and the Royal Navy in the Battle of the Atlantic were virtually the same, the only difference being that the United States was not yet in the shooting war. But everyone expected it soon would be.

The Washington talks wrapped up at the end of March. Then, on 11 April (one day after the *Niblack* attacked U-52), Roosevelt informed Churchill that henceforth the United States neutrality zone would begin not at 60 degrees west longitude, but at 25 degrees west longitude, thus taking in the Azores and several tens of thousands of square miles more of ocean. He asked Churchill to ensure that the Royal Navy, "in great secrecy," inform the United States about convoy movements so that U.S. ships and aircraft might "seek out any ships or planes of aggressor nations operating west of the new line of the security [that is, neutrality] zone." He undertook to "immediately make public to you position [of] aggressor ships or planes when located in our patrol area." Roosevelt asked Churchill to keep this new policy secret and told him that he was not certain he would even make "a specific announcement. I may decide to issue necessary naval operations orders and let time bring out the existence of the new patrol area."[49]

Henceforth, the U.S. Navy would be additional eyes and ears for the Royal Navy within the entire area from 25 degrees west longitude to the Atlantic coast and, by virtue of the United States' prior agreement with Denmark to protect Greenland, most of the Arctic waters that German raiders would pass through to reach the convoy lanes. The Americans would not shoot on sight just yet, but they would make it impossible for German warships or submarines to effectively conduct operations in the vicinity of U.S. ships. The Germans would have to shoot at the Americans if they were to evade the British. U.S. warships sailing in the newly extended neutrality zone would be going in harm's way and taking direct part in the Battle of the Atlantic.

Roosevelt's decision was a major point of departure for the U.S. Navy; within weeks, the details of internavy liaison and cooperation were being worked out. In late April Roosevelt sent Admiral Ghormley back to London to resume his old job as the president's special naval representative to the British Admiralty. It was Ghormley's task to coordinate the growing collaboration between the United States Navy and the Royal Navy. Henceforth, until his transfer to the South Pacific in the spring of 1942, Ghormley was the London contact man between the two navies, responsible for setting up and maintaining the operational links. Roosevelt was satisfied with Ghormley's progress. He told Churchill at the beginning of May that "liaison between the two naval services is being established satisfactorily."[50] The eastward patrols of U.S. warships, including the two Atlantic Fleet battleships *Texas* and *New York*, were extended. From the beginning of May onward, the two battleships made regular training and reconnaissance cruises from their East Coast bases. On 5 May the *Texas* and three destroyers weighed anchor out of Newport, Rhode Island. The task force steamed for five days, until it was some 800 miles southeast of Cape Farewell, Greenland, then returned to Newport and moored on 25 May—ten days out and ten days back. On 23 May the *New York* raised anchor from Norfolk, Virginia, and, accompanied by three destroyers, headed for the same spot. This alternating schedule ensured that there would always be a U.S. battleship at sea somewhere in the western Atlantic. No doubt both Admiral King and the Royal Navy would have preferred to have had a third battleship to ensure that a U.S. capital ship was always on station south of the Denmark Strait, as the two navies had discussed at the recent staff talks in Washington, but there was no third battleship available.

On 4 May Roosevelt informed Churchill that he had just "added all of our heavier units" of the United States Coast Guard to the jurisdiction of the United States Navy, putting the *Northland*, the *Modoc*, and other, larger cutters under Admiral King's command.[51] Even so, King's Atlantic fleet was hard-pressed to meet the commitments Roosevelt had already made. The United States had not started construction of any new destroyers from 1920 until the eight destroyers of the *Farragut* class had been laid down in 1932. As overseas conditions deteriorated in the thirties, more destroyers were built, but the vast bulk of them were assigned to the West Coast or Pearl Harbor. The United States also suspended battleship and battle cruiser construction after the Washington Naval Conference of 1920–21. It had been building six battle cruisers, each of which was to approximate HMS *Hood* in size and gun power, but four were scrapped and the remaining two were converted into the aircraft carriers *Lexington* and *Saratoga*. No new battleships were started until the USS *North Carolina* and the USS *Washington* were laid down in 1937 and 1938. These two ships, completed in 1941, displaced 46,000 tons at full war load and mounted nine 16-inch guns as main armament. They had a top speed of just over 28 knots and were certainly the equal of Admiral Tovey's *King George V*. But both were assigned to West Coast operations. King could expect no new battleships for a long time.

The *Texas* and the *New York* were among the oldest operational battleships still in commission anywhere in the world. Both ships had been laid down in 1911 and commissioned in April 1914. With ten 14-inch guns in five double turrets, they packed a powerful punch for World War I-era dreadnoughts, but by 1941 they were thoroughly obsolete for anything other than heavy shore bombardment. They were among the last U.S. Navy warships with reciprocating engines. Their top speed was a mere 21 knots. They had formed part of Rear Admiral Hugh Rodman's battleship squadron attached to the Royal Navy's Grand Fleet at Scapa Flow after the United States had entered the First World War. In the interwar years, both the *Texas* and the *New York* had undergone minor modifications to their spotting towers and superstructures and had additional antiaircraft guns fitted, but neither was suitable for a gunfight at sea with a modern battleship. They were too slow, their armor was too thin, and their guns were too small and would not elevate sufficiently to engage an enemy farther than 20,000 or so yards. Their wartime complements of 1,200 to 1,500 men were sitting ducks for the *Bismarck*.

On the day that HMS *Hood* and HMS *Prince of Wales* departed Scapa Flow to steam toward Iceland, the USS *New York* made final preparations to put to sea under the command of Captain J. G. Ware. Anchored in Narragansett Bay, off Newport, Rhode Island, the *New York* swung at anchor among the other moored warships of Admiral King's Atlantic Fleet. Those blue jackets not engaged in cleaning or stowing gear leaned over the railings smoking and talking as the day brightened across the bay. Not far from them was the old battleship *Wyoming*, long ago stripped of most of her armor and main armament and turned into a gunnery practice vessel. King's flagship, the heavy cruiser *Augusta*, the newest capital ship in the fleet, rode at anchor closer to shore. Old four-stacker destroyers and newer destroyers of the *Sims*, *Benham*, and *Benson* classes were spotted around the harbor. The sailors could easily see the Luce Hall cupola of the Naval War College, one of the points they used to adjust their magnetic compasses before putting to sea. Just before noon, an oil lighter pulled alongside and began to pump the first of 486 tons of fuel oil into the *New York*'s bunkers. That took four hours. Other barges pulled alongside, and bluejackets manned cranes to lift produce aboard: half a ton of apples, 800 pounds of cauliflower, 31 pounds of garlic, a quarter ton of celery, 522 pounds of bananas, three-quarters of a ton of cabbage, 6 tons of potatoes. Someone was going to peel an awful lot of potatoes on the twenty-day voyage.

The President was still sleeping at 6:30 A.M. on 23 May when a long telegram from Churchill was delivered to the White House via the decoding rooms in the Navy Department. The message had three parts: a request from the Admiralty for the U.S. Navy to increase its patrols in a belt of ocean about 400 miles wide from the Denmark Strait to the equator, especially to shore up the Royal Navy's defense against surface raiders; a report to FDR on the increasingly unfavorable developments surrounding the German assault on Crete; and a warning that something big was about to break in the North Atlantic.

> Yesterday, twenty-first, BISMARCK, PRINCE [*sic*] EUGEN and eight merchant ships located in Bergen. Low clouds prevented air attack. Tonight they have sailed. We have reason to believe that a formidable Atlantic raid is intended. Should we fail to catch them going out your Navy should surely be able to mark them down for us. KING GEORGE V, PRINCE OF WALES, HOOD, REPULSE and aircraft carrier VICTORIOUS with auxiliary vessels will be on their track. Give us the news and we will finish them off.[52]

Given that Roosevelt had already brought the U.S. Navy to the brink of war with Nazi Germany in the Battle of the Atlantic, FDR could not have wasted a moment sharing the news with Knox or Stark. Chief of Naval Operations Stark knew that the *New York* was about to depart. The Atlantic Fleet commander, King, was no doubt alerted and passed the word to Captain Ware. There were no quickly scribbled notes of instructions, no hurried last-minute orders to the bridge of the *New York*. There did not have to be. The orders were passed in face-to-face meetings or in whispered telephone conversations. After his private talks with King, Ware was under no illusions concerning the seriousness of the *Bismarck* putting out to sea or of what was expected of him.

Ware and his senior officers spent the day poring over charts and trying to discern the latest news of the *Bismarck*'s whereabouts as the *New York* made ready to depart. This was the final opportunity for new crew members to be transferred aboard, others to depart. Five sailors left the ship to attend elementary fire-control school at the

Washington Navy Yard; seven were assigned to shore patrol duty in Newport; one officer was sent off for flight training. At 10:39 A.M. on the morning of 23 May the last garbage lighter pulled away, and the *New York* made ready for sea. Three of her four main boilers were lit off. When there was sufficient steam pressure, the high-pressure steam lines were opened from the boilers to the engines. At 7:10 P.M. the *New York*'s escort began to move—the *Sims*-class destroyers USS *O'Brien*, USS *Hughes*, and USS *Russell*. An hour and ten minutes later Captain Ware gave the order for the *New York* to depart. She slipped past the Brenton Reef lightship and headed toward the open sea with the *Hughes*, the *Russell*, and the *O'Brien* taking screening positions in the van. The sea was calm, but a line of rain squalls hung ahead of the ships. Ware called for 12 knots and a course of 120 degrees as night fell and the four-ship flotilla entered a squall. It was 9:10 P.M. local time on 23 May. The *New York* was only a few miles from the East Coast of the United States, but she was bound for the mid-Atlantic south of the Denmark Strait. Ware knew the *Bismarck* was at sea. He also knew that he was now obliged under presidential order to help the Royal Navy in any way that he could, from unmasking the *Bismarck*'s tankers and supply ships to tracking the giant battleship itself if need be. His little task group would not last more than an hour at most if the *Bismarck* opened fire on them. What Ware did not know at that moment was that the HMS *Hood* had less than four hours to live.

Winston Churchill left London in late afternoon on Friday, 23 May for the drive to Chequers, the prime minister's country residence. He planned, as usual, to dine with his wife, Clementine, their daughter Sarah, her husband, Victor Oliver, and General Hastings Ismay, his chief of staff and primary link to the British Chiefs of Staff Committee. Averell Harriman was also invited for the weekend and given an upstairs bedroom across the hall from Ismay's. The household was tense; regular reports of the fighting on Crete and in the surrounding sea reached Churchill. The battle was not going well. German paratroopers had landed three days before, and although they had suffered heavy casualties, they had taken the key airfield at Maleme and started to fly in support troops of the Fifth Mountain Division. On the 23rd, the first Luftwaffe fighters had landed on Crete, and German artillery units had started to arrive. The Commonwealth forces under New Zealand general Bernard Freyburg were hard-pressed on land, while at sea the Royal Navy had already lost three destroyers—two on the 23rd alone—and two cruisers, while the old battleship HMS *Warspite* had been heavily damaged.

Most of the discussion at dinner and far into the night, however, was of the *Bismarck*. Churchill and his guests ate dinner, drank brandy, smoked cigars, and talked while, 2,000 miles to the west, Vice Admiral Sir Lancelot Holland and his task group groped their way toward Admiral Lütjens in the half-light, snow showers, and ice fog of an Arctic night. Churchill had faith in Admirals Tovey and Pound. Tovey knew where the *Bismarck* was and had powerful forces at his disposal to destroy her. He could also count on the Americans. But war was never predictable, and Churchill would not rest easily until he had a message in his hands confirming that the German ship had been sent to the bottom. At 3:00 A.M. he gave in to fatigue and retired to his bedroom. He was sleeping soundly three hours later when the *Bismarck*'s shells found their mark and blew the *Hood* in half.

When the *Hood* blew up, Rear Admiral Wake-Walker ordered his chief yeoman of Signals to send the message out immediately. From the *Norfolk*'s powerful transmitter four momentous words reached across the North Atlantic to Tovey's flagship, the *King George V*, to the Admiralty, and then to every ship in the fleet: "*Hood* has blown up." On the bridge of the *King George V*, Commander Jacobs, the fleet radio officer, literally yelled the news to Tovey, who replied, "All right Jacobs, there's no need to shout," before sending him back into the radio room to check the accuracy of the message and of the decoding.[53] There was no mistake. About two hours later Ismay was awakened by the sound of conversation in Harriman's room at Chequers: "I jumped out of bed to see the Prime Minister's back disappearing down the corridor. Averell's door was ajar and I went in. He looked puzzled."[54] Churchill had come into Harriman's room only a few minutes before "in a yellow sweater, covering a short nightshirt, his pink legs exposed." "Hell of a battle going on," Churchill had told Harriman. "The *Hood* is sunk, hell of a battle." Harriman asked him about the *Prince of Wales*. "She's still at her," Churchill replied, then retreated down the hall.[55] An hour or so later, Churchill heard the news that HMS *Prince of Wales* had broken off the action.

It was just after 3:00 A.M. in Washington when Harold "Betty" Stark was given the the news that the *Hood* had been sunk. Stark knew that a moment of truth had arrived for Roosevelt, for the United States Navy, and for the nation. The British were still hot on the *Bismarck*'s trail, but the almost instant destruction of the Royal Navy's most powerful and most famous warship sent shivers through every navy man who fully thought through the implications of that event. Roosevelt had given the British an almost blank check; now Churchill had every right to try to cash it.

SEARCH AND DESTROY

THE *BISMARCK* CONTINUED HER lonely run toward St. Nazaire in France. Throughout the late afternoon and into early evening of 24 May, rain showers and fog, as well as a hostile heavy cruiser, HMS *Suffolk*, and a battleship, which the Germans still believed to be HMS *King George V*, trailed her. As far as Admiral Günther Lütjens knew, the heavy cruiser *Prinz Eugen* had escaped. The *Bismarck* had had no such luck. "Enemy maintains contact," the fleet chief tersely informed German shore commands.[1]

The torpedo bomber attack by HMS *Victorious*' Swordfish in the opening minutes of 25 May had badly shaken Lütjens. Up to that attack, and despite the damage to his ship, he had been both elated and worried about the day's events. The *Bismarck* had destroyed the world's greatest warship, HMS *Hood*, and damaged another, HMS *Prince of Wales*. He also knew that the *Prinz Eugen* had successfully broken out into the Atlantic to raid Allied convoys, and that St. Nazaire was being readied to receive the *Bismarck*. By morning the next day, she would come within range of German bombers. There was enough fuel—some 5,100 tons—to shape course for western France along a curve through the mid-Atlantic. And a quick plot showed that the aircraft carrier HMS *Ark Royal* of Force H out of Gibraltar could not reach the *Bismarck* before the evening of 26 May. Thus there was every prospect that the battleship would safely reach St. Nazaire by the morning of 27 May. From there the *Bismarck* eventually could hook up with the 11-inch battleships *Scharnhorst* and *Gneisenau* (undergoing repairs at Brest), as well as the *Prinz Eugen* (eventually heading for Brest)—perhaps also with the newly completed sister battleship *Tirpitz*—and renew Rhine Exercise with an even more powerful squadron. Lütjens, undoubtedly having been recently apprised that 1,000 tons of fuel were inaccessible in the flooded forward compartments, decided to reduce speed to 21 knots. Once more, his refusal to top off with fuel oil either in the Grimstadfjord or from the tanker *Weissenburg* in the Norwegian Sea came back to haunt the task force commander.

Even before the Swordfish attack, Lütjens had been growing increasingly skeptical about the information coming from Naval Group Command West. At first the incoming radio traffic seemed to confirm that everything was going well. At 7:50 P.M. on the evening of the 24th, General Admiral Alfred Saalwächter from Paris sent "heartiest congratulations" on the sinking of the *Hood* and informed Lütjens that both St. Nazaire and Brest were being readied for the battleship. Three destroyers would be sent out to escort the *Bismarck*, and bombers and reconnaissance aircraft would range as far as 14 to 25 degrees west to cover her approach. And then a strange comment from Saalwächter: "In case you succeed in shaking off shadowers, a prolonged stay [of 10 to 14 days] for *Bismarck* in a remote part [of the Atlantic] seems purposeful."[2] Obviously, Naval Group Command West had not yet received the *Bismarck*'s battle report. And then, at 8:42 P.M., Lütjens received the most incredible news out of Paris: "Aerial reconnaissance Scapa today reveals three battleships . . . possible decoys." No British admiral would have remained in port after the sinking of the *Hood*. And then, to confirm his suspicions, Naval Group Command West informed him just after 11 P.M. that the report had been in error, that there were at best "two probably light cruisers" at Scapa Flow. And it had advised Lütjens that one of his shadowers most likely was the *Prince of Wales*.[3] Best not to count on naval intelligence, Lütjens grumbled. And also best to inform Paris that a prolonged stay in a remote part of the Atlantic was out of the question, given the *Bismarck*'s battle damage and fuel situation. At 8:56 P.M. Lütjens radioed Naval Group Command West: "Shaking off contacts impossible due to enemy radar. Must head for St. Nazaire due to fuel oil [shortage]."[4]

The signal was received in Paris at 9:32 P.M. It struck like a bolt out of the blue. For the first time, shore command became aware of the battleship's dangerous situation. For hours, both Admiral Saalwächter and Vice Admiral Karl Dönitz, commander in chief of U-boats, had been anxiously awaiting word from Lütjens concerning his intentions. In fact, the "Great Lion," as Dönitz was reverently called by his submariners, already had contacted Saalwächter to ascertain whether he should reposition the U-boats, sent out to a point south of Greenland to support Rhine Exercise, closer to the *Bismarck*. The commander of Naval Group Command West had been unable to respond. "I will finalize my wishes as soon as the fleet chief has reported,"[5] Saalwächter had testily replied.

In fact, when Lütjens had discussed Operation Rhine Exercise with Dönitz on 8 April at Paris, the fleet chief eschewed direct cooperation and instead suggested that Dönitz dispose of his forces "according to the normal requirements of U-boat warfare." But when news finally arrived at Paris late on 24 May concerning Admiral Lütjens' intention to put into St. Nazaire for repairs, Dönitz at 9:31 P.M. ordered U-93, U-43, U-46, U-557, U-66, and U-94 to take up new positions along the *Bismarck*'s line of march by 6 A.M. the next day. U-556 was instructed to act as scout. Just to be safe, Dönitz set a second trap in the Bay of Biscay, 420 miles west of Lorient, with U-97, U-48, U-98, and U-556, the latter two to serve as lookouts for the other boats. On the following night, 25 May, Dönitz also ordered U-108 and U-552 out from Lorient to reinforce the snare. U-74, returning from an Atlantic patrol and severely damaged by depth charges, volunteered to join the *Bismarck* rescue attempt. In all, the Great Lion committed seventeen boats to Greenland and eight to the Bay of Biscay. It was the largest concentration of "gray sharks" in any action since the invasion of Norway in March 1940.

In Berlin, Grand Admiral Erich Raeder summarized the situation that 24 May in his war diary: "At the conclusion of this eventful day, the proud feelings about the sinking of the 'Hood' mingle with . . . concern whether 'Bismarck' will be able to shake her pursuers and reach the west coast of France safely."[6]

Out at sea, the *Bismarck*'s damage-control teams worked throughout the night of 24 May and into the dawn of 25 May to repair the damages inflicted by the *Prince of Wales*. In the bowels of the great ship, Chief Engineer Walter Lehmann struggled to prevent the seawater that had flooded the port no. 2 boiler room from salting up the feedwater system of turbo-generator no. 4. This could have resulted in unevaporated water being carried along with steam into the propulsion turbines, destroying the turbine blades. It was not until late in the evening of 25 May that Commander Lehmann could report that the danger had passed, as the ship's four freshwater condensers and auxiliary boiler produced sufficient freshwater. Another damage-control crew set about to reinforce the collision matting that had been placed in the holes in the forecastle. As the *Bismarck* slowed to 12 knots, divers entered the flooded forward compartments and placed fresh collision matting against the gaping holes. They even managed to connect two hoses to the forward fuel-tank valves and to pump a few hundred tons of precious fuel oil to the after tanks.

Then came a brief moment of levity on board the *Bismarck*. As Saturday gave way to Sunday, 25 May 1941, the *Bismarck*'s loudspeakers blared out: "The crew congratulates the fleet chief on his birthday!"[7] Günther Lütjens had just turned fifty-two.

Aboard the *King George V*, Tovey pondered the situation. He knew the Germans had suffered damage in their encounter with the *Hood* and the *Prince of Wales*; the oil slick trailing the German battleship was a sure sign that something was wrong, but he had no idea how the *Bismarck*'s fighting ability might have been impaired by that encounter. He had marveled at the news that the mostly green pilots from the *Victorious* had indeed attacked the *Bismarck* and, even more remarkably, had returned to make night landings onto a pitching flight deck. There were reports of one hit, but Tovey doubted a single hit had done anything to impair the *Bismarck*'s fighting ability. The *Bismarck* was steaming more slowly than before her encounter with the *Hood* and the *Prince of Wales*, but that was no guarantee that she had suffered serious damage. From her two encounters with Rear Admiral W. F. Wake-Walker's ships during that long Friday, it appeared she was as dangerous as ever. That bore remembering, because Tovey expected to encounter the *Bismarck* at about 8 A.M. if Wake-Walker's ships continued to drive the German vessel toward him. Tovey decided he would close on the *Bismarck* from the southeast, as Vice Admiral Lancelot Holland had tried to do. Tovey had to worry about the vulnerable *Repulse*, as Holland had had to worry about the *Hood*. And although the *King George V* was not so untried as the *Prince of Wales*, Tovey nevertheless had gnawing doubts about how well his main guns would work. He also worried more each minute about the diminishing fuel supply in his fleet. Most of his own destroyers had already dropped out of the chase; HMS *Repulse* had about 24 hours of steaming at the most, then would have to peel off to Iceland to refuel. The *Victorious* was running low too, and there was no telling how quickly Vice Admiral Sir James Somerville's high-speed steaming with Force H was draining his fuel tanks.

To add to his difficulties, Tovey was certain just who was commanding this complex operation, spread out over thousands of miles of ocean and encompassing dozens of major British fleet units. Throughout much of the day he had gazed with dismay at the radio messages passing back and forth between Wake-Walker and the Admiralty. He could not communicate with either as long as he kept his all-important radio silence, but it galled him to know that

Admiral Sir Dudley Pound, probably at Prime Minister Winston Churchill's direct instigation, was trying to tell Wake-Walker what to do from the safety of the Admiralty's Operations Control Center. The first sea lord had no idea what constraints Wake-Walker was dealing with, nor how badly smashed up the *Prince of Wales* was. At one point that afternoon, Tovey had considered transmitting a message to London to tell Pound to back off. But Wake-Walker's reply, giving the specific details of how serious the damage to the *Prince of Wales* was, seemed to solve the problem, so Tovey had kept his silence.

John Tovey had spent more days and nights at sea on the open bridges of British warships than he cared to remember. On a very few heart-pounding occasions over the years those bridges had resounded to the calls of excited men conning ships into battle while the shell splashes of the enemy erupted close by. But most of the time the hours passed slowly, with nothing but the humdrum of watch routine, or small talk, to disturb the immense loneliness of rolling ocean and endless sky. Day or night, it was always the same except for those times when the wind screamed through the masts and antennas and howled around the superstructure, and when ships pitched and rolled in heavy weather with green seas cascading off the bows and water rolling up the decks almost to the forward turrets—before draining away over the sides and through the scuppers. Tovey knew that in those long empty watches the best thing a commander could do was to rest, even to sleep if he could, so that he could be as alert as possible when he was really needed. So it was that Tovey retired to his sea cabin on HMS *King George V* in the early-morning hours of 25 May, after one of the most disappointing days in his many years at sea.

At that moment Captain H. C. Bovell, commanding the *Victorious*, was making sure that his eight undamaged Swordfish torpedo bombers were being serviced and rearmed in the carrier's hangar decks; there was to be another torpedo attack at first light, around 5:00 A.M. But the *Victorious* herself was showing signs of wear in this, her first sea chase. Aside from her armored sections, she had been lightly built for a ship of her size. The weather and seas, though moderate in Bovell's opinion, were causing structural damage, including hull leaks. He also found that the *Victorious* had a permanent 4.5-degree list, making it very difficult to handle aircraft on the flight deck and positively dangerous in high winds.[8]

Ahead, in the dark, HMS *Norfolk* plowed steadily on. Rear Admiral Wake-Walker was dead tired, exhausted almost beyond the point of comprehension by the events that had come so quickly from the moment HMS *Suffolk* had spotted the *Bismarck* late on the 23rd. For the remainder of that night and through the dawn hours of the 24th, he had stood on the open bridge of the *Norfolk* and guided both his cruisers as they held tightly to the tiger's tail. Before his eyes, the *Hood* had been destroyed the next morning, and he then had to take the badly wounded *Prince of Wales* under his charge. The chase had continued all day and into the night; he had had no rest. Nor had his captains. The indomitable Captain A. J. L. Phillips, always at his side, ready to assume instant control of the *Norfolk* from the officer of the watch, had argued when Wake-Walker insisted that the two of them split bridge duties. But then Phillips had relented, and each man passed half the night on the bridge while the other slept. But when both were awake, they could, at least, talk to each other and test their ideas about what the *Bismarck* was up to.

Some miles to the southwest of the *Norfolk*, and ahead of the *Prince of Wales*, on the *Suffolk*'s bridge, Captain R. M. Ellis was virtually alone all the time. The windows of his winterized bridge had been smashed from the recoil when his forward turrets had opened fire on the *Bismarck* in the recent gun action, and now there was no protection between him and the weather. He was cold, wet, and dead tired. Wake-Walker had given him freedom to decide how to trail the *Bismarck*, though all three ships were positioned to detect a possible *Bismarck* turn to port, toward the French or Spanish coast. Ellis might have kept tabs from a position just in line with the *Bismarck*'s stern, but instead he chose to position the *Suffolk* off the *Bismarck*'s port beam. That was risky. The three British warships had entered waters that might hide U-boats and were zigzagging on their base course to throw off stalking subs. That meant that the *Suffolk* steamed for ten minutes or so outward from the base course, then turned to steam for the same length of time inward. Positioned where she was, off the *Bismarck*'s port beam, the *Suffolk* was always out of radar range when she reached the last few miles of the port, or outward, leg of her zigzag.

In his cabin aboard the *Bismarck*, Lütjens, as always, was alone with his thoughts. It was his birthday, yet the fleet chief found little time to celebrate. He had been in action continuously since sighting the *Hood* and the *Prince of Wales* just before 6 A.M. on the morning of 24 May. He was dead tired. He had not been able to shake his pesky pursuers. It was time to try again. Since the British ships continued to dog him off his port quarter, and since they had begun to zigzag 30 degrees either side of their base course every ten minutes, he decided to make a run to starboard. Perhaps he could at least shake visual, if not electronic, contact. At 3 A.M. on 25 May Lütjens ordered Captain Ernst Lindemann to bring the *Bismarck* up to best speed, 28 knots. Lütjens then instructed Lindemann to steer to the west, then to the northwest, and finally to the north. The German battleship began to turn just as the *Suffolk* reached the outward limit of her port zigzag. Captain Ellis expected the *Bismarck* to reappear on his radar screen as the *Suffolk* swung back to her base course. That had happened several times already that night. But it did not happen now. At 3:06 A.M. the *Bismarck*'s echo had appeared reassuringly on the *Suffolk*'s radar screen; by 3:30 the echo had disappeared. The *Bismarck* was gone.[9] She had run virtually a complete circle before settling on a southeasterly course toward St. Nazaire. Lütjens had unknowingly cut back across the track of his pursuers as they rushed blindly by in the semidarkness of the northern twilight.

Ellis' first thought was to try to regain contact alone. Obviously, the *Bismarck* had slipped away westward. Maybe she was still headed in that direction. He ordered revolutions for 25 knots and steady on a course of 230° away from the brightest part of the twilight. He waited about half an hour before breaking the news to his fleet admiral. Then, at 4:01 A.M., his message crackled through the predawn: "Enemy has either worked around to eastward under stern of shadowing ships or has turned westward—am acting on latter assumption." His intention was to follow the *Bismarck* to the west, then resume his earlier course in the belief that the *Bismarck* had made a high-speed turn to starboard to shake the *Suffolk* when the heavy cruiser had been out of radar range but that the German ship would go back to her base course right afterward.

Rear Admiral Wake-Walker was asleep in his sea cabin aboard the *Norfolk* when the urgent message from the *Suffolk* came through. He slipped on his boots, coat, and cap and rushed to join Captain Phillips on the bridge. It was even colder and grayer than the previous day, and the wind from the northwest was piling the waves even higher. He was frustrated, even angry—not so much at Ellis, but at the whole damned situation. Where had the *Bismarck* gone? It must have been to the west somewhere. He told Captains Phillips and Ellis, as well as Captain J. C. Leach on the *Prince of Wales*' badly damaged bridge, that as soon as it was light enough to visually detect the Germans they would fan out over an arc from west to south. The *Prince of Wales* would head almost due south, eventually to join Admiral Tovey, while the *Norfolk* steamed directly west and the *Suffolk* southwest.

Tovey slept in his sea cabin, four levels above the main deck at the very forward part of the *King George V*'s superstructure. The pitching and yawing of the ship in heavy weather was much more apparent here than in Tovey's spacious quarters in the stern, just under the main deck. But here he was just a few steps from the chart house, the plotting office, and both the upper and lower bridges. He could join Captain W. R. Patterson in a moment or two if needed. So he slept with his sea boots at the ready beside his bunk, his duffle coat flung over a chair, his cap hanging on a hook, a voice tube to the upper bridge open above his head. He slept until he was awakened just after first light by the second worst piece of bad news he had received in twenty-four hours—the *Bismarck* had disappeared.

The *King George V* was about 100 miles to the southeast of the

Bismarck's last reported position. Tovey quickly climbed the two levels to the plotting office, where his chief of staff, Commodore E. J. P. "Daddy" Brind, and the rest of his staff joined him. Now, just as he had done in Scapa Flow, he weighed the possibilities. Much of his Home Fleet was scattered over thousands of square miles of ocean. About half of his ships were almost out of fuel. The *Hood* was gone. Radio silence had to be maintained if at all possible. The pesky low-pressure system south of Iceland had intensified overnight, and gale-force winds were expected as far south and east as the Bay of Biscay. It would be almost impossible to conduct carrier operations and almost as bad for searches by long-range coastal command aircraft.

John Tovey knew that the *Bismarck* could be almost anywhere and that his safest course was to assume she had not been badly damaged by any of the previous day's gun actions, nor by the night torpedo attack. That led to the further assumption that she was still a great danger to the Atlantic convoys. He decided to concentrate his search to the west, because if, the *Bismarck* indeed had made course for France after crossing her own wake in the night, at least they'd find her when she showed up in Brest, St. Nazaire, or even a Spanish port. But if she had gone west, to refuel from a tanker in the Davis Strait or elsewhere, or if she was steaming straight on to the mid-Atlantic, he would find her.[10]

The messages went out. Rear Admiral Wake-Walker was to continue his search to the west and south. Rear Admiral Alban Curteis, commanding the Second Cruiser Squadron from HMS *Galatea*, dispatched to escort the *Victorious* to within striking range of the *Bismarck* the previous afternoon, was to search from west to north. Curteis ordered the *Galatea* and her consorts, the *Aurora*, the *Hermione*, and the *Kenya*, to plot a search arc, and he told Captain Bovell on the *Victorious* to send his Swordfish to supplement that search. Bovell was convinced that the *Bismarck* was heading for the Bay of Biscay, but he had no choice except to carry out his orders. If the *Victorious* had had a normal complement of Swordfish aboard, he might easily have convinced Curteis and Tovey to conduct a full

360-degree search, but he had left Scapa Flow with only nine operational torpedo bombers; one had been damaged in the previous night's attack, and now another had failed to start. So west it had to be.

The Royal Navy had one other aircraft carrier at its disposal that morning, the *Ark Royal*, even though she was still at least twenty-four hours' steaming from the main areas that had to be searched. Unlike the *Victorious*, the *Ark Royal* was a veteran. She displaced about 27,000 tons with a full war load and carried almost 1,600 officers and ratings. Her normal complement of aircraft, including both Fulmar fighters and Swordfish torpedo bombers, was sixty, but as she pushed north in company with the battle cruiser *Renown* and the light cruiser *Sheffield*, she could muster but twenty Swordfish. Still, her aircrew had been in many sea fights, both in the South Atlantic and in the Mediterranean. Well-trained and bloodied, they could be counted upon to give everything they had if the opportunity arose.

At 3:30 in the morning, while Tovey slept and the *Bismarck* slipped away from the *Suffolk*, Vice Admiral Somerville received new orders. He was to forget about meeting troop convoy WS.8B. Instead, he was to steer to intercept the *Bismarck* and, for the time being, continue on his course of 310 degrees, or west of north, and maintain his speed of 24 knots. His new destination was the eastern Atlantic, due west of the Bay of Biscay and equidistant from Cape Finisterre, Brest, Land's End, and the southern tip of Ireland. At the very moment Tovey and his staff were meeting in the *King George V*'s plotting office, Somerville's ships were plunging northward under a complete overcast, heading into gale-force winds and heavy seas. By midmorning on the 25th, Somerville had been forced to detach all six of his destroyers to Gibraltar to refuel.[11]

As word flashed that the *Suffolk* had lost the *Bismarck*, the battleship HMS *Rodney* and her three tribal-class destroyers were proceeding southwest to where the *Rodney*'s commander, Captain Frederick Dalrymple-Hamilton, believed Tovey to be. The *Rodney* was not in the best of shape. Originally she had been heading for Boston for a refit, and crates of spare parts, machinery, and tools had been secured to her decks; as well, about five hundred additional personnel were making the passage with her. She was way overdue for the fitter's yard. Her engines were constantly cranky and her best speed was a mere 21 to 22 knots. But she had nine 16-inch guns—the heaviest main guns in the Royal Navy—and her armor plate was thick and tough. If the *King George V* was to go into action against the *Bismarck*, it was the *Rodney* that was wanted as her consort, and not the battle cruiser *Repulse*, which parted company with Tovey at 9:06 A.M. on the 25th to steam to Newfoundland to refuel.

Dalrymple-Hamilton was fortunate in his passengers because aboard the *Rodney* in the early-morning hours of 25 May were two men whose sea smarts were as good as his. One of them was Lieutenant Commander Joseph H. Wellings, the United States' assistant naval attaché to the United Kingdom, returning to the States after a stint in the embassy in London. The other was Captain Cuthbert Coppinger, RN, traveling to the United States to take command of the Royal Navy battleship *Malaya*, then being repaired on the U.S. East Coast. Dalrymple-Hamilton formed a sort of executive committee with these two men, not to make command decisions regarding the daily operations of the *Rodney*, but to give him their best advice as to what they thought the *Bismarck* might do.[12]

Since Dalrymple-Hamilton was operating under strict radio silence, all his information about the sea chase came directly from the Admiralty, which was not known for either complete accuracy or objectivity in relaying information—or in attempting to guide the king's ships at sea. In the night, even before he heard that the *Bismarck* had slipped surveillance, Dalrymple-Hamilton had ordered his chief engineer officer to make best possible speed, even leaving his bucking destroyers behind, so as to place the *Rodney* squarely across the most likely route the *Bismarck* might take if she broke from Wake-Walker's ships and headed for the French coast. When he arrived at that spot, he slowed, waited for his destroyers to catch up, then broke radio silence to let Tovey and the Admiralty know where he was. For the better part of the day, Dalrymple-Hamilton cruised slowly southwest, across the *Bismarck*'s suspected path. Then he turned back, in the opposite direction, to continue the waiting.

Far to the west, the American battleship *New York*, in company with her destroyers, steamed through the early watches of 25 May heading just north of due east. It was raining, but the sea was relatively calm as the *New York* proceeded slowly toward a mid-Atlantic high-pressure ridge and better weather. She was making 12 knots, and her crew conducted a variety of night exercises as she steamed eastward. From 1:00 A.M. until dawn, her navigation lights glowed far out to sea as her destroyers kept station, sweeping for U-boats. As dawn broke under leaden skies, the morning routine began. Breakfast was doled out in the messes, morning signals were checked, and Captain J. G. Ware scanned the latest dispatches from Newport. The Royal Navy had informed Admiral Harold Stark, chief of naval operations, that they had lost track of the *Bismarck* in the middle of the night. Ware no doubt wondered what effect that event might have on his little task group. The *Bismarck*'s last known position was about 1,400 miles to the northeast, so he probably gave it barely a second thought. He might have paused somewhat longer if he had known that the *New York* was about the same distance from the *Bismarck*'s last known position as was Vice Admiral Somerville's Force H.

Each day the British ambassador to the United States, Lord Halifax, met either with a senior member of the State Department or—when momentous events were afoot—with the president. He always carried with him a succinct summary of the previous day's war news. On the morning of 25 May, his news was doubly bad. Not only had the *Hood* been destroyed the previous morning, but "at 0306 our shadowing forces lost touch with the enemy."[13] The time had clearly arrived for President Franklin D. Roosevelt to fulfill his commitments to Churchill. From the White House to the Navy Department to Admiral Ernest J. King, commander in chief of the Atlantic Fleet, the word went out: Help find the *Bismarck*. The *New York* was ordered to begin stopping and searching unidentified merchantmen that might be the *Bismarck*'s supply ships; at Argentia,

U.S. Navy PBY-5 Catalina seaplanes were ordered to join the search, flying as far east as 30 degrees longitude. Roosevelt followed the chase with great interest.

While the British and the Americans began to search desperately for the *Bismarck*, the only man in this great sea chase who did not know that the *Bismarck* was indeed "lost" was Admiral Lütjens himself. For almost five hours the *Bismarck* steamed south on a course of 180 degrees, unaware that she had eluded her pursuers. Lütjens remained convinced that the British warships continued to track him with their "Dete" gear (radar). At 7 A.M. Lütjens, a pathological radio signaler—he had sent out no fewer than twenty-two messages since HMS *Norfolk* had first sighted him in the Denmark Strait—was back again on the air. To Naval Group Command West: "0700 hours. Quadrant AK 55, one battleship, two heavy cruisers continue to maintain contact."[14] In this nascent period of electronic surveillance, the battleship's one functioning rear FuMO-23 radar-detection set continued to pick up radar impulses from its pursuers. No one on board the *Bismarck* appreciated that, to be effective, the radar impulses also had to return to their sender. HMS *Suffolk* was now some 22 miles astern the *Bismarck*, and her Type 284 radar had an effective range of only 15 miles.[15]

Naval Group Command West desperately sought to inform the fleet chief that he was in the clear. At 8:46 A.M. Admiral Saalwächter sent a most critical signal: "Last report of enemy contact 0213 *Suffolk*. Thereafter continuation of three-digit tactical radio signals but no more open position reports. Have impression that contact has been broken."[16] Obviously, Paris appreciated that the *Bismarck* had eluded her pursuers, but Lütjens continued to question the accuracy of the B-Dienst reports.

It was cool and showery at Churchill's country residence on Sunday morning, 25 May; the news from the Atlantic added to the gloom. All day Churchill was beside himself with anger at A. V. Alexander, the first lord of the Admiralty, and at Admiral Pound, but most of all at Rear Admiral Wake-Walker and Captain Leach for not attacking the *Bismarck* when they had had the chance. The Royal Navy seemed more interested in saving its ships than in fighting. The news from Crete added to his anger at the navy. In that crucial battle—still raging, though close to lost—he berated Admiral Andrew B. Cunningham's failure to see that "the loss of half the Mediterranean fleet would be worth while to save Crete."[17] He paced about his study, trying to dictate letters and memos, but thinking constantly of what he would do when he returned to London, to the Cabinet War Rooms in Whitehall, and especially to the Admiralty, where he was determined to take personal charge of the search for the *Bismarck*.

In London that rainy morning, the Admiralty was abuzz with the news that the *Bismarck* had slipped her pursuers. Admiral Pound arrived early at the Operational Control Centre; First Lord Alexander rushed in just behind him. With Vice Admiral Sir Tom Phillips, the vice chief of naval staff, and others, they looked desperately at the great wall map where the current positions, courses, and speeds of all Royal Navy fleet units at sea were indicated. They were not quite sure where some of those units were, due to radio silence, and of course they had no idea at all where the *Bismarck* was. Their first task, then, was to help Admiral Tovey find her; their second was to deploy their units in such a way as to box her in. They had to do that before she either slipped away into the Atlantic for months of attacking convoys or turned back to the French coast and slipped into port under the Luftwaffe's air umbrella.

Then, just after 7:00 A.M., powerful high-frequency direction-finding (HF/DF) receivers on the British coast began to detect the rapid dots and dashes of a ship transmitting far out to sea. Thinking he was still being electronically shadowed, Admiral Lütjens had decided to send yet another message to Naval Group Command West. This one was a detailed, half-hour situation report:

> Presence of radar apparatus on enemy ships, range at least 35,000 yards; has the severest possible effect on Atlantic operations. Ships

> had been contacted in the Denmark Strait in thick fog and contact was never broken. Attempts to break off failed despite favorable weather conditions. . . . Running battle between 23,000 and 19,000 yards. Adversary *Hood* . . . destroyed by explosion after five minutes; thereafter, shift target to *King George V*, which veered off making smoke after several clearly-observed hits, and was out of sight for several hours. Own ammunition expenditure: 93 shells. *King George V* thereafter accepted battle only at most extreme range. *Bismarck* twice hit by *King George V*, one of these below side armor, Sections XIII and XIV. Hit Sections XX and XXI reduced speed and caused ship to be down by the bows and loss of oil tanks. Detachment of *Prinz Eugen* made possible by battleship engaging cruiser and battleship in fog. Own radar-detection set subject to disturbances, especially when firing.[18]

Every Allied radio direction-finder set in Britain, Greenland, Iceland, and Ireland tuned in. British Y stations immediately picked up Lütjens' signal—even before he had completed it. The signals were in code and could not be read, but the men at the receiving consoles had heard the call sign of this ship before, just after the *Hood* had been sunk. The giant antennas of the HF/DF receivers swung slowly until the signal was at its loudest and the instruments in the radio shack showed it at its greatest strength. Then they took a bearing. The bearings from several stations were immediately sent to the Admiralty's Operational Intelligence Centre, where they were plotted on a map of the North Atlantic. Was it the *Bismarck*? It had to be. And then, once again, a second series of bearings came in about two hours later. It was the same ship. The *Bismarck* was breaking her own radio silence.

High-frequency direction finding, or "Huff Duff" as it was called, worked best when bearings could be taken by stations as far apart as possible. Later in the war, HF/DF receivers at sea tracked U-boat transmissions on the Canadian, American, British, and even West African coasts at the same time. Taking all those bearings, the Allies could work out a U-boat's position to within 50 miles at most. And when smaller HF/DF sets were installed on destroyers, frigates, and corvettes, they often pinpointed U-boats transmitting near convoys and fixed their positions to within a mile or so. Some of Admiral Tovey's destroyers were already equipped with these small sets, but on the morning of 25 May they were on their way to Iceland to refuel.

Admiral Lütjens' radio transmissions were picked up by British shore stations—which were not thousands or even hundreds of miles apart, but close together. They were not detected by stations in Canada or Gibraltar. When plotted on maps at the Admiralty, they gave a pretty good indication of the *Bismarck*'s latitude, but virtually no idea of her longitude. Still, they provided hard evidence that the *Bismarck* was somewhere to Tovey's east, not to his west. At 8:54 A.M. the first of these bearings was sent to the *King George V*, where they were plotted by Tovey's master of the fleet, Captain Frank Lloyd, on an ordinary Mercator projection. Quickly done, Lloyd's calculations showed the *Bismarck* to the northeast. That could mean only one thing: the German ship was heading back to the North Sea either through the Denmark Strait or, more likely, through the Iceland-Faeroes gap. At 10:47 A.M. Tovey turned back on his track and headed northeast on a course of 55 degrees, speed 27 knots.

At midday on Sunday, 25 May 1941 the battleship *Bismarck* was as safe from the Royal Navy as she was ever likely to be. Tovey was steaming fast to the northeast, but *Bismarck* was heading southeast and the distance between pursued and pursuer was opening by the minute.[19] Across the ocean search areas, British ships were burning fuel at a prodigious pace, as they had been for three days of high-speed steaming, and their tanks were now emptying fast. Like Salome's veils, the ships were shed one by one as they headed to Newfoundland, Iceland, Ireland, or Gibraltar to refuel. The *Victorious*, the *Suffolk*, the *Norfolk*, the *Hermione*, and the *Prince of Wales* would leave before evening. The *Galatea* and the *Aurora* were due to depart for Iceland an hour or so after midnight. The *Repulse* was already on her way to Newfoundland. In less than eighteen hours the *King*

George V would be the only ship left from the mighty Home Fleet that had sallied forth on the two successive nights of 21 and 22 May. Tovey himself was kept regularly informed by the *King George V*'s chief engineer how much fuel was left in his flagship's tanks, how fast she was burning it up, and when they themselves would have to turn back. At that moment, with Tovey 165 miles to the west of the *Bismarck* and headed in the wrong direction, the Home Fleet posed no threat to the German ship.

To the southeast, off the coast of Spain, Force H was coming on as fast as it could, but Vice Admiral Somerville's ships were steaming hard into a gale. HMS *Ark Royal* was pitching wildly as Captain L. E. H. Maund struggled to keep her stem into the wind. He knew that it was going to be close to impossible to conduct flight operations under these conditions. It would be slow and dangerous just to bring the Swordfish up from the hangar deck to the flight deck by the ship's main deck elevator, a task that had to be done dozens of times as the *Ark Royal*'s twenty operational torpedo bombers were readied for flight. Somerville anxiously watched the clock and the barometer, knowing that he needed to slow down to make life—and fighting—less difficult, but also knowing that every knot less was one more chance for the *Bismarck*, wherever she was, to reach safety.[20]

HMS *Rodney* was still in the picture at noon on the 25th, and even though she was old, slow, and much in need of repair, she was still the most lethal weapon in Tovey's arsenal. The *Rodney*'s nine 16-inch guns could throw a broadside of 10 tons of armor-piercing shells every forty-five seconds. But the *Rodney* alone was too slow to stop the *Bismarck*, even if Captain Dalrymple-Hamilton and his "committee" could guess the exact spot where they might intercept the German battleship. And without precise intelligence as to the *Bismarck*'s course, speed, and destination, that would be virtually impossible.

The heavy cruiser *Dorsetshire*, commanded by Captain B. C. S. Martin, was also joining the hunt. The *Dorsetshire* was on convoy duty when word came that the *Bismarck* had disappeared from the fleet's radar screens; Martin decided at once to leave the convoy and to rush to Tovey's assistance. He still had lots of fuel and thought the commander in chief could always use another heavy cruiser.[21] But unless the *Bismarck* was located within thirty-six hours at most, no ship on earth was going to enable the Royal Navy to bring her to account.

When Admiral Lütjens' radio signals arrived at Paris they sent Naval Group Command West into further fits of frustration. Why in the world did the task force commander not realize that he was in the clear? Why did he continue to overestimate British radar capabilities? And why did he continually dash off radio signals? By now the B-Dienst on board the *Prinz Eugen* likewise concluded that the *Bismarck* had shaken off her pursuers. Captain Helmuth Brinkmann could not understand why the fleet chief continued to believe that he was still being tracked. He had been given a second birthday present—loss of contact by the enemy—but somehow refused to take advantage of it.

At that moment the men in the British Admiralty's Operational Control Centre were as confused as Lütjens. When they had plotted the *Bismarck*'s radio transmissions, they had concluded that the *Bismarck* was southeast of Tovey; they could not understand why the commander in chief of the Home Fleet was rushing away to the northeast. They did not realize that his HF/DF destroyers were long gone. Maybe he knew something they didn't about where the *Bismarck* was headed. Churchill wandered in and out of the Operational Control Centre all day. He had decided—strictly on a hunch—that the *Bismarck* was steaming back to the North Sea.[22] His was "a powerful presence," to say the least, and Alexander and Pound ignored his views at their peril.[23] Indeed, they were barely able to restrain him much of the day from sending his few remaining ships hither and yon across the seascape. Hence Tovey was not told for seven precious hours that he was probably steaming in the wrong direction. At one point, in fact, the Admiralty radioed Dalrymple-Hamilton on the *Rodney* to proceed northeast to join

Tovey. Dalrymple-Hamilton thought better of the order and, risking his career, defied it to continue patrolling across what he thought would be the *Bismarck*'s path.

In the meantime, evidence mounted that the *Bismarck* apparently was steaming toward the area of Brest. In midmorning Vice Admiral Phillips sent Captain C. S. Daniel, director of plans, and Captain R. A. B. Edwards, director of operations, to each make a separate and independent evaluation of where they thought the *Bismarck* was headed. An hour or two later both reported their view that she was headed for Brest. That fitted in with other intelligence. From Brest itself came news from a French naval officer working under cover for British intelligence that the port was being readied for the *Bismarck*'s arrival.[24] And even though Bletchley Park could not read the *Bismarck*'s Enigma-encoded signals without several days' delay, German radio traffic along the French coast suddenly seemed to reach fever pitch. Apparently every German naval and air force radio from the Cotentin Peninsula to Cape Finisterre had suddenly lit up shortly after the *Bismarck* had been lost.[25] On the basis of these factors, First Sea Lord Pound issued new orders for Force H. At 11:00 A.M. Somerville was told to act on the assumption that the *Bismarck* was headed for Brest and to alter course to due north. Somerville calculated that the *Ark Royal* would be close enough to Brest by the next morning to begin aerial reconnaissance across the Bay of Biscay.[26] An hour and fifteen minutes later he decided to change course to 345 degrees, or a little west of due north, so that the *Ark Royal* would be in the best possible position for an early-morning air search. It mattered little that the *Bismarck* was, in fact, heading for St. Nazaire. The distance between the two French ports was about 93 miles and, given the *Bismarck*'s almost direct approach from a position some 250 miles west-northwest of the ports, the *Ark Royal*'s air sweep would adequately cover the approaches to either port.

Although the code breakers at Bletchley Park could not read German naval Enigma traffic quickly enough to provide an up-to-the-minute picture of what was happening aboard the *Bismarck*, they could read the much less complex Luftwaffe Enigma virtually within the hour. Now, at a few minutes past 6:00 P.M., a message was broken from General Hans Jeschonnek, staff chief of the Luftwaffe, to Berlin. Jeschonnek was in Athens overseeing the Luftwaffe's part in the Battle of Crete. His son was a midshipman on the *Bismarck*, and Jeschonnek wanted to know where he was. Luftwaffe authorities, still unaware of Admiral Lütjens' intention to make for St. Nazaire, replied at once in their own Enigma cipher that the *Bismarck* would soon berth at Brest.[27] There was no longer any real doubt in London where the *Bismarck* was headed.

For most of the 25th Admiral Tovey steamed in the wrong direction, wasting time and fuel in a fruitless chase. As evidence mounted from the bits and pieces of intelligence that came into the *King George V* by radio that he was embarked on a wild-goose chase, he began to reassess his position. He sent the ship's navigation officer, Master of the Fleet Lloyd, back to the plotting office to recalculate the bearing reports that had come from the Admiralty that morning. Captain Lloyd emerged a few minutes later with the sheepish admission that he had been wrong, that the bearings showed the *Bismarck* to the southeast of where the *King George V* had been at midmorning, not northeast. And that had been many long hours ago. Tovey developed a sickening feeling that he was heading in the wrong direction, but could he—should he—change course on his own and head for the Bay of Biscay? If he was heading in the right direction, why wasn't everyone else? If he was heading in the wrong direction, why was the Admiralty not telling him to do otherwise? At 3:48 P.M., uncertain of what he ought to do, Tovey ordered Captain Patterson to change course to 80 degrees; then he waited. Finally at 4:21 P.M. he broke radio silence and signaled the Admiralty: "Do you consider that enemy is making for Faeroes?"

In the bridge receiving room, the *King George V*'s radio operators waited desperately for the dots and dashes that would give the commander in chief the Admiralty's answer. Hour after hour they sat by their sets, but there were no messages addressed to the *King*

George V's call sign. At 6:05 P.M. a radio transmission from the Admiralty to HMS *Rodney* was intercepted, canceling Admiral Pound's earlier instructions to head for the northeast, instructions that Captain Dalrymple-Hamilton had ignored anyway. But nothing for Tovey. He could wait no longer. He already doubted that he could make up the time the Admiralty's confusion had cost him. He was using fuel at a prodigious rate. He was by nature decisive, and he hated this waiting around. He decided to damn the consequences of not waiting for Pound to tell him what to do. At 6:10 P.M. Tovey told Patterson to alter course again, this time to the southeast. The orders were passed; the *King George V* heeled over and settled on a course of 117 degrees, speed 24 knots. Tovey radioed the change to the Admiralty five minutes later. Ten minutes after that the Admiralty's first answer was decoded in the receiving room: the *Bismarck* was probably heading for the west coast of France. Finally, at 7:24 the definitive word arrived as the Admiralty broadcast to all its ships at sea: "Information received graded A1 that intention of 'Bismarck' is to make for the west coast of France."[28]

At noon on Sunday, 25 May Admiral Lütjens decided to break his customary silence and address the *Bismarck*'s crew. The men deserved praise for sinking the *Hood* and some word about their next destination. In his speech, Lütjens first recalled the Battle of Iceland: "Seamen of the battleship 'Bismarck'! You have covered yourself with great glory! The sinking of the battle cruiser 'Hood' has not only military, but also moral value, for 'Hood' was the pride of England." The men's beaming faces reflected the glorious weather. Then, ever the brutal realist, Lütjens offered a rigorous analysis of their present situation: "The enemy will now seek to concentrate his forces and to deploy them against us. Thus, I released 'Prinz Eugen' yesterday so that it can conduct commerce warfare in the Atlantic. She has managed to evade the enemy." Next, the admiral offered insight into his plans: "We, on the other hand, have received orders [*sic*] because of the hits we took to proceed to a French port." Happiness all around the *Bismarck*'s decks. And then Lütjens dashed the crew's visions of a quick cruise to the coast of France:

> On the way there, the enemy will gather his forces and force us to do battle with him. The German Folk is with you and we will fire until the barrels glow red-hot and until the last shell has left its barrel. For us seamen, there is now but one cry: "Victory or Death."[29]

The speech had the effect of a cold shower. It spread gloom and doom throughout the ship.[30] Morale plummeted. Ordinary seamen as well as staff officers began to wear open life jackets to their duty stations. A "contagious" depression gripped the crew. The first signs of fatalism, of sullen introspection appeared. There was even talk among the ratings of being under a "death sentence." The dour, phlegmatic Lütjens had chosen the wrong moment for the wrong speech. And he had given it to the wrong audience: mostly young men, only recently members of the Hitler Youth, they were easily swayed one way or another.

In fact, Lütjens had acted true to character. His dour, dry, almost colorless personality was well known to the *Bismarck*'s men, as was his silent, inflexible, taciturn style of command. The "man with the iron mask," the sailors had called him, even before leaving Gotenhafen. And they knew that in the service he was not known as a lucky commander; the epithet "Jonah" had followed him from one senior command to the next. But Lütjens' birthday oration surpassed all that. It was a haunting, fatalistic speech, one that revealed the fleet chief in a state of serious depression. The *Bismarck* had enough fuel to reach port, was on a direct course for France, and was fully operational in terms of both her power plant and her armament. She had taken the full measure of the *Hood* and the *Prince of Wales* to her advantage, had (unknowingly) eluded her pursuers, and was leading Admiral Tovey's Home Fleet on a merry chase. But there was Lütjens speaking of a final battle to the death, of guns glowing red-hot, of the *Bismarck* fighting to the last shell, and offering the men the lurid alternative of "Victory or Death." The days without sleep, the fury of battle, the weight of isolated decision making, the euphoria of victory, and the constant proximity of death and defeat had obviously taken their toll on the fleet chief.

Captain Lindemann was furious. On 24 May Lütjens had denied

him the opportunity to hunt down the damaged the *Prince of Wales*. Later that day he had rejected Lindemann's suggestion that the *Bismarck* shape course for Bergen, Norway, rather than St. Nazaire. And now, the admiral had poisoned the crew's morale. Within an hour of Lütjens' near-funereal address, the *Bismarck*'s skipper briefly spoke to the men over the ship's loudspeakers, assuring them they would "put one over on the enemy and soon reach a French port."[31] Lindemann as well as his officers and senior petty officers thereafter made the rounds, assuring the men they had every chance of reaching port.

As well, Lindemann decided to take the crew's mind off the fleet chief's depressing speech by assigning them a new task. As the *Bismarck* steamed ever southward in the early afternoon of 25 May, the captain issued orders for the crew to construct a dummy funnel from wood, canvas, and sheet metal, and to paint it battleship gray, like the *Bismarck*'s single funnel. British as well as American battleships mounted two funnels, and thus future air patrols might mistake the *Bismarck* for a *King George V*–class or a *New York*–class battleship. Soon officers joked that the ship's smokers ought to take up residence inside the funnel so that it would actually smoke. The duty crew in the signal room set about to compose English-language Morse signals to throw off future enemy contact by surface vessels.

Lütjens, perhaps feeling chastised by Lindemann's efforts to raise morale, spent the afternoon informing the crew of the latest intelligence. He noted that Force H had left Gibraltar; that the British battleship they had damaged on 24 May had been the *Prince of Wales* and not the *King George V*; and that the *Bismarck* was being pursued by a hostile armada that included the *King George V*, the *Rodney*, the *Ramillies*, the *Repulse*, and a host of cruisers and destroyers.[32]

All that day, birthday congratulations arrived on board the *Bismarck*. At 12:28 P.M. Grand Admiral Raeder, who still believed it best for the *Bismarck* to seek safety in the wide expanses of the Atlantic, radioed: "Heartiest congratulations on your birthday! After the last great feat of arms, may you be granted many more successes in your new year." And at 4:47 P.M. a cold, formal communiqué from the Führer: "I send you best wishes on your birthday today. Adolf Hitler."[33] The rest of the day and evening were uneventful. A signal late in the evening announcing that the U.S. Coast Guard cutters *Modoc* and *Mojave* were in quadrant CB 61 caused little stir.

About 4:30 A.M. on 26 May an announcement from the bridge spread cheer and joy throughout the ship:

> We have now passed three-quarters of Ireland on our way to St. Nazaire. Around noon we will be in the U-boats' operational area and within the range of German aircraft. We can count on the appearance of Condor planes after 1200.[34]

The *Bismarck* was still alone and undetected. The Admiralty knew approximately where she was headed and when she would get there but could do nothing to stop her. She was on a southerly course, making about 21 knots. Ahead lay St. Nazaire.

At the Admiralty's Operational Control Centre, Captain R. A. B. Edwards, director of operations, had been at his post at least since the morning of the 24th. Like the other Admiralty men and women involved in the *Bismarck* pursuit, he snatched a few minutes' sleep whenever he could and ate bully beef sandwiches and drank tea as he worked tirelessly on the many problems that had to be resolved to give Admiral Tovey the information and the resources he needed. One problem of growing importance as the 25th wore on was the lack of escort for the cruisers, battleships, and aircraft carriers that were searching for the *Bismarck*. All Vice Admiral Somerville's destroyers screening Force H had been detached to refuel; so had Tovey's Home Fleet screen. The *Rodney*'s three destroyers—the *Mashona*, the *Somali*, and the *Tartar*—had enough fuel for possibly another day's steaming, but that was all. And now the British capital ships were entering waters easily reached by U-boats from their bases on the Biscay coast. Edwards was desperate to find fresh destroyers to throw into the fray. But there were none in port close enough to make any difference. The only destroyers at sea that might be sent to help were the five of the Fourth Destroyer Division, Captain Philip L. Vian commanding, that were escorting troop convoy WS.8B to the Middle East. Could he strip yet more protection from that convoy, carrying thousands of soldiers, and risk a slaughter at sea?

War forces terrible choices on those who fight them; the lives of several thousand soldiers weighed against the possibility of a German submarine sinking the *King George V*, the *Rodney*, or the *Ark Royal*, thereby virtually guaranteeing the *Bismarck*'s escape. If the *Bismarck* entered a French harbor, joined the *Gneisenau* and the *Scharnhorst* and most likely rejoined the *Prinz Eugen*, then came out to raid the convoy lanes, possibly in company with the soon-to-be-seaworthy *Tirpitz*, what losses might Britain suffer? Perhaps the Battle of the Atlantic itself, and then the war. Captain Edwards forced from his mind the thought of thousands of soldiers blown to bits by torpedoes or dying slowly in the North Atlantic. There were no confirmed reports of German submarines in the area. The convoy would have to make do. Edwards contacted Admiral Sir Percy Noble, the Commander-in-Chief Western Approaches, who was in command of all convoy escorts, and asked for Captain Vian's destroyers. At a minute before 2:00 A.M. on the morning of the 26th the orders crackled out from Noble's headquarters in Liverpool: Captain Vian's Fourth Destroyer Division, escorting the military convoy WS.8B, was detached from duty and ordered to provide an antisubmarine screen for the battleships.[35]

At forty-seven, Philip Vian had already made his name as a man in the tradition of Elizabethan captains such as Sir Walter Raleigh or Sir Martin Frobisher, who had humbled the Spanish Armada in 1588. He had first come to public notice in February 1940 when he was commanding the *Tribal*-class destroyer HMS *Cossack*. At Churchill's order, he had taken his ship into then-neutral Norwegian territorial waters to investigate the German supply ship *Altmark* and discovered 299 prisoners transferred to the *Altmark* by the *Graf Spee* before she was scuttled in Montevideo Harbor the previous

December. After a short fight in the fjord, Vian's men liberated the prisoners; the *Cossack* then brought them home in triumph. Now, as commander of the Fourth Destroyer Division, Vian's flag still flew from the *Cossack*. He also had under command three other *Tribal*-class destroyers—the *Maori*, the *Zulu*, and the *Sikh*—and the Free Polish destroyer *Piorun*.

Vian's *Tribals*, built in the late 1930s, were among the most powerful destroyers afloat. They could make 36 knots and were heavily armed with eight 4.7-inch guns and four torpedoes. They packed almost as much punch as a light cruiser. The *Piorun* was a British-built N-class destroyer, which had been transferred to the Polish government-in-exile in October 1940. She was smaller and lighter than Vian's *Tribals*, with fewer guns, but just as quick, and she carried ten torpedoes to their four.

In addition to the desperate shortage of destroyers, the Admiralty also had to decide where to send reconnaissance aircraft once dawn broke on the 26th. Vice Admiral Somerville's Swordfish were going to fly out over the Bay of Biscay, and the Americans were keeping watch west of longitude 30 degrees, which was probably not where the *Bismarck* was going in any case. Coastal Command had been searching fruitlessly all day on the 25th; the next morning, at the Admiralty's direction, two PBYs would leave from Lough Erne, in Northern Ireland, and fly a search pattern from northeast to southwest over the area the *Bismarck* was most likely to steam through on her way to Brest or St. Nazaire.

PBY Z from Coastal Command's No. 209 Squadron lifted off from Loch Erne at 3:45 A.M. on the 26th. It was pitch dark as Flying Officer Dennis Briggs struggled through the overcast to bring the twin-engine patrol bomber to 3,000 feet. The seaplane bounced and jolted this way and that as the big engines mounted on the wings dragged it through the rain and mist. When he reached the west coast of Ireland, Briggs turned southwest and descended to his assigned search altitude of 500 feet. At that height, Briggs and his crew could not possibly miss anything as large as a 50,000-ton battleship. But the sky was almost completely overcast, with clouds down to the deck in many places along their route. The crew was dead tired. Early-morning flying operations never seemed to discourage late-night revelries. They were all young men in the most adventurous time of their lives, but they always paid the following morning as they droned over the sea hour by hour. It was hard to stay awake. Briggs' copilot, United States Navy Ensign Leonard B. "Tuck" Smith, didn't even bother to try. As soon as the PBY reached 500 feet and Briggs switched on the autopilot, Smith nestled down in his seat and dozed off.[36]

As an officer in a neutral nation's navy, Smith ought not to have been in the starboard seat in the cockpit of that PBY. But then the *Modoc* ought not to have helped the *Victorious*' torpedo bombers find the *Bismarck*, as it no doubt had on the night of 24 May, and the *New York*'s task force ought not to have started to seek out the *Bismarck*'s tankers and supply ships by stopping and searching lone merchantmen. Smith and sixteen other American navy volunteers had agreed earlier that year to accompany a few dozen brand-new Lend-Lease PBY Catalina seaplanes to the United Kingdom to train the Royal Air Force in their use. In fact, the other PBY in the air that morning, aircraft M of No. 240 Squadron, carried another of Smith's colleagues, United States Navy Lieutenant (jg) J. E. Johnson. Johnson's PBY was assigned to patrol an area due north and adjacent to the one Smith's aircraft was patrolling.

As Smith dozed, Briggs kept watch as "George," the autopilot, kept the PBY straight and level. A gray dawn crept over the seascape, and somewhere in the rear of the PBY, a crewman lit the primus stove to begin frying the crew's bacon-and-egg breakfast. The smell of food and fresh coffee woke Smith up. He ate his breakfast as he watched the sea slide by below him. Visibility was not good, ranging from zero to 5 miles. They were bucking a northwest wind and making barely 80 knots. The sea was a heaving plane of dark gray mottled with whitecaps, when they could see it. They reached their assigned search area at 9:45 A.M. and began to fly a crossover search pattern. The sky cleared a bit; below 800 feet they could see up to 10 miles.

A few minutes after 10:00 A.M. Briggs climbed out of his seat and went to the back of the aircraft. Ten minutes later Smith saw something. It was 8 miles away, off his port bow, at the limit of his visibility. There were no destroyers accompanying it, and British ships always had destroyers with them. He grabbed the wheel, disengaging the autopilot, and called Briggs. Briggs scrambled forward and clambered into his seat. There it was: a very large ship steaming furiously to the southeast. Briggs shouted to get closer, to fly up the ship's stern. Smith pushed the throttles forward, then pulled the PBY around into a tight banking turn to the right, spiraling upward into the cloud base. Briggs went back to the radio compartment as the PBY flew through the cloud. Smith hoped to drop out of the overcast far enough away to keep sight of the vessel, then shadow it without getting into gun range. Yoke forward, the PBY broke from the overcast, right on top of the ship. The sky exploded with antiaircraft fire. The sound of bullets hitting wings, airframe, and Perspex announced the jagged holes that suddenly appeared in the fuselage skin. One large hole was punched in the floor between Smith's seat and Briggs'. The flak explosions threw the PBY about the sky. Pans and dishes crashed in the galley. An off-duty crewman was hurled from his bunk. The gunners hung on for dear life. Then they lost sight of the ship in the overcast.

Aboard the *Bismarck*, Monday, 26 May broke gray and foreboding. Low clouds scudded across the horizon. Visibility was 10 miles or less. The wind from the north-northwest grew to 40 miles an hour, a moderate to fresh gale. White foam from the breaking waves began to blow in well-marked streaks. The ocean swell reached formidable proportions; the *Bismarck*'s stern rose and fell more then 30 feet. A major storm was brewing in the eastern Atlantic. But both wind and swell drove the *Bismarck* toward her goal. On deck, the crew continued work on raising the dummy funnel. Others set about painting the tops of the gun turrets yellow as a ruse against enemy flyers, but the breakers washed the paint off as soon as it was applied.

Then a piece of crushing news: at 10:25 A.M. Naval Group Command West signaled Lütjens that Luftwaffe air support would not be up that day due to heavy weather in the Bay of Biscay—40- to 50-mile-per-hour winds, showers, visibility 6 to 8 miles. In fact, Paris cautioned Lütjens not to expect Luftwaffe protection until he was close to shore. Might the fleet chief consider putting into a Spanish port, such as Ferrol? Admiral Saalwächter wished to know. Lütjens was crestfallen. Exactly six hours earlier he had apprised the *Bismarck*'s crew that they could expect Focke-Wulf 200 Condors to fly over by noon. The news had occasioned widespread joy and had raised morale immeasurably.

"Aircraft Alarm! Aircraft to port!" The cry from the bridge ripped Admiral Lütjens out of his dark musings. It came from the *Bismarck*'s alert antiaircraft gunners. Out of a ragged hole in the clouds, they saw Briggs' PBY approach the battleship from the stern. Captain Lindemann immediately opened fire, driving the Catalina off—and broadcasting to the British that he was a hostile. Lindemann considered sending up the Arado196 aircraft, but the heavy seas made recovery unlikely. Quickly the *Bismarck*'s B-Dienst deciphered Briggs' transmission from the Catalina: "One battleship bearing 240° five miles, course 150°, my position 49° 33' north, 21° 47' west. Time of origin, 1030/26."[37] At first, in the confusion, Smith thought he had seen two German ships, and he and Briggs miscalculated the enemy's ship before losing her position by 20 miles under the clouds. After testing the PBY for possible serious damage, Smith and Briggs flew on, again searching for the ship that could only be the *Bismarck*. They couldn't find her. The other PBY joined them, but the battleship eluded both aircraft under the overcast. No matter; the *Bismarck* was spotted again an hour later by an *Ark Royal* Swordfish, flying on the carrier's second early-morning sweep. Then the second PBY spotted her again. Now two aircraft kept visual contact with the *Bismarck*; between Coastal Command's PBYs and the *Ark Royal*'s Swordfish, they never again would lose her.[38] When the *Bismarck*'s crew spotted the Swordfish, they knew there was an aircraft carrier in the vicinity. Lütjens at once notified Paris: "Enemy aircraft maintains contact in quadrant BE 27; wheeled aircraft!"[39]

All afternoon on 26 May a Catalina flying boat and aircraft from the *Ark Royal* flew surveillance over the *Bismarck*. Continually the task force commander apprised Naval Group Command West of the contacts. Swordfish after Swordfish seemed to be in the sky all at once. Lütjens informed the *Bismarck*'s crew of the obvious: "Aircraft carrier nearby." At around 5:40 P.M. the *Bismarck* also sighted HMS *Sheffield*, Captain Charles Larcom commanding. The *Sheffield* was a light cruiser. She could make 32 knots when running "both ahead, full," but she was lightly armed. She had nine main guns of only 6-inch bore, throwing a shell that was considerably lighter than her heavy cruiser cousins. Her armored protection over her most vital areas was a mere 1 to 4 inches. She was easy meat for the *Bismarck*.

But the *Sheffield* had not arrived to fight. With low clouds and rain squalls blowing across the seascape in the *Bismarck*'s vicinity, it would be easy for the shadowing aircraft to lose her again. Vice Admiral Somerville had detached the *Sheffield* from Force H at 1:26 P.M. with orders to "close and shadow enemy." Somerville thought the signal flags hoisted to the *Renown*'s yardarm would make the announcement to the *Sheffield*. That was standard practice because the *Ark Royal* would then see it also and know that the *Sheffield* was being sent ahead. But the chief yeoman of signals used the signal light instead, and no effort was made to specifically ensure that the *Ark Royal* knew the *Sheffield*'s whereabouts. In the bad weather and the confusion of maneuvering to send off and take on aircraft, no one in the *Ark Royal*'s flying operations center realized the *Sheffield* had gone.[40]

After leaving the *Renown* and the *Ark Royal*, the cruiser steamed through heavy seas at 28 knots to reach the *Bismarck*. It was a hard ride. With the wind blowing against the port bow, she tended to corkscrew as she plowed her stem under, then rose with green seas streaming off her forecastle. In the mess decks, plates and crockery smashed to the deck to mix with seawater, bits of paper, sodden books and magazines, and vomit. Sleeping was impossible for the men off watch. Besides, everyone was tense with both excitement and foreboding. When the *Sheffield* hove in sight of the German battleship at 5:40 P.M. to begin trailing her, her company were the first British seamen to catch sight of her in forty hours.

And then, at 7:03 P.M., Naval Group Command West at Paris received another one of Lütjens' customarily matter-of-fact shock signals: "Fuel situation urgent—when can I expect replenishment?"[41] Not a word more. How much fuel did the *Bismarck* have? Admiral Saalwächter wondered. And why was she even short on fuel? Had Lütjens not topped off in Norway? All available tankers at sea were headed for the *Prinz Eugen*. Whom to send?

The Royal Navy now knew the *Bismarck*'s whereabouts but was faced with a daunting task. By late morning of the 26th it obviously had a much better chance of getting the *Bismarck* than it had had just twenty-four hours before; Tovey and the Admiralty at least knew where she was, where she was headed, and how long it would take her to get there. But they also knew that if she continued on her current heading at a speed of 20 knots or so, they had only perhaps eighteen hours to bring her to bay before swarms of Luftwaffe bombers took to the air from their French bases to provide coverage for the last leg to France. The *Bismarck* was about 130 miles ahead of the *King George V* and the *Rodney*, which had started steaming a course converging with that of the *King George V* at about 9:00 A.M. that morning. When Captain Dalrymple-Hamilton caught sight of Tovey just about 3:20 P.M., he swung in behind; Tovey was forced to slow to a bit more than 21 knots to enable the *Rodney* to keep up. The *Bismarck* and her two battleship pursuers were then about seven hours of steaming apart; if the *Bismarck* was not slowed down, that gap would never be bridged. Tovey knew something else—even if the Luftwaffe did not appear in swarms the next morning, his fuel was rapidly running out. The time was quickly approaching when he would have to choose between abandoning the chase altogether or allowing his tanks to run dry and his ship to go dead in U-boat-infested waters. Neither was a happy thought.

Captain Vian's five destroyers were coming up fast, but even though they could easily catch the *Bismarck* before dawn with their 37-knot speed—and use their modern radar to attack her with torpedoes—their primary assignment was to protect the *King George V* and the *Rodney* from U-boats after their destroyers were detached to refuel, and also to guard Vice Admiral Somerville's Force H. Besides, British naval torpedoes were rather short-ranged, and the only way that Vian's flotilla might be effective against the *Bismarck* was to mount a tightly coordinated attack—at night, in heavy seas, at ranges well within the reach of the *Bismarck*'s main guns and her secondary armament. If a single 15-inch shell found its mark, scratch one destroyer and most of its 160-to-200-man company.

In fact, Somerville's Force H was really the only British force capable of standing between the *Bismarck* and succor by midafternoon on the 26th. HMS *Renown*, with the *Ark Royal* in company, was about 75 miles east of the *Bismarck*. The *Ark Royal* would not stand up to the *Bismarck*'s shellfire for more than a few minutes. The *Renown* was even older than the *Hood* had been, smaller, less powerful, and with all the weaknesses of a battle cruiser. Even so, Somerville seriously considered sending the *Renown* into battle against the *Bismarck*, a suicide mission if ever there was one. As he later reported: "Should it be desirable for RENOWN to attack unsupported it was my intention to do so from upwind and astern with the object of causing him to turn and thus slow up his retreat, and also full use to be made of smoke."[42] In other words, Somerville would try to draw the *Bismarck* westward and give Admiral Tovey a chance to catch her, even though such a move would have put 1,500 British lives on the line. But Somerville was spared this grave decision. At 11:45 A.M. the Admiralty sent him a message not to engage the *Renown* unless the *King George V* and the *Rodney* were in company.[43]

Sir James Somerville had a personal stake in stopping the *Bismarck*. Like Tovey, he too had been frustrated by Lütjens two months earlier during Operation Berlin. On 20 March 1941, when Lütjens had approached the Biscay coast with the 11-inch battleships *Gneisenau* and *Scharnhorst*, a dusk air patrol flying off the *Ark Royal* had spotted the German flotilla just before nightfall. But Lütjens' ships had been 130 miles to the north of the carrier—too far to attack before dark. Somerville had lost his chance to block them, and Tovey never caught up. That had been an opportunity missed.[44] This time it was going to be different.

Somerville had no choice but to order Captain Maund to send his Swordfish to attack the *Bismarck*. Neither man believed they could sink her with those small 18-inch aerial torpedoes, but perhaps they might damage her enough to slow her up. Somerville and Maund both knew that was not going to be easy. Sea and sky conditions were about as close to making air operations impossible as they might be without actually shutting the air attack down. There was a 35-mile-per-hour wind blowing from the northwest, pushing the sea into 10-foot whitecapped waves. The sky was overcast, and visibility was 10 to 12 miles at best. The *Ark Royal*'s stern was rising and falling 56 feet at times, and the flight deck was slippery with sea spray. It was difficult for the flight deck and hangar crews to even manhandle the Swordfish onto the flight deck, let alone carry out all the necessary preflight preparations. Maund watched from the bridge as twenty men moved a Swordfish laboriously from the hangar deck elevator to the takeoff position. One moment they were pushing the airplane up a steep incline; the next they were breaking into a canter, holding on to the torpedo bomber for dear life, trying to keep their feet and prevent the aircraft from going over the stern or crashing into another parked aircraft. And each time the elevator disgorged another Swordfish, the deadly tango of men and plane on a wet, pitching flight deck began again, until fifteen aircraft were waiting to take off.

By 2:50 P.M. all reconnaissance and antisubmarine patrol aircraft flown off earlier had been recovered and stored in the hangar deck. It was time to launch the first strike of fifteen aircraft. Captain Maund watched intently from the bridge, his heart in his mouth, as the frail biplanes lifted off the pitching carrier deck and clawed for altitude. On the bridge of HMS *Renown*, Vice Admiral Somerville peered through his binoculars and waited until all fifteen had gotten off before turning back to the plotting table. The Swordfish wheeled over the *Ark Royal* as they formed into five subgroups of three planes each, then banked left and headed off to the southwest. Under each was an 18-inch torpedo with a duplex firing pistol set for 30 feet. This pistol was supposed to explode the torpedo on contact when it smashed into the side of its target, or explode it by magnetic influence when it slipped under the keel of its target. Blowing up under a ship's keel would do far more damage, because the effect of the explosion would be greatly magnified by the pressure of the seawater, much like a depth charge explosion.

The *Bismarck* was estimated to be 52 miles distant. With a strong crosswind, the Swordfish struggled to maintain course and keep speed at 80 knots.[45] They calculated they'd be onto the *Bismarck* in about forty-five minutes. The first aircraft in the No. 4 subflight, piloted by Sub-Lieutenant M. J. Lithgow, was equipped with an ASV (air search) radar watched intently by observer Sub-Lieutenant N. C. Cooper. As they droned through clouds and mist, Cooper spotted something on his screen. Against the roar of the engine he shouted the contact course and speed through the voice tube connecting him to Lithgow. Then he stood up into the slipstream and signaled the rest of the squadron that he had picked up a radar contact about 20 miles to starboard. He swung his arm to indicate the direction. The squadron banked sharply to settle on the new course. In the second aircraft of Lithgow's subflight, the officer commanding the squadron, Lieutenant Commander J. A. Stewart-Moore, thought that the contact did not correspond with the position of the *Bismarck* as given to the pilots in the carrier ready room. But, "as there were said to be no British ships in the area, it had to be German."[46] Then they saw a dark gray shape on the sea sliding by gaps in the clouds. It looked more like a cruiser than a battleship. Was it the *Prinz Eugen?* The Royal Navy pilots took up attack position, dove through the clouds, lost sight of each other as they descended, then poked through the cloud bottoms. Stewart-Moore's pilot, Lieutenant H. de G. Hunter, yelled through the voice tube, "It's the *Sheffield!*"

With her twin funnels, the *Sheffield* looked nothing like the *Bismarck*, but the adrenaline was flowing and the blood was up. Hunter pulled up and waggled his wings. Neither his Swordfish, nor any of the others were equipped with radios to talk to each other; they could speak only to the *Ark Royal*. One by one the other aircraft executed their attacks in textbook fashion as Hunter and Stewart-Moore looked on in horror. The Swordfish dove toward the British cruiser, flattened out near the water, held their speed and altitude, then dropped. One by one the torpedoes entered the water as the men aboard HMS *Sheffield* watched, transfixed by the terrible fate about to overwhelm them. In his fury and frustration, Captain Larcom was sorely tempted to order his antiaircraft gunners to open fire. But the immediate job was to save the *Sheffield*. He tensed and waited for the torpedoes to hit the water, ready to bark out orders to the coxswain to turn this way and that to comb the tracks and avoid the deadly fish.

Then, a miracle. One by one all the torpedoes except one or two exploded within a minute of hitting the water. The *Sheffield* easily avoided the rest. The duplex pistols had malfunctioned. Perhaps this was due to a quirk in the earth's magnetic field, or to tired, seasick men in the *Ark Royal*'s hangar deck who had failed to set them properly. Maybe the extreme turbulence on the sea had tossed the torpedoes about, upsetting the delicate firing mechanism. But whatever it was that gave a hint of divine intervention, it saved the *Sheffield*. The aircraft maintenance crews on the *Ark Royal* quickly exchanged duplex pistols for contact detonators when the next flight went out to attack the *Bismarck*.

The first strike force returned to the *Ark Royal* at 5:20 P.M., flying over four of Captain Vian's destroyers and reporting their presence. Immediately every available torpedo bomber was scraped together for a second attack. Maund and Somerville hoped against hope that they might get a third attack in before darkness and weather closed flying operations, but neither one was really optimistic about it. One by one the aircraft were laboriously refueled, rearmed, and checked for damage, all on the open, sea-swept flight deck. Again, fifteen aircraft were to be sent out. The weather had not improved from earlier in the day, when the first strike had been launched, but at 7:10 P.M. the first of the aircraft lifted ponderously off the flight deck, directly into the spray thrown up by the *Ark Royal*'s bow, and climbed to the cloud base. Fourteen other aircraft followed. They formed up, flew over the *Renown* at 7:25, and headed under the cloud layer for the *Sheffield*—this time not to attack her, but to use her as a reference point from which to attack the *Bismarck*. At 7:55 they spotted the *Sheffield*, calculated their direction and distance from the *Bismarck*, then climbed into the cloud layer for the run to the German battleship. At 8:47 P.M. the squadron began to lower through the clouds.

"Aircraft! Alarm!" The cry cut short Admiral Lütjens' musings about his precarious situation and the Luftwaffe's failure to start from their Biscay bases. Spotters on the *Bismarck* saw fifteen Swordfish torpedo bombers overhead, swooping down through the violent rain squalls and heavy clouds. But then, once more, they were gone as quickly as they had appeared. At that moment the *Bismarck*'s great 15-inch guns spewed out their deadly fire—at HMS *Sheffield*. Commander Adalbert Schneider's first salvo splashed into the Atlantic short of the light cruiser. His second salvo straddled the ship; four further salvos fell close. Lethal shell fragments caused a dozen casualties, three of them fatal. The *Sheffield* at once began to lay down dense smoke and to flee the scene at flank speed.

"Aircraft! Alarm!" Time: 8:30 P.M. Another wave of Swordfish torpedo bombers dove out of the clouds, singly and in pairs, recklessly coming at the *Bismarck* from all angles. Once more, the battleship became a mountain of fire. First Gunnery Officer Schneider ordered his main as well as secondary armament to fire at the bubbling tracks approaching the *Bismarck* just below the surface of the sea, hoping to explode some of the incoming torpedoes. At the same time, the four hundred men of the flak sprang into action with their heavy 4-inchers, as well as lighter 1.5-inch and .75-inch "pom-pom" guns. Soon the barrels became red-hot and what little paint remained blistered. The Swordfish were so close, Seaman Georg Herzog remembered, that he was ordered to send up barrage fire rather than to target single craft. Suddenly the *Bismarck* began to heel violently from side to side. Next she lost speed. On the captain's bridge, Lindemann once more was barking out furious commands: "All ahead full!" "All stop!" "Hard a-port!" "Hard a-starboard!" On and on, the staccato commands went, for fully fifteen minutes. One after another, the *Bismarck* evaded the deadly torpedoes.

Seaman Herzog, manning his port third 1.5-inch flak gun, saw three Swordfish approach the *Bismarck* from astern, at 270 degrees, then bank hard right, to 180 degrees. They were flying too low to allow accurate antiaircraft fire. Most of the planes were concentrating on the battleship's port side. Then Herzog saw two other torpedo bombers on the port beam. They also banked right to come at the ship from starboard, and at 875 yards off the *Bismarck*'s stern they released their torpedoes. Two of the "fish," only 13 to 20 feet apart, were headed to cross the battleship's projected course.[47] Captain Lindemann, afraid that a torpedo might hit his bow, thus seriously impairing the *Bismarck*'s maneuverability, screamed at his coxswain: "Hard a-port!" Perhaps he could cut in front of the expected track of the torpedoes. From the captain's bridge, Lindemann anxiously watched as the *Bismarck* and the bubble tracks closed on each other second by second.

The last group of Swordfish were met with immediate and intense antiaircraft fire. The No. 1 subflight went in first. They dropped. No hits. They scampered away, fishtailing, yawing, and corkscrewing over the seascape to get away from the intense antiaircraft fire. Then the No. 3 subflight went in, against the battleship's port beam, scoring a hit about one-third the length from the stern. The three Swordfish escaped. Next the No. 2 subflight, down from 9,000 feet, went against the *Bismarck*'s starboard beam. Two misses and another hit amidships. The No. 4 subflight, joined by another aircraft, attacked on the port side. One Swordfish took a hundred flak hits but managed to limp home to the carrier. The No. 5 subflight got separated from the other attackers and from each other. One of the aircraft saw a torpedo hit the *Bismarck* on the starboard side, but no one was quite sure where, or who had launched it. In a half hour it was over. Torpedoes expended, the exhausted and sorely tried crews struggled back to the *Ark Royal*, where all landed safely. Some of the aircraft were so badly shot up they would never fly again. It was too late in the day for another strike, but Captain Maund reported "one and probably two hits."[48]

Maund underestimated the impact of the attack. The first explosion, near Section VII amidships, did little more than raise a giant waterspout into the air. But another blast, this one near Section II at the *Bismarck*'s stern, lifted the ship up by the stern and rocked her from side to side. A number of survivors recalled their fears that the *Bismarck* might actually capsize. But after what seemed an eternity, she righted herself on the water.

Down in the battleship's engine rooms, near-panic ensued. Men were knocked down. Floor plates in the center engine room buckled upward a foot and a half. Welds split. Cable protectors stripped. Water poured in through the port shaft well. The safety valve in the starboard engine room closed and the engines shut down. The big ship was temporarily without power. The first damage-control team, consisting of men released from the *Bismarck*'s antiaircraft and secondary batteries, rushed aft and informed Captain Lindemann that the hole blasted in the *Bismarck*'s hull by the torpedo was so large that all the steering rooms were flooded and had to be evacuated. Seamen near the after armored hatch over the steering mechanism gazed down onto the open sea.

Seaman Herzog returned to his station; he recalled the sheer terror of the next few announcements over the ship's loudspeakers. "Rudder system fouled. Rudder jammed hard a-starboard. Ship slows to 19 knots." Then, "Ship steaming in a circle. Ship slows to 17 knots." And finally, "Ship slows to 13 knots."[49] The *Bismarck*'s fourth gunnery officer, Lieutenant Burkard von Müllenheim-Rechberg, on duty in the after firing-control station, sat almost on top of the torpedo hit. He heard the blast of the explosion and then got what he remembered as a "sickening feeling." He knew the *Bismarck* had been hit; "My heart sank." Müllenheim-Rechberg stared at the rudder indicator: "Left 12 degrees." Seconds went by. Still the same: "Left 12 degrees."[50] The *Bismarck* increasingly began to list to starboard. She was in a continuous counterclockwise turn. "Left 12 degrees." The rudder indicator was frozen at that setting. Speed had fallen to 13 knots. The howling nor'wester whipped the crests of the gigantic Atlantic breakers over the ship's deck. "Left 12 degrees." The rudder indicator was like a magnet, with all eyes aft riveted to it.

And then the full reality hit: the *Bismarck*'s twin parallel rudders were jammed. The battleship was turning wide circles in the middle of the Atlantic. St. Nazaire seemed an eternity away. Admiral Lütjens, laconic as always, signaled Paris at 9:05 P.M.: "Quadrant BE 6192; torpedo hit in stern!" And then at 9:15 P.M.: "Ship no longer maneuverable!"[51]

THE KILL

ON THE *BISMARCK*'S STERN Captain Ernst Lindemann rushed down from the bridge to supervise repairs. Two engineers, Lieutenants Gerhard Junack and Hermann Giese, along with a master carpenter's team, shored up the transverse bulkhead and sealed the broken valves and tubes. Next Lindemann sent men from the starboard gun turrets to the quarterdeck to try to place collision matting over the hole in the ship's hull, but the torrents of incoming seawater could not be stemmed. From the command center, First Officer Hans Oels repeatedly called Giese for up-to-the-minute damage assessment reports. When would the *Bismarck* resume way? Oels demanded to know.[1] On the admiral's bridge, Fleet Chief Günther Lütjens anxiously paced up and down, demanding instant damage reports from Lindemann.

The main problem, of course, was with the jammed parallel rudders. Junack and Giese and a master's mate came up with a plan: They would don diving gear, make their way through an armored hatch to the upper platform deck, and disengage the rudder-motor coupling. But each time they opened the armored hatch over the steering gear, the seawater blew them back—and then threatened to suck them down as the ship rose on the crest of a giant Atlantic breaker. Over and over, the same pattern: a torrent of water as the *Bismarck* plunged into a trough, then a sucking down as she rode the next wave crest. There was nothing to do but to close the hatch.

The *Bismarck* was now wallowing on an erratic course, roughly northwest, into 40-to-50-mile-per-hour winds and toward the enemy. Back on the bridge, Captain Lindemann, practically, tried to use the three main engines to steer the ship. "Port engines half ahead, center and starboard engines stop!" "Port and center engines half ahead, starboard engines back slow!" "Port engines full ahead, starboard engines stop!" No combination of ahead and astern power worked. When Lindemann ordered the starboard engine to run at a higher speed than the port engine, for example, he could force the *Bismarck* to turn to port. But as soon as some speed was attained, the twin rudders, each with an area of 24 square yards, would bite into the sea and drive the ship back to starboard. Moreover, Lindemann's repeated "Stop!" and "Full Power!" commands raised boiler pressure past prescribed limits. Temperature in the engine room climbed to 122 degrees Fahrenheit, as neither doors nor ventilators could be opened since the ship was still in a cleared-for-action state of readiness.[2] The great ship's hull vibrated noticeably throughout the ordeal.

A plan to send divers down to cut off the *Bismarck*'s rudders or to set charges to sever them was abandoned, as the violent seas were too high and the alternating pressure and suction of incoming and outgoing water allowed no one to get to the steering gear on the upper platform deck. Another plan, to weld the Arado floatplane's hangar door to the starboard side of the stern at a 15-degree angle—which would correspond to a rudder position of 12 degrees—likewise had to be abandoned due to the high seas and roaring gale. And a third proposal, to send divers down to uncouple the starboard rudder, failed when the divers discovered that the coupling was so badly damaged that it could not be budged.[3]

Hourly damage-control teams struggled to clear the *Bismarck's* fouled electric steering gear and rudders. Some even put forward the idea that a U-boat could be taken in tow as a steering drag, but Lindemann realized that a 700-ton submarine would be like a cork on the ocean.

Lütjens remained on the admiral's bridge, alone with his thoughts. His cold, analytical mind allowed only one conclusion: The great ship was doomed. Neither the *Scharnhorst* nor the *Gneisenau* at Brest was seaworthy. Destroyers could make little headway in the heavy seas and against such a strong headwind. Tugs could not possibly reach the *Bismarck* for forty hours. U-boats could barely stay afloat on the raging sea. The British most likely would wait until dawn to move in for the kill. There was no need to pretend otherwise. The admiral's staff—composed of experienced officers who had served with the pocket battleship *Graf Spee* off Montevideo in 1939 and with the battleship *Gneisenau*, as well as the heavy cruiser *Blücher*, during the Norway operation in 1940—most likely shared the task force commander's assessment of his dire predicament.[4]

A veteran of World War I, Lütjens was too painfully aware of the High Sea Fleet's inglorious rebellion in 1917, revolution in 1918, and scuttling in 1919. And then there was December 1939, when Captain Hans Langsdorff had scuttled the *Graf Spee* off the River Plate rather than sortie against three British cruisers.[5] For the stiff, duty-bound Lütjens, there could be no talk of scuttling or of surrendering his ship. If 2,220 officers and men had to be sacrificed, then that was the price the task force commander was willing to pay.

In April 1941 Lütjens had discussed Rhine Exercise with several colleagues and a former fleet chief. Admiral Wilhelm Marschall, his predecessor, had warned Lütjens not to stick too closely to Raeder's rigid orders but rather to improvise as conditions warranted. Lütjens, aware that Raeder had already fired two fleet chiefs for alleged "temerity," vowed that he would not be the third. When Admiral Conrad Patzig, Lütjens' mate from the Naval Academy Crew of 1907, had urged caution, Lütjens replied: "I am of the opinion that I should have to sacrifice myself sooner or later. I have closed out my private life."[6] His flagship now was not capable of maneuver, but her machinery, armaments, and crew were intact. The time had come for Lütjens to sacrifice himself. At 9:40 P.M.—just half an hour after the fatal torpedo strike—he informed Naval Group Command West of the inevitable: "Ship unable to maneuver. We will fight to the last shell. Long live the Führer."[7] The suddenness and the finality of the signal stunned both his fleet staff and the radiomen. There is no indication that Lütjens discussed this signal with Captain Lindemann.

Admiral Lütjens' melodramatic signal arrived in Germany about midnight. Grand Admiral Raeder and his staff quickly assessed the situation. Neither the *Scharnhorst* nor the *Gneisenau* was available for rescue. Neither the weather nor the distance to the *Bismarck* (400 nautical miles) allowed airplanes from Air Fleet 3 in France to reach the crippled ship in time. The weather also prevented a suicidal charge by German destroyers. Even the U-boats were too far removed and too battered by the gale to be of help. On 26 May and again on 27 May, Raeder entered his sober analysis into his war diary: "Given these circumstances, the ship's situation is hopeless."[8] To Lütjens, Raeder dispatched a somber message: "All our thoughts are with you and your ship. We wish you success in your desperate struggle." Admiral Alfred Saalwächter from Paris also added what amounted to condolences: "Our thoughts and good wishes are with our victorious comrades." And from Naval Group Command North, Admiral Rolf Carls also acknowledged the inevitable: "We think of all of you with loyalty and pride."[9] Behind the scenes, Raeder requested the Spanish government to dispatch the cruiser *Canarias* and two destroyers from Ferrol to assist what would be the *Bismarck* survivors. Hitler was furious; the request meant loss of prestige for the Third Reich.

Hitler was still at his alpine retreat at the Berghof in Bavaria, along with Major Nicolaus von Below, his Luftwaffe adjutant. At 12:36 A.M. Hitler was handed Lütjens' dramatic note. He at once dictated to Below a reply to Lütjens: "All of Germany is with you. Whatever can be done, will be done. Your sense of fulfilling your duty will strengthen our Folk in its struggle for survival. Adolf Hitler."[10] Then silence fell on the duumvirate at the Berghof as the harsh reality of the pending loss of the *Bismarck* set in. Finally Hitler asked about the number of lives at stake: roughly 2,300, Below replied. Hitler then became livid. "During the night," Below recalled, "Hitler became ever angrier and more enraged. He stated that he would never let another battleship or cruiser out into the Atlantic." The Führer excused himself sometime between 2 and 3 A.M. Below returned to his quarters "profoundly shocked": with the expected loss of the *Bismarck*, the Third Reich would suffer its first major setback in the war.[11]

Out in the raging Atlantic, some 400 miles north of Brittany, Captain Lindemann struggled to maintain at least some semblance of control over his ship. He realized that the *Bismarck* had to be kept under way to prevent her from wallowing and yawing helplessly in the 45-foot breakers. Lindemann discovered that he could steady the *Bismarck* only by holding her into the wind, that is, on a northwesterly course—over the same waters she had just traversed en route to St. Nazaire—at dead slow speed, 5 to 7 knots. Lindemann could not help but recall the urgency with which he had pressed both ship and crew into battle maneuvers in the Baltic Sea. Then, his ship had been green, his crew green. There had been so little time for workup, so little time for emergency drills. He had practiced the hit-in-the-steering-gear battle problem time and again, and each time the great ship had not responded well to his efforts to steer with the main engines. Now that practice had turned into deadly reality.

Sometime around midnight Captain Lindemann abandoned attempts to repair the rudders. Throughout the ship, as news of the jammed rudders made the rounds, a mood of despondency and despair returned. Late that night Lindemann announced to the crew that they could help themselves to anything they wanted from the ship's stores. The older hands had no illusions; most made their peace with their maker, while some faced the inevitable end with total indifference. The younger hands clung to the slender straws of hope: the promise of aircraft, tugs, tankers, and U-boats. They listened with fierce intensity to the loudspeakers: "Watch for our planes!" "Watch for our U-boats!"[12] Hope surged among many of them. Would Vice Admiral Karl Dönitz's "gray sharks" arrive in time to rescue them? Indeed, shortly before 8 P.M. Admiral Lütjens had received word from Paris that *U-48* was on her way to operate against HMS *Sheffield*. Could other boats be far behind?

The first Swordfish to return to the *Ark Royal* from the second strike wave began to arrive over the pitching carrier at 10:05 P.M. By ones and twos, the badly shot-up torpedo bombers approached the *Ark Royal*'s stern gingerly as Captain L. E. H. Maund's coxswain struggled to keep her stem into the wind. Flying directly into the gale, the pilots wrestled with stick, rudder bar, and throttle, trying to meet the bucking flight deck at precisely the right moment. If they made it, they cut throttles, and as their arrester hooks grabbed one of the six cables strung across the aft flight deck, they applied brakes to pitch to a stop. Most did make it. But a few of the "Stringbags" were badly damaged when the flight deck slammed into them from below just before touchdown. By the time all aircraft were taken aboard, it was far too late to launch a third strike. But Vice Admiral Sir James Somerville wanted his aircraft up at the crack of dawn, so flight deck personnel manhandled the aircraft below while mechanics, riggers, and armorers worked to prepare the Swordfish for a dawn launch. Miraculously, they had six aircraft rearmed and refueled, and back on the flight deck, within the hour. While the aircraft were being readied or repaired, pilots and observers were hustled to the ready room for postflight interrogation. They added little to what Captain Maund already knew. Sea conditions, the storm, and nightfall had made it all but impossible to assess the full extent of the damage to the German ship.[13]

That was bad news for Admiral Sir John Tovey, still about 100 miles to the northwest. With HMS *Rodney* now steaming purposefully behind HMS *King George V*, the commander in chief of the Home Fleet was literally running out of gas. Five and a half hours earlier the chief engineer had showed Tovey his calculations on how much fuel remained and how far it would carry them. The *King George V* had used up 68 percent of her fuel since departing Scapa Flow, and the remaining 32 percent, or 1,184 tons, would be enough for only about 1,350 miles of steaming at a relatively economical 20 knots. That was not good enough. At a leisurely 10 knots, the *King George V* could steam 14,000 miles, but at double that speed her engines swallowed fuel at a much greater rate, restricting her range to some 4,300 miles. Since turning southwest toward the Biscay coast the previous afternoon, the *King George V* had been steaming at 25 knots, gulping fuel at more than 100 gallons per minute. Then, at about the time the *Ark Royal* launched her first air strike at the *Bismarck*, Admiral Tovey had ordered Captain W. R. Patterson to slow to 22 knots. That was much too slow to close the gap on the *Bismarck*, but even that speed was too fast, too fuel-consuming, to allow Tovey to stay in the chase much longer. Moreover, Tovey feared that U-boats were closing in, while the Admiralty warned him that heavy German air attacks might descend on his ships after dawn on the 27th. John Tovey wanted revenge for the *Hood* as much as any man alive, but he had a duty to king and country to preserve the *King George V*, which he knew was now Britain's "only effective capital ship in home waters." Not long after 9:00 P.M. he radioed the first sea lord, Admiral Sir Dudley Pound, that he was going to break off the chase at midnight unless the *Bismarck*'s speed had been significantly reduced.[14]

What Tovey did not realize as his radio signals sparked across a thousand miles of ocean to the Admiralty's giant receiving towers was that two Swordfish were still droning through the sky above the *Bismarck*. These were the trackers sent from the *Ark Royal* to dog the German ship and help the light cruiser *Sheffield* maintain contact. They had watched from a distance as the second strike force attacked; then, when the attackers departed and the antiaircraft fire died away, they went back to tracking the *Bismarck*. The two aircraft ducked in and out of huge cloud banks as the pilots fought against side winds and headwinds, while the observers struggled to keep the giant battleship in sight until total darkness. These four cold, wet, and tired men were sorely tested just to keep their supper down. As the gale tossed their aircraft about, it was almost impossible to keep the *Bismarck* in sight long enough to calculate her course and speed. But at 9:15 P.M. one of the two Swordfish radioed the *Ark Royal*: "Enemy course 090." In the carrier's radio room the message was duly written down and brought to Captain Maund, still on the bridge. At first he could hardly believe the news. The course was 90 degrees? The *Bismarck* was steaming due east? But then Maund realized that there was nothing unusual about that. No doubt she would quickly swing back to her base course of 120 degrees. She had just been attacked by torpedo bombers, after all, and was probably just coming out of her high-speed avoidance maneuvers.

Another message from one of the tracking Swordfish followed the first seven minutes later: "Enemy course 000." This made absolutely no sense. The *Bismarck* would not possibly have changed course to due north. The observation must be in error. Maund felt more than a touch of sympathy for his flyers, out in that raging, darkening twilight, holding on for dear life in open cockpits, trying to keep the enemy in sight and the chase alive. But six minutes later another message was placed into his hands: "Enemy changed course to port." And two minutes after that: "Enemy course 340." Why, *Bismarck* had turned a complete circle. She had steamed all the way around the compass and had come back to almost due north. She was now closing on the *King George V* and the *Rodney*. Captain Maund and his staff quickly studied the charts. There was no mistake. The *Bismarck*'s movements made no rational sense. As they huddled over the chart table, another message from one of the Swordfish: "Enemy laying smoke." That was the clincher for Maund. The *Bismarck* was hurt, badly hurt, maybe even out of control, wallowing in the storm, making smoke to conceal herself from the tracking aircraft and from the *Sheffield*. Five minutes later, another message: "Enemy course 330." She was still turning to port.

Then at 9:36 P.M. the *Sheffield*'s powerful radio boomed out a message that absolutely confirmed the information coming from the two Swordfish: *Bismarck* was steering 340 degrees and turning to port. Four minutes later the *Sheffield* radioed again—the *Bismarck* was now steaming due north. There was no way on God's earth that Admiral Lütjens was deliberately choosing to head back along his track to challenge Tovey's Home Fleet, not with British cruisers, destroyers, and a carrier hard on his heels. When Somerville, Tovey, and the Admiralty picked up the *Sheffield*'s two transmissions, there was jubilation. The cause for celebration was confirmed by 11:35 P.M., when the two tracking Swordfish landed on the *Ark Royal* and the crews reported that the *Bismarck* had made two complete circles at slow speed after being hit by a torpedo. The *Ark Royal*'s "String-bags" had done their job. At the last possible moment, they had struck the *Bismarck* a crippling blow. For the moment, the *Bismarck* was in the bag. The question was, for how long?[15]

For the first time in the ninety-six hours that had elapsed since the main body of the Home Fleet had sortied from Scapa Flow, Admiral Tovey had the upper hand. He did not know how long that happy situation would last. His first thought was to go after the *Bismarck* right away. He was about four hours away. With the *Rodney* behind him and the *Bismarck* unable to maneuver, the battle was a foregone conclusion. At 9:42 P.M. he ordered Captain Patterson, commanding the flagship, and Captain F. H. G. Dalrymple-Hamilton, commanding the *Rodney*, to shape course for 180 degrees—due south—to close and engage without delay.[16] But having made that decision, Tovey now gathered with his staff for the umpteenth time since that long-ago morning of 21 May to take their counsel. They were as dog-tired as he was. Captain Patterson had hardly slept in four days; Commodore E. J. P. "Daddy" Brind, his chief of staff, had done little better. For the first time since those two could recall, Tovey himself appeared rumpled and a bit disheveled. But although fatigue had corroded their physical and mental alertness, the knowledge that the *Bismarck* was finally within their reach was all the tonic they needed to see this great chase through to the end.

They discussed the variables. They knew the men in the enemy ship were working feverishly to repair whatever damage had caused them to lose control of the *Bismarck*. They knew a modern battleship had many resources with which to patch itself together long enough to reach safe harbor. They were also certain that Hitler would drive his commanders hard to send every U-boat, every tug, every destroyer, and every plane to the scene. Night was falling fast; total darkness would soon be upon them. The sea was in a frenzy, driven by high winds. The sky was obscured by rain squalls and low clouds. The *King George V* and the *Rodney* would reach the *Bismarck* while it was still pitch dark. Was it not better to open the battle at dawn, ships carefully positioned to keep the *Bismarck* fixed while she was pounded from all sides?

Admiral Tovey's once-powerful fleet had shrunk due to fuel depletion, but the *Sheffield* was still shadowing the *Bismarck*, and the *Ark Royal* was less than an hour's flying time from the German vessel and would be ready to launch aircraft whenever light conditions and weather permitted. Captain Benjamin Martin, commanding the heavy cruiser *Dorsetshire*, was pushing through heavy seas to join them. Even the *Norfolk* was on her way. She had been making for Portsmouth to refuel when the *Bismarck* had been relocated; after all the heartache she and her company had spent trying to bring the *Bismarck* to bay, Rear Admiral Frederick Wake-Walker was desperate to be in on the finish. Finally, Captain Philip Vian's destroyers were coming on fast. Even without direct radio contact with Vian, Tovey reckoned the destroyer commander would ignore his by-now irrelevant instructions from the Admiralty to shield the *Rodney*, the *King George V*, and Vice Admiral Somerville's ships from German subs and would make directly for the *Bismarck*. The destroyers ought to make visual contact with the *Bismarck* within the hour. The *Bismarck* was not going anywhere. Best to wait until dawn before closing on her. Tovey ordered Patterson and Dalrymple-Hamilton to turn east, to steam to the north-northeast of the *Bismarck*'s position. They would then work around to engage the German from the west at dawn. They would go straight at her out of the still-dark western sky; she would be visible to them against the early-morning twilight.[17] The new course was set at 11:06 P.M.: due eastward. The *King George V* and the *Rodney* swung to port in the heavy swell, and with a strong wind pushing on their port bows, they made for the spot from which they would begin their attack run at dawn.

As the *King George V* and the *Rodney* turned, the USS *New York* plodded eastward at 15 knots. Some 2,100 miles west-southwest of the battle zone, she was well out of the way of any possible confrontation with the *Bismarck* now. That no doubt relieved her commanding officer, Captain J. G. Ware. The *Bismarck* would have made short order of this old, slow, thinly armored, outgunned battleship. But the *Bismarck*'s imminent destruction did not end the *New York*'s involvement in the episode. There were German tankers and supply ships out there to be discovered and marked off for the Royal Navy. The *New York* had already sent her destroyers to stop and inspect two mysterious merchantmen early on the morning of 26 May. More such inspections would follow in the next few days. Perhaps the *Prinz Eugen* would steam into the *New York*'s patrol area. In London, Admiral Robert L. Ghormley was coordinating U.S. Navy and Royal Navy cooperation. President Franklin D. Roosevelt was keenly following the *Bismarck* chase; so were Navy Secretary Frank Knox, Chief of Naval Operations Admiral Harold R. Stark, and Admiral "Ernie" King, commander in chief of the Atlantic Fleet.[18]

The *New York* steamed on into the night; the wind from the southwest increased to 40 miles per hour and the seas mounted. On her flanks, her three destroyers rose and fell in the heavy seas, pitching from side to side as their bows knifed into the waves. The task force pressed on for five more days, until it reached the farthest point in its patrol at 8:00 P.M. on 31 May. As they approached longitude 30 degrees, the limit of the president's newly expanded neutrality zone, they prepared to turn back. When they did so, the *New York* was less than 100 miles southeast of the position the *Bismarck* had thundered past on her run to the French coast just four days earlier. Given Roosevelt's orders to his navy to do everything short of war to help the British, and Lütjens' determination to fight his way through the neutrality zone, those four days had been the margin of the *New York*'s survival. They also allowed the United States seven more months of official peace.[19]

At 8:00 P.M. on 26 May 1941 Lieutenant Herbert Wohlfahrt brought U-556 to the surface in a gale and a heaving, rolling sea. Winds of 45 to 50 miles per hour whipped up the Atlantic with dense streaks of foam. Before him, "bow right, 10 degrees," lay the aircraft carrier *Ark Royal* and the battle cruiser *Renown* of Force H from Gibraltar.

Known throughout the U-boat service as "Sir Parsifal," Herbert Wohlfahrt was one of "Volunteer Corps Dönitz's" most skilled and cold-blooded hunters.[20] During the period from 5 to 21 November 1939, the U-boats' longest dry spell in the war, Wohlfahrt, commanding the old "duck" U-137, in an audacious night surface attack had torpedoed four ships totaling 13,300 tons out of a Gibraltar convoy bound for Britain. During the "happy time" of May to December 1942 Wohlfahrt had sunk seven more ships, for another 25,440 tons. By the end of 1941 the zealous skipper with U-14 and U-137 had dispatched nineteen Allied ships, for a total of 47,919 tons. Dönitz had rewarded Wohlfahrt with a new Type VIIC boat, U-556.

On 6 February 1941 U-556 was formally commissioned at the Blohm & Voss Shipyard at Hamburg. Wohlfahrt was disappointed that the yard had not provided a military band for the occasion. He spied the *Bismarck* undergoing final workup and requested that her skipper supply the fleet band. Captain Lindemann agreed. In return, Wohlfahrt handed the *Bismarck*'s skipper a formal sponsorship document:

> We, the U-556 (500 tons) hereby declare before Neptune, the ruler of the oceans, seas, lakes, rivers, brooks, ponds, and rills, that we will stand beside our big brother, the battleship *Bismarck* (42,000 tons), whatever may befall her from water, land, or in the air.[21]

On 28 February *U-556* received ammunition, fuel, provisions, and torpedoes at Kiel for her maiden voyage. It was to be a memorable patrol.[22] Already en route to the killing grounds of the North Atlantic, Wohlfahrt warmed up to the task at hand. He attacked and sank the unarmed Faeroe Island fishing schooner *Emanual*, killing three of its crew of eight fishermen by gunfire. In a later radio broadcast from Berlin, Wohlfahrt described the blazing schooner as "a most beautiful sight to see."

Shortly after midnight on 10 May, *U-556*, standing east of Greenland, well beyond the reach of Iceland-based Allied air forces, attacked convoy Outbound 318, guarded by the Third Escort Group. At 4:42 A.M. Wohlfahrt fired a single torpedo; a second eel followed one minute later. Both struck their designated targets amidships—the 8,500-ton tanker *British Sovereign* and the 5,000-ton freighter *Hercules*. As dawn arrived, Wohlfahrt was content to break off the hunt. "Suddenly, a single steamer approaches from behind." At 7:52 A.M. he fired a double spread from tubes two and three at the intruder. Both eels struck home. Wohlfahrt recorded that *U-556* had destroyed a 13,000-ton British tanker (which in reality turned out to be a 4,900-ton freighter). Later that morning, he fired the torpedo in the stern tube at a convoy steamer. It darted under its intended victim. By now, Outbound 318 had scattered in all directions.

At noon *U-556* submerged and reloaded her torpedoes. At 8:37 P.M. that night Wohlfahrt came across a straggler and fired a single eel from tube two. It crashed into the target under the bridge, but the 5,100-ton Belgian freighter *Gand* refused to sink. In panic, her crew took to the lifeboats. Wohlfahrt circled his wounded victim at periscope depth. She carried a single deck gun. He pounced in for the kill. "Set the steamer ablaze with artillery fire to help it sink. Steamer sunk." Four enemy ships destroyed—it had been a good night's work.

For the better part of a week, *U-556* joined seven other boats in a "west group" south-southeast of Cape Farewell, Greenland. Just after midnight on 19–20 May Wohlfahrt decided to break off the patrol and head home. "I am down to 35 tons of fuel. I can no longer tarry here, if I want to take advantage of possible opportunities to attack on the way home." He shaped course for the Bay of Biscay, with no radio signal to alert the enemy. "I will not report in until tomorrow night so as not to betray the position of the boats." But at 6:36 P.M. his Enigma board lit up. First, Lieutenant Herbert Kuppisch in U-94 had discovered another convoy, HX 126, screened by a single auxiliary cruiser. Second, from Paris, Vice Admiral Dönitz, the "Great Lion," congratulated Wohlfahrt on having been awarded the coveted Knight's Cross. "Now, especially," Wohlfahrt recorded in the war log, "at him!" But the convoy refused to zigzag and instead steamed due west, away from U-556. "Almost impossible to close with it, as that would put me ever further from home base."

The 20th of May broke heavy with fog and rain. Visibility was poor. By noon Wohlfahrt was despondent. "Will have to abandon the search for the convoy in 1 hour." Suddenly Kuppisch was back on the Enigma: "Convoy in sight." Wohlfahrt smelled blood. "He has led us by the nose for too long; now it is his turn!"[23] In short order, HX 126 became a blazing hell. At 2:48 P.M. Wohlfahrt fired a double spread from tubes one and two at an 8,000-ton tanker. "Both torpedoes hit." But there was no time to observe the kill. At 2:50 P.M. he fired a third eel at yet another tanker. He was so close that not even an error in setting the target angle mattered; the torpedo ran but twenty-five seconds. "The tanker was struck amidships and immediately burst into bright flames." A third tanker was discernible in the convoy's outer column. Again, there was no time to set a proper angle for the torpedo in tube four. "2:54 P.M. *Fired despite this*, for the eels must be expended now. [Low] fuel level will not allow me to leap ahead of the convoy." But the torpedo missed as the tanker suddenly swerved. "The convoy now steamed wildly in all directions, and I had to be careful not to get run over." The inferno raged on. "The oil from the two tankers has spread over the water. The entire sea is on fire. In its middle, looming gigantically, the burning tanker. It is dreadfully beautiful."[24] In desperation, the convoy ships hurled fog canisters into the ocean.

Time to reload the bow tubes. At 3:16 P.M. a fourth torpedo

from tube one struck "a beautiful 5,000-ton tanker, its decks loaded with large crates, most likely automobiles and aircraft."[25] The target sank after an internal boiler explosion. Chaos continued all around U-556. Her radioman reported four torpedoes running close by in the direction of the convoy. "Then four detonations." One rocked the U-boat and short-circuited several of its ammeters. "Probably a munitions ship or a tanker has exploded." By now U-556 was down to 21 tons of fuel oil. Wohlfahrt ordered propulsion reduced to one screw. A last look back at the carnage: "The entire northern horizon is a sea of smoke and flame." At 5:38 P.M. Sir Parsifal reported to Lion Heart (Dönitz) the sinking of seven ships totaling 49,900 tons, including the auxiliary cruiser *Cheshire*. Time to return to base. The Great Lion agreed.

Ever so slowly U-556 pointed southeast for Lorient. Then, at 4:56 P.M. on 24 May, Dönitz ordered Wohlfahrt to assist the *Bismarck*. U-556 used her last fuel reserves to reach her "sponsor" in time. At 3:31 P.M. on 26 May Wohlfahrt was attacked from the air. Just as suddenly, the intruder disappeared. As he dove in heavy seas half an hour later, Wohlfahrt heard several explosions, "Like artillery fire." Up above, the *Bismarck* was shaping a course for 115 degrees in a fresh gale, slightly northwest of the U-boat patrol line. By 7:48 P.M. Wohlfahrt had brought his craft up to periscope depth. Quadrant BE 5332, visibility moderate to good, 40-to-50-mile-per-hour winds. He could hardly believe the sight that greeted him:

> Alarm! Through the haze from abaft the beam, a battleship of the King George class and an aircraft carrier, probably *Ark Royal*, hove into view at high speed. Bow right, 10 degrees. If only I had torpedoes now!!!! I would not even have to plot an approach, but already am properly positioned to attack. Without destroyers, without zigzagging!! I could squeeze in between them and finish both off concurrently.[26]

"The carrier," he recorded, "is abuzz with torpedo-planes." They were Swordfish ordered to strike the *Bismarck* a second time.

Lieutenant Wohlfahrt thought back on the eels that had misfired as well as on those that had struck "mere" freighters, and on his zeal to expend all his torpedoes. The opportunity of a lifetime, and U-556 was out of torpedoes. All Wohlfahrt could do was to send Dönitz sighting reports on the British warships, which he did frantically at 8:43, 8:52, 9:07, 9:47, and 10:06 P.M. Radio transmissions instead of torpedoes.

The only other U-boat to be in position possibly to help the *Bismarck* was U-74. At 6:30 A.M. on 27 May Wohlfahrt had given her commander, Lieutenant Eitel-Friedrich Kentrat, the battleship's position. But Kentrat couldn't make headway against the rolling swell, and his bridge was constantly underwater, allowing almost no visual observation. "It is an abominable night," Kentrat wrote in his war log. At 7:26 A.M. a cruiser and a destroyer forced him to crash-dive and to run north with the swell. When U-74 resurfaced at 9:22 a.m., the sea was empty. The wind had fallen to a moderate gale, but the sea ran high as ever. Clouds and rain pelted the small craft. U-Boat headquarters near Lorient signaled: "U-Kentrat, retrieve KTB *Bismarck*!" Reluctantly, Kentrat replied: "Retrieval of *Bismarck*'s KTB no longer possible." Finally, a melodramatic entry into the war log: "Powerless and with our hands tied, we faced the unleashed forces of nature's might—without being able to help our brave *Bismarck*."[27]

On the surface, the men on the *Bismarck* had been oblivious to U-556's rescue attempts. Captain Lindemann could barely hold her 50,000 tons on a steady northwesterly course. Giant breakers broke over her bow and against her superstructure, rising as high as the fire-control center in the foretop. Ever so slowly, the "pride of the navy" wallowed toward certain destruction. It was a dark, sinister, moonless night.

That darkness, and the rain squalls that intensified the gloom, occasionally hid the *Bismarck* from the lookouts clinging to HMS *Sheffield*'s upper works. No one realized that the *Bismarck*'s erratic course was bringing the two ships closer and closer. Suddenly, at 9:40 P.M.—

bare moments after the *Sheffield* radioed that the *Bismarck* was out of control—great flashes of light flared behind the cloud and drove away the darkness. Fortunately for the *Sheffield*, the *Bismarck*'s first salvo of 15-inch shells fell short. Seconds later came the unmistakable rushing roar that heavy shells make when they split the air in flight. Then six massive columns of water exploded upward as shells from the *Bismarck*'s main guns straddled the cruiser. No direct hits, but one explosion sent lethal shell splinters flying across the unprotected after part of the *Sheffield*. On the bridge, Captain Charles Larcom shouted orders: "Full ahead both! Make smoke! Hard a-port." The coxswain swung the wheel, the engine room telegraphs rang, the engineers threw the steam valves fully open, and the *Sheffield* turned desperately away, gathering speed with every second and heeling over as she escaped. Three men were dead, two were seriously injured, three slightly injured. The *Sheffield*'s main radar went dead from a splinter in the main mast; the damage-control party counted some forty splinter holes above the waterline. In her wild escape from certain destruction, she lost visual contact with the *Bismarck*, and now, with her radar screen gone dark, she could not reacquire it. Captain Larcom set course to the north of the *Bismarck*'s estimated position, running in the darkness before slowing to take full stock of the damage. At 11:10 P.M. he estimated the *Sheffield* as 14 miles off the *Bismarck*'s port beam. Visibility was "treacherous," and he made no effort to close. The *Sheffield* never again made contact with the *Bismarck*. Later, after dawn, the ship's company heard the sound of heavy shelling as they sighted the *Renown* and the *Ark Royal* and rejoined Force H.[28] With the *Sheffield* gone, it was Philip Vian's task to keep tabs on the *Bismarck* through the night.

On the bridge of the *Cossack*, Vian was both the ship's commander and the "Captain (D)" or division commander of the four Royal Navy tribal-class destroyers and the Polish (British-built N-class) destroyer *Piorun*. He knew the *Bismarck* was crippled, going nowhere, and that the *King George V* and the *Rodney* were going to engage at first light. He had received the *Sheffield*'s last sighting report and knew approximately where the German battleship was.

The order went out to the other destroyer captains: a high-speed approach in line-abreast, 2.5 miles apart, at right angles to the *Bismarck*'s estimated course. Running ahead of the heavy seas, the destroyers buried their bows into the monster waves as they cut toward the enemy. The *Piorun*, on the far left of the charging destroyer line, sighted the *Bismarck* first, at 11:38 P.M. Four minutes later the *Bismarck*'s secondary guns opened up; the destroyer's decks were showered with shell splinters. The impudent Pole returned fire with her puny 4.7-inch guns as she skidded away, laying down smoke. She then struggled around to the north in the heavy swell, steaming up-sea of the *Bismarck*. The *Maori* was next to come under fire. Charging at the *Bismarck* between the *Piorun* on her port beam and the *Cossack* to starboard, she came under the *Bismarck*'s guns just moments after the *Piorun*. Her captain, Commander H. T. Armstrong, ordered a hard turn to port, doubled back on his track, then circled back to the southwest of the *Bismarck*. The *Cossack*, the *Sikh*, and the *Zulu* raced past untouched. The flotilla, less the *Piorun*, then reformed about 10 miles to the south of the battleship as Vian weighed his options.

At first Vian had thought only of tracking and containing the *Bismarck*, but now he decided to attack. He ordered his destroyers to charge in to launch their 21-inch torpedoes; as flotilla commander, he went first. Midnight came and went, and the 26th of May dissolved into the 27th. The order went out from the *Cossack*'s bridge: "Full ahead both. Midships. Prepare to launch torpedoes." The *Cossack* picked up speed, closely followed by the *Zulu*, the *Sikh*, and the *Maori*.

Through the driving rain squalls, the *Bismarck*'s lookouts spotted Vian's charging destroyers almost immediately. The range shortened by the minute: 8,000 yards, 6,000 yards, 4,000 yards. First Gunnery Officer Adalbert Schneider and Second Gunnery Officer Helmut Albrecht immediately opened up on the *Cossack* and the *Sikh* with their 6-inch antidestroyer guns. Once again, the *Bismarck*'s superior firepower was brought to bear: Vian's destroyer was straddled immediately and splinters destroyed her main aerials. Vian put his wheel over and ran off. Next, Schneider and Albrecht targeted the *Zulu*, this time with the 15-inch main armament. Again, the first salvo was a straddle. Splinters wounded three men, and the *Zulu*, like the *Cossack* before her, was forced to turn away. At 12:25 A.M. the *Bismarck* shifted target to the *Sikh*. Incredibly, she once again straddled the target with her first salvo. The *Sikh* also had to put her wheel hard over to escape. It was unbelievable shooting: the *Bismarck* was rolling on the heavy sea, the night was pitch dark with rain squalls and powder smoke obscuring accurate viewing, and without rudders she was swinging some eighty points between northwest and northeast.[29]

Shortly after 1 A.M. the *Maori* took her turn. Commander Armstrong illuminated his target with several shots of star shell—high-arcing white illumination rounds. "Fire on the bow!" came the cry from one of the *Maori*'s lookouts. Some of the star shell had landed on the battleship's forecastle. Armstrong then closed to 3,200 yards to bring his torpedo gear into play. The *Maori* launched two torpedoes, and then Armstrong also had to put her wheel over and seek safety. The mêlée lasted until 3 A.M., when Vian decided that he could not possibly launch a coordinated attack on the still-powerful *Bismarck*. Final shots were exchanged at 7 A.M., when the *Maori* once more tried to torpedo the battleship—only to be straddled again repeatedly. Captain Lindemann sought to lift the spirits of the *Bismarck*'s crew by inaccurately informing them that one destroyer had been sunk and two severely damaged and set on fire.[30] Admiral Lütjens sent a terse signal to Paris, stating the obvious: "Ship fully intact in terms of armaments and machinery. But cannot be steered with engines."[31]

The frenetic action with Vian's destroyers had caused near-pandemonium in the *Bismarck*'s engine rooms. Without pause, Captain Lindemann had ordered "Full speed ahead!" then "Full speed astern!" Next came "Stop!" for the starboard engine, followed by "Ahead!" for the center and port engines. The throttles on the turbines leapt from "Open!" to "Close!" to "Reverse!" in a bewildering succession that lasted about four hours. Desperately Lindemann struggled to evade Vian's steady barrage of torpedoes. The *Bismarck*'s fourth artillery officer, Burkard von Müllenheim-Rechberg, later recalled the scene:

> The men, sweat oozing from every pore, had hardly a dry stitch on their bodies. A sweatband around the head, a slice of lemon in the right corners of the mouth, a cigar or pipe in the left—they looked comical and their mood matched their appearance.[32]

One turbine froze. Steam pressure rose to fifty-eight atmospheres and reached 750 degrees Fahrenheit. Finally the blades turned.

Wohlfahrt's submerged submarine heard the muffled noises of the deadly action on the surface. He was helpless. At midnight he surfaced in a pitch-black, rainy night. "But what can I do for *Bismarck?*" Nothing. He observed star shell and the long-range artillery duel between the *Bismarck* and her pursuers. "What a horrible feeling, to be so close and not to be able to do anything, since I have neither torpedoes nor fuel."[33] At 6:30 A.M. on 27 May Wohlfahrt again registered the heavy artillery fire. He sent the Great Lion his last position report.

As if to torment him further, Dönitz at 8:35 A.M. (Paris time) on 27 May sent Wohlfahrt a funereal order: "U-556 proceed to *Bismarck* and retrieve fleet war diary." Admiral Lütjens, painfully aware that the history of Rhine Exercise would be written by Grand Admiral Raeder and his staff, had tried desperately to get one of the Arado 196 floatplanes to fly the *Bismarck*'s war diary to France so that his account of his actions could be fully weighed. But the Arado could not take off because the catapult's tracks and hydraulic lines had been broken—most likely by the hit on the nearby service boat during the Battle of Iceland. Since it was fully fueled, the aircraft was dumped overboard, drifting off on the ocean, floats up. Next, Lütjens requested that a U-boat pick up the war diary. But U-556 was so low on fuel that Wohlfahrt doubted whether he could even steam back to the wreck. At 14:02 P.M. Paris received the disheartening news: "Retrieval of war diary impossible due to fuel shortage for return leg."[34] Wohlfahrt headed for Lorient, which he made on 30 May. Undoubtedly remembering his sponsorship pact with the battleship in February, he ruefully added to the war log: "Perhaps I could have helped *Bismarck*."

In the *King George V*, Tovey followed Vian's struggle. When it was obvious that the heavy sea and bad visibility were making it almost impossible for the four destroyers to make a concerted and coordinated attack against the *Bismarck*, Tovey radioed Vian to make sure the Germans' position was marked throughout the night hours. This was important; Tovey would have to begin making his approach run before dawn if he was to appear before the *Bismarck* at precisely the right moment, with darkness behind him and the *Bismarck* backlit by the first glow of the coming day. To do that, he needed to know where the *Bismarck* was every minute of the night. At first the destroyers fired star shell over the battleship in the hope the pyrotechnics would be seen for many miles over the seascape and Tovey would know where the *Bismarck* was. But every salvo brought retaliation from the *Bismarck*. Then the destroyers tried to mark their position—and the *Bismarck*'s—by medium-frequency radio transmissions that could be fixed from Force H and the Home Fleet's two battleships. But the destroyers' radio antennas had been badly shot up and the *Zulu*'s deck insulator smashed—every time she tried to transmit, she threw off large sparks, marking her position for the *Bismarck*'s gunners. Tovey decided that although he had a good general idea of where the *Bismarck* was, he did not have an accurate enough fix to attack at dawn. He told Captains Patterson and Dalrymple-Hamilton that they would open the action only after full light.[35] That would come at about 8:30 A.M., less than four hours from the time when they would have to turn back due to their dwindling fuel supplies. Their gunnery would be aided by the *Norfolk*, just taking up position to the north of the *Bismarck*, which was given the job of flank marking, or calling the fall of shot to the two British battleships as they fired at the *Bismarck*.

Admiral Tovey retired to his sea cabin to rest, maybe to catch a few moments of sleep if he could. The ship's storm-tossed movement combined with the constant throb of the giant boilers and turbines from seven decks below and the continuous chatter of men coming and going to the chart house, the plotting office, or the bridge conspired against sleep. So did his own fears. He knew they would get the *Bismarck*, but how many of his own men would yet die in the effort? He had been through this many times before, the calm before the storm, as the fiction writers loved to put it. But this was not fiction. He knew that the apparent solidity of the bulkheads and decks surrounding him was an illusion, that the *Bismarck*'s huge armor-piercing shells could blow that illusion apart in an instant. He knelt beside his simple bunk and prayed for guidance and help. As he murmured words of devotion and beseechment, his anxieties melted away. He felt as if all responsibility for the final outcome was being lifted from his shoulders. He knew everything would turn out all right.[36]

After Vian's destroyers ceased their attacks, an eerie silence descended over the *Bismarck*. At 7:22 A.M. a gray dawn broke over the heavy seas. In the engine rooms, the men, five days and nights now without sleep, fell into an exhaustion-induced sleep. In the turrets, gunners fell asleep at their posts. On the bridge, Commander Schneider and several other officers slumped down on the floor also, dead asleep.

And then, a ray of hope. Naval Group Command West informed the fleet chief that three tugs and three bomber groups would start from France between 5 and 6 A.M. Rumors of impending rescue spread like wildfire throughout the *Bismarck*. Admiral Lütjens, ever the brutal realist, moved quickly to head off further scuttlebutt. He called on Captain Lindemann: "Please inform the crew that early in the morning 81 *Junkers-87* [*sic*] aircraft will join us; in addition, two tugs and one tanker. The U-boats have received orders to close with *Bismarck*."[37] But there was no room for hope in Lütjens' dour and depressed mind. At 2:58 A.M. he again signaled Hitler: "We will fight to the last, believing in you, my Führer, and with unshakable faith in Germany's victory."[38]

At the Berghof in the Bavarian Alps, Major von Below composed several replies for Hitler, who had retired for the night. To Lütjens: "I thank you in the name of the entire German Folk." To the crew of the *Bismarck*: "All of Germany is with you. What can still be done, will be done. Your performance of your duty will strengthen our Folk in its belief in our struggle for existence."[39] Each communiqué from the Führer was relayed to the *Bismarck*'s crew. Finally, Lütjens requested that Commander Schneider be awarded the Knight's Cross for sinking the *Hood*. At 3:51 A.M. Grand Admiral Raeder signaled the *Bismarck* that Hitler had consented to the decoration.[40] In the gray twilight of dawn, Tuesday, 27 May 1941, Naval Group Command West informed the *Bismarck* first that two Focke-Wulf 200 reconnaissance aircraft had taken off at 3:30 A.M. and, second, that fifty-one bombers had started between 5:20 and 6:45 A.M. For a fleeting moment the news, when announced to the crew over the loudspeakers, raised hopes and expectations yet again. Some broke out in song.

The great battleship continued to roll on the heavy seas—ever closer to Admiral Tovey's battleships, cruisers, and destroyers. The wind continued to howl at about 50 miles per hour. Around 8 A.M. Lieutenant von Müllenheim-Rechberg took leave of his after gunnery station and paid a visit to the bridge. He found Lindemann in the forward conning tower, being served breakfast by his steward, Arthur Meier. The *Bismarck*'s skipper was wearing an open life jacket. He neither returned Müllenheim-Rechberg's salute nor acknowledged his presence. "This was not the Lindemann we all knew." Only four hours earlier Lindemann, "beaming with delight" and chain-smoking cigarettes as ever, had congratulated his first gunnery officer on having been awarded the Knight's Cross. Now Lindemann just sat there in sullen gloom. After fifteen hours on the bridge, much of it spent directing the *Bismarck* out of harm's way from Captain Vian's torpedoes, Lindemann was exhausted and crestfallen. He had commanded the battleship for 277 days, the last nine of these in action-packed deadly drama. His relations with the fleet chief had been anything but smooth. Now the end was near. When Engineer Gerhard Junack that morning had requested permission to put the *Bismarck*'s overheated engines on "Ahead slow!" Lindemann had offered only resignation: "Oh, do as you like."[41] On the way back to his duty station, Müllenheim-Rechberg unexpectedly ran into Lütjens and his second staff officer, Commander Paul Ascher. The fleet chief stiffly returned Müllenheim-Rechberg's salute, then disappeared without a word.

The *Rodney* and the *King George V* steamed west-southwest in the predawn darkness as Admiral Tovey began his run. He planned to get well to the west of the *Bismarck*, then swing about, run eastward until he sighted her, and finally begin maneuvering to gain the best firing position. Weather and sea conditions were as bad as they could possibly be for a major gun action; the wind whipped the seascape from the northwest at 50 miles an hour. The waves, some 50 feet from trough to crest, had their tops blown off by the gale-force wind, the foam from the whitecaps spewing across the water like blowing snow across a windswept Arctic plain. The dark sky was completely overcast, with rain squalls. Visibility, when not obscured by the squalls, was about 12 miles.[42]

Tovey thought about how he was going to approach the *Bismarck*. Up to now he had made every key decision by erring on the side of caution. But not now. This was no time to adhere to the letter of the Admiralty's Fighting Instructions. As the sodden sky grew lighter in the east with the onrushing sunrise, he signaled his instructions to Captain Dalrymple-Hamilton on the *Rodney*. The signal light blinked out the message across the short distance between the two battleships:

> Am changing course to look for enemy. Keep station 1200 yards or more as you desire and adjust your bearings. If I do not like the first setup I may break off the engagement at once. Are you ready to engage?[43]

The *Rodney* was ready. The two ships swung to port, still in line-ahead, the *King George V* leading. Then, as they began a second turn to port, to start heading for the *Bismarck*'s approximate position, the *Rodney* swung out to take position off the *King George V*'s port quarter, about 1,200 yards distant.

Tovey gave Dalrymple-Hamilton much room to maneuver. He was to keep station with the *King George V* during the run in, but he was free to adjust his own bearings when and where he thought necessary in the course of the fight. Tovey's approach was in direct contrast to the instructions Vice Admiral Lancelot Holland had given Captain John Leach in the *Prince of Wales* the night before their encounter with the *Bismarck*: to stay nailed to the *Hood*'s flank in a vain attempt to concentrate fire. But Tovey did not fight his ships differently than Holland had because he was learning from Holland's mistakes. In fact, he had little idea of what had transpired on the morning of the 25th; the only evidence he had to go on was the *Prince of Wales*' radio transmission made at 8:00 that morning, which had loosely described the *Hood*'s fate. Tovey chose the course he did because, unlike Holland, he knew when to break the rules.

The two battleships came out of their turn at 7:37 A.M. and straightened on a course of east-northeast. They were steering 110 degrees, steaming at 19 knots. Ahead of them, on the northeast horizon, was the first patch of open sky they had seen for days. The intense low-pressure system that had dominated sea and sky from the afternoon of 22 May was moving off to the east; a mid-Atlantic ridge of high pressure was beginning to spread eastward toward the southwest corner of the British Isles and the Bay of Biscay. To the southeast, however, where Force H lay just over the horizon, the sky was still heavily overcast. There would be no air strike now. Neither radar nor human eye could detect the *Bismarck* ahead. Tovey made another course change, first to the southeast, then almost due east. At 8:08 A.M. the lookouts spotted the *Norfolk* 14 miles dead ahead. The *Norfolk*'s signal light blinked rapidly: "Enemy 130°, 16 miles."

The *King George V* and the *Rodney* heeled to starboard, then turned to port, now steering southwest as they bore in on the *Bismarck*'s estimated position. Side by side they raced downwind. Tovey planned to go straight at the German battleship until his two ships were about 8 miles distant; then they would turn due south, parallel to the *Bismarck*'s meandering course, open A arcs, and let her have the full broadsides of the *Rodney*'s nine 16-inch guns and the *King George V*'s ten 14-inch guns.[44] Since the *Bismarck* was steaming in a northerly direction and they would be steering to the south, Captains Patterson and Dalrymple-Hamilton would have only a few minutes to begin scoring hits before the *Bismarck* temporarily drew out of range. As the two battleships raced toward the *Bismarck*, the *Rodney* veered slightly to port to open the distance between her and the flagship. Then, at 8:43 A.M., a lookout on the *King George V* saw the *Bismarck*'s dark and massive shape: "Enemy in sight." In both ships, the men on the bridge donned their flat-brimmed helmets. The *Bismarck* was heading right for them, 25,000 yards distant, well within range. Everyone knew that main-gun firing was but moments away.

In the closed-up compartments, in the boiler rooms, in the engine rooms, in the damage-control offices, in the radio and radar rooms, at the ammunition hoists, in the main gun turrets, in the magazines of the *Rodney* and the *King George V*, the tension grew as the two battleships raced on. As the gun directors began to train on the target, the turrets swung toward the *Bismarck*, and the power grappling gear and the shell hoists sprang to life, some of the men were too busy to think about the chances of instant and terrible destruction. Inside the turrets men shouted instructions, guns were elevated, powder bags were placed on their shoots and rammed home, and the giant shells were loaded and breeches slammed shut. In the boiler rooms and the engine rooms the stokers and engine-room artificers kept close watch on valves, steam lines, spinning shafts, reduction gear, and the telegraphs from the bridge. But in other areas of the ships, men could only await their fate. Most were far belowdecks; few had any real idea what was going on six or seven decks up, where the men with gold braid were making decisions that would determine the fate of them all.

At 8:47 A.M. the *Rodney*'s two forward turrets opened fire. With each of the six guns firing in very rapid succession, it would have seemed to the untrained observer as if the *Rodney* had simply loosed one massive salvo. The effect was virtually the same, as 15,000 pounds of armor-piercing shells blasted from her barrels and rocketed toward the *Bismarck* at about 2,400 feet per second. It took less than sixty seconds for the shells to plunge into the sea around the *Bismarck*. By then the *King George V* had also opened fire.

"Alarm!" "Two battleships port bow!" On board the *Bismarck*, the two British battleships were sighted in line-abreast at a range of

24,000 yards. At 8:48 A.M. columns of water 150 feet high erupted ahead of the *Bismarck* as shells from the *Rodney*'s 16-inch guns plunged into the sea. One minute later, more columns of seawater from the *King George V*'s shells sent tons of water cascading across the *Bismarck*'s decks. The *Bismarck*'s 15-inch fore turrets replied at 8:50 A.M. Admiral Lütjens ordered that fire be concentrated first against the *Rodney* and then the *King George V*. But the battleship's after turrets could not be brought to bear on the target. In fact, Captain Lindemann could turn his ship northward toward the enemy only by engaging his port engine. The two sides were closing at a combined speed of 25 knots; range quickly fell to 20,000 yards. In his gunnery-control post in the foretop, Commander Schneider was steady as ever. He routinely informed his gunners of the accuracy of the first three salvos: "Short!" "Straddling!" "Over!" His gunnery skills had not abated one iota: one shell from the second salvo that straddled the *Rodney* had landed a mere 60 feet off her bridge, showering the decks with tons of seawater.

Deep inside the bowels of HMS *Rodney*, Sam Davis manned his post in the battleship's damage-control headquarters. Neither he nor the men around him had any idea of what was happening up top as the battle raged. As Davis later wrote: "All we had were the frequent rumbles and shakes as the salvoes left us. For something to do I recorded the times of firing."[45] As the *Rodney* fired, the concussion from her guns wreaked havoc from stem to stern. Water pipes burst, cast-iron fittings cracked, tile decking lifted or shattered, beams cracked, water leaks sprang from a hundred places, bolts and rivets popped loose, furniture and lockers were torn loose to slide across the decks as the ship lurched and rolled, light bulbs smashed, wires were torn loose, urinals were blown off bulkheads, ceramic toilets were smashed.[46] The *King George V* suffered much less damage from her own guns, but those guns soon began to give the same trouble that the *Prince of Wales*' guns had produced on the morning of the 25th. At one point, A turret had to cease firing for half an hour due to mechanical malfunction—all four guns in this turret were thus put out of action. Y turret was completely out of action for seven minutes. In addition, individual guns went out of action when a shell rammer failed, flash doors jammed, or a shell hoist seized up. Parts fractured. Other parts were found to be missing altogether. Breech mechanisms jammed. A cordite bag failed to explode, putting its gun out of action for thirty minutes.[47]

As the three heavy ships slugged it out at diminishing range, the *King George V* heeled to starboard, firing heavy salvoes as she turned due south. The *Bismarck* was passing her on her port beam, about six miles away, heading north. All four turrets on Tovey's flagship swung round to the left to follow the German ship. By now the secondary armament was also hammering away. The *Norfolk* opened up from 10 miles away with her 8-inch guns. The *Dorsetshire* hove into sight from the southwest and opened fire. When the *King George V* turned south, Dalrymple-Hamilton kept the *Rodney* steaming due east, approaching the *Bismarck*'s track at right angles, closing the range even further as she hammered away. Then he too turned to starboard, swinging south before turning eastward, crossing the *Bismarck*'s track and coming up alongside the *Bismarck*'s starboard beam, firing all the way. His three forward main turrets swung rapidly on their turret rings as the *Rodney* crossed the *Bismarck*'s track. Tovey urged Captain Patterson to get closer. He needed to see more hits. He needed to see this beast die under his guns, from close up. He needed to make sure it never again menaced him, his ships, his men, his cause.

Unable to maneuver, the *Bismarck*, almost dead and wallowing in the swells, offered an easy target. Lindemann could neither steer a course nor evade hostile fire. Schneider and Albrecht simply fired as best they could with the battleship's main and secondary armament, hoping to score a lucky hit. Shells were landing all around the *Bismarck* now. Fountains of water rose as high as Schneider's post in the foretop. Then at 9:02 A.M. a 16-inch shell from the *Rodney* slammed into the *Bismarck*'s upper deck forward. Sheets of fire engulfed her superstructure. Hundreds of men died at their battle stations. The forward turrets were reduced to "shambles of riven metal."[48] Round after round landed on the *Bismarck*, mostly amidships. White smoke rose from her funnel. The officers' quarters were engulfed by flames. There is no survivors' testimony that Lütjens ever considered signaling Admiral Tovey "Cease fire!" to end the carnage.

Lieutenant von Müllenheim-Rechberg, at his duty station in the after fire-control center, was suddenly called to the control telephone. It was the *Bismarck*'s gunfire-plotting officer, Lieutenant Friedrich Cardinal, the man who had briefed Hitler on the *Bismarck*'s main armament back at Gotenhafen. Miraculously, a single telephone line had escaped the terrible pounding that the *Bismarck* was taking. The main fire-control station in the foretop could not be contacted, Cardinal informed Müllenheim-Rechberg; turrets Anton and Bruno were out of action. Could the fourth gunnery officer take over control of the after turrets, Cäsar and Dora? According to the *Bismarck*'s survivors, the *Rodney*'s lethal salvo at 9:02 A.M. most likely killed Admiral Lütjens and Captain Lindemann.

"Action circuit aft!" Müllenheim-Rechberg shouted, at the same time scanning the horizon through his port director. There, abaft the *Bismarck*'s beam at 11,000 yards and steaming on a reciprocal course, was the *King George V*. "Passing fight to port, target is the battleship at 250°." As soon as he received the reply "Ready!" from below, Müllenheim-Rechberg ordered, "One salvo!" The 15-inch shells roared out of their barrels. Twenty seconds later the fire-control room reported: "Attention fall! Two questionably right, two right wide, questionably over." Not much help. Müllenheim-Rechberg adjusted ten left, down four. Another salvo. "Middle over." The next salvo: "Middle short." And another: "Three over, one short."

It was to be the last directed salvo. An incoming shell slammed into the fire-control center, shattering the aft director. The gun crew was now blind. Müllenheim-Rechberg raced up the ladder to the cupola to check on the large range finder—it was gone. A heavy shell had ripped through the middle of the cupola. There was nothing to do but to let the two after turrets operate independently and at will. At 9:31 A.M. the *Bismarck* fired her last shell.

As shell after shell plunged into the *Bismarck*'s superstructure and a great pall of black smoke rose from her flaming decks, the British seamen watched, transfixed, as the ship they had feared and hunted for six days was blown apart. Shells of every size blasted away huge bits of superstructure, antiaircraft and secondary guns, antennas and masts, boats and floats and deck fittings. Gaping holes appeared as the heavy armor-piercing shells from the British main guns cut deep into the *Bismarck*'s decks and exploded inside. Smoke and flame could be seen through the tears and gashes that now marred this once-beautiful ship. They knew that men were dying horrible, painful deaths inside that flaming, smoking hulk, but Lütjens' flag still flew, as did the naval insignia with its swastika. So the shells still rumbled in. The battle would continue as long as her colors snapped from their poles, or until it was obvious that the German commander had ordered "abandon ship."

By 10:00 A.M. the *Bismarck*'s superstructure and decks were in shambles. The *Rodney* had fired 380 16-inch shells and 716 6-inch shells at her, the *King George V* 339 rounds of 14-inch and 660 rounds of 5.5-inch ammunition. The *Norfolk* and the *Sheffield* had pumped 780 rounds of 8-inch shell at her.[49] She was littered with maimed and dead bodies and body parts. Boats and lockers had been shot to pieces. Antiaircraft positions were recognizable only by the seats of their erstwhile gunners. Twisted machinery and instruments littered the decks. Gas and smoke billowed from what once were mighty 15-inch turrets. The mainmast had crashed down over the ship. A heavy shell set off the ready-use ammunition near one of the 4-inch heavy flak stations, killing the crews who were using its base as shelter. Another shell ripped open the back-wall of turret Bruno and set it on fire. Reddish fire and yellow fumes quickly consumed it. The guns of Anton turret were at full depression; those of Bruno were trained to port, one barrel pointing skyward. The hangar for the Arado aircraft was furiously ablaze. The *Bismarck* was blowing off steam, a thick oily smoke rising from the base of her funnel. She was listing 20 degrees to port, with starboard being the lee side. Her stern was beginning to sink and breakers were rolling over her from the port quarter, washing countless seamen overboard. All the while, the enemy kept the burning hulk in a murderous crossfire. Range fell to 3,000 yards, no longer even target practice. At 10:15 A.M. a pair of heavy shells from the *King George V* shattered the *Bismarck*'s forward superstructure, producing a firestorm that swept up to her bridge. No one could have survived that explosion on the captain's or the admiral's bridge.

Conditions belowdecks were almost indescribable.[50] Shell after shell slammed through the decks and exploded below. Red-orange flames came up through the ventilators. Fumes and nitrogen gas generated by bursting shells permeated the great and deep caverns inside the *Bismarck*'s hull, forcing the men to put on gas masks. Paint burned off the bulkheads and suffocated those without masks. Splinters shot through the compartments. Safety valves blew off and condenser intakes exploded. Armored hatches and doors, ladders and companionways, were stove in or buckled, twisted in every shape and jammed. Many passageways were no longer wide enough to allow men with their inflated life jackets to pass through. Seaman after seaman ripped off his life jacket and ran topside. Screams of "I am dying, I am dying" reverberated throughout the interior of the battleship. The *Bismarck*'s doctors and corpsmen could do little but give the worst cases morphine injections.

The *Bismarck*'s first officer, Commander Oels, took command of damage control down below. At first Oels urged the men to put out the countless fires raging throughout the ship. But he quickly realized that this was a labor of Sisyphus. As Oels made his way to Section XIII on the battery deck, he exhorted his sailors to fend for themselves. "Comrades, we can no longer fire our guns and anyway we have no more ammunition. Our hour has come. We must abandon ship. She will be scuttled. All hands to the upper deck."[51] In the engine room, Lieutenant Junack assumed command. He ordered all bulkhead doors to the shaft alleys opened and nine-minute fuses set for the scuttling charges. "Prepare ship for scuttling!" Junack then also ordered his men up to the main deck.[52]

Up top, fires burned out of control. Heavy smoke lay over the *Bismarck*'s deck like a deadly pall. Many who made it up from below were blinded by the thick smoke and fell back down through the gaping shell holes as they raced across her deck. The *Bismarck* was heeling dangerously to port, and water began to cascade down ventilators and shell holes on the port side. A direct hit on the after dressing station killed many of the medical staff and the wounded who had sought refuge there. In the forward canteen, some two hundred sailors were trapped. When a hatch to the upper deck was freed and hope seemed at hand, another direct hit crashed through the deck, "transforming the canteen into a charnel house."

Some crews were trapped in munition magazines. As the flames on deck increased in intensity, the temperature in the magazines rose to dangerous levels. Machinist Josef Statz came upon the ammunition chamber for a 4-inch heavy flak turret and estimated it to have reached 175 degrees Fahrenheit. The ammunition would go off at any minute. In vain, Statz tried to open the chamber bulkheads. Chief Petty Officer Gerhard Sagner immediately ordered the magazines to be flooded. "But there are still people in there!" Statz pleaded. "For Führer, Folk, and Fatherland," Sagner shouted back, "it's got to be, otherwise we'll all go sky-high."[53] They flooded the chamber, drowning the men inside.

Someone, from somewhere on the deck, gave the order: "Abandon ship! Ship is to be sunk!" Elsewhere, survivors also recalled hearing, "Clear ship for scuttling; apply explosive charges." Those who heard the "Abandon ship!" order gathered in small groups, hurled lifeboats off the upper deck into the ocean, and then jumped off the battleship's quarterdeck. By 10:20 A.M. the small groups had grown to a vast throng. A raging sea, fouled by fuel oil rushing from the battleship's ruptured tanks, heaved those who jumped off her port side back against the ship's steel hull, crushing their bodies instantly. Numerous sailors dove over the starboard rails headfirst—only to break their necks upon hitting the bilge keel. A small contingent of three seamen, having been ordered, "Destroy telephones! Inflate lifejackets!" sought shelter behind the smoldering ruins of turret Dora. There they found a rubber dinghy, hurled it off the starboard quarter, and jumped into the sea after it.

With the time-fused scuttling charges having been set in the turbine rooms, boiler rooms, and auxiliary machine rooms, First Officer Oels charged through the *Bismarck*'s compartments, urging men to head for the upper deck.[54] Watertight compartment doors and flooding valves had all been left open. Then the seacocks were opened. "Scuttling procedure!" Oels screamed above the din. "Everyone overboard!" As he raced through the port bulkheads toward the stern, Oels continued to implore the men to head up. "We have nine or ten minutes' time!" In Section XIII of the battery deck, he found a crowd of about three hundred men surging toward the ladders. Acrid yellowish green smoke was everywhere. Violent coughing and retching racked those without gas masks. "Get out, get out," Oels yelled at the top of his lungs. "Everyone off the ship, She's being scuttled." At that moment a green flash burst into a lurid fireball. Bodies flew through the air and crashed against steel walls; body parts slid onto the floor plates. About one hundred sailors were killed instantly—including First Officer Oels.[55]

Wild stories about the *Bismarck*'s end abounded during later interrogation on land. Some survivors remembered officers shooting men who abandoned their posts. Others recalled that the Luftwaffe officers on board shot themselves with their service pistols. Still others swore that many seamen jumped from the *Bismarck* with shouts of "*Sieg Heil!*" or "Three Cheers for Germany and the Führer." Some apparently sang the national anthem as they leaped into the ocean swell. One survivor swore that a "propaganda company" from Dr. Joseph Goebbels' Ministry of Propaganda had filmed the entire final battle.[56] And several swimmers ahead of the *Bismarck*'s bow even claimed that they saw Captain Lindemann, standing on the forecastle, hand to his white cap, go down with his ship.[57]

Müllenheim-Rechberg left his after gunnery station and made his way forward through the fire and the debris. "It was chaos and desolation." The *Bismarck*'s antiaircraft guns and searchlights had disappeared without a trace. Whitish smoke, like a fog, rose from gaping holes in the ship's deck where incoming shells had penetrated—a sure sign that devastating fires were raging below. Turret

Dora was burning, sheets of flame still shooting skyward. A heavy shell burst had shredded its right barrel. Men, some on fire, were running in all directions. Off the starboard quarter stood the *Rodney*, a menacing 2,500 yards away.[58] Fortunately for Müllenheim-Rechberg, the enemy stopped firing at 10:21 A.M. In the course of her final encounter, the *Bismarck* had 2,878 rounds fired at her. It had taken the best efforts of five battleships, three battle cruisers, two aircraft carriers, four heavy and seven light cruisers, and twenty-one destroyers to hunt her down.

From just 2 miles away, Admiral Tovey watched the *Bismarck* in her death throes. This was point-blank range, and his ships had turned the *Bismarck* into a slaughterhouse. Still, the hulk that Hitler had hailed as the "pride of the navy" refused to sink. But Tovey now saw the men begin to swarm over the wreck, jumping overboard, "preferring death by drowning in the sea to the appalling effects of our fire," he later wrote.[59] He had stayed on the scene many hours longer than he had originally intended, and now he had to run for home to refuel. He was "confident that *Bismarck* would never get back to harbour and that it was only a matter of hours before she would sink."[60] At 10:36 he ordered the *Dorsetshire* to finish the battleship off with her torpedoes. Captain Martin fired his first two torpedoes into the *Bismarck* amidships and stern. He then circled his prey and launched a third torpedo. Colors still flying, the great ship heeled over to port, turned turtle, and continued to go down stern first. As the *Bismarck* went down, her tower mast, funnel, and rear mainmast broke away from their bases. Other debris from the decks as well as the heavy anchors from both sides of the ship broke loose and sank. As the *Bismarck* turned fully over, her four main gun turrets, each weighing 1,900 tons, slid out of their barbettes and sank to 2,500 fathoms below the ocean.[61] Finally, at about 10:40 A.M., the bow disappeared beneath the heavy seas. Position: 48° 09' north, 16° 07' west. Admiral Günther Lütjens, Captain Ernst Lindemann, and about 2,100 other officers and men died that day. It took thirty secretaries three days to notify relatives of the dead and missing.

Hundreds of the *Bismarck*'s officers and men were bobbing like corks on the Atlantic breakers. Many were injured, others were badly burned; all were covered with a foul-smelling coat of fuel oil welling from the wreck. The lucky ones kept afloat until HMS *Dorsetshire,* which had given the *Bismarck* the coup de grâce, could reach them. Her skipper ordered that ropes be lowered off the ship's sides. Most survivors could not hold on to the slippery, oil-soaked rope ends, and Captain Martin eventually lowered rope ladders as well. Next, HMS *Maori* hove in sight and also began rescue actions. Then, suddenly, at 11:40 A.M. Martin ordered *Dorsetshire* to make way, leaving hundreds of *Bismarck* survivors in the heavy cruiser's wake—a certain death sentence. Spotters on the cruiser's bridge thought they had made out a suspicious "smoking discharge" on the horizon. No one could say what it was, but Martin was not about to risk his ship for the men who had killed the *Hood,* then led the Royal Navy on a chase halfway across the Atlantic. He decided that the risk of an approaching U-boat was too great to continue the rescue effort. In all, the *Dorsetshire* recovered eighty-five men and the *Maori* twenty-five.[62] Few, if any, German authors writing of the *Bismarck*'s sortie have accepted Martin's reason for abandoning the rescue. There was no U-boat within the vicinity of the *Dorsetshire.*

In Church House, London, temporary home to the House of Commons while bomb damage to the Parliament buildings at Westminster was being repaired, Prime Minister Winston Churchill stood to report to the Members of Parliament that Admiral Tovey had brought the *Bismarck* to heel and that a great sea battle was raging at that very moment. He then sat down. A moment later, there was a bustle on the government side of the House as one of his ministers handed him a piece of paper that had just been brought into the chamber. Churchill glanced at it, rose again, and announced: "I have just received news that the *Bismarck* is sunk." The tension in the House snapped and the members roared their approval.[63] Not long after, on the admiral's bridge of the *King*

George V, Tovey was also handed a piece of paper, a message conveyed to him by Admiral Pound that had come directly from Churchill. It was an answer to Tovey's signal the night before that he might have to break off the chase and return for fear of leaving the *King George V* wallowing helplessly in the waves, out of fuel. It read: "We cannot visualise the situation from your signals. *Bismarck* must be sunk at all costs and if to do this it is necessary for the *King George V* to remain on scene then she must do so, even if it subsequently means towing *King George V*." To John Tovey, this was "the stupidest and most ill-considered signal ever made."[64]

In the search area, neither the Spanish cruiser *Canarias* nor her destroyer escort found any survivors. On the German side, for most of 27 May Lieutenant Kentrat in U-74 and Lieutenant Wilhelm Schütte of the weather ship *Sachsenwald* steamed through the field of debris where the *Bismarck* had gone down. Sometime between 7:30 and 8:20 P.M. Kentrat discovered three men in a small rubber dinghy—they were Seamen Georg Herzog, Herbert Manthey, and Otto Höntzsch, the sailors who had taken shelter behind turret Dora and then jumped overboard with their rubber dinghy.[65] The rescue was dangerous and time-consuming in the heavy swell. The sudden appearance of a hostile aircraft forced U-74 to break off the search.

Around noon on 28 May U-74, having resurfaced in quadrant BE 6152, crossed paths with the *Sachsenwald*. Both continued to search the debris-littered sea. "Starting at 1 P.M. we sighted corpses and debris in the northwest corner of quadrant BE 6145," Kentrat noted in his war log. "On a zigzag course, around 5 P.M. I sighted individual corpses, wooden boards, and rafts." And again, around midnight: "Sighted corpses and parts of a cutter." It was grisly work. "All in all, sighted about 40 corpses. All were bobbing up and down in their life jackets, with their heads down in the water."[66] At about the same time, Lieutenant Schütte spied three red flares. He turned the *Sachsenwald* into the moderate gale and toward the light. At 10:30 P.M. Schütte came upon a rubber raft with two occupants. "Are you German?" he shouted. A cry of relief came from the raft: "*Ja*, hurrah!" Schütte lowered a Jacob's ladder and hauled Seaman Otto Maus and Machinist Walter Lorenzen on board.[67] These were the last five rescued survivors out of a complement of 2,200 officers and men.

Epilogue

As soon as some of the *Bismarck*'s few survivors were hauled out of the fouled waters of the Atlantic 400 nautical miles west-northwest of Brest on 27 May 1941, the British warships departed. Short of fuel, desperate to escape the Luftwaffe attacks, which were sure to come, they steamed to safe harbor as quickly as they could without draining their tanks. The *King George V* and the *Rodney* shaped course for Loch Ewe, on the west coast of Scotland, accompanied by the destroyers *Cossack*, *Sikh*, and *Zulu*. Eleven more destroyers joined the weary veterans as they made their way home. They entered port at 12:30 P.M. on 29 May to the cheers of thousands and the "woop, woop" of moored warships' signal horns. That same day, 1,500 miles to the south, Vice Admiral Sir James Somerville's Force H hove in sight of the Rock of Gibraltar. They had departed the scene of the *Bismarck*'s destruction just as three Luftwaffe bombers finally arrived. A Heinkel dropped a stick of bombs into the sea near the *Ark Royal*, then flew off. As the *Ark Royal* glided into the roadstead off the Rock two days later, every boat in the harbor went out to welcome her home.[1]

The three German bombers that menaced the *Ark Royal* on 27 May were part of a much larger force. Air Fleet 3 launched three strikes of 128 aircraft from airfields on the French coast between 10 A.M. and 3 P.M.[2] With the exception of the handful that located the *Ark Royal*, they found nothing. More aircraft swept Admiral John Tovey's route home on the 28th, but Tovey's two battleships and escorting destroyers were long gone. West of Ireland, Hermann Göring's bombers found the destroyers HMS *Tartar* and HMS *Mashona*.[3] Plodding slowly homeward to preserve fuel, the two warships fended off attacks all morning. By noon, the *Mashona* had sunk, with the loss of forty-seven men; the *Tartar* managed to save the *Mashona*'s commanding officer and 170 others before leaving the scene. She arrived in Londonderry, Northern Ireland, the next day with but 5 tons of fuel remaining.[4] After the ships departed the scene of the last battle, the intense low-pressure system that had dominated the weather since the *Bismarck*'s breakout drifted eastward to the Baltic and then to Russia. The skies over the mid-Atlantic and the Bay of Biscay cleared, and the sea rolled calmly.

Out in the Atlantic, Captain Helmuth Brinkmann, commanding the heavy cruiser *Prinz Eugen*, failed to cover himself with glory. Brinkmann spent most of the period after separating from the *Bismarck* on 24 May refueling, avoiding sea traffic, and writing lengthy memoranda explaining his lack of action since separating from the "big brother" *Bismarck*. At best, he hoped to encounter and sink stragglers from some distant convoy. He found none. Instead, Brinkmann rested his crew and evaluated his ship's machinery. The damage-control reports were not encouraging. A high-pressure steam leak prevented the port engine from developing full power. Noise from a chipped propeller blade—damage likely inflicted by ice floes in the Denmark Strait—interfered with sonar. Most ominously, the port turbine emitted strange rumblings, leading to the suspicion of a misalignment problem caused by the mine explosion off Kiel.[5]

Prime Minister Winston Churchill saw in the *Prinz Eugen*'s continuing survival somewhere at sea a golden opportunity to bring the United States into the war. In the early-morning hours of

28 May, he had more reason to hope for that outcome than at any time since the start of the war. That was because at 10:30 P.M. Washington, D.C., time on the night of 27 May, President Franklin D. Roosevelt had addressed the American people from the East Room of the White House. Across the nation Americans sat silently by their radio sets and listened—the largest radio audience in U.S. history. The president told them that he had decided to take all measures he thought necessary to ensure that the war materials the United States was shipping to Britain under the Lend-Lease Act would get through. There would be more American warships, more American planes, more American fighting men devoted to the cause of helping the British. This, he said, was America's best defense. Finally, he revealed the news that he had just issued a proclamation declaring "an unlimited national emergency," which required strengthening the defenses of the United States "to the extreme limit of our national power and authority."[6] Just before the speech, FDR had wired Churchill:

> I hope you will like the speech tonight. It goes farther than I thought was possible even two weeks ago and I like to hope it will receive general approval from the fairly large element which has been confused by details and unable to see the simpler facts. All of us are made very happy by the fine tracking down of the *Bismarck* and that she is literally gone for good.[7]

After the broadcast, Churchill penned a memorandum to the first lord of the Admiralty, A. V. Alexander, as well as to the first sea lord, Admiral Sir Dudley Pound:

> The bringing into action of the PRINZ EUGEN and the search for her, raise questions of the highest importance. It is most desirable that the United States Navy should play a part in this. It would be far better, for instance, that she be located by a United States ship, as this might tempt her to fire upon that ship, thus providing the incident for which the United States Government would be so thankful.
>
> Pray let this matter be considered from this point of view, apart

> from its ordinary naval aspect. If we can only create a situation where the PRINZ EUGEN is being shadowed by an American vessel, we shall have gone a long way to solve the largest problem.[8]

Alexander and Pound assured the prime minister that every effort was being made to involve the Americans, that they had already sought the help of U.S. Navy ships operating in the waters east of Newfoundland and U.S. aircraft flying out of Argentia.[9] But the confrontation between American warships and the *Prinz Eugen* that Churchill so devoutly wished for was not to be. At midnight on 30 May Brinkmann scribbled a laconic entry into the *Prinz Eugen*'s war diary: "March east."[10] He then shaped a course of 90 degrees for port to undertake repairs. At 7:30 P.M. on 1 June the *Prinz Eugen* docked at Brest. She had covered 7,000 nautical miles at an average speed of 24 knots.[11]

In the next seven months the United States edged closer to war with Nazi Germany. On 7 July American troops relieved British and Canadian forces occupying Iceland; twelve days later Roosevelt ordered the US Navy to begin escorting convoys to and from Iceland. On 10 August Roosevelt and Churchill met in the waters off Argentia to sign the Atlantic Charter. Roosevelt steamed to the meeting aboard Admiral Ernest J. King's flagship, USS *Augusta*, while Churchill arrived aboard the just-refurbished HMS *Prince of Wales*.

Then the war became "hot" for the Americans. On 1 September the U.S. Navy assumed general escorting responsibilities, and just three days later U-652 fired torpedoes at the destroyer USS *Greer* but missed. Roosevelt declared this to be an act of "piracy," and from this day on the United States was engaged in a de facto naval war with Germany. On 11 September the president issued an order to U.S. ships to "shoot on sight" any Axis vessels that entered the Neutrality Zone. On 17 October torpedoes from U-568 struck the destroyer USS *Kearney*, escorting a convoy to the United Kingdom. The *Kearney* survived but suffered eleven dead and twenty-two injured—the first casualties of the U.S. Navy in the Second World War. Two weeks later U-552 torpedoed and sank USS *Reuben James*, an old four-stacker destroyer, 600 miles west of Ireland. The first U.S. naval vessel lost in the war, the "Rube" sank with the loss of 115 men. All the while public support grew for greater U.S. intervention in the war at sea. But in the end, it took Japan's attack on Pearl Harbor and Hitler's moronic decision to declare war on the United States on 11 December 1941 to bring America fully in.

In the final chapter of Rhine Exercise, the Royal Navy mopped up the *Bismarck*'s tankers and supply ships. It was short shrift. Aided by ULTRA decrypts of the German "Home Waters" naval Enigma, seven of the support vessels were hunted down and destroyed by 21 June; another seven by 11 July 1941.[12] They included the tankers *Belchen, Friedrich Breme, Lothringen, Esso-Hamburg,* and *Gedania,* and the supply ship *Gonzenheim*. As well, the British were able to round up four Atlantic weather ships. Still, the German Naval Communications Service refused to acknowledge that its Enigma codes had been broken. As late as 13 July 1942, its chief, Captain Ludwig Stummel, insisted that "unlucky circumstances, [chance] encounters with convoy escorts, increased surveillance of the approaches to the Bay of Biscay, treason in home bases, and other causes" had led to the ships' rapid capture. The Enigma remained secure. "It is not necessary to put the blame on a breach of security as regards the code and cipher tables."[13]

At the Berghof, high in the Bavarian Alps, Adolf Hitler was in a foul mood. The loss of the *Bismarck* had confirmed his worst fears about the susceptibility of the big ships to hostile aircraft—a fear that he had raised aboard the battleship at Gotenhafen on 5 May. On 2 June he met the Italian dictator, Benito Mussolini, at the Brenner Pass and vented fully his fury over Rhine Exercise. "The German U-boats," Hitler assured Mussolini, "will force England to capitulate!"[14]

On 6 June Grand Admiral Erich Raeder arrived at the Berghof to face his Führer's wrath. Hitler did not disappoint. He insisted on a private meeting with Raeder and cut straight to the heart of the matter. "Why did the fleet chief not commence the march home after the battle with the *Hood?*" Moreover, "Why did *Bismarck*, after sinking the *Hood*, not rely on its fighting power to attack the *Prince of Wales* anew, in order—with full engagement—to destroy it?" The failure to do so made no sense to Hitler. "Even given the loss of the *Bismarck* after such a battle, the end result would have been 2 Engl[ish] losses against one German." And when Raeder began anew to lay before Hitler visions of Atlantic sorties in the early fall of 1941, the Führer cut these musings short. "It makes no sense to expose the surface fleet to greater risks unless there are prospects of certain greater successes." Not even Raeder's presentation of the gripping depositions taken from the three seamen rescued by U-74 had an impact on the Führer. Major Gerhard Engel, Hitler's army adjutant, recalled: "It is striking how little, when he comes to speak of it, the fate of the *Bismarck* appears to affect F[ührer]."[15] Finally, Hitler lectured Raeder that he would in future brook no opinions on the war at sea that differed from his own, and he threatened to take a more active role in naval matters. "The dispatch of further forces into the Atlantic was forbidden." Commander Karl Jesko von Puttkamer, Hitler's naval adjutant, noted in his memoirs that "a chapter of the war at sea" had ended.[16]

Puttkamer's observation reflected the naked fear at German naval headquarters that Atlantic sorties would indeed end. General Admiral Otto Schniewind, Lütjens' successor, at once reiterated the navy's faith in future Atlantic operations by battle groups—as did General Admiral Alfred Saalwächter, head of Naval Group Command West, and Vice Admiral Hubert Schmundt, the newly appointed commander of cruisers. Schmundt crowed that with the *Bismarck*'s heroic last stand, the Kriegsmarine at least would not have to hear from the Wehrmacht and the Luftwaffe that it lacked the will to sacrifice in this war.[17] The lone voice of dissent belonged to General Admiral Rolf Carls, head of Naval Group Command North, who argued that, excluding the sinking of the *Hood*, the surface fleet had destroyed only 250,000 tons of enemy shipping. "The present war at sea is for us a struggle of dwarves against giants."[18] Like Admiral Reinhard Scheer after the Battle of Jutland in 1916, Carls hinted that Britain could be defeated only by the U-boats.

In their postmortem, Raeder's minions uncovered mistakes heaped upon mistakes. The operation had been rushed by not waiting for the *Tirpitz*, the *Scharnhorst*, and the *Gneisenau*. Intelligence had been abysmal. Swedish, Danish, or Norwegian agents obviously had spotted the task force in the Belts and the Norwegian fjords. Some form of new British "Dete" gear (radar) apparently had come into play. And there had been an unusual amount of plain "bad luck"—in being sighted by the Swedish cruiser *Gotland* in the Baltic Sea; in being spotted off Bergen, Norway; in being discovered in the Denmark Strait. Above all, it was "bad luck" that a torpedo from a Swordfish flying off the *Ark Royal* had struck the *Bismarck*'s Achilles' heel, her twin parallel rudders.

And there was the psychological factor. The army had marched triumphantly across Europe—and it was expected to do the same in the Soviet Union. Its operational plans called for victory in nine weeks at best, in seventeen at worst.[19] The navy had played no major role in the conquest of Poland, the Low Countries, Denmark, or France. It had lost a large portion of its fleet during the invasion of Norway in April 1940. Could it sit on the sidelines in the summer of 1941 and simply watch as the Wehrmacht crushed the Soviet Union? If so, how would it ever receive its fair share of future armaments resources? Thus, in Raeder's mind, the *Bismarck* had to go out in May 1941; otherwise, the last vestiges of German sea power would slip from view. And just to rub salt into the wound, Reinhard Heydrich, head of the Security Service (SD) of the Schutzstaffel (SS), crowed that his agents had found thousands of propaganda leaflets dropped on German cities, linking the demise of the *Bismarck* to a newly emerging Anglo-American special relationship. "American aircraft found the *Bismarck*," the leaflets informed Germans, "and when she tried to get away, brought the British fleet into contact with her."[20]

Nemesis came at the end of 1942. On 31 December Vice Admiral Oskar Kummetz, commanding the heavy cruiser *Lützow* and the pocket battleship *Hipper* as well as six destroyers, failed to deal effectively with the weakly guarded convoy JW51B near Bear Island in the Polar Sea, for fear of encountering British heavy units in the process.

This was the final link in a long chain of failures for Hitler. On 3 January 1943 he subjected Raeder to a ninety-minute tirade, the Führer accusing the navy's leaders of lack of will and determination during both world wars. Arguing that "we cannot permit our large ships to ride idly at anchor for months," Hitler decided "to scrap the large ships" and to use their heavy guns as shore batteries.[21] Erich Raeder resigned on 30 January. Karl Dönitz, promoted to the rank of grand admiral, succeeded him. The future now lay with the U-boats.

The war against the U-boats was the Royal Navy's finest hour. The experts on naval warfare had forecast prior to the beginning of the war that U-boats would pose no threat because of the invention of sonar. With its far-flung empire and oceanic lifelines, the Royal Navy built dozens of heavy ships with big guns and aircraft carriers that came into action in 1939. After the sinking of the *Bismarck*, the Royal Navy acquired more and better aircraft for its carriers—mostly from the United States. It developed ship-to-ship refueling capability, improved the performance of its big guns and their radar, and outstripped German intelligence-gathering capability. It suffered heavy losses at the beginning of the war against Japan, but eventually won the battle for naval supremacy in the Mediterranean even though Crete was lost on 1 June 1941.

The great irony of the war was that the Royal Navy's most important battle and victory was the Battle of the Atlantic. It was the Royal Navy's escort carriers, destroyers, frigates, sloops, minesweepers, and corvettes, complemented by the growing Royal Canadian Navy and the aircraft of Coastal Command, that bore the brunt of victory in the Atlantic. The U.S. Navy was too busy fighting Japan in the Pacific to put any real effort into the war against the U-boats until the spring of 1943, and although the Royal Navy certainly might not have prevailed over the U-boats without American help, Britain arguably was the ultimate victor.

The destruction of the *Bismarck* ended the surface phase of the Battle of the Atlantic for Nazi Germany. But the desperate struggle continued for the men who had sailed into history from Gotenhafen on 18–19 May 1941. To be sure, Günther Lütjens and Ernst Lindemann rested in their iron coffin on the floor of the Atlantic Ocean. There was to be no criticism of the two commanders. They had met heroic deaths against impossible odds. The *Bismarck*, as Raeder had demanded in 1939 after the inglorious scuttling of the *Graf Spee*, had fought to the last shell and gone down with colors flying. Thus why question Lütjens' refusal to top up the *Bismarck*'s fuel tanks? Or his constant refusal to share information with subordinates? Or his refusal to hunt down the *Prince of Wales*? Or his decision to head for France rather than to return via German-occupied Norway? Or his decision not to run at best speed for St. Nazaire after the hit by HMS *Victorious*' torpedo bombers?

No one dared question why Lütjens had sacrificed some 2,100 officers and men after the *Bismarck* had lost all maneuverability and become a sitting duck. The man had done what was expected of him. He had executed Raeder's orders. He had led from the front. He had died transmitting heroic signals: "Long Live the Führer!" In March 1969 the West German navy honored Lütjens' memory by naming a class of guided-missile destroyers after him. Ironically, given the Kriegsmarine's pathological hostility toward the United States, the ships were of the American *Charles F. Adams* class, built at Bath Iron Works, Maine.[22]

No such heroic lore shielded Erich Raeder. Brusquely called on the carpet by Hitler concerning the lack of value of the big ships, on 30 January 1943 the Kriegsmarine's commander in chief since 1928 chose retirement in the face of disgrace. He was arrested by the Allies and put on trial at Nürnberg; the International Military Tribunal on 1 October 1946 convicted Raeder of conspiracy, crimes against peace, and war crimes. He was sentenced to life imprisonment but was released from Spandau Prison at Berlin on 26 September 1955 due to ill health. Erich Raeder died at age eighty-four on 6 November 1960 at Kiel. Admiral Erich Förste ghostwrote his memoirs, a whitewash of the Nazi criminal regime.

Raeder's successor, Grand Admiral Karl Dönitz, got his chance to show what the U-boats could do after assuming command on

30 January 1943. During the Battle of the Atlantic, his "gray sharks" ravaged the world's oceans, sinking 2,603 merchant ships totaling 13.5 million tons and killing 20,248 merchant seamen. As well, they torpedoed 175 Allied naval vessels. But the costs were high: of the 1,162 U-boats built, 784 were lost at sea, and of the roughly 48,000 men recruited for the "Volunteer Corps Dönitz," some 29,000 lost their lives and 5,000 were taken prisoner. The endless bronze tablets at the U-Boat Memorial at Möltenort, near Kiel, that bear the names of every man lost on every boat are a grisly reminder of Dönitz's dedication to his Führer.

Indeed, a sycophantic Nazi to the end, Dönitz was rewarded for his dogged loyalty when Hitler in his Last Will and Testament on 30 April 1945 appointed the admiral Reich president and supreme commander of the armed forces. Dönitz established his "acting government" at the Navy School at Flensburg-Mürwik, from which he had graduated in 1910. He was captured by the British on 23 May 1945 and placed in the same docket as Raeder at Nürnberg. The "last Führer" cleverly succeeded in convincing the tribunal that he had been kept ignorant of the "final solution"—the murder of some six million Jews in the concentration camps and death camps. As well, the court failed to implicate him in the forced recruitment of millions of workers from across Europe to build his war machines. Still, on 1 October 1946 Dönitz was sentenced to ten years' incarceration for crimes against peace and war crimes. Released in 1956, the erstwhile Great Lion died at age eighty-nine on 22 December 1980 at Aumühle, near Hamburg. He refused to the end to believe that the cryptanalysts at Bletchley Park had cracked his beloved Enigma, the *Schlüsselmaschine M*.

General Admiral Alfred Saalwächter retired in November 1942. He was taken to the Soviet Union as a prisoner of war and, according to the Russian Red Cross, died there in December 1945 at age sixty-two. General Admiral Rolf Carls continued as head of Naval Group Command North. In January 1943 Raeder recommended both Carls and Dönitz to Hitler as possible successors; Hitler chose the latter. Carls retired in March 1943. He was killed by enemy fire on

15 April 1945. Captain Helmuth Brinkmann commanded the heavy cruiser *Prinz Eugen* until 31 July 1942. Thereafter Dönitz assigned him to a series of ever-diminishing naval commands: chief of staff to Naval Group Command South; commanding admiral, Black Sea; and finally second admiral, Baltic and North Sea. Brinkmann was promoted to vice admiral in February 1944, arrested by the Allies in May 1945, and returned in November 1947. He died at Dießen, Bavaria, on 26 September 1983. And Lieutenant Herbert Wohlfahrt, the cold-blooded commander of *U-556* who on the evening of 26 May 1941 had surfaced between HMS *Ark Royal* and HMS *Renown*, but out of torpedoes, was depth-charged on 27 June 1941 by the Royal Navy corvettes *Celandine, Gladiolus,* and *Nasturtium*. Forced to the surface, Wohlfahrt surrendered just before his boat sank; he was released from an Allied prisoner-of-war camp in July 1947.

Of the men of the Royal Navy, First Lord of the Admiralty A. V. Alexander stayed at his post, serving always in Churchill's shadow, until the end of the war. He was eighty when he died in 1965. Admiral of the Fleet Sir Alfred Dudley Pound died of cancer, still in harness, at the age of sixty-six in 1943. His brush with disaster when the *Bismarck* nearly got away left him a troubled man. In late June 1942, when he believed that Arctic convoy PQ 17 was about to be attacked by the *Bismarck*'s sister ship *Tirpitz*, he withdrew the Royal Navy's escorting warships over Admiral Tovey's strenuous objections and ordered the convoy to scatter. The individual merchantmen were abandoned to their fate. Forced to make for Murmansk alone or in small groups, they were subjected to ceaseless air and submarine attack in the white nights of the far north. Just eleven out of thirty-seven ships survived.

Admiral of the Fleet Sir John Cronyn Tovey served as commander in chief, Home Fleet, until 1943, when he was made commander in chief, the Nore, a post he held until he retired from the Royal Navy in March 1946. He was involved in charitable and religious work for a time after that, growing more reclusive as his memory began to fail. He lived to eighty-six and died in 1971. William Frederick Wake-Walker hauled down his flag in February 1942 and went to the Admiralty as controller of the navy and third sea lord. He was still in the Royal Navy and about to take up a promotion to commander in chief, Mediterranean, when he died suddenly at the age of fifty-seven in late September 1945.

Sir James Somerville narrowly escaped forced retirement from the Royal Navy for a second time in 1942; he survived the chop to assume command of the Royal Navy's Eastern Fleet from 1942 to 1944, when he went to Washington as head of the British Admiralty delegation. He retired in 1945 and died in 1949 at the age of sixty-seven. Frederick Dalrymple-Hamilton went ashore as naval secretary to the first lord of the Admiralty in 1942, serving in a variety of command and staff positions until he retired in 1950. He died in 1974 at the age of eighty-four. Philip Vian played a vital role in the planning and execution of the Normandy invasion of 6 June 1944. He then commanded the Royal Navy's carrier forces sent to the southwest Pacific and Japanese home waters toward the close of the Pacific war. After the war he served for a time as fifth sea lord and commander in chief, Home Fleet. His memoirs, *Action This Day,* are among the best of their genre. He died at the age of seventy-two in 1968.

U.S. Navy Admiral Robert Lee Ghormley left Washington to become commander, South Pacific Area and South Pacific Force, for the United States Navy in June 1942. He commanded the landings at Guadalcanal but proved a better staff officer than operational commander. He was relieved by Vice Admiral William F. "Bull" Halsey in October 1942. He retired in 1947 and died at the age of seventy-four in 1958.

Of the ships deployed in Rhine Exercise, the *Bismarck* rests 3 miles beneath the surface of the Atlantic, some 400 miles west-northwest of the coast of Brittany. There, Robert Ballard found her on 9 June 1989. The *Prinz Eugen*, on the other hand, went on to an incredible service career. Bombed at Brest by the Royal Air Force on 1 July 1941, she took part in Operation Cerberus, the famous "Channel dash" from Brest to Germany on 11–13 February 1942. Eventually berthed in the Grimstadfjord (where she had lain up with the *Bismarck* in May 1941), the heavy cruiser was torpedoed by the British submarine SS *Trident* on 23 February 1942. Captain Brinkmann brought his heavily damaged ship to Kiel for major repairs on 16–18 May 1942. In the summer of 1943 the heavy cruiser tried twice to break through to Norway; both times she was detected by the British and returned to Gotenhafen. In the summer and fall of 1944 the *Prinz Eugen* operated in support of the Wehrmacht in the Gulf of Finland and the Gulf of Riga. Returned to Wilhelmshaven under Royal Navy escort 24–26 May 1945, she became U.S. Navy property in December. On 22 January 1946 the *Prinz Eugen* arrived in Boston after suffering a complete machinery breakdown under her U.S. Navy crew. On 1 July 1946 the heavy cruiser (along with USS *New York*) survived Atomic Test Able at Bikini Atoll in the South Pacific. She finally capsized—rusted and at anchor—on Enubuj Reef, Kwajelein Atoll, in December 1946. She is still there, radium-contaminated.

Many of the most important Royal Navy warships that hunted down and destroyed the *Bismarck* suffered the ravages of a war that would be waged for another four years. The *Ark Royal* was the first to go, sunk by just one torpedo from U-81 in the Mediterranean on 13 November 1941. Less than one month later, on 10 December, the *Prince of Wales* and the *Repulse* were caught by Japanese bombers while steaming north from Singapore off the east coast of Malaya. Without air cover, both warships were destroyed. Admiral Sir Tom Phillips, who had masterminded the chase of the *Bismarck* from the Admiralty's Operational Control Centre, and Captain J. C. Leach, still in command of the *Prince of Wales*, perished. Captain Philip Vian's flagship, the *Tribal*-class destroyer *Cossack*, was torpedoed by U-563 in the North Atlantic in October 1941 and sank with heavy casualties. Vian had left her bridge before that date. The *Dorsetshire*, too, was a casualty of war, sunk by Japanese dive-bombers off Ceylon (today Sri Lanka) on 5 April 1942. All the other principal British ships—the *Rodney*, the *King* the *George V*, the *Victorious*, the *Norfolk*, and the *Suffolk*—ended their days in the scrap yards; all had contributed immeasurably to the Allied victory.

The *Bismarck* saga continues to grip the imagination. She was in service for only 277 days, and her one combat operation lasted just

215 hours. But not since Admiral Horatio Nelson's pursuit of the French Admiral Pierre Villeneuve from Toulon to the West Indies and back in 1805 had a major surface operation covered such vast distances—almost 3,000 sea miles.[23] Never in the annals of naval warfare had the pursuit of a single ship mobilized such a powerful and vast armada as the one that finally tracked the *Bismarck* down and destroyed her. Never had such virulent national passions—from the highest echelons of government to the public at large—been engendered by a single sortie. Never had a mere 215 hours brought such highs and lows of alternating optimism and pessimism, of dramatic victory and equally dramatic defeat. It was a battle that pitted the epitome of World War II warships—fast, heavily armored, heavily gunned—against each other, aided by the most modern products of mankind's technological genius for war—radar, high-frequency direction finding, aircraft. It was a fight for mastery of the Atlantic and of the commerce that could bring victory to one side, defeat to the other. But most of all it was a clash of will, of genius, of imagination, of determination, of dedication, of doggedness, of instinct, fought out against the rolling sea as the future of civilization hung in the balance.

Notes

Chapter 1

[1]For the personal recollections of the visit by a German naval officer, see Burkard Baron von Müllenheim-Rechberg, *Battleship Bismarck: A Survivor's Story* (Annapolis, 1990), pp. 96–8.
[2]Adolf Hitler, *Zweites Buch*, ed. Gerhard L. Weinberg (Stuttgart, 1961), p. 171.
[3]Jochen Brennecke, *Schlachtschiff Bismarck* (Herford, 1960), p. 52.
[4]In battleships, the British had 15 to Germany's 2; in aircraft carriers, 6 to 0; in pocket battleships, 3 to 0; in heavy cruisers, 15 to 2; in light cruisers, 49 to 6; in destroyers and torpedo boats, 183 to 34; and submarines, 57 to 57.
[5]Cited in Brennecke, *Schlachtschiff Bismarck*, p. 50.
[6]Raeder declined to discuss his absence, or even Hitler's visit, in his memoirs. Erich Raeder, *Mein Leben. Von 1935 bis Spandau 1955* (2 vols., Tübingen, 1956–57), vol. 2, pp. 265ff.
[7]Müllenheim-Rechberg, *Battleship Bismarck*, p. 278.
[8]Ibid., p. 98.
[9]Charles S. Thomas, *The German Navy in the Nazi Era* (Annapolis, 1990), pp. 52–7, 154.
[10]The following stems from what remains of Admiral Lütjens' service records at

the Deutsche Dienststelle (WASt) in Berlin. In 1947 the British Admiralty inexplicably destroyed Lütjens' personnel files. See Paul Schmalenbach, "Admiral Günther Lütjens," *Leinen Los!* 14 (1968), p. 26.

[11]*Das Deutsche Reich und der Zweite Weltkrieg*, vol. 6, *Der Globale Krieg. Die Ausweitung zum Weltkrieg und der Wechsel der Initiative* 1941–1943 (Stuttgart, 1990), p. 382, n. 230.

[12]From Captain Lindemann's remaining service records at the Deutsche Dienststelle (WASt) in Berlin.

[13]Bundesarchiv-Militärarchiv (hereafter BA-MA), Freiburg, RM 20/880 Generalkommandos, 25 May 1938.

[14]These ships were announced by Germany as falling within the 10,000-ton restriction imposed by the Treaty of Versailles (1919). In fact, fully loaded the *Deutschland*, *Admiral Scheer*, and *Admiral Graf Spee* displaced almost 16,000 tons. In German they were dubbed simply *Panzerschiffe* (armored ships).

[15]See the detailed account in Max Domarus, ed., *Hitlers Reden und Proklamationen* (4 vols., Würzburg, 1963), vol. 2, pp. 1077–80.

[16]Ibid., vol. 2, p. 1118.

[17]Ibid., pp. 1118–9.

[18]Ibid., p. 1127.

[19]Raeder's comments to fleet officers at Wilhelmshaven, 18 June 1939. Cited in Michael Salewski, *Die deutsche Seekriegsleitung* 1935–1945 (3 vols., Frankfurt, 1970), vol. 1, pp. 65–7.

[20]Reader's "Gedanken des Oberbefehlshabers der Kriegsmarine zum Kriegsausbruch 3. 9. 1939." BA-MA, I. SKL. Teil C VII. Überlegungen des Chefs der SKL und Niederschriften über Vorträge und Besprechungen beim Führer, pp. 1–3.

[21]Order of 22 December 1939. BA-MA, I. SKL. Teil C VII, p. 5.

[22]See Krancke's report of 4 April 1941 in *Kriegstagebuch der Seekriegsleitung* 1939–1945, ed. Werner Rahn and Gerhard Schreiber (68 vols., Herford, 1988–97), vol. 20, pp. 45–6.

[23]Dated 14 November 1940. BA-MA, I. SKL. Teil C VII, p. 5.

[24]"Gedanken zur Kampfführung gegen England." Ibid.

[25]Salewski, *Die deutsche Seekriegsleitung*, vol. 1, p. 387.

[26]"Vortrag des Ob.d.M. beim Führer am 27.12.40"; and "Vortragsnotiz" of 26.8.40. Ibid.

[27]Stig H:son Ericson, *Knopar på logglinan* (Stockholm, 1966), pp. 150ff. Also, Gunnar Richardson, *Beundran och fruktan. Sverige inför Tyksland* 1940–1942 (Stockholm, 1996). I am indebted to Dan Harris of Ottawa, a member of the British Legation at Stockholm in 1940, for this information.

[28]Müllenheim-Rechberg, *Battleship Bismarck*, pp. 29, 30–4, 50.

[29]Given that virtually all books detailing the *Bismarck*'s technical data introduce minute differences, for the sake of consistency I have taken the following data

from a single source, Siegfried Breyer and Gerhard Koop, *Schlachtschiff Bismarck. Eine technikgeschichtliche Dokumentation* (Augsburg, 1996). See also Gerhard Koop and Klaus-Peter Schmolke, *Battleships of the Bismarck Class: Bismarck and Tirpitz: Culmination and Finale of German Battleship Construction* (London and Annapolis, 1998).

[30]The following is taken from Koop and Schmolke, *Battleships of the Bismarck Class*, pp. 151–4.

[31]The German navy's radar development concentrated on radar fire control for their surface ships and not, like the Allies, on the development of search radar. Thus Germany never developed and produced an effective search radar. Later in the war, much of their effort went into producing radar warning devices such as the Metox and the Hagenuk—that is, devices designed to warn against the approach of Allied radar-equipped ships or aircraft. Nor did the Germans ever develop centimetric (or microwave) 271 radar, which was based on the magnetron power valve.

[32]Discussion of 7 February 1941. BA-MA, PG 31762d, Oberkommando der Marine. Lagevorträge des Oberbefehlshabers der Marine vor Hitler.

[33]War diary entries for September 1940. BA-MA, PG 47896 Kriegstagebuch des Schlachtschiffes "Bismarck." Hereafter cited as: KTB *Bismarck*; BA-MA, PG 47896.

[34]Ibid.

[35]Ibid.

[36]Ibid.

[37]KTB *Bismarck*, 16 to 30 November 1940. Ibid.

[38]Randolph S. Churchill and Martin Gilbert, *Winston S. Churchill* (8 vols., London, 1966–88), vol. 6, pp. 848–50.

[39]Müllenheim-Rechberg, *Battleship Bismarck*, pp. 54–5.

[40]Ibid., p. 243.

[41]Paul Schmalenbach, *Kreuzer Prinz Eugen . . . unter drei Flaggen* (Hamburg, 1998), pp. 23–4. Prince Eugene of Savoy-Carignan (1663–1736) had been a field marshal of the old Holy Roman Empire.

[42]Technical data from M. J. Whitley, *German Cruisers of World War Two* (London, New York, Sydney, 1985); and Schmalenbach, *Prinz Eugen*.

[43]24 January 1941; Anlage 1 (Maschine) to war diary. KTB *Bismarck*; BA-MA, PG 47896.

[44]27–28 December 1940. KTB *Bismarck*; ibid.

[45]16–28 February 1941. KTB *Bismarck*; ibid.

[46]See Wilhelm M. Carlgren, *Svensk underrättelsetjänst 1939–1945* (Stockholm, 1985). The authors are indebted to Dr. Marianne Lindvall of the Germanic Languages Department at the University of Alberta for translating the pertinent passages into English.

[47]7 March 1941. KTB *Bismarck*; BA-MA, PG 47897.

[48]8 March 1941. KTB *Bismarck*; ibid.

[49]12 March 1941. KTB *Bismarck*; ibid.

[50]War diary entry by Captain Wiegmink, 15 March 1941. BA-MA, Kriegstagebuch der Bordfliegerstaffel 1/196 auf "*Bismarck*," 14 to 30 March 1941.

[51]19 March 1941. KTB *Bismarck*; BA-MA, PG 47897.

[52]Müllenheim-Rechberg, *Battleship Bismarck*, pp. 45–6.

[53]Breyer and Koop, *Schlachtschiff Bismarck*, pp. 42–54.

[54]18–30 April 1941. KTB *Bismarck*; BA-MA, PG 47897.

[55]18–30 April and 16–30 April 1940. KTB *Bismarck*; ibid.

[56]Raeder's directive of 2 April 1941. BA-MA, RMD 4/601, Operationen und Taktik. Heft 3, Die Atlantikunternehmung der Kampfgruppe "Bismarck"-"Prinz Eugen," p. 5.

[57]Entry for 6 March 1941. *Kriegstagebuch der Seekriegsleitung*, vol. 20, p. 73.

[58]Entry for 7 March 1941. Ibid., p. 90.

[59]Entry for 10 April 1941. Ibid., p. 127.

[60]Entry for 19 April 1941. Ibid., p. 271.

[61]Entry for 11 April 1941. Ibid., pp. 139–40.

[62]Entry for 14 April 1941. Ibid., pp. 190–1.

[63]See Siegfried Breyer, *Battleship "Tirpitz"* (West Chester, PA, 1989); and Jochen Brennecke, *Schlachtschiff "Tirpitz". Das Drama der "Einsamen Königin des Nordens"* (Biberach, 1953).

Chapter 2

[1]Entry for 8 April 1941. Bundesarchiv-Militärarchiv (hereafter BA-MA), Freiburg, PG 48345 Kriegstagebuch des Kreuzers "Prinz Eugen." Hereafter cited as: KTB *Prinz Eugen*; BA-MA, PG 48345ff.

[2]23 April 1941. KTB *Prinz Eugen*; BA-MA, PG 48346.

[3]24 April 1941. KTB *Prinz Eugen*; ibid.

[4]Entry for 24 April 1941. *Kriegstagebuch der Seekriegsleitung* 1939–1945, ed. Werner Rahn and Gerhard Schreiber (68 vols., Herford, 1988–97), vol. 20, p. 346.

[5]Entry for 26 April 1941. Ibid., pp. 370–1.

[6]Ibid., p. 372.

[7]Cited in Jochen Brennecke, *Schlachtschiff Bismarck* (Herford, 1960), p. 47.

[8]Ibid., p. 50.

[9]Cited in Burkard Baron von Müllenheim-Rechberg, *Battleship Bismarck: A Survivor's Story* (Annapolis, 1990), p. 86.

[10]Brennecke, *Schlachtschiff Bismarck*, p. 47.
[11]Ibid., p. 265.
[12]War diary entries for 16–30 April 1940. BA-MA, PG 47896 Kriegstagebuch des Schlachtschiffes "Bismarck." Hereafter cited as: KTB *Bismarck*, BA-MA, PG 47897.
[13]The following is from "Appendix A: Naval Gunnery," in Robert J. Winklareth, *The Bismarck Chase: New Light on a Famous Engagement* (Annapolis, 1998), pp. 173–82.
[14]Paul Schmalenbach, *Kreuzer Prinz Eugen . . . unter drei Flaggen* (Hamburg, 1998), pp. 118–21.
[15]26 April 1941. KTB *Bismarck*; BA-MA, PG 47897.
[16]BA-MA, RMD 4/601, Operationen und Taktik. Heft 3, Die Atlantikunternehmung der Kampfgruppe "Bismarck"-"Prinz Eugen," p. 6.
[17]28 April 1941. KTB *Bismarck*; BA-MA, PG 47897.
[18]*Eichenkranz* = "oak wreath"; *Meeresgott* = "Neptune"; *Zwerghuhn* = "bantam hen"; *Bilderbuch* = "picture book"; *Antilope* = "antelope."
[19]Entry for 12 May 1941. *Kriegstagebuch der Seekriegsleitung*, vol. 21, p. 155.
[20]Entry for 13 May 1941. Ibid., pp. 168–9.
[21]Entry for 14 May 1941. Ibid., p. 185.
[22]Starting on 14 May 1941, the *Bismarck*'s war diary is a meticulous reconstruction undertaken after the battleship's demise on 27 May. Lieutenant Hans-Henning von Schultz, the *Prinz Eugen*'s chief wireless officer, based the reconstruction on the heavy cruiser's war diary, the records as well as signals traffic of Naval Groups North and West, all existing B-Dienst messages, and the central files at naval headquarters in Berlin.
[23]BA-MA, Marinegruppenkommando West. Battle orders for 5th Destroyer Flotilla, 13 May 1941. English translations for the ships' code names are: *Dattelpalme* = "date palm"; *Opernhaus* = "opera house"; *Dreschflegel* = "flail"; *Känguruh* = "kangaroo"; *Tigerfell* = "tiger skin"; *Walzerkönig* = "waltz king"; *Obstgarten* = "orchard"; *Lebertran* = "cod-liver oil."
[24]14 May 1941. KTB *Bismarck*; BA-MA, PG 47897. Lütjens had received the "Marburg" decoding instructions on 25 April 1941; BA-MA, PG 36782 Marine-Gruppenkommando.
[25]16 May 1941. KTB *Bismarck*; BA-MA, PG 47897. The telegram is in BA-MA, PG 36782 Marine-Gruppenkommando Nord. Operationsbefehl Nr. 16. Ausmarsch "Bismarck" und "Prinz Eugen" in den Atlantik.
[26]Entry for 16–17 May 1941. BA-MA, PG 30070/2 Kriegstagebuch des Unterseebootes "U 74." Six days earlier, Kentrat had fired three torpedoes at a passing convoy; all three "eels" had run under their targets.
[27]Entry for 17 May 1941. KTB "U 74," ibid.
[28]Entry for 16 May 1941. *Kriegstagebuch der Seekriegsleitung*, vol. 21, pp. 227–30.
[29]Raeder's "general orders" of 22 April 1941 are in BA-MA, PG 36782 Marine-Gruppenkommando Nord, Operationsbefehl Nr. 16. Ausmarsch "Bismarck" und

"Prinz Eugen" in den Atlantik. (Unternehmen "Rheinübung"); and reproduced in Müllenheim-Rechberg, *Battleship Bismarck*, pp. 431–4.

[30]*Laubfrosch* = "tree frog"; *Maikäfer* = "cockchafer"; *Ruhekissen* = "pillow"; *Puderdose* = "powder box."

[31]The orders for the individual support ships are from BA-MA, PG 36782 Marinegruppenkommando West.

[32]The various intelligence reports are in *Kriegstagebuch der Seekriegsleitung*, vol. 21, passim, and run almost daily.

[33]The following is from Operational Directive, Group West, 14 April 1941. BA-MA, RM 7/1448 K-2. Oberkommando der Marine. Entwurf Atlantik-Unternehmen der Kampfgruppe "Bismarck"-"Prinz Eugen."

[34]18 May 1941. KTB *Prinz Eugen*; BA-MA, PG 48348. Also 18 May 1941. KTB *Bismarck*; BA-MA, PG 47897.

[35]See Raeder's "Operational Instruction" to Lütjens of 14 April 19141. BA-MA, PG 36782 Marinegruppenkommando West 1803/41.

[36]18 May 1941. The best account is in the original KTB *Prinz Eugen*; BA-MA, PG 48348.

[37]Lindemann's words should be taken for their meaning, not literally, as they were relayed much later by the *Bismarck*'s survivors in BA-MA, Marinegruppenkommando West, gKods. 3156/41 A1.

[38]Entry for 18 May 1941. *Kriegstagebuch der Seekriegsleitung*, vol. 21, p. 255.

[39]20 May 1941. KTB *Bismarck*; BA-MA, PG 47897.

[40]See Wilhelm M. Carlgren, *Svensk underrättelsetjänst 1939–1945* (Stockholm, 1985). Translations again kindly provided by Marianne Lindvall. For details on the *Gotland*, see Curt Borgenstam, *Kryssare. Med svenska flottans kryssare under 75 år* (Stockholm, 1993).

[41]Müllenheim-Rechberg, *Battleship Bismarck*, p. 104.

[42]Interview with Dan Harris at Ottawa, 19 June 1999.

[43]Roscher Lund took the name of his contact, who likely was a member of the Swedish naval establishment, to the grave with him. Interview with Dan Harris at Ottawa, 19 June 1999. Müllenheim-Rechberg, *Battleship Bismarck*, p. 105, suggests the contact may have been Lieutenant Commander Egon Ternberg.

[44]C. G. McKay, *From Information to Intrigue: Studies in Secret Service Based on the Swedish Experience 1939–45* (London, 1993), pp. 106–7.

[45]Cited in Henry Denham, *Inside the Nazi Ring: A Naval Attaché in Sweden 1940–1945* (New York, 1984), p. 85.

[46]British messages were graded by the letters A (complete reliability) to E (reliability unknown), and given numbers from 1 (completely reliable) to 5 (reliability unknown) as well.

[47]Information courtesy of Dan Harris, Ottawa, 19 June 1999. Harris received the

information from Professor Jürgen Rohwer, Germany's foremost expert on the war at sea 1939–45.

[48]On Bletchley Park's role in the hunt for the *Bismarck*, see especially John Winton, *Ultra at Sea* (London, 1988), pp. 22ff.; and Ralph Erskine, "Naval Enigma: The Breaking of Heimisch and Triton," *Intelligence and National Security* 3 (January 1988), pp. 164–5.

[49]Müllenheim-Rechberg, *Battleship Bismarck*, p. 108. These actions were critical since Admiral Lütjens' (intercepted) Enigma message at 11:36 A.M. reporting the sighting by the *Gotland* was not decrypted by Bletchley Park until after the *Bismarck* had been sunk.

[50]Ibid., pp. 108–9.

[51]21 May 1941. KTB *Bismarck*; BA-MA, PG 47897.

[52]Ibid.

[53]21 May 1941. KTB *Prinz Eugen*; BA-MA, PG 48348.

[54]Entry for 21 May 1941. *Kriegstagebuch der Seekriegsleitung*, vol. 21, p. 308.

[55]21 May 1941. KTB *Bismarck*; BA-MA, PG 47897.

[56]Radiograms of 21 May 1941 in BA-MA, PG 36782.

[57]21 May 1941. KTB *Prinz Eugen*; BA-MA, PG 48348.

[58]Müllenheim-Rechberg, *Battleship Bismarck*, p. 84.

[59]2 June 1941. Interviews of survivors Manthey, Herzog, and Hoentzsch. KTB *Bismarck*; BA-MA, PG 47897.

[60]Cited in Müllenheim-Rechberg, *Battleship Bismarck*, p. 116.

[61]Winton, *Ultra at Sea*, p. 26.

[62]Carls' diary of 22 May 1941. BA-MA, PG 47895 Oberkommando der Kriegsmarine. Entwurf Atlantik-Unternehmen der Kampfgruppe "Bismarck"-"Prinz Eugen."

[63]While the *Bismarck*'s clocks remained on standard Central European Time throughout Operation Rheinübung, times given in this account are in German Summer Time, which equates to double British Summer Time, to avoid confusion with British accounts of the operation.

[64]22 May 1941. KTB *Bismarck*; BA-MA, PG 47897.

[65]22 May 1941. KTB *Prinz Eugen*; BA-MA, PG 48348.

[66]22 May 1941. KTB *Bismarck*; BA-MA, PG 47897. For "Merkur," see *Das Deutsche Reich und der Zweite Weltkrieg* ed. Militärgeschichtliches Forschungsamt, vol. 3, *Der Mittelmeerraum und Südosteuropa* (Stuttgart, 1984), pp. 500ff.

[67]22 May 1941. KTB *Prinz Eugen*; BA-MA, PG 48348.

[68]22 May 1941. KTB *Prinz Eugen*; ibid.

[69]Müllenheim-Rechberg, *Battleship Bismarck*, p. 118.

[70]Churchill to Roosevelt, 23 May 1941. Warren F. Kimball, ed., *Churchill & Roosevelt: The Complete Correspondence* (3 vols., Princeton, 1984), vol. 1, p. 192.

[71]All three messages of 22–23 May 1941 are in KTB *Bismarck*; BA-MA, PG 47897.

[72]BA-MA, RMD 4/601, Heft 3, p. 14.

[73]22 May 1941. KTB *Bismarck*; BA-MA, PG 47897.

[74]Ibid.

[75]Entry for 22 May 1941, *Kriegstagebuch der Seekriegsleitung*, vol. 21, p. 325.

[76]22 May 1941. KTB *Bismarck*; BA-MA, PG 47897.

[77]Hitler-Raeder conference, 22 May 1941. BA-MA, I. S.K.L. Teil CVII. Überlegungen des Chefs der S.K.L. und Niederschriften über Vorträge und Besprechungen beim Führer.

[78]See Karl Jesko von Puttkamer, *Die unheimliche See. (Hitler und die Kriegsmarine)* (Vienna and Munich, 1952), pp. 47–8.

[79]The talks of 22 May 1941 are in BA-MA, I. S.K.L. Teil CVII; also, *Lagevorträge des Oberbefehlshabers der Kriegsmarine vor Hitler 1939–1945*, ed. Gerhard Wagner (Munich, 1972), pp. 227–38.

[80]Hitler's comments noted by his naval adjutant, Puttkamer, and cited in Müllenheim-Rechberg, *Battleship Bismarck*, p. 98.

Chapter 3

[1]John Costello and Terry Hughes, *Jutland 1916* (New York, 1976), pp. 157–8.

[2]Admiral Sir W. M. James, *The British Navies in the Second World War* (London, 1946), p. 64.

[3]Ibid., p. 67; Stephen Roskill, *The Navy at War: 1939–1945* (London, 1990), p. 105.

[4]All three quotes are taken from Correlli Barnett, *Engage the Enemy More Closely: The Royal Navy in the Second World War* (New York, 1991), p. 287.

[5]Public Record Office, Kew (hereafter cited as PRO), ADM 1/10617, "Methods of Attack on German Ships *Bismarck* and Graf Zeppelin," 27 March 1940.

[6]PRO, CAB 106/333, *Supplement to The London Gazette of Tuesday, the 14th of October, 1947.* This is Tovey's official report to the Admiralty of his actions in the search and destruction of *Bismarck*. See also Donald McLachlan, *Room 39: A Study in Naval Intelligence* (New York, 1968), pp. 143–62.

[7]Graham Rhys-Jones, *The Loss of the Bismarck: An Avoidable Disaster* (Annapolis, 1999), pp. 38–9.

[8]Roskill, *The Navy at War*, pp. 122–4; Barnett, *Engage the Enemy More Closely*, p. 279; James, *The British Navies*, pp. 161–3; and Cajus Bekker, *Hitler's Naval War* (New York, 1977), pp. 209–13.

[9]*Supplement to The London Gazette, Tuesday, 14 October 1947.*

[10]Rhys-Jones, *The Loss of the Bismarck*, p. 97.

[11]Ernie Bradford, *The Mighty Hood: The Life and Death of the Royal Navy's Proudest Ship* (London, 1961), pp. 104–5.

[12]PRO, ADM 234/325, Battle Summary #9, "The Action off Cape Spartivento, 27th November, 1940"; Barnett, *Engage the Enemy More Closely*, pp. 239–41; Captain Donald McIntyre, *Fighting Admiral: The Life of Admiral of the Fleet Sir James Somerville, G.C.B., G.B.E., D.S.O.* (London, 1961), pp. 93–7.

[13]Battle Summary #9, "The Action off Cape Spartivento, 27th November, 1940," p. 7.

[14]Barnett, *Engage the Enemy More Closely*, pp. 239–41.

[15]Battle Summary #9, "The Action off Cape Spartivento, 27th November, 1940," p. 13.

[16]Russell Grenfell, *The Bismarck Episode* (London, 1949), p. 198.

[17]Quoted in Barnett, *Engage the Enemy More Closely*, p. 52.

[18]James Levy, "Ready or Not? The Home Fleet at the Outset of World War II," *Naval War College Review*, Autumn 1999, pp. 90–108.

[19]Ibid.

[20]Ibid., p. 7.

[21]Andrew Lambert, "Seapower 1939–1940: Churchill and the Strategic Origins of the Battle of the Atlantic," in Geoffrey Till, ed., *Seapower: Theory and Practise* (London, 1994), p. 105.

[22]PRO, ADM 223/619, Rear Admiral Sir John Godfrey's unpublished war memoirs.

[23]Ibid.

[24]These schemes, and Churchill's interventions, are covered in Richard Lamb, *Churchill as War Leader* (New York, 1991).

[25]Ibid., p. 66.

[26]Rhys-Jones, *The Loss of the Bismarck*, pp. 145–6, n. 18.

[27]MacIntyre, *Fighting Admiral*, p. 99.

[28]Lamb, *Churchill as War Leader*, p. 241.

[29]Grenfell, *The Bismarck Episode*, pp. 198–201; Peter Hodges, *The Big Gun: Battleship Main Armament, 1860–1945* (Greenwich, 1981), pp. 93–5, 103–4.

[30]Levy, "Ready or Not?," p. 4; C. P. Gallimore, "The Development of Propulsive Machinery for Surface and Submarine Warships," *Royal United Services Institute Journal*, August 1951, pp. 385–400.

[31]All these factors and more are extensively discussed in Geoffrey Till, *Air Power and the Royal Navy: 1914–1945, A Historical Survey* (London, 1979).

[32]PRO, HW 3/140, "History of naval section . . ."; Anthony Wells, "Naval Intelligence and decision making in an era of technical change," in Bryan Ranft, ed., *Technical Change and British Naval Policy, 1860–1939* (London, 1977), pp. 123–45.

[33]Grenfell, *The Bismarck Episode*, pp. 30–5; Rhys-Jones, *The Loss of the Bismarck*, pp. 102–5.

[34]*Supplement to The London Gazette, Tuesday, 14 October 1947.*

Chapter 4

[1]War diary, 23 May 1941. Bundesarchiv-Militärarchiv (hereafter BA-MA), Freiburg, PG 48349 Kriegstagebuch des Kreuzers "Prinz Eugen." Hereafter cited as: KTB *Prinz Eugen*; BA-MA, PG 48349.

[2]War diary, 23 May 1941. BA-MA, PG 47896 Kriegstagebuch des Schlachtschiffes "Bismarck." Hereafter cited as: KTB *Bismarck*; BA-MA, PG 47896.

[3]Cited in Burkard Baron von Müllenheim-Rechberg, *Battleship Bismarck: A Survivor's Story* (Annapolis, 1990), p. 130.

[4]Cited in Jochen Brennecke, *Schlachtschiff Bismarck* (Herford, 1960), pp. 85–6.

[5]Derek Howse, *Radar at Sea: The Royal Navy in World War 2* (Annapolis, 1993), pp. 91–2.

[6]23 May 1941. KTB *Prinz Eugen*; BA-MA, PG 48349.

[7]BA-MA, PG 47895. Oberkommando der Kriegsmarine. Entwurf Atlantik-Unternehmen der Kampfgruppe "Bismarck"-"Prinz Eugen."

[8]Entry for 23 May 1941. *Kriegstagebuch der Seekriegsleitung 1939–1945*, ed. Werner Rahn and Gerhard Schreiber (68 vols., Herford and Bonn, 1988–97), vol. 21, p. 344.

[9]Naval Intelligence Division, "German Battleship 'Bismarck': Interrogation of Survivors." August, 1941. C.B. 4051 (24), p. 12.

[10]23 May 1941. KTB *Prinz Eugen*; BA-MA, PG 48349.

[11]Brennecke, *Schlachtschiff Bismarck*, p. 87.

[12]Rear Admiral Joseph H. Wellings, *On His Majesty's Service*, ed. John B. Hattendorf, (Newport, 1983), pp. 193–4.

[13]Müllenheim-Rechberg, *Battleship Bismarck*, p. 134.

[14]23 May 1941. KTB *Prinz Eugen*; BA-MA, PG 48349.

[15]Ibid.

[16]Müllenheim-Rechberg, *Battleship Bismarck*, pp. 70–1.

[17]Wellings, *On His Majesty's Service*, p. 194.

[18]Public Record Office, Kew (hereafter cited as PRO), Admiralty (ADM) 199/1188, "Engagement of Hood and Prince of Wales . . . 24th May, 1941." Memorandum of 26 June 1941.

[19]Jon Tetsuro Sumida, " 'The Best Laid Plans': The Development of British Battle-Fleet Tactics, 1919–1942," *International History* (November 1992), pp. 681–700.

[20]Naval Staff History, Second World War, Battle Summary No. 5, *The Chase and Sinking of "Bismarck,"* pp. 7–10; PRO, Cabinet (CAB) 106/333, *Supplement to The London Gazette, Tuesday, 14 October 1947*, Report of Admiral Tovey, pp. 4849–50; Correlli Barnett, *Engage the Enemy More Closely: The Royal Navy in the Second World War* (London, 1991), pp. 289–91.

[21]Ludovic Kennedy, *PURSUIT: The Chase and Sinking of the Bismarck* (London, 1974), p. 66.

[22]Ibid., p. 75.

[23]24 May 1941. KTB *Prinz Eugen*; BA-MA, PG 48349. After-action report of Lieutenant Schmalenbach.
[24]24 May 1941. KTB *Prinz Eugen*; BA-MA, PG 48349.
[25]Ibid.
[26]Ibid.
[27]Ibid. Schmalenbach's after-action report, 24 May 1941.
[28]Brennecke, *Schlachtschiff Bismarck*, p. 96.
[29]24 May 1941. KTB *Prinz Eugen*; PG 48349. Schmalenbach's after-action report.
[30]Naval Staff History, *The Chase and Sinking of Bismarck*, pp. 7–10; *London Gazette*, Report of Admiral Tovey, pp. 4849–53; Barnett, *Engage the Enemy*, pp. 289–93; Robert J. Winklareth, *The Bismarck Chase: New Light on a Famous Engagement* (Annapolis, 1998), pp. 76–101.
[31]24 May 1941. KTB *Prinz Eugen*; PG 48349. Schmalenbach's after-action report p. 80.
[32]Ibid., p. 82.
[33]BA-MA, Marinegruppenkommando West, B.Nr. gKdos. 3156/41 A1. Depositions of 14 June 1941.
[34]Winklareth, *The Bismarck Chase*, pp. 88–89.
[35]Naval Intelligence Division, German Battleship "Bismarck": Interrogation of Survivors, C.B. 4051 (24), August 1941, p. 13.
[36]Müllenheim-Rechberg, *Battleship Bismarck*, p. 139.
[37]"German Battleship 'Bismarck': Interrogation of Survivors," C.B. 4051 (24), p. 13.
[38]Cited in Nathan Miller, *War at Sea: A Naval History of World War II* (New York, 1995), p. 156.
[39]Müllenheim-Rechberg, *Battleship Bismarck*, p. 141.
[40]Ulrich Elfrath and Bodo Herzog, *The Battleship Bismarck: A Documentary in Words and Pictures* (West Chester, PA, 1989), p. 108.
[41]24 May 1941. KTB *Prinz Eugen*; BA-MA, PG 48349.
[42]Barnett, *Engage the Enemy More Closely*, p. 293.
[43]Rear Admiral Hubert Schmundt, commander of cruisers, in his after-action report severely criticized Brinkmann for this "very brave" but utterly "unorthodox" behavior. BA-MA, Oberkommando der Kriegsmarine. Entwurf Atlantik-Unternehmung der Kampfgruppe "Bismarck"–"Prinz Eugen," PG 47895.
[44]24 May 1941. KTB *Prinz Eugen*; BA-MA, PG 48349.
[45]Brennecke, *Schlachtschiff Bismarck*, p. 100.

Chapter 5

[1]The experiences of the *Hood's* survivors can be found in Public Record Office (hereafter cited as PRO), Admiralty (ADM) 116/4351, Loss of HMS *Hood*: Report of the First Board of Inquiry.

[2]Nathan Miller, *War at Sea: A Naval History of World War II* (New York, 1995), p. 157.

[3]War diary, 24 May 1941. Bundesarchiv-Militärarchiv (hereafter BA-MA), Freiburg, PG 48349 Kriegstagebuch des Kreuzers "Prinz Eugen." Hereafter cited as: KTB *Prinz Eugen*; BA-MA, PG 48349.

[4]Burkard Baron von Müllenheim-Rechberg, *Battleship Bismarck: A Survivor's Story* (Annapolis, 1990), p. 142.

[5]Ibid., p. 143.

[6]Ibid., p. 144.

[7]BA-MA, Marinegruppenkommando West, B.Nr. gKdos. 3156/41 A1. 14 June 1941.

[8]Generaladmiral Rolf Carls, head Naval Command West, later chastised Brinkmann for his "*horrid* failure" to engage the ship's "*primary*" weapon. BA-MA, PG 47895, Oberkommando der Marine. Entwurf Atlantik-Unternehmung der Kampfgruppe "Bismarck"–"Prinz Eugen."

[9]War diary, 24 May 1941. KTB *Prinz Eugen*; BA-MA, PG 48349.

[10]Ibid: After-action reports by Schmalenbach and Jasper, 24 May 1941.

[11]Ibid.

[12]Cited in Müllenheim-Rechberg, *Battleship Bismarck*, pp. 149–50.

[13]"German Battleship 'Bismarck': Interrogation of Survivors," C.B. 4051 (24), p. 13.

[14]Ibid.

[15]"German Battleship 'Bismarck': Interrogation of Survivors," C.B. 4051 (24), p. 13. After-action report by Korvettenkapitän Jasper, 24 May 1941.

[16]Richard Hough, *Former Naval Person: Churchill and the Wars at Sea* (London, 1985), p. 172.

[17]Correlli Barnett, *Engage the Enemy More Closely: The Royal Navy in the Second World War* (New York, 1991), p. 209.

[18]War diary, 24 May 1941. KTB *Prinz Eugen*; BA-MA, PG 48349.

[19]See Jochen Brennecke, *Schlachtschiff Bismarck* (Herford, 1960), pp. 109ff.

[20]BA-MA, Oberkommando der Marine, Lagezimmer G.Kdos.-Akte "Bismarck," PG 47892. Also, war diary 24 May 1941. BA-MA, Kriegstagebuch des Schlachtschiffes "Bismarck." Hereafter cited as: KTB *Bismarck*; BA-MA, PG 47896.

[21]War diary, 24 May 1941. KTB *Prinz Eugen*; BA-MA, PG 48349. Brinkmann's after-action report.

[22]Cited in Müllenheim-Rechberg, *Battleship Bismarck*, p. 152.

[23]Brennecke, *Schlachtschiff Bismarck*, pp. 121–2. The German rank of Generaladmiral

does not have an English equivalent; it lies between the ranks of admiral and fleet admiral.

[24]Ibid., p. 122; and Nicolaus v. Below, *Als Hitlers Adjutant 1937–45* (Mainz, 1980), p. 275.

[25]Cited in Müllenheim-Rechberg, *Battleship Bismarck*, p. 149.

[26]War diary, 24 May 1941. KTB *Bismarck*; BA-MA, PG 47896.

[27]BA-MA, Oberkommando der Marine, RMD 4/601. Operationen und Taktik. Auswertung wichtiger Ereignisse des Seekriegies, Heft 3, Die Atlantikunternehmung der Kampfgruppe "Bismarck"-"Prinz Eugen," pp. 17–8.

[28]Ibid., p. 19.

[29]Müllenheim-Rechberg, *Battleship Bismarck*, p. 157.

[30]Naval Intelligence Division, C.B. 4041 (24). German Battleship "Bismarck": Interrogation of Survivors; August, 1941, p. 15.

[31]War diary, 24 May 1941. KTB *Prinz Eugen*; BA-MA, PG 48349.

[32]Ibid.

[33]Naval Staff History, Second World War, Battle Summary No. 5, *The Chase and Sinking of "Bismarck,"* p. 10. Also, PRO, Cabinet (CAB) 106/333, *Supplement to The London Gazette, Tuesday, 14 October 1947*, Report of Admiral Tovey, pp. 4850–52.

[34]War diary, 24 May 1941. KTB *Prinz Eugen*; BA-MA, PG 48349.

[35]BA-MA, Oberkommando der Kriegsmarine, Lagezimmer G.Kdos.-Akte "Bismarck."

[36]War diary, 24 May 1941. KTB *Bismarck*; BA-MA, PG 47896.

[37]Cited in Müllenheim-Rechberg, *Battleship Bismarck*, pp. 162–3.

[38]War diary, 24 May 1941. KTB *Prinz Eugen*; BA-MA, PG 48349.

[39]Ibid.

[40]Ibid.

[41]Ibid.

[42]War diary, 25 May 1941. KTB *Bismarck*; BA-MA, PG 47896.

[43]War diary, 26 May 1941. KTB *Prinz Eugen*; BA-MA, PG 48349.

[44]Paul Schmalenbach, *Kreuzer Prinz Eugen . . . unter drei Flaggen* (Hamburg, 1998), p. 127.

[45]Cited in Müllenheim-Rechberg, *Battleship Bismarck*, p. 164.

[46]War diary, 24 May 1941. KTB *Bismarck*; BA-MA, PG 47896.

Chapter 6

[1]All particulars of the *Modoc*'s voyage are from Ship's Log Book, U.S. Coast Guard cutter *Modoc* for the month of May 1941, National Archives, Washington, D.C.

[2]United States Coast Guard, material supplied by R.M. Browning, Jr., Historian, U.S. Coast Guard, Letters of Richard Davies, Davies to Ralph Moore, 9 May 1989.

[3]Stetson Conn, Rose C. Engelman, and Byron Fairchild, *United States Army in World War II, The Western Hemisphere, Guarding the United States and Its Outposts* (Washington, D.C., 1964), pp. 442–58.

[4]United States Coast Guard, Historical Section, *The Coast Guard at War: Greeenland Patrol II*, unpublished ms., July 1945, pp. 20–2.

[5]*Modoc* log, 20 May 1941.

[6]The fate of HX 126 is found in Clay Blair, *Hitler's U-Boat War: The Hunters, 1939–1942* (New York, 1996), pp. 286–7.

[7]*The Coast Guard at War: Greeenland Patrol II*, p. 24.

[8]Ibid., p. 26.

[9]*Modoc* log, 24 May 1941.

[10]Royal Navy, Naval Staff History, B.R. 1736 (3/50), Battle Summary No. 5, *The Chase and Sinking of the "Bismarck"* (Admiralty: Tactical and Staff Duties Division, 1949), p. 14.

[11]T. R. Sargent and B. M. Chiswell, " 'We Was Dere, Charlie!', or Saga of the CGC MODOC's Encounter with the German Battleship Bismarck," in United States Coast Guard Alumni Association, *The Bulletin*, March/April 1980, p. 25.

[12]Davies Letters, Davies to Mary Margaret, 25 May 1941.

[13]*Modoc* log, 24 May 1941.

[14]Davies Letters, Davies to Mary Margaret, 25 May 1941.

[15]See Charles Lamb, *To War in a Stringbag* (Garden City, NY, 1977), pp. 45–8.

[16]Battle Summary No. 5, *The Chase and Sinking of the "Bismarck,"* p. 15.

[17]Thompson's report is to be found in National Archives, Washington, D.C., Office of U.S. Naval Intelligence, Enclosure "F" of "Operations and Battle of German Battleship Bismarck, 23–27 May, 1941, 1 July 1941.

[18]Bundesarchiv-Militärarchiv (hereafter BA-MA), Freiburg, Marinegruppenkommando West. B.Nr. gKos. 3156/41 A1. Deposition of 14 June 1941.

[19]Herzog deposition; ibid.

[20]War diary, 25 May 1941. BA-MA, PG 47896 Kriegstagebuch des Schlachschiffes "Bismarck." Hereafter cited as: KTB *Bismarck*; BA-MA, PG 47896.

[21]War diary, 24 May 1941; ibid.

[22]BA-MA, PG 47892 Oberkommando der Kriegsmarine. Lagezimmer gKdos.-Akte "Bismarck."

[23]Ibid.

[24]*Modoc* log, 24 May 1941.

[25]Davies Letters, Davies to Mary Margaret, 25 May 1941.

[26]Sargent and Chiswell, " 'We Was Dere, Charlie!,' " p. 25.

[27]Thomas B. Buell, *Master of Sea Power: A Biography of Fleet Admiral Ernest J. King* (Boston, 1980), p. 140.

[28]Ibid.

[29]Ludovic Kennedy, *PURSUIT: The Chase and Sinking of the Bismarck* (London, 1974), p. 235.

[30]Details of the sorties of USS *New York* and USS *Texas* are from the ships' logs for May 1941 at the National Archives, Washington D.C.

[31]Martin Gilbert, *Winston S. Churchill* (8 vols., London, 1966–88), vol. 6, p. 690.

[32]Correlli Barnett, *Engage the Enemy More Closely: The Royal Navy in the Second World War* (New York and London, 1991), p. 184.

[33]National Archives, Washington, D.C., U.S.-British Staff Conversations, R. L. Ghormley, "Notes on Conversation with the First Sea Lord," 19 November 1940.

[34]Ibid., Ghormley to Stark, 7 January 1941.

[35]Ibid., "Record of a meeting held at the Admiralty on 22nd November, 1940."

[36]National Archives, Washington, D.C., Director (Naval) War Plans Division to Chief of Naval Operations re: "New York and Texas increased gun elevations," 28 November 1940.

[37]Ibid.

[38]National Archives, Washington, D.C., memo from CNO to BuShips and BoUrd, 7 December 1940.

[39]Gilbert, *Churchill*, vol. 6, p. 762 and note.

[40]W. Averell Harriman and Elie Abel, *Special Envoy to Churchill and Stalin, 1941–1946* (New York, 1975), p. 11.

[41]Samuel Eliot Morison, *History of United States Naval Operations in World War II*, vol. 1, *The Battle of the Atlantic: September 1939–May 1943* (Boston, 1962), p. 14, Appendix V.

[42]Buell, *Master of Seapower*, p. xx.

[43]Ibid., p. 139.

[44]Theodore Roscoe, *Tin Cans: The True Story of the Fighting Destroyers of World War II* (New York, 1960), p. 12.

[45]The *Niblack*'s encounter with U-52 is reconstructed from Blair, *Hitler's U-Boat War*, pp. 269–270; and Roscoe, *Tin Cans*, pp. 15–6.

[46]Harriman and Abel, *Special Envoy*, p. 57.

[47]Ibid., pp. 22–3.

[48]The talks are summarized in Richard Hough, *Former Naval Person: Churchill and the Wars at Sea* (London, 1985), p. 170. Quotes are from National Archives, Washington, D.C., U.S.-British Staff Conversations, minutes of a meeting on 6 March 1941.

[49]Franklin D. Roosevelt Library, Hyde Park, New York, Roosevelt-Churchill Correspondence, Roosevelt to Churchill, 11 April 1941.

[50]Ibid., Roosevelt to Churchill, 1 May 1941.

[51]Ibid., Roosevelt to Churchill, 4 May 1941.

[52]Ibid., Churchill to Roosevelt, 23 May 1941.

[53]Kennedy, *PURSUIT*, pp. 102, 223n.

[54]Gilbert, *Churchill*, vol. 6, p. 1094.
[55]Harriman and Abel, *Special Envoy*, pp. 33–4.

Chapter 7

[1]Cited in Burkard Baron von Müllenheim-Rechberg, *Battleship Bismarck: A Survivor's Story* (Annapolis, 1990), p. 164.
[2]War diary, 24 May 1941. Bundesarchiv-Militärarchiv (hereafter BA-MA), Freiburg, PG 47896 Kriegstagebuch des Schlachtschiffes "Bismarck." Hereafter cited as: KTB *Bismarck*; BA-MA, PG 47896.
[3]Ibid.
[4]Ibid.
[5]Cited in Jochen Brennecke, *Schlachtschiff Bismarck* (Herford, 1960), p. 131.
[6]Entry for 24 May 1941. *Kriegstagebuch der Seekriegsleitung* 1939–1945, ed. Werner Rahn and Gerhard Schreiber (68 vols., Herford, 1988–97), vol. 21, p. 365.
[7]War diary, 25 May 1941. KTB *Bismarck*; BA-MA, PG 47896.
[8]Public Record Office (hereafter PRO), Admiralty (ADM) 199/838, "HMS 'Victorious'—Report of Operations 24th May up to Destruction of the 'Bismarck,' " pp. 565–6.
[9]Royal Navy, Naval Staff History, B.R. 1736 (3/50), Battle Summary No. 5, *The Chase and Sinking of the* "Bismarck" (Admiralty: Tactical and Staff Duties Division, 1949), p. 16.
[10]PRO, Cabinet (CAB) 106/333, *Supplement to The London Gazette, Tuesday, 14 October 1947* (Tovey's official report of the chase and sinking of the *Bismarck*), pp. 4854–5.
[11]PRO, ADM 234/509, "HMS 'Ark Royal'—Report of Proceedings, 24 May 1941, To the Destruction of 'Bismarck.' "
[12]Rear Admiral Joseph H. Wellings, *On His Majesty's Service*, ed. John B. Hattendorf (Newport, 1983), pp. 189ff.
[13]Roosevelt Library, Hyde Park, NY. Roosevelt-Churchill correspondence, telegram received from London, 25 May 1941.
[14]BA-MA, PG 37823 German Naval Group Command West, Operation "Rheinübung," General Communications File. Hereafter referred to as BA-MA, PG 37823, General Communications File.
[15]See Brennecke, *Schlachtschiff Bismarck*, p. 146.
[16]Cited in Müllenheim-Rechberg, *Battleship Bismarck*, p. 177.
[17]Martin Gilbert, *Winston S. Churchill* (8 vols., London, 1966–88), vol. 6, p. 1095.

[18]BA-MA, PG 37823, General Communications File.

[19]Donald McLachlan, *Room 39: A Study in Naval Intelligence* (New York, 1968), pp. 152–3; John Winton, *ULTRA at Sea* (London, 1988), p. 29.

[20]PRO, ADM 234/509, "HMS 'Ark Royal'—Report of Proceedings, 24 May 1941, To the Destruction of 'Bismarck.' "

[21]Robert J. Winklareth, *The Bismarck Chase: New Light on a Famous Engagement* (Annapolis, 1998), p. 131.

[22]R.F. Jessel, "The *Bismarck* Operation—The German Aspect," in *Journal of the Royal United Services Institute*, February 1953, p. 26.

[23]Correlli Barnett, *Engage the Enemy More Closely: The Royal Navy in the Second World War* (New York, 1991), p. 303.

[24]Ludovic Kennedy, *PURSUIT: The Chase and Sinking of the Bismarck* (London, 1974), pp. 133–5.

[25]McLachlan, *Room* 39, p. 132.

[26]National Archives Washington, Washington, D.C., Records of the Department of the Navy, Intelligence Report from the Naval Attaché at Madrid, 3 July 1941, containing Somerville's report of 4 June 1941: "Destruction of German Battleship 'Bismarck' " of 27 May 1941.

[27]Winton, *ULTRA at Sea*, p. 30; Nathan Miller, *War at Sea: A Naval History of World War II* (New York, 1995), p. 162. "A" (completely reliable) and "1" (completely reliable) were the highest grades of intelligence information.

[28]Ibid., p. 30. The timing as given in Winton is suspect; the Admiralty's general broadcast to all ships that *Bismarck* was headed for Brest was made at 7:24 P.M.

[29]War diary, 25 May 1941. KTB *Bismarck*; BA-MA, PG 47896. Lütjens himself had made the decision to make for France.

[30]See the depositions of 14 June 1941 by Machinist Walter Lorenzen and Seamen Apprentices Otto Maus, Otto Höntzsch, Georg Herzog, and Herbert Manthey. BA-MA, Marinegruppenkommando West. B.Nr. gKods. 3156/41 A1.

[31]Müllenheim-Rechberg, *Battleship Bismarck*, pp. 182–4.

[32]Ibid., p. 185.

[33]BA-MA, PG 37823, General Communications File.

[34]Müllenheim-Rechberg, *Battleship Bismarck*, p. 192.

[35]Winklareth, *The Bismarck Chase*, p. 131.

[36]Kennedy, *PURSUIT*, pp. 152–3; PRO, AIR 15/415, "Battle of the Denmark Straits and Sinking of the German Battleship Bismarck."

[37]Wellings, *On His Majesty's Service*, pp. 209–11.

[38]Winklareth, *The Bismarck Chase*, p. 194.

[39]War diary of 26 May 1941. KTB *Bismarck*; BA-MA, PG 47896.

[40]Churchill College, Cambridge, Somerville papers, Somerville's list of comments re manuscript of Russell Grenfell's book *The Bismarck Episode*.

[41]War diary of 26 May 1941. KTB *Bismarck*; BA-MA, PG 47896.
[42]National Archives, Washington, D.C., Records of the Department of the Navy, Intelligence Report from the Naval Attaché at Madrid, 3 July 1941, containing Somerville's report of 4 June 1941: "Destruction of German Battleship '*Bismarck*'" of 27 May 1941.
[43]Ibid.
[44]Graham Rhys-Jones, *The Loss of the Bismarck: An Avoidable Disaster* (Annapolis, 1999), p. 69.
[45]National Archives, Washington, D.C., Records of the Department of the Navy, Intelligence Report from the Naval Attaché at Madrid, 3 July 1941, containing Somerville's report of 4 June 1941: "Destruction of German Battleship 'Bismarck'" of 27 May 1941.
[46]PRO, ADM 234/509 "HMS 'Victorious'—Report of Operations 24th May up to Destruction of the 'Bismarck.'"
[47]Ibid.
[48]Deposition of 21 June 1941. BA-MA, Marinegruppenkommando West. B.Nr. gKos. 3156/41 A1.
[49]Ibid.
[50]Müllenheim-Rechberg, *Battleship Bismarck*, p. 208.
[51]BA-MA, PG 37823 German Naval Group Command West. Operation "Rheinübung," General Communications File.

Chapter 8

[1]Burkard Baron von Müllenheim-Rechberg, *Battleship Bismarck: A Survivor's Story* (Annapolis, 1990), pp. 210–1.
[2]Ibid., p. 212.
[3]Ibid., p. 214. See also Appendix D on the rudder; ibid., pp. 438–44.
[4]Jochen Brennecke, *Schlachtschiff Bismarck* (Herford, 1960), p. 281.
[5]See Chapter 1.
[6]See Chapter 1.
[7]Bundesarchiv-Militärarchiv (hereafter BA-MA), Freiburg, PG 47892 Oberkommando der Marine. Lagezimmer G.Kdos-Akte "Bismarck." The admiral's sudden references to his "Führer" should not be read in terms of a newfound conversion to Nazism or slavish obedience to Hitler, as some scholars have suggested, but rather in terms of his continuing deference and obedience to the Reich's head of state and commander of its armed forces.

[8]*Kriegstagebuch der Seekriegsleitung* 1939–1945, ed. Werner Rahn and Gerhard Schreiber (68 vols., Herford, 1988–97), vol. 21, pp. 392, 405.
[9]BA-MA, PG 47892 Oberkommando der Marine. Lagezimmer G.Kdos.-Akte "Bismarck."
[10]Ibid.
[11]Nicolaus v. Below, *Als Hitlers Adjutant* 1937–45 (Mainz, 1980), p. 276.
[12]Müllenheim-Rechberg, *Battleship Bismarck*, pp. 226–7.
[13]Public Record Office (hereafter PRO), Kew, Admiralty (ADM) 234/509, "HMS Ark Royal Report of Proceedings, 24th May, 1941 Up to Destruction of Bismarck," p. 49.
[14]PRO, Cabinet (CAB) 106/333, *Supplement to The London Gazette, Tuesday,* 14 *October* 1947, p. 4857.
[15]Rear Admiral Joseph H. Wellings, *On His Majesty's Service*, ed. John B. Hattendorf (Newport, 1983), p. 219; ADM 234/509, "HMS *Ark Royal* Report of Proceedings, 24th May, 1941 Up to Destruction of *Bismarck*," p. 49.
[16]Naval Staff History, B.R. 1736 (3/50), Battle Summary No. 5, *The Chase and Sinking of the 'Bismarck,'* p. 30.
[17]Ibid.; *Supplement to The London Gazette, Tuesday,* 14 *October* 1947, p. 4857.
[18]Franklin D. Roosevelt Library, Hyde Park, New York, Roosevelt-Churchill correspondence. Churchill to Roosevelt, 28 May 1941.
[19]National Archives, Washington, D.C. Logbook, USS *New York*, 26–31 May 1941, 1–5 June 1941.
[20]See *Der U-Boot-Krieg* 1939–1945. *Die Deutschen U-Boot-Kommandanten* (Hamburg, Berlin and Bonn, 1996), pp. 258–9.
[21]Cited in Müllenheim-Rechberg, *Battleship Bismarck*, p. 234.
[22]The following description of U-556 is taken from BA-MA, PG 30591/1, Kriegstagebuch des Unterseebootes "U 556," 6.2.41—30.5.41.
[23]KTB entry for 12:45 P.M., 20 May 1941; ibid.
[24]Ibid.
[25]Ibid.
[26]KTB entry for 3:31 P.M., 26 May 1941; ibid.
[27]KTB entries for 27 and 28 May 1941. BA-MA, PG 30070/2 Kriegstagebuch des Unterseebootes "U 74."
[28]ADM 234/509, "Enclosure No. 6 to Flag Officer Commanding Force H," 4 June 1941.
[29]Müllenheim-Rechberg, *Battleship Bismarck*, p. 218; *Supplement to The London Gazette, Tuesday,* 14 *October* 1947, p. 4858.
[30]War diary, 26 May 1941. BA-MA, PG 47896 Kriegstagebuch des Schlachtschiffes "*Bismarck*."
[31]Ibid.
[32]Müllenheim-Rechberg, *Battleship Bismarck*, p. 218.

[33]KTB entry for midnight, 26–27 May 1941; ibid.
[34]KTB entries for 11:29 A.M., 27 May 1941; ibid. The original electronic signals, with correct times, are in the appendix to the KTB.
[35]*Supplement to The London Gazette, Tuesday, 14 October 1947*, p. 4858.
[36]Naval Staff History, B.R., 1736 (3/50), Battle Summary No. 5, *The Chase and Sinking of the 'Bismarck,'* p. 30; Correlli Barnett, *Engage the Enemy More Closely: The Royal Navy in the Second World War* (New York and London, 1991), p. 311.
[37]Survivor's diary, Naval Intelligence Division, C.B. 4051 (24). German Battleship "*Bismarck*": Interrogation of Survivors; August, 1941, pp. 20, 59. Hereafter cited as Naval Intelligence Division, C.B. 4051 (24).
[38]BA-MA, PG 47892 Oberkommando der Marine. Lagezimmer G.Kdos.-Akte "*Bismarck.*"
[39]Ibid.
[40]Ibid.
[41]Account by *Bismarck* survivors: BA-MA, Marinegruppe West, B.Nr. gKos. 3156/41 A1.
[42]*Supplement to The London Gazette, Tuesday, 14 October 1947*, p. 4859.
[43]Ibid.; Wellings, *On Her Majesty's Service*, p. 225.
[44]Ludovic Kennedy, *PURSUIT: The Chase and Sinking of the Bismarck* (London, 1974), pp. 200–1; Naval Staff History, B.R. 1736 (3/50), Battle Summary No. 5, *The Chase and Sinking of the 'Bismarck,'* pp. 31–32.
[45]Directorate of History and Heritage, Department of National Defence (Ottawa), "Davis Reminiscences."
[46]Wellings, *On Her Majesty's Service*, p. 234.
[47]ADM 234/509, *King George V*, narrative of the action, "Gunnery," pp. 147–8.
[48]Barnett, *Engage the Enemy More Closely*, p. 312.
[49]Ibid., p. 313.
[50]Based on survivors' reports in Naval Intelligence Division, C.B. 4051 (24), p. 24.
[51]Müllenheim-Rechberg, *Battleship Bismarck*, p. 267.
[52]See the detailed description in Brennecke, *Schlachtschiff Bismarck*, pp. 202–6, 214–6.
[53]Müllenheim-Rechberg, *Battleship Bismarck*, p. 270.
[54]Survivors' testimony. Naval Intelligence Division, C.B. 4051 (24), p. 25.
[55]Müllenheim-Rechberg, *Battleship Bismarck*, pp. 269–70.
[56]Survivors' testimony. Naval Intelligence Division, C.B. 4051 (24), pp. 25–6.
[57]Müllenheim-Rechberg, *Battleship Bismarck*, pp. 277–8.
[58]Ibid., pp. 256–7.
[59]*Supplement to The London Gazette, Tuesday, 14 October 1947*, p. 4859.
[60]Ibid.

[61]See Robert D. Ballard, *Exploring the Bismarck* (New York, 1991). Ballard and his team from the Woods Hole Oceanographic Institute on Cape Cod discovered the wreck of the *Bismarck* on the morning of 9 June 1989 (almost forty-seven years after her sinking) at a depth of just over 15,000 feet.
[62]Graham Rhys-Jones, *The Loss of the Bismarck: An Avoidable Disaster* (Annapolis, 1999), pp. 211–2, 231; Robert J. Winklareth, *The Bismarck Chase: New Light on a Famous Engagement* (Annapolis, 1998), pp. 160–1.
[63]Martin Gilbert, *Winston S. Churchill* (8 vols., London, 1966–88), vol. 6, pp. 1095–6.
[64]Barnett, *Engage the Enemy More Closely*, pp. 314–5.
[65]Entry for 27 May 1941. BA-MA, KTB des Unterseebootes "U 74."
[66]Ibid.
[67]Schütte's detailed report is in BA-MA, PG 47898 Kriegstagebuch des Schlachtschiffes "*Bismarck*": Fischdampfer "*Sachsenwald*." Bericht über den Einsatz bei der Rettungsaktion "*Bismarck*" 30.5.1941.

Epilogue

[1]Ludovic Kennedy, *PURSUIT: The Chase and Sinking of the Bismarck* (London, 1974), p. 221.
[2]Bundesarchiv-Militärarchiv (BA-MA), Freiburg, RMD 4/601, Operationen und Taktik. Auswertung wichtiger Ereignisse des Seekrieges, Heft 3, Das Atlantikunternehmen der Kampfgruppe "Bismarck"-"Prinz Eugen" Mai 1941. See also Jochen Brennecke, *Schlachtschiff Bismarck* (Herford, 1960), pp. 237–42.
[3]Entry for 28 May 1941. *Kriegstagebuch der Seekriegsleitung* 1939–1945, ed. Werrner Rahn and Gerhard Schreiber (68 vols., Herford, 1988–97), vol. 21, p. 423.
[4]Kennedy, *PURSUIT*, p. 221; Naval Staff History, Second World War, B.R. 1736 (3/50), Battle Summary No. 5, *The Chase and Sinking of the "Bismarck,"* p. 35.
[5]War diary, 29 May 1941. BA-MA, PG 48349 Kriegstagebuch des Kreuzers "Prinz Eugen."
[6]Doris Kearns Goodwin, *No Ordinary Time: Franklin & Eleanor Roosevelt: The Home Front in World War II* (New York, 1994), pp. 238–40.
[7]Franklin D. Roosevelt Library, Hyde Park, NY, Roosevelt/Churchill Correspondence. Roosevelt to Churchill, 27 May 1941.
[8]Public Record Office, Kew, Admiralty 199 /1933, First Lord's Records. Churchill to First Lord and First Sea Lord, 28 May 1941.

[9]Ibid., Alexander to Churchill, 29 May 1941.

[10]War diary, 30 May 1941. BA-MA, PG 48349 Kriegstagebuch des Kreuzers "Prinz Eugen."

[11]War diary, 1 June 1941; ibid.

[12]BA-MA, Marinegruppenkommando West, B.Nr. gKdos. 3355/41, Verlust Versorgungsschiffe. See also F. H. Hinsley, *British Intelligence in the Second World War: Its Influence on Strategy and Operations* (3 vols., London, 1979), vol. 1, p. 345; and John Winton, *ULTRA at Sea* (London, 1988), pp. 33–9.

[13]Stummel's report is in BA-MA, PG 37823 German Naval Group Command West. Operation Rheinübung, General Communications file.

[14]Max Domarus, *Hitler. Reden und Proklamationen 1932–1945* (3 vols., Munich, 1965), vol. 2, p. 1722; Andreas Hillgruber, *Staatsmänner und Diplomaten bei Hitler. Vertrauliche Aufzeichnungen über Unterredungen mit Vertretern des Auslandes 1939–1941* (Frankfurt, 1967), pp. 559ff.

[15]Cited in Burkard Baron von Müllenheim-Rechberg, *Battleship Bismarck: A Survivor's Story* (Annapolis, 1990), p. 262.

[16]Karl Jesko von Puttkamer, *Die unheimliche See. (Hitler und die Kriegsmarine)* (Munich, 1952), pp. 48–9.

[17]See Michael Salewski, *Die deutsche Seekriegsleitung 1935–1945* (3 vols., Frankfurt, 1970), vol. 1, pp. 451–4.

[18]Undated memorandum. BA-MA, PG 47895 Oberkommando der Kriegsmarine. Entwurf Atlantik-Unternehmung der Kampfgruppe "Bismarck"-"Prinz Eugen."

[19]See Andreas Hillgruber, *Deutschlands Rolle in der Vorgeschichte der beiden Weltkriege* (Göttingen, 1967), p. 105.

[20]Report of 28 July 1941, Chef der Sicherheitspolizei und des RSHA-Amt III (SD-Hauptamt). Bundesarchiv Koblenz, R 58/144–194 Meldungen aus dem Reich.

[21]See Holger H. Herwig, *Politics of Frustration: The United States in German Naval Planning, 1889–1941* (Boston and Toronto, 1976), pp. 243–4.

[22]*Jane's Fighting Ships 1969–70* (London, 1969), p. 116.

[23]Russell Grenfell, The *Bismarck* Episode (London, 1949), p. 193.

Glossary

Abaft. To the rear of; aft of; in the direction of the stern.

ABC-Staff Agreement. An agreement of March 1941 that committed the United States to a "Europe first" strategy in the event that it became involved in a war in both Europe and Asia.

Abeam. At right angles to the fore-and-aft line.

Aft. Close to or toward the stern.

Aircraft carrier. A warship equipped with a deck for the taking off and landing of aircraft and with storage decks for aircraft.

Amidships. In or at the part of the ship midway between bow and stern.

Arado 196. German two-seat maritime reconnaissance floatplane outfitted to the *Bismarck*. A 960-hp BMW engine gave best speed of 193 mph; range was 665 miles at 157 mph. Armed with two rapid-fire 20-mm machine guns in wings.

Ark Royal. British *Courageous*-class aircraft carrier, launched April 1937. Displacement: 22,000 tons; 27,700 full load. Machinery: 3-shaft Parsons geared turbines for 102,000 shp; best speed 31 knots. Range: 7,600 nm at 20 knots. Guns: 16 4.5-in. Aircraft: 60 normal; 72 in May 1941. Complement: 1,600. Delivered the critical air strikes against *Bis-*

marck on 26 May 1941; torpedoed by U-81 off Gibraltar, 14 November 1941.

ASV. Air to Surface Vessel; British airborne radar device to detect ships; introduced in 1940.

Athwartships. From one side of a ship to the other.

B-Dienst. German radio intelligence (*Beobachtungsdienst*); responsible to monitoring and interpreting enemy signal traffic.

Battle cruiser. A large, heavily armed warship that is lighter, faster, and more maneuverable than a battleship.

Battleship. Any of a class of warships that are equipped with the most powerful armament and are the most heavily armored.

***Bismarck*.** German battleship, launched February 1939. Displacement: 41,200 tons; 50,5000 full load. Machinery: 3-shaft Curtis steam turbines for 150,170shp; best speed 30 knots. Range: 8,500 nm at 19 knots. Armament: 8 15-in (38-cm) guns; 12 6-in (15-cm) guns; 8 21-in (53.3-cm) torpedo tubes. Main belt armor up to 12.6 in; deck armor to 3.15 in. Complement: 2,200. Sunk by enemy actions on 27 May 1941.

Bletchley Park. British "Government Code and Cypher School" in Buckinghamshire. By May 1940 it had broken the Luftwaffe Enigma machine cipher.

Bow. The forward part of a ship; **bow-on**, with the bow foremost.

Cape Spartivento. Naval clash between British and Italian forces on 27 November 1940. Involved on the British side were Admirals Sir James Somverville and Lancelot Holland of Force H.

Condor. See **Focke-Wulf 200 Condor.**

Convoy. A ship of group of ships traveling together and usually accompanied by a protective escort of warships.

Cordite. A smokeless, slow-burning powder composed of nitroglycerine, nitrocellulose, and mineral jelly.

Coxswain. Steersman; seaman in charge of a ship in the absence of an officer.

Crow's nest. Platform or shelter for a lookout at or near the top of a mast.

Cruiser. Any of a class of warships of medium tonnage and designed for high speed and long cruising radius.

Denmark Strait. The waters between Iceland and Greenland. Normally 180 to 200 miles wide, the strait in May 1941 was reduced to 60 miles because of pack ice.

Destroyer. A fast, relatively small warship armed mainly with five-inch guns; in World War II used as an escort in convoys and in antisubmarine duties.

"Destroyers-for-bases" deal. Announced August 1940, the United States transferred to Britain and Canada 50 World War I "four-piper" destroyers in return for 99-year leases on British territory from Newfoundland to the Caribbean.

"Dete." German Admiral Günther Lütjens' term for British radar.

Direction finder. A loop antenna receiver rotating on a vertical axis designed to ascertain the direction of incoming radio waves. See also **FuMo**.

***Dorsetshire*.** British *Norfolk*-class heavy cruiser, launched January 1929. For specifications, see **Norfolk**. Fired three torpedoes into the wreck of the *Bismarck* on 27 May 1941; sunk by aircraft of the Japanese 1st Carrier Fleet off Hondra Head, Ceylon (today Sri Lanka), 5 April 1942.

Eel. German slang term for a torpedo. The British equivalents were **fish** and **kipper.**

Enigma. Electro-mechanical enciphering machine, much like a typewriter, with 3 (later 4) wheels used to encode day-to-day secret communication. First marketed in 1923 and used by the German navy (*Schlüsselmaschine* "M") in 1926, the German army in 1929, and the German air force in 1934. Each branch of the armed services had its own Enigma cipher.

Escort. Any of a number of classes of warships designed to protect merchant ships arranged in convoy for their journey.

Faeroes. Faeroe Islands, a self-governing community of the kingdom of Denmark, between Iceland and the Shetland Islands.

Fire control. Technical supervision of naval gunfire on a target, as for range, elevation, and the like.

Flagship. A ship bearing the flag officer or the commander of a fleet, squadron, or flotilla and displaying his flag.

Flak. Antiaircraft fire directed at hostile aircraft. The word was adopted during World War II from the German acronym for *Flieger-Abwehr-Kanone* (aircraft defense gun).

Flotilla. A group of usually small naval vessels, usually composed of at least two squadrons.

***Flygplankryssare*.** See **Gotland**.

Focke-Wulf 200 Condor. German maritime reconnaissance bomber made operational January 1940. Four 1,200-hp BMW engines gave best speed of 224 mph; range 2,206 miles. Main armament: one 15-mm and one 20-mm machine gun.

Foc's'le. Abbreviation for *forecastle;* a superstructure either at or immediately aft of the bow of a vessel, and used either for storage or as quarters for seamen.

Force H. British naval squadron based at Gibraltar under Vice Admiral Sir James Somverville. The aircraft carrier *Ark Royal*, the battle cruiser *Renown*, and the light cruiser *Sheffield* were all involved in the final phase of the hunt for the *Bismarck*.

FuMO. German "Seetakt" radar-detection sets, formally called *Funkmeßortungsgerät*, often mistaken for radar-surveillance devices. The *Bismarck*'s three FuMO-23 sets had an effective range of about 15.5 miles; the *Prinz Eugen* mounted two FuMO-27 sets.

Funnel. A smokestack of a ship; a flue, tube or shaft used for ventilation.

Gneisenau. German *Scharnhorst*-class battleship, launched December 1936. For specifications, see ***Scharnhorst***. Laid up at Brest during Rhine Exercise; bombed by the Royal Air Force after the "Channel dash," February 1942; scuttled as a blockship at Gotenhafen 27–28 March 1945.

Gotenhafen. German naval port off Danzig in the Baltic Sea; today Polish Gdynia.

Gotland. Swedish flight-deck cruiser, placed in service September 1933. Displacement: 4,775 tons. Machinery: 2-shaft geared turbines for 33,000 shp; best speed 27.5 knots. Armament: 6 6-in guns; 4 3-in guns; 6 21-in torpedo tubes. 8 floatplanes. Complement: 540. Spotted the *Bismarck* and *Prinz Eugen* off Sweden on 20 May 1941.

Graf Spee. German pocket battleship, launched June 1934. Displacement: 13,600 tons; 15,900 full load. Machinery: 8 MAN 3-shaft diesels for 54,000 shp; best speed 26 knots. Range: 18,650 nm at 15 knots. Armament: 6 11-in (28-cm) guns; 8 6-in (15-cm) guns; 8 50-cm (21-in) torpedo tubes. Main belt armor 2.4 in; deck armor 1.6 in. Complement: 950. Scuttled by Captain Hans Langsdorff off Montevideo 17 December 1939, resulting in Grand Admiral Erich Raeder's general order that a German warship fight "until the last shell, until it is victorious or goes down with flag flying."

Grid, Diagraph, or Quadrant. Standard German naval charts, drawn to Mercator projection, were based on a system of artificial squares (grids, diagraphs, quadrants), each about 486 nm, covering the globe's surface. The *Hood* sank in AD 73; the *Bismarck* last reported her position as BE 6192.

Halyard. Any of various lines or tackles used to hoist a spar, sail, or flag into position for use.

Heavy cruiser. A naval cruiser armed with 8-in guns as its main armament.

High explosive. Bursting charges in bombs or shells with an explosive (such as trinitrotoluene, or TNT) in which the reaction is so rapid as to be practically instantaneous.

High-frequency direction finder (HD/DF). A radio receiver that can indicate from which direction a signal is being sent. "Huff-Duff," as it was commonly called, helped the Admiralty locate the *Bismarck* on 25 May 1941.

Hood. British battle cruiser, launched August 1918. After modifications in 1931 and 1939—Displacement: 42,670 tons; 48,350 full load. Machinery: 4-shaft Brown-Curtis geared turbines for 160,000 shp; best speed 32 knots. Range: 7,500 nm at 14 knots. Armament: 8 15-in guns; 12 5.5-in guns; 6 21-in torpedo tubes. Main belt armor to 12 in; deck armor to 3 in. Complement: 1,480. Sunk by *Bismarck* during Battle of Iceland.

"HOOD." Admiral Günther Lütjens' code word for *Prinz Eugen* to separate from *Bismarck* 24 May 1941.

Hvalfjord. Fjord northwest of Reykjavik, Iceland, used by the British as a supply station in 1941. Icelandic: **Hvalförđur.**

Hydrophones. See **Sonar**.

Incendiary. Bombs or shells containing thermite or some other substance that burns with intense heat.

"JOTDORA." The German signal, "JD," for permission to open fire.

King George V. British battleship, launched February 1939. Displacement: 38,000 tons; 44,800 full load. Machinery: 4-shaft geared turbines for 125,000 shp; best speed 29 knots. Range: 15,600 nm at 10 knots. Armament: 10 14-in guns; 16 5.25-in guns. Main belt armor to 15 in; deck armor to 6 in. Complement: 1,650. Admiral Sir John Tovey's flagship, she hunted the *Bismarck* and severely damaged her on 27 May 1941; broken up January 1958.

Knot. A unit of speed equal to about one nautical mile or 1.15 statute miles per hour.

Kriegsmarine. German term for the navy of the Third Reich.

Lend-Lease. United States legislation, passed March 1941, that authorized the president to "exchange, lend, lease or otherwise dispose of" war materials to foreign governments for use in a manner "vital to the defense of the United States."

Light cruiser. A naval cruiser mounting 6-in guns as its main armament.

Luftwaffe. German term for the air force of the Third Reich.

Maryland. Glenn Martin Maryland; a twin-engine American Martin Model 167 bomber, taken over by the Royal Air Force as the Maryland Mk. I and II. Maximal speed 275 mph; range 1,300 miles; armament six 7.5-mm machine guns; bomb load two 624-pound or eight 116-pound bombs.

Mers el-Kebir. Near Oran, North Africa, site of the British destruction or crippling of the French battleships *Bretagne* and *Provence* as well as the battle cruisers *Strasbourg* and *Dunkerque* with the loss of 1,297 sailors on 3 July 1940. Ordered by Prime Minister Winston Churchill, the attack was carried out by Vice Admiral Sir James Somverville and Force H.

Messerschmitt. The Messerschmitt Bf.109 was developed in 1935 and became the archetype of World War II fighters. Armed with two machine guns, it maximal speed was 342 mph and it had a range of 410 miles. The Bf.110 had a maximal speed of 348 mph and range of 695 miles; it was armed with five 7.9-mm machine guns.

Modoc. United States *Mojave*-class Coast Guard cutter, launched October 1922. Displacement: 1,780 tons. Best speed: 15 knots. Guns: 2 5-in, and 2 3-in. Complement: 140. In the vicinity of the *Bismarck* (at times as close as 6 miles) from 24 to 27 May 1941. Decommissioned in 1947, scrapped as the private ship *Machala* in Ecuador 1964.

Naval attaché. Naval officer assigned to a diplomatic post to gather technical information concerning the country in which he is stationed.

Naval Group Command North. German shore command at Wilhelshaven, *Marinegruppenkommando Nord* was headed during Rhine Exercise by General Admiral Rolf Carls. The latter supervised Rhine Exercise until the ships passed the line between southern Greenland and the northern Hebrides.

Naval Group Command West. German shore command at Paris, *Marinegruppenkommando West* was headed during Rhine Exercise by General Admiral Alfred Saalwächter. The latter supervised Rhine Exercise after the ships had passed the line between southern Greenland and the northern Hebrides.

Neutrality Act. United States, September 1939. A defensive ring (neutrality zone) extending 300 miles out to sea and maintained by a Neutrality Patrol of mostly World War I warships.

New York. United States battleship (BB34), launched October 1912. After 1928 modification—Displacement: 28,700 tons; 29,159 full load. Machinery: 2-shaft triple expansion engines for 28,100 shp; best speed 19.7 knots. Range: 15,000 nm at 10 knots. Armament: 10 14-in guns; 16 5-in guns. Main belt armor to 12 in; deck armor to 2 in. Complement: 1,042. The *New York* supported Allied landings in North Africa November 1942 and Iwo Jima February 1945; she, like the *Prinz Eugen*, survived the atomic blast at Bikini Atoll and was attacked and sunk during a fire exercise off Pearl Harbor in July 1948.

Niblack. United States Navy *Gleaves*-class destroyer, launched May 1940. Displacement: 1,625 tons; 2,060 full load. Machinery: steam turbines for 50,000 shp; best speed 37 knots. Range: 3,630 nm at 20 knots. Armament: 5 5-in guns; 10 21-in torpedo tubes. Complement: 250. On 10 April 1941 almost engaged U-52 off the coast of Iceland. After supporting Allied landings on Sicily and in southern France, she was decommissioned June 1947 and struck from the lists July 1968.

Norfolk. British heavy cruiser, launched December 1928. Displacement: 9,925 tons; 14,600 full load. Machinery: 4-shaft Parsons geared turbines for 80,000 shp; best speed 32.3 knots. Armament: 8 8-in guns; 8 21-in torpedo tubes. Complement: 784. Shadowed *Bismarck* throughout Rhine Exercise; paid off 1949 and broken up 1950.

Northland. United States Coast Guard cutter (or cruising class of gunboat), launched February 1927. Specially designed for Arctic operations. Displacement: 2,065 tons. Guns: 2 3-in. Complement: 105. In the *Bismarck*'s operational area from 20 to 23 May 1941; decommissioned March 1946.

Oberkommando der Marine. German Supreme Naval Command at the Tirpitzufer in Berlin; seat of the commander in chief, Grand Admiral Erich Raeder, and his staff.

Obersalzberg. Adolf Hitler's Alpine retreat, the Berghof, near Berchtesgaden in Bavaria.

Oerlikon. A variety of Swiss-developed 20-mm automatic aircraft or antiaircraft guns; named after the Oerlikon arms manufactory near Zürich.

Operation Barbarossa. German invasion of the Soviet Union on 22 June 1941.

Operation Berlin. German raid on Allied commerce in the Atlantic, January to March 1941; in command, Admiral Günther Lütjens with the 11-in battleships *Scharnhorst* and *Gneisenau.*

Operational Intelligence Centre. A section of the British Admiralty's Naval Intelligence Division; gathered and analyzed operational intelligence from all sources and provided this to the naval staff and to operational commanders at sea. In the Admiralty Building overlooking Horseguards Parade, it was often called "the Citadel."

PBY-5 Catalina. U.S. patrol bomber flying boat. Two 1,200-hp Pratt & Whitney engines gave best speed of 200 mph. Maximum range 1,895 miles. Main armament: one 0.5-in machine gun each in nose and turret; four depth charges; two torpedoes or four 1,000-lb bombs.

Perspex. A clear plastic prepared by the polymerization of methyl methacrylate; used as a windshield on Allied aircraft.

Pocket battleship. A small heavily armed and armored German warship serving as a battleship because of limitations imposed by international treaty.

Port. The left-hand side of a ship, facing forward; **a-port**, to turn or shift to the port, or left, side.

Prince of Wales. British battleship of the *King George V* class, launched May 1939. For specifications, see ***King George V***. Damaged by the *Bismarck* during Battle of Iceland, she was sunk by aircraft of the Japanese 22nd Naval Air Flotilla off Kuantan, Malaya, 10 December 1941.

Prinz Eugen. German *Hipper*-class heavy cruiser, launched August 1938. Displacement: 14,271 tons; 18,700 fully loaded. Machinery: 3-shaft La Mont/Brown-Boverie turbines of 133,631 shp; best speed 32.5 knots. Range 5,050 nm at 15 knots. Armament: 8 8-in (20.3-cm) guns, 12 4.1-in (10.5-cm) guns; 12 21-in (53.3-cm) torpedo tubes. Complement: 1,500. Main belt armor 3.2 in; deck armor 2 in. *Bismarck*'s only escort until 24 May 1941; sank December 1946 at Kwajelein Atoll after surviving an atomic bomb explosion at Bikini Atoll.

Quadrant. See **Grid**.

Radar. Acronym formed from radio detection and ranging. Developed by both sides shortly before 1939, it is most often associated with the British scientist Robert Watson-Watt. In May 1940 the British heavy cruiser *Suffolk* carried 50-cm Type 284 radar, with effective range of about 24 km.

Range finder. Any of various instruments used to determine the distance from the observer to a particular object; as for sighting a gun.

Ratings. Crew members having certain ratings; especially the enlisted personnel in the British Navy.

Renown. British battle cruiser, launched March 1916. After modification in 1939—Displacement: 32,000 tons; 37,400 full load. Machinery: 4-shaft steam turbines for 130,000 shp; best speed 29 knots. Range: 6,580 nm at 18 knots. Armament: 6 15-in guns; 20 4.5-in guns. Main belt armor to 9 in; deck armor to 3 in. Complement: 1,200. Joined the hunt for *Bismarck* 25 May 1941; broken up 1948.

Repulse. British *Renown*-class battle cruiser. For specifications, see ***Renown***. Part of the hunt for the *Bismarck* in May 1941, she was sunk by aircraft of the Japanese 22nd Naval Air Flotilla off Kuantan, Malaya, 10 December 1941.

Rheinübung. See **Rhine Exercise**.

Rhine Exercise. *Rheinübung*, as it was called in German, was a planned raid of Atlantic convoys with battleships and pocket battleships; in May 1941 it was reduced to *Bismarck* and *Prinz Eugen*.

Rodney. British *Nelson*-class battleship, launched December 1925. Displacement: 33,960 tons; 38,000 full load. Machinery: 2-shaft geared turbines for 45,000 shp; best speed 23 knots. Range: 5,500 nm at 23 knots. Armament: 9 16-in guns; 12 6-in guns; 2 24.5-in torpedo tubes. Main belt armor to 14 in; deck armor to 6.25 in. Complement: 1,640. Severely damaged *Bismarck* on 27 May 1941; broken up 1948.

Rudder. A vertical blade at the stern of a ship for turning horizontally to change the ship's direction when in motion; the *Bismarck* mounted two balance-type parallel rudders.

Scharnhorst. German battleship, launched June 1936. Displacement: 35,540 tons; 36,108 full load. Machinery: 3-shaft Brown-Boverie geared turbines for 160,080 shp; best speed 32 knots. Range: 9,020 nm at 15 knots. Armament: 9 11-in (28-cm) guns; 12 6-in (15-cm) guns; 14 4-in (10.5-cm) guns. Main belt armor to 14 in; deck armor to 2 in. Complement: 1,700. Laid up at Brest for repairs during Rhine Exercise; sunk 26 December 1943 by British battleship *Duke of York* with Force 2 off North Cape.

Seekriegsleitung. German Naval War Staff. Rear Admiral Kurt Fricke headed its operations division during the *Bismarck*'s Atlantic sortie.

Sheffield. British *Southampton*-class light cruiser, launched 1936. Displacement: 9,100 tons; 11.350 full load. Machinery: 4-shaft Parsons geared turbines for 75,000 shp; best speed 32 knots. Range 9,000 nm at 15 knots. Armament: 12 6-in guns; 6 21-in torpedo tubes. Complement: 748. Joined in the hunt for *Bismarck* 26 May 1941; broken up 1967.

Smoke screen. A mass of dense smoke produced and disseminated from the funnel(s) to conceal a ship from the enemy.

Sonar. Sound detection of submerged submarines; either passive (hydrophones) or active (British original term ASDIC).

Spitfire. The Supermarine Spitfire was an all-metal British fighter. Designed in 1936, the aircraft had a maximal speed of 355 mph, range of 500 miles, and mounted eight machine guns. The first units used for aerial reconnaissance (Mk.IV) appeared in 1940.

Squadron. A detachment of warships; a subdivision of a fleet; often a detachment of four warships.

Starboard. The right-hand side of a ship, facing forward; **a-starboard**, to turn or shift to the starboard, or right, side.

Star shell. A shell or bomb that upon bursting releases a shower of brilliant stars; used by the Royal Navy to illuminate the *Bismarck* at night.

Stern. The after part of a ship; to the back or rear.

Suffolk. British *Kent*-class heavy cruiser, launched February 1926. Displacement: 10,900 tons; 15,000 tons full load. Machinery: 4-shaft Parsons geared turbines for 80,000 shp; best speed 31.5 knots. Range 13,300 nm at 12 knots. Armament: 8 8-in guns; 8 21-in torpedo tubes. Complement: 784. First detected the *Bismarck* in the Denmark Strait with her Type 284 radar; paid off 1946, broken up 1948.

Sunderland. The Short Sunderland was a British reconnaissance flying boat developed in 1937; more than 700 were built during the war.

Superstructure. Any construction built above the main deck of a ship as an upward continuation of the sides.

Swordfish. British (Fairey-built) carrier-based torpedo bomber. One 690 hp Pegasus engine gave best speed of 139 mph; range 546 miles. Armament: one Vickers gun forward and one Lewis gun aft; one 18-in 1,1610 lb torpedo. On board HMS *Victorious* and *Ark Royal* during hunt for *Bismarck*.

Task force. A temporary grouping of warships under one commander, formed for the purpose of carrying out a specific operation or mission.

Texas. United States *New York*–class battleship (BB35), launched May 1912. For specifications, see **New York**. The *Texas* supported Allied operations in North Africa in October/November 1942 and Pointe du Hoc, Normandy, 6 June 1944; decommissioned April 1948.

Tirpitz. German battleship, launched April 1939. For specifications, see ***Bismarck***. *Tirpitz* did not complete her workup in the Baltic Sea in time to take part in Rhine Exercise; sunk by RAF Lancaster bombers in Kaafjord, Norway, 12 November 1944.

Torpedo boat. A small, fast, and highly maneuverable boat used for torpedoing enemy shipping; a German term often used for a destroyer.

Tracking Room. British Admiralty center where the movements, locations, and intentions of enemy ships (especially U-boats) were displayed and plotted.

***Tribal*-class.** British destroyers, launched 1937. Displacement: 1,800 tons; 1,927 full load. Machinery: 2-shaft geared turbines of 44,000 shp; best speed 36 knots. Range 1,500 nm at economical speed. Main armament: 8 4.7-in guns. Complement: 190. HMS *Cossack*, *Maori*, *Zulu*, and *Sikh* attacked *Bismarck* the night of 25–26 May 1941.

Turret. A towerlike, heavily armored structure usually revolving horizontally, within which guns are mounted; **superimposed turrets**, a set of usually two turrets, placed one above the other.

Type 284. See **Radar**.

U-boat. German term (*Unterseeboot*), literally "undersea boat," for a submarine. Most German U-boats cited were of the Type VIIC class. Basically 700-to-800-ton boats, twin MAN diesel motors produced 2,800 shp for a best speed of 17 knots on the surface (8 knots submerged); range about 6,300 nm. Main armament: 5 53.3-cm (21-in) torpedo tubes and one 8.8cm (3.5-in) deck gun.

ULTRA. Short title and message prefix for Special Intelligence; top-secret information secured from breaking enemy codes at Bletchley Park from 1939 to 1945; operation kept secret until 1974.

Vichy. French Nazi collaborationist government under Marshal Henri Pétain, based at the spa of Vichy.

Victorious. British *Illustrious*-class aircraft carrier, launched September 1939. Displacement: 23,170 tons; 28,210 full load. Machinery: 3-shaft Parsons geared turbines for 111,000 shp; best speed 30.5 knots. Range: 11,000 nm at 14 knots. Guns: 16 4.5-in. Aircraft: 33. Complement: 1,200. Launched first air attack against the *Bismarck* the night of 24–25 May 1941; rebuilt 1950 and again 1958, sold for breaking up June 1969.

Vormars. German term for the fore upper direction tower high up on a warship's superstructure; the *Bismarck*'s main artillery command post.

Walrus. British three-seat, spotter-reconnaissance aircraft. One 450-hp engine gave best speed of 124 mph; armed with one Vickers gun forward and one Lewis gun aft. On board HMS *Prince of Wales* before Battle of Iceland.

Warrant officer. An officer in the U.S. armed forces of one of four grades ranking above enlisted men and below commissioned officers.

Wehrmacht. German term for the armed forces of the Third Reich.

Z-Plan. German blueprint of January 1939 to construct, by 1948 at the latest, a blue-water fleet of 10 battleships, 15 pocket battleships, 4 aircraft carriers, 49 cruisers, 68 destroyers, and about 300 U-boats.

Table of Equivalent Naval Ranks

Kriegsmarine	*United States Navy*	*Royal Navy*
Grossadmiral	Fleet Admiral	Admiral of the Fleet
Generaladmiral	—	—
Admiral	Admiral	Admiral
Vizeadmiral	Vice Admiral	Vice-Admiral
Konteradmiral	Rear Admiral	Rear-Admiral
Kommodore	Commodore	Commodore
Kapitän zur See	Captain	Captain
Fregattenkapitän	—	—
Korvettenkapitän	Commander	Commander
Kapitänleutnant	Lieutenant	Lieutenant
Oberleutnant zur See	Lieutenant j.g.	—
Leutnant zur See	Ensign	Sub-Lieutenant
Oberfähnrich zur See	—	—
Fähnrich zur See	Midshipman	Midshipman
—	—	Cadet

A NOTE ON SOURCES

I. Primary Sources

The German documents pertaining to Rhine Exercise are at the Bundesarchiv-Militärarchiv (BA-MA) at Freiburg; some of these are also available on microfilm through the National Archives, Washington, D.C. Details of the operation can be gleaned from "Marine-Gruppenkommando Nord B.Nr. 237/41, Operationsbefehl Nr. 16, Aufmarsch 'Bismarck' und 'Prinz Eugen' in den Atlantik. (Unternehmen: 'Rheinübung')"; as well as "Marine-Gruppenkommando West, Operative Weisung für Flottenkommando zum Einsatz des Schlachtschiffes 'Bismarck' und des Kreuzers 'Prinz Eugen' (Deckbezeichnung 'Rheinübung')." The *Bismarck*'s war log (Kriegstagebuch, or KTB) was lost at sea on 27 May 1941, but it was later painstakingly reconstructed by naval planners in Berlin from nine various naval command records. The KTB constitutes the heart of the documentary record: "Marinegruppenkommando Nord, Kriegstagebuch des Schlachtschiffes 'Bismarck,' " 14 to 27 May 1941. The German Naval High Command later reconstructed the task force's sortie on the basis of the available documentary record: Oberkommando der Kriegsmarine. Entwurf: Atlantik-Unternehmung der Kampfgruppe "Bismarck"-"Prinz Eugen." This was printed for internal use only: RMD 4/601, Operationen und Taktik. Auswertung wichtiger Ereignisses des Seekrieges. Heft 3, Die Atlantikunternehmungen der Kampfgruppe "Bismarck"-"Prinz Eugen," Berlin, October 1942. The *Prinz Eugen*'s original war diary is at the BA-MA: Kriegstagebuch des Kreuzers "Prinz Eugen," PG 48345ff. The countless ship-to-shore and shore-to-ship electronic messages are also at the BA-MA: Oberkommando der Kriegsmarine. Lagezimmer G. Kdos.-Akte "Bismarck"; Oberkommando der Kriegsmarine, Operation "Rheinübung," PG 37823; and German Naval Staff, Battleship *Bismarck*, File of All Signals Sent and Received from Ships Taking Part in the Action 24–27.5.1941, PG 47892. The service records of Admiral Günther Lütjens and Captain Ernst Lindemann were reconstructed from the documentary files of the Deutsche Dienststelle, Berlin.

Testimony by *Bismarck* survivors taken on board U-74 came from BA-MA, Marinegruppenkommando West, B.Nr. gKos. 3156/41 A1, Vorläufige Vernehmungen über Unternehmung Schlachtschiff 'Bismarck,'" 14 June 1941. The attempts by U-556 and U-74 to rescue the ship's war log stem from "Kriegstagebuch des Unterseebootes 'U 556,' 6.2.41—30.5.41" as well as from "Kriegstagebuch des Unterseebootes 'U 74', 12.4.1941—30.5.1941." These were checked against Admiral Karl Dönitz's war diary: RM 87, vol. 4, Großadmiral Karl Dönitz, BdU. Kriegstagebuch. Workup details of the *Bismarck*'s Arado aircraft are from: Kriegstagebuch der Bordfliegerstaffel 1/196 "Auf Bismarck"; naval air training was reconstructed from "Kriegstagebuch der Bordfliegerstaffel 1/196 'Auf Bismarck.'" The fate of the German supply ships is documented in Marinegruppenkommando West, B.Nr. gKdos. 3355/41. Finally, the SS' reading of the public's reaction to the *Bismarck* saga is from Bundesarchiv-Koblenz, R 58/144–194 Meldungen aus dem Reich.

American sources on the Kriegsmarine included: British interrogation of survivors, Naval Intelligence Division, Washington, D.C., "German Battleship '*Bismarck*,' Interrogation of Survivors," C.B. 4051 (24),

August, 1941; and National Archives, Washington, D.C., "Operations and Battle of the German Battleship BISMARCK, 23–27 May 1941," Commander, Scouting Forces (RG 313).

For the British side of the ledger, most of the primary materials are at the Public Record Office (PRO), Kew. Cabinet (CAB) 106/333 contains Admiral Tovey's official report to the Admiralty of his actions in the search and destruction of the *Bismarck: Supplement to The London Gazette, Tuesday,* 14 *October* 1947. The Admiralty (ADM) files begin with an evaluation of Vice Admiral Holland's actions earlier in the war: ADM 234/325, Battle Summary #9, "The Action off Cape Spartivento, 27th November, 1940." They also include Rear Admiral Sir John Godfrey's unpublished war memoirs, ADM 223/619; and "Methods of Attack on German Ships *Bismarck* and Graf Zeppelin," ADM 1/10617. The Battle of Iceland is covered in ADM 116/4351 and 4352, Loss of HMS *Hood*: Report of the First and Second Boards of Inquiry. There are various sources on the destruction of the *Bismarck*: Battle Summary No. 5, *The Chase and Sinking of the "Bismarck,"* part of the Royal Navy, Naval Staff History, B.R. 1736 (3/50), is also in ADM 234/321; ADM 199/1187 and 1188 Pursuit and Destruction of German Battleship *Bismarck*; and ADM 234/322, "The Chase and Sinking of the German Battleship "'Bismarck.'" Individual ships' operations against the *Bismarck* are in ADM 199/838, "H.M.S. Victorious—Report of Operations 24th May Up to Destruction of the Bismarck"; ADM 234/509, "HMS Ark Royal—Report of Proceedings 24th May 1941, Up to the Destruction of 'Bismarck'"; and ADM 234/509, King George V, narrative of the action, "Gunnery." The air effort against the *Bismarck* is in AIR 15/204 "Sinking of the German Battleship 'Bismarck' "; and AIR 15/415 "Battle of the Denmark Straits and Sinking of the German Battleship 'Bismarck'." ADM 234/509 contains "Enclosure No. 6 to Flag Officer Commanding Force H," 4 June 1941. Finally, the papers of Vice Admiral Sir James Somverville are at Churchill College, Cambridge; and his report of 4 June 1941 on the *Bismarck* operation is in National Archives, Washington, D.C., Records of the Navy, Intelligence Report from the Naval Attaché at Madrid, 3 July 1941.

Research on the American side was conducted primarily at the National Archives, Washington, D.C. All particulars of the *Modoc*'s and the *Northland*'s incredible voyages are from Ship's Log Book, U.S. Coast Guard Cutter *Modoc* and U.S. Coast Guard Cutter *Northland* for the month of May 1941; the Letters of Richard Davies were supplied by R. M. Browning Jr., U.S. Coast Guard; and the U.S. Coast Guard, Historical Section, in Washington provided the unpublished manuscript *The Coast Guard at War: Greenland Patrol II* (July 1945). Details of the sorties of USS *New York* and USS *Texas* as well as of the destroyer *Niblack* are from the ships' logs for May 1941 at the National Archives. The records of the Director (Naval) War Plans Division regarding gun details of the two battleships, as well as those of the Chief of Naval Operations on the vessels, likewise are at the National Archives. At the political level, the National Archives yielded the U.S.-British Staff Conversations in general and Admiral Robert L. Ghormley's notes in particular. As well, what the United States knew of the Battle of Iceland and its aftermath was gleaned at the National Archives from Office of the U.S. Naval Intelligence, Enclosure "F" of "Operations and Battle of German Battleship *Bismarck*, 23–17 May, 1941." The Roosevelt-Churchill Correspondence was investigated at the Franklin D. Roosevelt Library, Hyde Park, New York. And in Canada, we consulted Directorate of History and Heritage, Department of National Defence (Ottawa), "Davis Reminiscences."

II. Printed Sources

The war logs of the *Bismarck* and the *Prinz Eugen* were compared to the Kriegsmarine's day-by-day operational diary: *Kriegstagebuch der Seekriegsleitung* 1939–1945, *Teil A*, ed. Werner Rahn and Gerhard Schreiber (Herford and Bonn, 1990), vols. 20–22. Further, they were checked against "German Naval High Command, Raeder's

Personal Files" (PG 31762), published in English as *Führer Conferences on Naval Affairs 1939–1945* (Annapolis, 1990); in German, *Lagevorträge des Oberbefehlshabers der Kriegsmarine vor Hitler 1939–1945*, ed. Gerhard Wagner (Munich, 1972).

With regard to Hitler, the texts of his speeches (other than the *Führer Conferences*) were taken from Max Domarus, ed., *Hitler. Reden und Proklamationen 1932–1945* (3 vols., Munich, 1962–63). Concerning the *Bismarck*, two memoirs by service adjutants were consulted: Karl Jesko von Puttkamer, *Die unheimliche See (Hitler und die Kriegsmarine)* (Vienna and Munich, 1952); and Nicolaus v. Below, *Als Hitlers Adjutant 1937–45* (Mainz, 1980). Rich in detail on the *Bismarck*'s first and only sortie are the recollections of her fourth gunnery officer, Burkard Baron von Müllenheim-Rechberg, *Battleship Bismarck: A Survivor's Story* (Annapolis, 1980, 1990). Likewise, for the *Prinz Eugen*, see the account by her second gunnery officer: Paul Schmalenbach, Kreuzer *Prinz Eugen... unter 3 Flaggen* (Herford, 1978).

Major published collections for the United States in the war on the Atlantic in 1941 begin with Samuel Eliot Morison, *History of United States Naval Operations in World War II*, vol. 1, *The Battle of the Atlantic: September 1939–May 1943* (Boston, 1962). The Churchill-Roosevelt correspondence has been edited by Warren F. Kimball, *Churchill & Roosevelt: The Complete Correspondence* (3 vols., Princeton, 1984). Concerning FDR's special missions to London in 1941, see W. Averell Harriman and Elie Abel, *Special Envoy to Churchill and Stalin, 1941–1946* (New York, 1975). Also relevant on the British side, Rear Admiral Joseph H. Wellings, *On Her Majesty's Service*, ed. John B. Hattendorf (Newport, 1983).

III. Printed Works

The technical details of the *Bismarck* were gleaned from Jochen Brennecke, *Schlachtschiff Bismarck* (Herford, 1960); Ulrich Elfrath and

Bodo Herzog, *The Battleship Bismarck: A Documentary in Words and Pictures* (West Chester, PA, 1989); and Siegfried Breyer and Gerhard Koop, *Schlachtschiff Bismarck. Eine Technikgeschichtliche Dokumentation* (Augsburg, 1996). See also Jochen Brennecke, *Schlachtschiff "Tirpitz." Das Drama der "Einsamen Königin des Nordens"* (Biberach an der Riss, 1953). An initial assessment of the *Bismarck*'s one and only sortie was undertaken by Gerhard Bidlingmaier, "Erfolg und Ende des Schlachtschiffes *Bismarck*," *Wehrwissenschaftliche Rundschau* IX (1975), pp. 261–81.

Allied intelligence concerning the *Bismarck* stems from Donald McLachlan, *Room 39: A Study in Naval Intelligence* (New York, 1968); F. H. Hinsley et al., eds., *British Intelligence in the Second World War: Its Influence on Strategy and Operations*, vol. I (London, 1979); Bradley F. Smith, *The Ultra-Magic Deals: And the Most Secret Special Relationship 1940–1946* (Novato, CA, 1994); and John Winton, *Ultra at Sea* (London, 1988). Good overviews of *Bismarck*'s sortie are Russell Grenfell, *The Bismarck Episode* (London, 1949); Ludovic Kennedy, *PURSUIT: The Chase and Sinking of the Bismarck* (London, 1974); and Graham Rhys-Jones, *The Loss of the Bismarck: An Avoidable Disaster* (Annapolis, 1999). A detailed analysis of naval gunnery during the confrontation between the *Bismarck* and the *Hood* has been provided by Robert J. Winklareth, *The Bismarck Chase: New Light on a Famous Engagement* (Annapolis, 1998). For the U-boats, see Clay Blair, *Hitler's U-Boat War: The Hunters 1939–1942* (New York, 1996). The British reconstructed the *Bismarck*'s interaction (or lack thereof) with the U-boats in Ministry of Defence (Navy), *German Naval History. The U-Boat War in the Atlantic 1939–1945* (London, 1989).

The "Swedish connection" concerning the *Bismarck*'s egress through the Danish Belts has been recounted by Henry Denham, *Inside the Nazi Ring: A Naval Attaché in Sweden 1940–1945* (London, 1984); C. G. McKay, *From Information to Intrigue: Studies in Secret Service Based on the Swedish Experience 1939–45* (London, 1993); Wilhelm M. Carlgren, *Svensk underrättelsetjänst 1939–1945* (Stockholm, 1985); and Curt Borgenstam et al., *Kryssare. Med svenska flottans kryssare under 75 år* (Stockholm, 1993). Last but not least, the *Bismarck*'s remains were discovered on the bottom of the Atlantic by Robert D. Ballard and described in *Exploring the Bismarck* (New York, 1991).

British histories of the war at sea 1939–1945 are numerous, and we relied mainly on the following: Correlli Barnett, *Engage the Enemy More Closely: The Royal Navy in the Second World War* (New York and London, 1991); Admiral Sir W. M. James, *The British Navies in the Second World War* (London, 1946); Stephen Roskill, *The Navy at War: 1939–1945* (London, 1990); and Nathan Miller, *War at Sea: A Naval History of World War II* (New York, 1995). More detailed studies included Ernie Bradford, *The Mighty Hood: The Life and Death of the Royal Navy's Proudest Ship* (London, 1961); Peter Hodges, *The Big Gun: Battleship Main Armament, 1860–1945* (Greenwich, 1981); Derek Howse, *Radar at Sea: The Royal Navy in World War 2* (Annapolis, 1993); and Geoffrey Till, *Air Power and the Royal Navy: 1914–1945, AQ Historical Survey* (London, 1979), as well as Till's *Seapower: Theory and Practise* (London, 1994). On Churchill: Richard Lamb, *Churchill as War Leader* (New York, 1991); Richard Hough, *Former Naval Person: Churchill and the Wars at Sea* (London, 1985); and Martin Gilbert's massive *Winston S. Churchill* (8 vols., London, 1966–88).

Of the numerous publications concerning Franklin D. Roosevelt, see especially Warren F. Kimball, *The Juggler: Franklin Roosevelt as Wartime Statesman* (Princeton, 1991); and Doris Kearns Goodwin, *No Ordinary Time: Franklin & Eleanor Roosevelt: The Home Front in World War II* (New York, 1994). For "Ernie" King, see Thomas B. Buell, *Master of Sea Power: A Biography of Fleet Admiral Ernest J. King* (Boston, 1980). The "neutrality zones" are detailed in Stetson Conn, Rose C. Engelman, and Byron Fairchild, *United States Army in World War II: The Western Hemisphere: Guarding the United States and its Outposts* (Washington, 1964). For small-craft action, see Theodore Roscoe, *Tin Cans: The True Story of the Fighting Destroyers of World War II* (New York, 1960).

INDEX

A

A arcs, 88, 149–50, 287
"abandon ship," 292, 293–5
ABC. *see* Cunningham, Sir Andrew Browne
ABC-Staff Agreement, 44
Achilles, *HMNZS* (light cruiser), 24
action stations, 86–7, 141–2, 147–8, 211–12, 288
Action This Day (Vian), 312
Admiral Hipper (heavy cruiser), 25, 43
Admiral Scheer (pocket battleship), 10, 19, 24–5, 43
Admiralty. *see* British Admiralty
Afrika Korps, 5
Ågren, Knut G. (Captain), 66
Air Fleet 3, 302
Air Fleet 5, 59
air support
  Arado floatplanes and, 34
  Messerschmitt 109 fighters, 40
  unavailable for *Bismarck*, 251–2
Ajax, *HMS* (light cruiser), 24
Albacore torpedo planes, 121
Albrecht, Helmut (Commander), 150, 280, 290
Alexander, A. V. (First Lord of the Admiralty)
  Churchill and, 236–7
  Churchill memorandum to, 303–4
  Churchill successor, 111
  death, 311
  news of *Bismarck* slipping away, 237
  Norfolk's first contact report, 134
Altmark (supply ship), 248–9
aluminum in aircraft skin, 182
American-British-Canadian (ABC-Staff Agreement), 44

Amphion, HMS (light cruiser), 83
Anglo-German Naval Agreement (1935), 32, 113–14
antiaircraft (flak) defense, 30, 33, 35, 87
"Antilope" (Fleet Command code name), 54
Arado196 (floatplane)
- aerial support with, 34
- *Bismarck* repair plan, 264
- Bismarck's complement of, 30–1
- plans for *Bismarck* war diary disposal, 282
- on *Prinz Eugen*, 38
- problems with, 40–2

Arethusa, HMS (light cruiser), 76, 99, 122, 174
Argentia (Newfoundland), 207–8, 235–6, 304
Ark Royal, HMS (aircraft carrier)
- action on 27 November 1940, 101–2
- affected by weather, 256
- after *Bismarck* destruction, 301
- capabilities against *Bismarck*, 255
- communiqué from Swordfish, 270
- description of, 136, 233
- destruction of, 313
- encounter with gale, 240
- estimated time for intercept of *Bismarck*, 224
- flying range of *Bismarck*, 272
- positioning for reconnaissance, 242
- *Renown* signal flags and, 253
- search for *Bismarck*, 233
- sighted by *Sheffield*, 279
- Spanish Intelligence Service message, 180
- Swordfish attack on *Bismarck*, 258–60
- Swordfish return from *Bismarck* strike, 268
- Swordfish return from *Sheffield* strike, 258
- Swordfish surveillance over *Bismarck*, 252–3
- U-556 sighting of, 274
- *see also* Maund, L.E.H. (Captain)

Arkansas, USS (battleship), 203, 205
armament
- on *Bismarck*, 29–30
- on British battleships, 86, 115
- C31 and C37 guns, 33–4
- design considerations, 116–17
- firing tests on *Bismarck*, 51–2
- HMS *Hood*, 97
- HMS *King George V*, 81
- Mediterranean battle, 87–8
- at mercy of tradition, 33
- on *Prinz Eugen*, 37–8

Armstrong, H.T. (Commander), 280–1
Arnold, H.A.P. (U.S. Army Air Force chief), 206
Ascher, Paul (Commander), 285
Asiatic Fleet, 205
ASV (air-to-surface-vessel) radar, 186, 257
Atlantic Fleet, 205–6, 208, 215–16
Atlantik (tug), 35
Atomic Test Able, 313
August Wriest (fishing boat), 59
Augusta, USS (heavy cruiser), 207, 217, 304
Aurora, HMS (light cruiser), 232, 239
Austin, B. L. (Lieutenant Commander), 202
Axelssen, Viggo, 68

B

Bacchus, Dick (Lieutenant (jg)), 186–7
Bailey, Sir Sidney (Admiral), 202
Baldwin, Prime Minister Stanley, 6

Ballard, Robert, 312
Barth, Edvard K. (professor), 69
Battle Cruiser Force, 73
battle cruisers, 97, 115–16
Battle of Britain, 1–2
Battle of Crete, 74, 220, 237, 243
Battle of Iceland, 125–64, 244
Battle of Jutland, 16–17, 72, 83–4, 97, 108
Battle of the Atlantic
- importance of, 7–8
- orders for U.S. Navy and Coast Guard vessels, 194
- Royal Navy and U-boats, 308–9
- U-94 and HX 126 convoy, 183–4
- U.S. and, 200–2, 209, 213–15

Battle of the River Plate, 24, 110, 140
Battleship "F." *see Bismarck* (battleship)
Battleship "G." *see Tirpitz* (battleship)
battleships, 21, 27, 29, 115–16, 203
bauxite, aluminum made from, 182
Bayern (dreadnought), 19
B-Dienst (German naval intelligence)
- capabilities of, 120
- intelligence report for Rhine Exercise, 60–1, 74
- message intercept (14 April 1941), 44
- radiograms from, 77
- urgent message to *Bismarck*, 69

Beatty, Sir David, 83–4
Belchen (tanker), 55, 60, 168, 176, 305
Belford, H. G. (Lieutenant Commander), 183, 185–7
Below, Nicolaus von (Major), 13, 266, 284
Benson, USS (destroyers), 195
Berwich, HMS (light cruiser), 102
"Bilderbuch" (Naval Group Command West code name), 54
Birmingham, HMS (light cruiser), 76, 99, 122, 174
Bismarck, Otto von, 21, 27–8
Bismarck (battleship)
- "abandon ship," 293–5
- attack on *Sheffield*, 278–9
- in Bloom & Voss docks, 39
- casualties/survivors, 290–7, 298–9
- Churchill telegram of sighting, 218
- code name "Eichenkranz," 54
- crew dissatisfaction, 166, 245
- crew gossip, 71, 192
- crew preparations for end, 267–8
- damage control, 169–70, 226, 261, 265
- damages to, 162–3, 171, 179–80, 190, 192, 261–2, 291–3, 295–6
- death throes, 295–6
- dummy funnel, 246, 251
- encounter with enemy aircraft, 189–93
- encounter with *Prince of Wales*, 161, 179, 192
- encounter with Royal Navy, 145–53
- encounter with Vian's destroyers, 279–81
- FDR wire to Churchill regarding, 303
- final attack on, 288–93
- first hit received, 149
- food supplies for, 35, 51
- fuel considerations, 105, 170–1
- Hitler's visit to, 13–15, 54
- ignoring *Modoc* signal, 187
- inclusion in Rhine Exercise, 15
- launching of, 21
- Lindemann final review of progress to date, 53–4
- Lütjens birthday, 226
- Lütjens instructions, 176
- Lütjens' push to St. Nazaire, 223–6

maiden voyage, 35–8
message from Hitler, 284–5
parting from *Prinz Eugen*, 177
personnel assigned to, 63
picking way through Denmark Strait, 125–7
preparations on, 27
problems plaguing, 40
problems with cranes, 41–2
repair plans, 263–5
resting place of, 312
rumors of impending rescue, 284
sighting of *Sheffield*, 253
slipping away, 230–1, 236, 239, 252
spartan training routine for men, 41
special victory rations, 170
specifications and cost, 28–34
statistics, 313–14
superiority of, 14
Swordfish attack, 259–62
U-boats rescue attempts, 277–8
wild stories about end, 295
Wohlfahrt's sponsorship document, 274, 282
wreck examined, 155
see also Lindemann, Ernst (Captain)

Bletchley Park, 44, 67–8, 120–1, 242–3
blockades, 82, 93
Blohm & Voss Shipyard, 21, 35, 274
Blücher (heavy cruiser), 265
Blue Pennant turn, 149
Boehm, Hermann (Admiral), 22
bombing raids, 2, 34–5, 48, 85
see also torpedo attacks
Bonin, Reimar von (Rear Admiral), 65–6
Bovell, H. C. (Captain), 228–9, 232–3
bracketing groups, firing as, 31–2
Breslau (light cruiser), 165
Brest, as sally port, 25–6
Briggs, A. E. (Ordinary Signalman), 156–7, 159
Briggs, Dennis (Flying Officer), 249–52
Brind, E.J.P. "Daddy" (Commodore), 95–6, 232, 271
Brinkmann, Helmuth (Captain)
after *Bismarck* separation, 302, 304
command from Lütjens, 176
death, 311
diminishing responsibilities, 311
evasive action with *Bismarck*, 131
Hood sinking, 158
Lütjens informed of sightings, 144
not understanding Lütjens' actions, 241
recognition of enemy, 150
relief noted in war diary, 74
reviewing options on separate course, 177–8
training and initial service, 38
see also Prinz Eugen (heavy cruiser)

Bristol, Arthur L., Jr. (Admiral), 205, 208
Britannic, *HMS* (passenger ship), 94–5
British Admiralty
formal investigations for *Hood* sinking, 155
function of, 107
Harriman's office in, 213
message to Somerville, 255
news of *Bismarck* slipping away, 237
Operational Control Centre, 241–2
Operational Intelligence Centre, 238–9
Operations Center, 134
response to *Hood* destruction, 174–5

British Chiefs of Staff Committee, 202–3
British Coastal Command, 71
British cryptoanalysts. *see* Bletchley Park
British Expeditionary Force, 3
British Home Fleet. *see* Home Fleet

British Intelligence Service for Scandinavia, 68
British Security, HMS (tanker), 184–5
British Sovereign, HMS (tanker), 275
Bromberg (tanker), 41
Brown Boverie turbines, 38
Budich, Hermann (Apprentice Machinist), 28
Burckhardt, Hermann (chief naval designer), 28
Byng, John (Admiral), 112–13

C

C31 guns, 33–4
C37 guns, 33–4
Canarias (Spanish cruiser), 266, 298
Cape Spartivento, 101–4
capital ships, limits on, 114
captain, functions during action stations, 87
Cardinal, Friedrich (Lieutenant), 14, 291
Carls, Rolf (Admiral)
- Admiral, 266
- displeasure over lack of communication, 73
- General Admiral, 306
- heading Naval Group Command North, 58
- important message from, 77
- Lütjens/St. Nazaire decision and, 168
- response to *Gotland* intrusion, 65
- retirement and death, 310–11

Case White, 22
Cassel, Isaac A. (Kommedör), 65
casualties/survivors
- from attack on *Kearney*, 304
- on *Bismarck*, 192
- from *Bismarck* attack on *Sheffield*, 279
- early 1940 sinkings, 8
- from final attack on *Bismarck*, 290–7, 298–9
- on *Hood*, 159
- from *Mashona*, 302
- rescuing *Bismarck* survivors, 297
- from *Saleir*, 210
- on *Sheffield*, 259
- U-556 and *Emanual*, 275
- Vian's destroyers attack on *Bismarck*, 280
- wild stories about *Bismarck end*, 295

CBS radio reports, 202
Celandine, HMS (corvette), 311
Cementite (Krupp), 30
Cesare (Italian battleship), 88
Chamberlain, Neville (Prime Minister), 3–4
Chapman, Alex C. (Captain), 99
Charles II (Preamble to the Articles of War), 106–7
Cheshire, HMS (auxiliary cruiser), 277
Chiswell, B. M. (communications officer), 194
Churchill, Clementine, 219
Churchill, Winston (Prime Minister)
- anger at Alexander, 236
- anger at Leach, 165
- anger at Pound, Leach, and Wake-Walker, 236–7
- Battle of the Atlantic, 8
- berating Cunningham, 237
- *Bismarck* sinking reported to Parliament, 297
- cable to Roosevelt, 76
- faith in Tovey and Pound, 220
- firing of Home Fleet commander in chief, 89
- first lord of the Admiralty, 109–13
- and Ghormley, 204
- and Harriman, 213

instructions for disabling battleships, 36
"liaison established," 215
message of additional ships from Roosevelt, 216
as military dictator, 111
missive to Roosevelt, 111
new U.S. neutrality zone, 214–15
news of *Hood*'s destruction, 164–5
Norfolk's first contact report, 134
opportunity in *Prinz Eugen* survival, 302–3
and Pound, 108, 112
"powerful presence," 241
quote, 1
replacement of Chamberlain, 3–4
Roosevelt compared with, 197
and Somerville, 112–13
telegram of *Bismarck* sighting to Roosevelt, 218
view on America, 6
weekend at Chequers, 219–21
winning over influential Americans, 204–5
as world's hope, 2–3
worries over dictator Franco, 5
CINCLANT, 205–6
Clydesdale, Marquess of, 55
Coastal Command, 76, 121, 122, 208, 249
code dates, 56
code names, 54–6, 60, 159, 177
Condors (German bombers), 9, 56–7, 252, 285
Conte di Cavour (Italian battleship), 102
convoy HX 126, 184–7, 276–7
convoy JW51B, 307
convoy OB 306, 210
convoy Outbound 318, 275
convoy PQ 17, 311
convoy WS8B (troop transport), 94, 233, 248
convoys
Bismarck as danger to, 98
Lend-Lease supplies, 7–8
from Malta, 85–9
Raeder hunting (1940), 24–5
Somerville's instructions to join, 134–5
U-boat instructions along Halifax (HX) routes, 56
Cooper, N. C. (Sub-Lieutenant), 257
Coppinger, Cuthbert (Captain), 234
Cossack, HMS (destroyer), 248–9, 279–81, 301, 313
Coventry, HMS (light cruiser), 102
coxswain, functions during action stations, 87
Crew of 1907, 38, 50, 265–6
Crew of 1913, 38, 45
cross the T, 138, 152
Cruiser J. *see Prinz Eugen* (heavy cruiser)
cruising watch, 86
cryolite, use for, 182
Cunningham, Sir Andrew Browne, 84–5, 90, 103–4, 237
Curteis, Alban (Rear Admiral), 232–3

D

Dalrymple-Hamilton, Frederick H. G. (Captain)
convergence on *Bismarck*, 254, 286–8
defying Admiralty orders, 241–2
final attack on *Bismarck*, 290
instructions to attack at dawn, 283
retirement and death, 312
search for *Bismarck*, 233–5
Tovey's plans for *Bismarck* destruction, 271
see also Rodney, HMS (battleship)

Daniel, C. S. (Captain), 242
Danish Belts, news-gathering network in, 44
Danzig Bay, 41–2, 55
"Dattelpalme" (*Belchen* code name), 55
Davies, Richard L., 181–2, 187, 194
Davis, Sam, 289
declarations of war, 2–6, 43–4, 85
Denham, Henry (Captain), 40, 44, 66–7, 95
Denmark
  Operation Weserübung, 24
  Roosevelt's decision to occupy Greenland, 43–4
Denmark Strait
  Bismarck and *Prinz Eugen* picking way through, 125–7
  Bismarck march to, 47–80
  British response to *Bismarck* march, 81–124
departure preparation, 99–101, 123–4
depth charges, setting, 211–12
Desert Fox, 5
Destroyer Division 13, 209
Destroyer Squadron 10, 205
destroyers-for-bases deal, 44, 207
"Dete" gear (British radar), 134, 236
Deutsche Werke, 47
Deutschland (pocket battleship). *see Lützow* (pocket battleship)
distress signal "SSS," 184
Dogger Bank (battle), 16–17
Dönitz, Karl "Great Lion" (Vice Admiral)
  command of U-boat fleet, 8
  confirmed *Modoc* location, 176
  congratulations to Wohlfahrt, 276
  desire for U-boat domination, 20–1
  "Great Lion," 225
  Kentrat's report to, 57
  and Lütjens, 225
  pleas for naval air arm, 34
  and Saalwächter, 225
  successor to Raeder, 308
  war trials and death, 309–10
  Wohlfahrt to retrieve *Bismarck* war diary, 282
  Wohlfahrt's report to, 277
Dorsetshire, *HMS* (heavy cruiser)
  destruction of, 313
  final attack on *Bismarck*, 290
  Force H ship, 136
  joining *King George V*, 272
  ordered to finish off *Bismarck*, 296
  rescuing *Bismarck* survivors, 297
  search for *Bismarck*, 240–1
  see also Martin, Benjamin C. S. (Captain)
double-pole strategy, 22–3
"Dreschflegel" (*Lothringen* code name), 56
Dry Dock C (Kiel), 40
Dundas, W. J. (Midshipman), 156–7, 159
Dunkirk, 3, 17, 112
Durgin, Edward R. (Lieutenant Commander), 209–12

E

Eagle, *HMS* (aircraft carrier), 85
Ebert, President Friedrich, 23
Edinburgh, *HMS* (light cruiser), 175
Edwards, R.A.B. (Captain), 242, 247–8
Eich, Adolf (Machinist Petty Officer), 149
"Eichenkranz" (*Bismarck* code name), 54
Ellis, R. M. (Captain), 73, 94, 127–8, 229–30, 230–1
  see also Suffolk, *HMS* (heavy cruiser)
Elsass (battleship), 19

Emanual (Faeroe Island fishing schooner), 275
Emmons, Delos C. (General), 200–1
encounters
air strike against *Bismarck*, 186–93
attack on *Mashona* and *Tartar*, 302
Bismarck and *Prince of Wales*, 161, 179, 192
Bismarck and *Prinz Eugen*, 131
Bismarck/Prinz Eugen and *Hood*, 145–53
Bismarck/Prinz Eugen and *Prince of Wales*, 159–65
in Brest harbor, 43
Cape Spartivento, 101–4
convoy from Malta, 85–9
in Denmark Strait, 127–30
destruction of Allied ships, 9–10, 25–6
fighting on Crete, 220, 237
first U.S. naval attack (*Niblack*), 209–12
in River Plate, 24
specifics of *Hood* destruction, 155–9
U-47 in Scapa Flow, 82–3
U-94 and convoy HX 126, 183–4
U-137 and Gibraltar convoy, 274
U-556 and *Emanual*, 275
Vian's destroyers firing on *Bismarck*, 279–81
see also torpedo attacks
Engadine, HMS (seaplane tender), 83–4
Engel, Gerhard (Major), 306
Enigma, 56–7, 63, 67–8, 73, 276, 305, 310
Enubuj Reef (Kwajelein Atoll), 313
Ericson, Stig (special envoy), 27
Ermland (tender), 56, 60
Escort Group 12, 184
Esmonde, Eugene (Acting Lieutenant Commander), 186–9, 193–6
Esso-Hamburg (tanker), 55, 60, 168, 305
executive officer, functions during action stations, 87
Exeter, HMS (heavy cruiser), 24
Externbrink, Dr. Heinz (meteorologist), 75

F

Fairey Swordfish biplane, 119
FDR. *see* Roosevelt, Franklin D. (President)
Fifth Mountain Division, 220
5th Destroyer Flotilla, 73
5th Minesweeping Flotilla, 68
fire lieutenant commander, 87
fire-control radar, 34
fire-control systems, 14, 31
First Cruiser Squadron, 94
first lieutenant, functions during action stations, 87
First Torpedo Boat Flotilla, 17–18
Fisher, Sir John A. "Jackie" (First Lord of the Admiralty), 109
flak. *see* antiaircraft (flak) defense
flank marking, 283
Fleet Air Arm, 119
Fleet Command (code name "Antilope"), 54
Flindt, Karlotto (Lieutenant), 134
floatplanes. *see* Arado196 (floatplane); S9 Hawker Osprey floatplane
flotillas
5th Destroyer Flotilla, 73
5th Minesweeping Flotilla, 68
First Torpedo Boat Flotilla, 17–18
24th U-Boat Flotilla, 47–8
Flygplankryssare, 65
Focke-Wulf FW200 Condors, 9, 56–7, 252, 285
Forbes, Sir Charles, 89, 113
Force B, 101–3

Force D, 101–3
Force F, 101–3
Force H
after *Bismarck* destruction, 301
capabilities against *Bismarck*, 255
description of, 135–6
Lindemann and, 53
major ships of, 136
new orders from Pound, 242
search for *Bismarck*, 240
Sheffield detached from, 253
skirmish on 27 November 1940, 101–3
Somerville command of, 112
welcome message about Crete, 74
Forshell, Anders (Captain), 39–40
Förste, Erich (Admiral), 309
Fourth Destroyer Division, 248
Franco, Francisco, 5, 19
Freese (fishing boat), 59
French Republic. *see* Vichy government
"Freya" (.9-in wave band), 34
Freyburg, Bernard, 220
Fricke, Kurt (Rear Admiral), 26, 48, 50
Friedrich Breme (tanker), 60, 168, 305
Frobisher, Sir Martin, 248
fuel considerations, 105–6, 141, 170–1, 239–40, 277
Fulmar fighters, 233
FuMO (radar detection sets), 31, 38, 126, 130, 153

G

G7a torpedo outfit, 160
Galatea, *HMS* (light cruiser), 232, 239
Gand (Belgian freighter), 275
Gedania (tanker), 60, 305
Gellert, Karl (Lieutenant), 176
George VI (appointment of Churchill), 111
German naval intelligence. *see* B-Dienst (German naval intelligence)
German navy, 18, 32–3
German Tactical Regulations, 153
Germania Shipyard (Kiel), 37
Germany, invasions by, 2–3, 24, 74
Ghormley, Robert Lee (Rear Admiral), 200–4, 213, 215, 273, 312
Gibraltar, 5, 62, 135, 274
Giese, Hermann (Lieutenant), 263
Gladiolus, *HMS* (corvette), 311
Gleaves, *USS* (destroyer), 195
Glenn Martin Maryland bomber, 75–6
Gloucester, *HMS* (cruiser), 85
Gneisenau (battleship)
breakout on 4 February 1941, 93
damaged in Brest harbor, 43
destruction of Allied ships, 10
inclusion in Rhine Exercise, 15
Lütjens assessment of *Bismarck* situation, 265
Lütjens service on, 18
Operation Berlin, 14, 255
plans to join *Bismarck*, 224
raiding mission (28 December 1940), 25
Goddard, Noel (Lieutenant), 76
Godfrey, Sir John H. (Rear Admiral), 95, 110, 120
Goeben (battle cruiser), 165
Gonzenheim (scout ship), 56, 168, 305
Göring, Hermann (Field Marshal), 21, 34
Gotenhafen Roads, 13, 41–2
Gotland (Swedish flight-deck cruiser), 64–5
Graf Spee (pocket battleship), 9, 140, 248–9
Graf Zeppelin (aircraft carrier), 43, 55
Graser (Commander), 48

Great Britain
British centrimetric radar, 34
declaring war on Germany, 2–3
Hitler's intentions to conquer, 4
importance of Gibraltar to, 5
King's views about, 206–7
mood of people, 3–4
Raeder's double-pole strategy against, 22–3
Raeder's view of Achilles' heel, 25
secret relationship with United States, 200–3, 212–15
Greenland, 43–4, 182–3, 209
Greenland Patrol, 183
Greer, *USS* (destroyer), 304
Grille (dispatch boat), 38
gun laying, 51–2
gunners, functions during action stations, 87, 147–8, 162–3

H

Halifax, Lord, 235
Halsey, William F. "Bull" (Vice Admiral), 312
Hamburg (yacht), 21
Hampshire, *HMS* (armoured cruiser), 82
Hannover (battleship), 19
Hansen, Hans (Seaman), 190
Haokon (Viking king), 82
Harriman, Averell
background, 212–13
Churchill and, 204
message on *Hood* sinking, 221
news of *Hood*'s destruction, 164–5
weekend at Chequers, 220–1
Harriman, Edward Henry, 212
Harris, Dan (Acting Lieutenant), 66–7
Harwood, Henry (Commodore), 110, 140
Hassell, Ilse von, 22
Heide (tanker), 60
Heinkel bomber, 301
hemispheric defense, 211
Hercules, *HMS* (freighter), 275
Hermione, *HMS* (light cruiser), 232, 239
Herzog, Georg (Seaman), 149, 189, 259, 260, 261, 298
Hess, Rudolf, 54–5
Hessen (battleship), 19
Heydrich, Reinhard, 307
HF/DF (high-frequency direction-finding) receivers, 237, 238–9
High Sea Fleet, 15–16
Hipper (heavy cruiser), 10, 307
Hitler, Adolf
assurances to Raeder, 20
birthday congratulations to Lütjens, 247
concerns with Rhine Exercise, 78–9
concerns with U.S. confrontations, 78–80
decision to declare war on U.S., 305
Dönitz in Last Will and Testament, 310
furious over expected *Bismarck* loss, 266–7
holiday outing on *Robert Ley*, 22
inspection of *Bismarck*, 13–15
as international renegade, 3
launching of *Tirpitz*, 21–2
meeting with Mussolini, 305
meeting with Raeder, 305–6
monologue aboard *Bismarck*, 15
opinion of High Sea Fleet, 16
provisional orders for Case White, 22
Raeder message about *Hood* sinking, 169
Raeder message about overseas supplies, 25
Raeder visit at Berghof, 78
Raeder's relations with, 17

response to *Graf Spee* scuttling, 24
tirade against Raeder, 308
views of battle fleets/ships, 19–20
Holland, Lancelot Ernest (Vice Admiral)
background, 101
Battle Cruiser Force, 73
convergence on *Bismarck*, 287
decisions after *Bismarck* sighting, 137–43, 146–7, 149–50
died in *Hood* destruction, 159
first force to sortie, 99
instructions to Leach, 141, 142
naval experiences, 101–3
patrolling Denmark Strait, 122
response to *Hood* damage report, 156
response to Rhine Exercise, 76
scrutiny over 27 November 1940 skirmish, 103–4
seizure of *München*, 104
strategy imparted to Leach, 140
Holland, Phyllis, 101
Home Fleet, 53, 72, 76, 81, 82
Höntzsch, Otto (Ordinary Seaman), 159, 298
"HOOD," 176–7
Hood, *HMS* (battle cruiser)
Battle Cruiser Force, 73
Churchill telegram of *Bismarck* sighting, 218
compared with *Bismarck*, 21
description of, 96—97
encounter with *Bismarck*, 145–53
eyewitness reports of destruction, 156–9
hits received by, 151–2
Holland's strategy with, 139–42
Lütjens message about, 238, 244
as part of Holland's sortie, 99
possible sighting of, 69
range compared with *Bismarck*, 29
readiness evaluation by Tovey, 96
sinking of, 153
specifics of destruction, 155–9
as "wet" ship, 152
see also Kerr, Ralph (Captain)
Hopkins, Harry, 204–5
Horthy de Nagybány, Nicholaus and Madgalena, 37
"Huff Duff." *see* HF/DF (high-frequency direction-finding) receivers
Hughes, *USS* (destroyer), 195, 219
Hull, Cordell (Secretary of State), 198
hull construction (*Bismarck*), 30
Hunter, H. de G. (Lieutenant), 257–8

I

Icarus, *HMS* (destroyer), 141
"ice fog," 62–3
Iceland, occupation of, 209
Illustrious, *HMS* (aircraft carrier), 208
Imperial German Navy, 16–17, 19
Indefatigable, *HMS* (battle cruiser), 97
intelligence gathering
Axelssen, Viggo, 68
Brinkmann concerns over radio traffic, 167–8
captured cipher material on *München*, 104
cleanup of *Bismarck* tankers and destroyers, 305
confirming *Bismarck* oil slick, 173
Enigma messages, 242–3
Glenn Martin Maryland bomber, 75–6
important messages, 76–7
intelligence gradings, 63, 95, 244
messages intercepted, 44, 56–7
receipt of Denham's report, 95
Royal Navy and, 120–1
sightings during Rhine Exercise, 64–8

Spanish Intelligence Service message, 180
see also reconnaissance
internationalism (Wilson's), 197
Invincible, HMS (battle cruiser), 97
Iron Chancellor, 21, 27–8
Ismay, Hastings (General), 219–20, 221
isolationism, United States and, 196–7

J

Jackal, HMS (destroyer), 83
Jacobs (Commander), 220–1
Jacob's ladders, 100
Japan, 5–6, 198, 305
Jasper, Paul (Commander), 143–4, 151–2, 161
Jellicoe, Sir John, 83
Jeschonnek, Hans (General), 243
Jodl, Alfred (General), 16, 25
Johnson, J. E. (U.S. Navy Lieutenant (jg)), 250
JOTDORA, 127
Junack, Gerhard (Lieutenant), 263, 285, 293
Jutland. *see* Battle of Jutland

K

"Känguruh" (*Nordmeer* code name), 56
Kapp Putsch, 23
Karlsruhe (light cruiser), 18
Kearney, USS (destroyer), 304
Keitel, Wilhelm (Field Marshal), 13
Kempff, Curt (Lieutenant Colonel), 65–6
Kennedy, Joseph P. (ambassador), 199
Kentrat, Eitel-Friedrich (Lieutenant), 57–8, 278, 298
Kenya, HMS (light cruiser), 232
Kerr, Ralph (Captain), 100, 156, 159
see also Hood, HMS (battle cruiser)
KGV. see King George V, HMS (battleship)
King, Ernest J. "Ernie" (Admiral)
Admiral, 273
and Arnold, 206
background, 206–8
CINCLANT, 205–6
commander in chief U.S. Atlantic Fleet, 194–5
and Marshall, 206
orders to find *Bismarck*, 235
and Stimson, 206
uncertainty over fleet's task, 209
understanding seriousness of *Bismarck* sighting, 218
views about Great Britain, 206–7
King George V, HMS (battleship)
after *Bismarck* destruction, 301
altering course for *Bismarck* search, 244
B-Dienst intelligence report, 60
Churchill telegram of *Bismarck* sighting, 218
convergence on *Bismarck*, 254, 273, 286–8
damages to, 289–90
description of, 81, 114–15
dispatched to sea, 122
disposition of, 313
final attack on *Bismarck*, 288–93
fuel considerations, 105, 254, 268–9
Lütjens message about, 238
response to Rhine Exercise, 73, 76
search for *Bismarck*, 231–2, 240
shadowing German task force, 176–7
see also Tovey, Sir John Cronyn (Vice Admiral)
Kirchberg, Kurt (Chief Petty Officer), 192
Kirk, Alan G. (Captain), 202
Kitchener, Lord H. H., 82
Kjølsen, Fritz (naval attaché), 27

Knight, Esmond (Lieutenant), 157, 161–2
Knox, Frank (Secretary of the Navy), 198, 273
Köln (light cruiser), 17
Königin Luise (minelayer), 83
Kota Penang (scout), 56, 168
Krancke, Theodor (Captain), 24–5
Kriegsmarine, 14, 43, 59, 65, 78–9
Krupp, Friedrich, 37
Krupp Cementite, 30
Kummetz, Oskar (Vice Admiral), 307
Kuppisch, Herbert (Lieutenant), 184, 276

L

Langsdorff, Hans (Captain), 9, 24, 265
Larcom, Charles (Captain), 253, 258, 279
  see also Sheffield, HMS (light cruiser)
"Laubfrosch" (*Friedrich Breme* code name), 60
Lauenberg (fishing boat), 59
Leach, J. C. (Captain)
  actions after *Hood* sinking, 159–65
  Churchill anger at, 165
  convergence on *Bismarck*, 287
  death, 313
  HMS *Prince of Wales* fit for duty, 95
  Holland's instructions to, 141–2
  Holland's strategy imparted to, 140
  search for *Bismarck*, 231
  see also Prince of Wales, HMS (battleship)
League of Nations, isolationism and, 196
"Lebertran" (*Kota Penang* code name), 56
Lee, Raymond (Commander), 204, 213
Lehmann, Walter (Commander), 29, 226
Lell, Rudolf (Lieutenant Commander), 68
Lend-Lease, 7–8, 205
Lexington, USS (aircraft carrier), 206, 216
Liebknecht, Karl, 23
Lilja, Nils-Hugo (Apprentice Radio Signalman), 65
Lindemann, Ernst (Captain)
  abandoned repair attempts, 267
  after-action and damage reports, 169–70
  awaiting orders, 39
  awards, 64–5
  band for U-556, 274
  Bismarck antiaircraft defense for Hamburg, 35
  Bismarck orders, 40
  clash with Lütjens, 165–6, 172–3
  at commanders' conference, 61
  commands while under attack, 259–60
  death, 291
  element of surprise forfeited, 65
  final review of *Bismarck* progress to date, 53–4
  frustrations with lack of clear orders, 42
  going down with ship, 295
  Hitler's inspection of *Bismarck*, 13–15
  Lütjens orders to, 230
  message to crew after torpedo hit, 192
  message to crew to help themselves, 267
  nonreceipt of messages, 131
  orders after *Bismarck* sighting, 129–30
  orders for enemy aircraft encounter, 190
  party for Ericson and Kjølsen, 27
  pending support, 284
  permission to fire request, 151
  reassuring crew, 244–5

response to sighting Briggs' PBY, 252
spartan routine for men, 41
state of mind, 72
steering limitations, 289
supervising *Bismarck* repairs, 263–5
training and initial service, 19
trying to life crew spirits, 281
uncharacteristic behavior, 285
von Müllenheim-Rechberg and, 285
see also Bismarck (battleship); Rhine Exercise (Operation Rheinübung)
Lithgow, M. J. (Sub-Lieutenant), 257
Lloyd, Frank (Captain), 239, 243
Loewenfeld-Bismarck, Dorothee von, 21
London Blitz, 1–2, 202
London Naval Treaty (1935), 81
Lorenzen, Walter (Petty Officer), 149, 159, 299
Lothringen (battleship)
code name "Dreschflegel," 56
destroyed, 305
Lindemann service on, 19
location of, 168
Lütjens instructions, 176
orders to, 60
Luftwaffe
arrival after *Bismarck* destruction, 301
and Battle of Crete, 243
nighttime bombings, 2
range during London Blitz, 1
task of destroying RAF, 4
time of expected support, 254
wild stories about *Bismarck* end, 295
Lund, Alfred Roscher (Colonel), 66–7
Lütjens, Günther (Admiral)
addressing crew, 244–7
adherence to primary goal, 166–7
after-action and damage reports, 169–70
analysis of decisions made by, 170–2
assessment of *Bismarck* situation, 179–80, 265–6
birthday on *Bismarck*, 226, 230, 246–7
Bismarck damage message, 262
clash with Lindemann, 165–6, 172–3
clocks to be set back, 74
command to Brinkmann, 176
damage reports from Lindemann, 263
death, 291
decision to proceed to St. Nazaire, 168
disposal of *Bismarck* war diary, 282
and Dönitz, 225
evasive actions in Scapa Flow, 132–3
"Execute *Hood*," 176, 177
expectations about *Bismarck*/St. Nazaire, 223–6
"fight to the last shell," 266
German Tactical Regulations ignored, 153
Hitler's inspection of *Bismarck*, 13–15
Hitler's message to, 266–7
ignoring pleas to fire, 148–9
layover at Bergen, 70
Lindemann's permission to fire request, 151
message regarding attack on *Bismarck*, 192
message regarding *Bismarck* condition, 281
message to Hitler, 284
namesake for class of destroyers, 309
Naval Group Command North messages, 76–7
Naval Group Command West messages, 192–3, 224–5, 236, 237–9, 252–4
no Luftwaffe support message, 251–2
Operation Berlin, 25
order for Skagerrak mine barrier, 68

orders during final attack upon *Bismarck*, 289
orders for new course, 149
promotions and commands, 17–18
recommend Schneider for Knight 's Cross, 285
relations with Hitler, 18
Rhine Exercise briefing, 61–2
Saalwächter and, 224
seeking advice about Rhine Exercise, 50–1
slipping away, 236
targeting orders, 152–3
training and initial service, 17
uncertainty over sightings, 144–5
"Victory or Death," 245
"wonderful ship" message to Brinkmann, 131
see also Rhine Exercise (Operation Rheinübung)
Lützow (pocket battleship), 51, 307
Luxemburg, Rosa, 23

M
Maclean, N. G. (Acting Lieutenant), 191
Mahan, Alfred Thayer, 15–16
"Maikäfer" (*Gedania* code name), 60
Malaya, HMS (battleship), 85, 208, 234
Manchester, HMS (light cruiser), 76, 99, 102–3, 122, 174
Manthey, Herbert (Seaman), 298
Maori, HMS (destroyer), 249, 279–81, 297
Marburg 5297, 56
Marburg 5724, 56
Marschall, Wilhelm (Admiral), 18, 50, 265
Marshall, George C. (U.S. Army Chief of Staff), 198, 206
Martin, Benjamin C. S. (Captain), 240–1, 272, 296–7
see also Dorsetshire, HMS (heavy cruiser)
Martin Maryland plane, 121–2
Mashona, HMS (destroyer), 247, 302
"mattresses" (mesh antennas as), 31
Maund, L.E.H. (Captain), 240, 256, 261, 270
see also Ark Royal, HMS (aircraft carrier)
Maus, Otto (Seaman), 159, 299
Mayo, USS (destroyer), 195
Mediterranean Fleet, 84–9, 101–3, 108, 111–12, 308
"Meeresgott" (*Prinz Eugen* code name), 54
Meier, Arthur (steward), 285
Mein Kampf, 55
Mers-el-Kebir, 111–12
Messerschmitt 109 fighters, 40, 69
Messerschmitt 110 fighters, 69
MG C/30 "pom-poms." *see* "pom-poms"
Ministry of Propoganda, 53, 295
Modoc, USS (Coast Guard cutter), 77, 176, 181–7, 191, 193, 216, 247
Mojave, USS (Coast Guard cutter), 247
Moresby, HMS (destroyer), 83–4
Morse code signals
HF/DF (high-frequency direction-finding) receivers, 237
"SSS," 184
Müllenheim-Rechberg, Burkard von (Lieutenant), 71, 75, 150, 158, 261, 281–2, 285, 291, 295–6
München (weather ship), 59, 104
Murrow, Edward R., 202
Mussolini, Benito, 305

N
Naiad, HMS (cruiser), 92–3
Nasturtium, HMS (corvette), 311
Naval Air Station Hatston, 121

naval aviation, 34, 119
Naval Defense Department, 38
Naval Group Command North
  code name "Zwerghuhn," 54
  critical messages from, 76–7
  headed by Rolf Carls, 58
  Lütjens message about intruder, 65
  received news of *Hood* destruction, 167
  refueling orders for *Weissenburg*, 73
Naval Group Command West
  Bismarck encounter with Swordfish, 192–3
  code name "Bilderbuch," 54
  instructions to Brinkmann, 178
  intelligence gathering by, 77
  Lütjens messages to, 236, 237–9, 254, 266
  message intercepted, 57
  messages to Lütjens, 224–5
  news of *Hood* destruction, 167
  no Luftwaffe support message, 251–2
  pending support message, 284
  Rhine Exercise orders finalized, 58
  Spanish Intelligence Service message, 180
Naval Gunnery School, 19
Naval Intelligence Division (NID), 120
Naval Personnel Office, 18
Naval Staff, 19
Naval War College, 217–18
Nelson, HMS (battleship), 60, 92, 115
Nelson, Horatio (Admiral), 314
Neptune, HMS (light cruiser), 85
Netzbandt, Harald (Captain), 61
Neuendorff, Wolf (Commander), 158
Neutrality Patrol, 198
neutrality policy
  instructions during Rhine Exercise, 61
  neutrality movement in U.S., 197–8
  Roosevelt radio address, 303
  secret US/UK relationship, 200–3, 212–15
  straining of, 195–6
  United States and, 79–80
  U.S. repair of Royal Navy warships, 208
  U.S. straining in Battle of the Atlantic, 209
Neutrality Zone, 273, 304
New York, USS (battleship), 195, 203, 205, 215–19, 235–6, 273, 313
Newcastle, HMS (light cruiser), 102
Newell (Able Seaman), 128–9
news-gathering network (Danish Belts), 44
Niblack, USS (destroyer), 208–12
No. 209 Squadron, 249
No. 210 Squadron, 250
No. 771 Squadron, 75–6
No. 825 Squadron, 186–9
No. 828 Squadron, 121–2
Noble, Sir Percy (Admiral), 248
Nomura, Naokuni (Vice Admiral), 43
Nordmeer (tanker), 56
Norfolk, HMS (heavy cruiser)
  assistance with *Bismarck* sighting, 188, 190–1
  Bismarck sighting, 287
  disposition of, 313
  final attack on *Bismarck*, 290, 292
  firing upon *Prinz Eugen*, 161
  Holland's battle strategy with, 140
  instructions to attack at dawn, 283
  joining *King George V*, 272
  patrolling Denmark Strait, 122
  plowing along, 229
  questions on *Bismarck* damage, 175
  reconnaissance in Denmark Strait, 94
  reconnaissance in Scapa Flow, 131–2

refueling needed, 239
repositioning after Battle of Iceland, 173–4
response to Rhine Exercise, 73, 76
search for *Bismarck*, 231
shadowing *Bismarck*, 192
see also Phillips, A.J.L. (Captain)
North Atlantic, Royal Navy superiority in, 62
North Carolina, *USS* (battleship), 216
North Sea Naval Station, 16–17
Northern Wave, *HMS* (rescue trawler), 185
Northland (U.S. Coast Guard cutter), 183–7, 216
Norway (Operation Weserübung), 24
Norwegian Narrows, 77
Nürnberg Racial Laws of 1935, 18
Nürnberg trials, 309, 310

O

O'Brien, *USS* (destroyers), 195, 219
"Obstgarten" (*Gonzenheim* code name), 56
Oels, Hans (Commander)
Bismarck first officer, 27, 35
Commander, 293
course correction, 64
death, 295
First Officer, 263
joy over *Hood* encounter, 159
supervision of departure, 63
Oerlikon guns, 190
OKW (Supreme Command of the Armed Forces), 13, 16
Oliver, Sarah, 219
Oliver, Victor, 219
Onslow, *HMS* (destroyer), 83–4
Operation Barbarossa, 43, 65–6
Operation Berlin, 14, 25, 255–6
Operation Catherine, 111
Operation Cerberus, 313
Operation Rheinübung. *see* Rhine Exercise (Operation Rheinübung)
Operation Sea Lion, 4
Operation Weserübung, 24
Operational Control Centre (British Admiralty), 241–2
Operational Orders 16–18: Rhine Exercise. *see* Rhine Exercise (Operation Rheinübung)
Operations Center (British Admiralty), 134
"Opernhaus" (*Esso-Hamburg* code name), 55

P

Pacific Fleet, 205
Pafford, A. W. (Paymaster-Captain), 95
Patterson, Wilfred R. (Captain)
commander *King George V*, 122
convergence on *Bismarck*, 287–8
instructions from Tovey, 290
instructions to alter course, 244
instructions to attack at dawn, 283
orders from Tovey, 269, 271
search for *Bismarck*, 231
see also King George V, *HMS* (battleship)
Patzig, Conrad (Admiral), 50, 265–6
PBY Catalina flying boats, 133, 161, 176, 207–8, 235–6, 249–50
PBY Z, 249–50
Pearl Harbor, 305
Pétain, Henri-Phillippe (Marshal), 5, 85
Petersén, Carl (Major), 66
Phillips, A.J.L. (Captain), 73, 131–2, 231
see also Norfolk, *HMS* (heavy cruiser)
Phillips, Sir Thomas (Admiral), 95, 134, 237, 242, 313
Pillau, lack of facilities at, 41–2
Piorun (Free Polish destroyer), 249, 279–80

plunging fire, 33
Poland, 2–3, 22
"pom-poms," 30, 38, 190, 259
Pound, Sir Alfred Dudley P. R. (Admiral of the Fleet)
background, 107–9
Churchill and, 112
Churchill memorandum to, 303–4
court-martial considerations, 165
death, 311
and Ghormley, 201, 204
news of *Bismarck* slipping away, 237
Norfolk's first contact report, 134
orders for Force H, 242
pressure to re-engage *Bismarck*, 175
Tovey "to break off chase" message, 269
Preamble to the Articles of War, 106–7
Prien, Günther (Lieutenant Commander), 78, 82–3
Prince of Wales, HMS (battleship)
assessment of condition, 175
Battle Cruiser Force, 73
B-Dienst intelligence report, 60
Churchill aboard, 304
Churchill telegram of *Bismarck* sighting, 218
compared with *Bismarck*, 27
convergence on *Bismarck*, 287
damage assessment, 173, 179
description of, 114–15
destruction of, 313
encounter with *Bismarck*, 179, 192
fuel considerations, 105
hits received, 153, 161–2
Holland's battle strategy with, 140
Holland's decision to change course, 139
as part of Holland's sortie, 99
readiness evaluation by Tovey, 96
refueling needed, 239
reported fit for duty, 95
search for *Bismarck*, 231
as "wet" ship, 152
see also Leach, J. C. (Captain)
Prinz Eugen (heavy cruiser)
after *Bismarck* separation, 304
Churchill memorandum regarding, 303–4
Churchill telegram of sighting, 218
close encounter with *Bismarck*, 131
code name "Meeresgott," 54
confirming *Bismarck* oil slick, 173
continuing delays, 52–3
crew gossip, 71
damages to, 302
description of, 37–8
fired upon, 130
fuel considerations, 105
Lütjens instructions, 176
Lütjens message about, 238
near miss with torpedoes, 160
parting from *Bismarck*, 177–9
personnel assigned to, 38
picking way through Denmark Strait, 125–7
plans to join *Bismarck*, 224
preparations and damage, 47–8
readiness for Rhine Exercise, 53–4
refueling, 47, 53, 71
service career, 312–13
see also Brinkmann, Helmuth (Captain)
Prinz Eugen Lied, 63–4
propulsion systems, 28–9, 33, 38, 118
"Puderdose" (*Heide* code name), 60
Puttkamer, Karl Jesko von (Commander), 13, 14, 80, 306

Q

quadrants, 59–60, 168, 178, 236
Queen Elizabeth, HMS (battleship), 60

Queen Mary, HMS (battle cruiser), 97
Quincy, USS (heavy cruiser), 205

R

radar detection
  ASV (air-to-surface-vessel) radar, 186
  on *Bismarck*, 31
  British "Dete" gear, 134, 236
  functions during action stations, 87
  German concerns over British, 170
  German concerns over improved British, 132–3
  on *Prinz Eugen*, 38
  Suffolk capabilities, 128
  Type 284 centrimetric radar, 94
radar industry, 34
radio transmissions
  Brinkmann concerns over, 167–8
  HF/DF (high-frequency direction-finding) receivers, 237, 238–9
  increased along French coast, 242
  mark *Bismarck* position by, 283
  Naval Group Command West concerns over clear, 241
  "SSS" Morse code signal, 184
  Tovey for *Bismarck* direction, 243–4
Raeder, Erich (Grand Admiral)
  absence from Hitler's visit to *Bismarck*, 14, 54
  admonition of June 1940, 50
  birthday congratulations to Lütjens, 246–7
  Bismarck christening, 21
  concerns about *Bismarck*, 226
  consultation with Admiral Carls, 69–70
  death, 309
  double-pole strategy, 22–3
  Gneisenau repair estimate, 43
  Hitler approved Schneider for Knight 's Cross, 285
  Hitler's assurances to, 20
  Lütjens and, 265–6
  meeting with Hitler, 305–6
  message about Achilles' heel, 25
  orders for Rhine Exercise, 62
  pleas for naval air arm, 34
  "problem U.S.A." treatise, 79
  promotions and commands, 22
  relations with Hitler, 17
  release of communiqué, 178
  resignation, 308
  response to Lütjens/St. Nazaire decision, 168–9
  Rhine Exercise task assignment, 61
  training and initial service, 16–17
  unveiling of new strategy, 26
  visit to Berghof, 78
  war diary impressions of attack on Poland, 23–4
  Z-Plan, 9
Ramillies, HMS (battleship), 60, 102–3, 174–5
range finding, 31, 38
Ranger, USS (aircraft carrier), 205
reconnaissance
  on 27 November 1940, 101–2
  Bismarck sighted, 176
  Coastal Command (May 1941), 95, 97
  decision for standing patrols, 94
  first-light, 104
  Home Fleet (23 May 1941), 136–7
  by Naval Air Station Hatston, 121–2
  No. 771 Squadron, 75–6
  Norfolk and *Suffolk* in Scapa Flow, 131–3
  Norwegian Sea passages, 122
  PBY Catalina flying boats for, 207–8

repositioning after Battle of Iceland, 173–4
search for *Bismarck*, 91–2, 235–52
Suckling film of battleships, 71
Swordfish spotting *Bismarck*, 252–3
see also intelligence gathering
Reichard, Kurt-Werner (Lieutenant Commander), 69
Renown, HMS (battle cruiser)
action on 27 November 1940, 101–3
B-Dienst intelligence report, 60
capabilities against *Bismarck*, 255
description of, 136
sighted by *Sheffield*, 279
signal flags, 253
Spanish Intelligence Service message, 180
Swordfish flyover, 258
U-556 sighting of, 274
Repulse, HMS (battle cruiser)
B-Dienst intelligence report, 60
Churchill telegram of *Bismarck* sighting, 218
destruction of, 313
escort for WS8B troop transport convoy, 94
interception attempt (23 January 1941), 92
refueling, 234
refueling needed, 239
rendezvous at Butt of Lewis, 122
response to Rhine Exercise, 76
at Tovey's disposal, 99
Tovey's worry over, 227
Reuben James, USS (destroyer), 208, 304–5
Revenge, HMS (battleship), 60, 175
Reynaud, Paul (President), 3
Rhine Exercise (Operation Rheinübung)
battle alert, 74
B-Dienst intelligence report, 60–1
British aircraft search for battleships, 72
code dates, 56
concerns over potential veto, 59–60
crew informed, 64
detailed tactical orders finalized, 58
encounter with British, 125–31
final commanders' conference, 61
intentions for, 15
Lindemann disappointment in delays, 52–3
Lütjens and improvisation, 265–6
Lütjens decision to abandon, 170–3
Lütjens reasoning for delay, 49
Lütjens seeking advice, 50–1
naval command structure, 58
official orders, 53
painting over aerial recognition markings, 74
painting over camouflage, 71
plans for *Bismarck* war diary disposal, 282
plans to renew, 224
postmortem, 307, 308–9
Raeder's anxiety about launch window, 48–9
Raeder's determination to launch, 44–5
Raeder's planning of, 42–3
secret blown, 69
two-months of destruction, 93
vessels available for, 55–6
Richter, Karl-Ludwig, 162–3, 169–70
Robert Ley (pleasure ship), 22
Rodman, Hugh (Rear Admiral), 217
Rodney, HMS (battleship)
after *Bismarck* destruction, 301
B-Dienst intelligence report, 60
convergence on *Bismarck*, 254, 273, 286

description of, 115, 234
disposition of, 313
escort for *Britannic*, 94
final attack on *Bismarck*, 288–92
interception attempt (23 January 1941), 92
repair in U.S. naval shipyard, 208
repositioning after Battle of Iceland, 174
search for *Bismarck*, 233–5, 240
at Tovey's disposal, 99
Tovey's service on, 84
see also Dalrymple-Hamilton, Frederick H. G. (Captain)
Rommel, Erwin (General), 5
Roosevelt, Franklin D. (President)
"act of piracy," 304
background, 196–7
cable from Churchill, 76
compared with Churchill, 197
decision to occupy Greenland, 43–4
dilemma in helping Allies, 198–200
extending U.S. Navy zone of activity, 79
following *Bismarck* chase, 273
and Ghormley, 215
message of additional ships to Churchill, 216
missive from Churchill, 111
new U.S. neutrality zone, 214–15
orders to find *Bismarck*, 235
radio address, 303
response to Italy's declaration of war, 4
vagueness with instructions, 209
view toward war, 6–7, 197
Roosevelt, Theodore (President), 196
Rotherham, G. A. (Commander), 122
Royal Air Force (RAF), 2, 4, 48, 104, 119, 250
Royal Canadian Navy, 8, 213
Royal Flying Corps, 119
Royal Naval Air Service, 119
Royal Navy
1941 fighting, 5
aircraft carriers and, 119–20
Battle of the Atlantic, 8
Bismarck located, 254
Bismarck's tankers and destroyers, 305
condition of, 26
discussions with United States, 213–15
fleet composition, 114–15
fuel considerations, 105–6
intelligence gathering and, 120–1
under King Charles II, 106–7
naval treaties handicapping, 113–14
peacetime neglect and, 106
period after 1920, 118
relationship with U.S. Navy, 194, 198
Scapa Flow as home base, 82
troubles, 113–21
U.S. repair of warships, 208
war against U-boats, 308
war strategy, 84–5
Royal Oak, HMS (battleship), 82–3
Royal Sovereign, HMS (battleship), 60, 85
rudders, 29, 262–4
"Ruhekissen" (*Weissenburg* code name), 60
Russell, USS (destroyers), 195, 219
Ryan, D. L. (Commander), 209, 211

S

S9 Hawker Osprey floatplane, 65
Saalwächter, Alfred (General Admiral)
Dönitz and, 225
General Admiral, 306
head of Naval Group Command West, 58

"heartiest congratulations," 224
Lütjens and, 236, 252, 266
Lütjens/St. Nazaire decision and, 168
prisoner of war in Soviet Union, 310
Rhine Exercise task assignment, 61
Sachsenwald (weather ship), 298
Sagner, Gerhard (Chief Petty Officer), 294
Saleir (Dutch freighter), 210
Salmann, Otto (Lieutenant), 210–11
San Francisco, USS (heavy cruiser), 205
Saratoga, USS (aircraft carrier), 216
Sargent, T. R. (engineering officer), 194
Scapa Flow
description of, 82, 90
High Sea Fleet scuttling at, 16
Home Fleet departure from, 123–4
Royal Navy superiority in, 62
Scharnhorst (battleship)
breakout on 4 February 1941, 93
destruction of Allied ships, 10
engine problems, 43
inclusion in Rhine Exercise, 15
Lütjens assessment of *Bismarck* situation, 265
Lütjens service on, 18
Operation Berlin, 14, 255
plans to join *Bismarck*, 224
raiding mission (28 December 1940), 25
at *Tirpitz* launching, 22
Scheer, Reinhard (Admiral), 72, 306
Schlesien (battleship), 17, 41
Schleswig-Holstein (battleship), 19
Schlüsselmaschine M. *see* Enigma
Schmalenbach, Paul (Lieutenant), 134, 143–5, 161, 177
Schmidt, Wilhelm (Warrant Officer), 169
Schmundt, Hubert (Vice Admiral), 306
Schneider, Adalbert (Commander), 280
antiaircraft orders, 189, 259
champagne toast to, 170
confusion over enemy identity, 150
final attack on *Bismarck*, 290
gun laying exercises, 51–2
gunnery practice, 31–2
Lütjens recommendations for Knight 's Cross, 285
orders during final attack upon *Bismarck*, 289
plea to fire, 148–9
targeting calculations, 145–6, 151
Schneider, Dr. Otto (medical officer), 72
Schniewind, Otto (General Admiral), 168, 306
Schulte-Mönting, Erich (Captain), 39
Schultz, Hans-Henning von (Lieutenant), 126–7, 133–4
Schulze-Hinrichs, Alfred (Commander), 73
Schütte, Wilhelm (Lieutenant), 298–9
Schutzstaffel (SS), 307
Scouting Forces, 16, 18
Second Cruiser Squadron, 232
Secretary of State (Cordell Hull), 198
Secretary of the Navy (Frank Knox), 198
Secretary of War (Henry Stimson), 198
Security Service (SD), 307
Seetakt. *see* FuMO (radar detection sets)
Seventh Cruiser Squadron, 86
Seydlitz (battle cruiser), 16–17
Sheffield, HMS (light cruiser)
action on 27 November 1940, 101–2
at anchor, 136
attacked by Swordfish, 257–8
B-Dienst intelligence report, 60
Bismarck sighting of, 253–4
confirmation of Swordfish communiqués, 270–1

final attack on *Bismarck*, 292
fired upon by *Bismarck*, 259, 278–9
to maintain contact, 269–70
shadowing *Bismarck*, 272
Swordfish flyover, 259
see also Larcom, Charles (Captain)
shipbuilding
armament design considerations, 116–17
Royal Navy's program, 114
United States Navy, 216
wet ships, 152
Sikh, HMS (destroyer), 249, 280–1, 301
6th Destroyer Fleet, 53
Skagerrak mine barrier, 68–9
Smith, E. H. "Iceberg" (Commander), 185
Smith, Leonard B. "Tuck" (U.S. Navy Ensign), 250–2
Somali, HMS (destroyer), 247
Somerville, Sir James (Vice Admiral)
Admiralty instructions (23 May 1941), 134–6
Churchill and, 112–13
Mediterranean Fleet, 101–3
message from Admiralty, 255
new orders from Pound, 242
orders for *Bismarck* search, 233
orders for Swordfish attack, 256
retirement and death, 312
Sheffield to shadow *Bismarck*, 253
strategy against *Bismarck*, 255
view on Holland's actions (27 November 1940), 103
watching Swordfish lift off, 256
sonar, functions during action stations, 87
songs, 13, 63–4
Southampton, HMS (light cruiser), 102–3
Soviet Union, 3–5, 43, 310
Spandau Prison, 309
Spanish Intelligence Service, 180
Spichern (tender), 56, 60, 168, 178–9
squadrons
Destroyer Squadron 10 (U.S.), 205
First Cruiser Squadron (U.K.), 94, 127
No. 209 Squadron (U.K.), 249
No. 210 Squadron (U.K.), 250
No. 771 Squadron (U.K.), 75–6
No. 825 Squadron (U.K.), 186–9
No. 828 Squadron (U.K.), 121–2
Second Cruiser Squadron (U.K.), 232
Seventh Cruiser Squadron (U.K.), 86
"SSS" (Morse code distress call), 184
St. J. Francourt, H. L. (Captain), 121–2
St. Nazaire, 170–2
Stalin, Joseph, 3
Standardization of Arms Committee, 200
star shell, 280, 283
Stark, Harold R. "Betty" (Admiral)
Admiral, 273
assignment of Lee to Admiralty, 213
Chief of Naval Operations, 198
decision on battleship modification program, 203
frustration with vagueness, 209
Ghormley as personal representative of, 201
informed that *Bismarck* contact lost, 235
message on *Hood* sinking, 221
Statz, Josef (Machinist), 294
Stewart-Moore, J. A. (Lieutenant Commander), 257–8
Stimson, Henry (Secretary of War), 198, 206
Stockholm (as center of intrigue), 65
Strong, George V. (Brigadier General), 200–1
Stummel, Ludwig (Captain), 305

submarines. *see* U-boats (gray sharks)
Sucking, Michael (Flying Officer), 71
Suffolk, HMS (heavy cruiser)
disposition of, 313
Holland's battle strategy with, 140
identified by Germans, 127
losing sight of *Bismarck*, 231
patrolling Denmark Strait, 122, 127–31
reconnaissance in Denmark Strait, 94
reconnaissance in Scapa Flow, 131–3
refueling needed, 239
repositioning after Battle of Iceland, 173–4
response to Rhine Exercise, 73, 76
search for *Bismarck*, 233–4, 236
shadowing *Bismarck*, 192
shadowing German task force, 176–7
trailing *Bismarck*, 229–30
see also Ellis, R. M. (Captain)
Sunderland flying boat, 173
Supermarine Spitfire fighters, 68
Support Force Atlantic Fleet. *see* Atlantic Fleet
Supreme Command of the Armed Forces. *see* OKW (Supreme Command of the Armed Forces)
survivors. *see* casualties/survivors
Swedish Combined Intelligence, 39–40
Swedish Defense Staff, 65–6
Swedish Intelligence, 27
Swedish Secret Military Intelligence, 66
Swordfish B, 191
Swordfish C, 190–2
Swordfish torpedo bombers
affected by weather, 256
air strike against *Bismarck*, 186–9
on *Ark Royal*, 233
attack on *Sheffield*, 257–8
attack procedure description, 188–9
communiqué to *Ark Royal*, 270
encounter with gale, 240
No. 1 subflight, 260
No. 2 subflight, 260
No. 3 subflight, 260
No. 4 subflight, 257
No. 5 subflight, 260
reconnaissance over Bay of Biscay, 249
return from *Bismarck* strike, 268
sighting Vian's destroyers, 258
Somerville orders for *Bismarck* attack, 256
tracking *Bismarck* after attack, 269–70
Wohlfahrt sighting of, 277

T

tanker placement, fuel considerations and, 106
Tartar, HMS (destroyer), 247, 302
task groups. *see* Force B; Force D; Force F; Force H
Tegetthoff, Wilhelm von (Commodore), 37
Tegetthoff (heavy cruiser), 37
Ternen (Greenland motor ship), 183
Texas, USS (battleship), 195, 203, 205, 207, 215–17
Third Escort Group, 275
Thompson, J. C. (Acting Sub-Lieutenant), 190–2
"Tigerfell" (*Ermland* code name), 56
Tilburn, R. E. (Able Bodied Seaman), 152, 157, 159
Tirpitz, Alfred von (Grand Admiral), 22
Tirpitz (battleship)
and convoy PQ 17, 311
fuel considerations, 105
Hitler's visit to, 54
inclusion in Rhine Exercise, 15
launching of, 21–2

mechanical breakdowns, 44
plans to join *Bismarck*, 224
Topp, Karl (Captain), 41, 44, 52
torpedo attacks
air strike at *Bismarck*, 189–93
attack procedure for, 188–9
Dorsetshire to finish off *Bismarck*, 296
firing pistols described, 257, 258
international distress call "SSS," 184
limitations of British naval torpedoes, 255
Maori on *Bismarck*, 281
official British version of encounter with *Bismarck*, 193–6
Swordfish attack on *Bismarck*, 256–9
Swordfish on *Bismarck*, 259–62
Swordfish on *Sheffield*, 257–8
U-137 and, 274
U-556 on convoy HX 126, 276–7
U-556 on convoy Outbound 318, 275
U-568 on *Kearney*, 304
U-652 on *Greer*, 304
see also encounters
Tovey, Aida, 89
Tovey, Sir John Cronyn (Vice Admiral)
action in Mediterranean, 85–6
after *Bismarck* destruction, 302
anticipation of Lütjens, 122
Battle of Jutland, 83–4
Churchill's response about breaking off chase, 297–8
commander in chief of Home Fleet, 72–3
convergence on *Bismarck*, 254
decisions made (20 May 1941), 98–9
delay in notification, 241
desperate for information, 75, 103–4, 121
final plans for *Bismarck* destruction, 271–3
first contact report received, 137
HMS *King George V* as flagship of, 81
instructions to Dalrymple-Hamilton, 286
instructions to Patterson, 290
instructions to Vian, 282–3
Lütjens and, 92
message on *Hood* sinking, 220–1
opinion of Holland's decisions, 141
orders for *Bismarck* air strike, 186
personal traits, 89–90
plans/worries about next *Bismarck* encounter, 226–36
promotions and commands, 84
reflections about Churchill, 90
response to court-martial considerations, 165
retirement and death, 311
sea battle conventions, 87–8
search for *Bismarck*, 231–2, 239
training and initial service, 83
uncertainty over direction of *Bismarck*, 243–4
view of Pound, 108, 227–8
vulnerability after Battle of Iceland, 174
watching *Bismarck* in death throes, 296
see also King George V, HMS (battleship)
triangulation, gun laying and, 51–2
Tribal-class destroyers, 248–9
Trident, SS (submarine), 313
Troubridge, Ernest (Admiral), 165
Troubridge, R.N.T. (Captain), 32
Tuscaloosa, USS (heavy cruiser), 205
24th U-Boat Flotilla, 47–8
Type 279 air-warning radar, 128
Type 284 centrimetric radar, 94, 128
Type 286M fixed-aerial radar, 128

U

U-14, 274
U-43, 225
U-46, 225
U-47, 78, 82–3
U-48, 225, 268
U-52 (Type VIIB), 210–11
U-66, 225
U-73 (Type VIIB), 210
U-74, 57, 225–6, 278, 298–9, 306
U-81, 313
U-93, 225
U-94, 183–4, 225, 276
U-97, 225
U-98, 225
U-108, 225
U-111, 77
U-137, 274
U-213 (Type VIIB), 210
U-552, 225, 304–5
U-556 (Type VIIC), 225, 274–7
U-557, 225
U-563, 313
U-568, 304
U-652, 304
U-boats (gray sharks)
  Bismarck repair plan, 265
  British evasive action, 230
  Carls view of, 306
  early 1940 sinkings, 8
  headquarters message to U-74, 278
  Hitler orders to hunt to Greenland, 209–10
  instructions for Rhine Exercise, 56
  instructions from Lütjens, 175–6
  King's own rules of engagement, 209
  largest concentration of, 225–6
  longest dry spell, 274
  Martin's reason for abandoning rescue, 297
  resentment over US/UK relationship, 211
  Royal Navy war against, 308
  superiority in, 26
  wolf-pack tactics, 8
  Z Plan and, 20
  see also specific U-boats
ULTRA (Special Intelligence), 73, 305
United Kingdom. *see* Great Britain
United States
  edging toward war, 304
  isolationism in, 196–7
  public opinion toward bombings, 7
  secret relationship with Great Britain, 200–3, 212–15
United States Atlantic Fleet, 194–5
United States Navy
  discussions with British, 213–15
  first casualties, 304–5
  first naval attack, 209–12
  fuel considerations, 105
  involvement with Royal Navy, 304
  neutrality zone and, 273
  orders for Battle of the Atlantic, 194
  responsibilities with Lend-Lease, 205
  shipbuilding for, 216
  zone of activity, 79
U.S. Army Chief of Staff (George C. Marshall), 198
U.S. Coast Guard, 194

V

Vian, Philip L. (Captain), 248–9, 254–5, 279–81, 312
Vichy government, 5
Victorious, HMS (aircraft carrier)
  air strike against *Bismarck*, 186–93
  Churchill telegram of *Bismarck* sighting, 218
  disposition of, 313

escort for WS8B troop transport convoy, 94
orders for *Bismarck* air strike, 186
readiness evaluation, 228–9
readiness evaluation by Tovey, 96
refueling needed, 239
response to Rhine Exercise, 73, 76
search for *Bismarck*, 232
at Tovey's disposal, 99
Tovey's marvel at deeds, 227
Villeneuve, Pierre (French Admiral), 314
Vincennes, USS (heavy cruiser), 205
Vittorio Veneto (Italian battleship), 102
VLR (very-long-range) antisubmarine Liberator patrol bombers, 206–7
Voss, Hans (Rear Admiral), 50–1

W

Wake-Walker, William F. (Rear Admiral)
agreement with Leach's decision, 173
Bismarck slipping away, 231
death, 311–12
exhaustion, 229
HMS *Arethusa* under command of, 99
joining for the finish, 272
message on *Hood* sinking, 220–1
Pound and, 227–8
pressured to re-engage *Bismarck*, 175
reconnaissance in Denmark Strait, 94, 127
search for *Bismarck*, 231–2
senior officer after *Hood* sinking, 163–4
viewed *Hood* destruction, 159
see also Norfolk, HMS (heavy cruiser)
Walrus seaplane, 140, 141
"Walzerkönig" (*Spichern* code name), 56
war trials. *see* Nürnberg trials
war zone, 79–80, 184
Ware, J. G. (Captain), 217–19, 235, 273
Warspite, HMS (battleship), 85, 88, 220
Washington, USS (battleship), 216
Washington Naval Conference, 216
Washington Naval Treaty (1922), 21, 113–14
Washington talks (US/UK), 213–15
wave bands, 34
Weissenburg (tanker), 60, 62, 73
Wellings, Joseph H., 234
Wilson, J. S. (Colonel), 68
Wilson, Woodrow (President), 196, 197
Wohlfahrt, Herbert "Sir Parsifal" (Lieutenant), 274–8, 282, 311
Wollin (tanker), 59, 71
World War II, events of winter of 1939-40, 3
Wright, USS (aircraft carrier), 206
"Würzburg" (19.7 inch wave band), 34
Wyoming, USS (battleship), 205, 217

Z

Z Plan (Ziel Plan), 9, 20–1
Zeiss range finders, 31
Zulu, HMS (destroyer), 249, 280, 283, 301
"Zwerghuhn" (Naval Group Command North code name), 54